# OECD Territorial Reviews: Valle de México, Mexico

OECD
BETTER POLICIES FOR BETTER LIVES

**Please cite this publication as:**
OECD (2015), *OECD Territorial Reviews: Valle de México, Mexico*, OECD Publishing, Paris.
*http://dx.doi.org/10.1787/9789264245174-en*

ISBN 978-92-64-24516-7 (print)
ISBN 978-92-64-24517-4 (PDF)

Series: OECD Territorial Reviews
ISSN 1990-0767 (print)
ISSN 1990-0759 (online)



**Photo credits:** Cover © SEDEMA 2015/Enrique Abe

Corrigenda to OECD publications may be found on line at: *www.oecd.org/about/publishing/corrigenda.htm*.

# *Foreword*

Across OECD countries, globalisation is increasingly testing the capacity of regional economies to adapt and exploit their competitive advantages, while also offering new opportunities for regional development. This is leading national and regional authorities to rethink their development strategies. As a result of decentralisation, central governments no longer have the sole responsibility for development policies, and different levels of government have to work effectively together to improve public service delivery. Metropolitan areas, because of their critical economic and environmental importance, are receiving particular attention. Metropolitan regions are the engines of social, economic and cultural development, and their dynamism – or lack thereof – has an impact on the overall national economic development agenda.

As highlighted in the 2015 *OECD Urban Policy Review of Mexico*, Mexico's well-being is closely tied to the functioning of its major cities and the quality of their governance. The Metropolitan Zone of the Valle de México produces the bulk of national wealth, but institutional capacity deficiencies, combined with a limited focus on strategic urban planning, prevent it from achieving its full potential. The mechanisms that should guide urban development are complex, fragmented and underdeveloped. Transforming the Valle de México into a functional urban area requires integrated regional planning frameworks applied at the metropolitan level. These frameworks should be buttressed by greater co-ordination and collaboration across and among levels of government, as well as by strong financing mechanisms. Stronger metropolitan governance, while no panacea for the Valle de México's complex problems, is a precondition for comprehensive urban policy.

OECD Territorial Reviews are conducted by the Regional Development Policy Committee (RDPC) through its Working Party on Urban Areas (WPUA), a unique forum for international exchange and debate. OECD Territorial Reviews are carried out in collaboration with national and/or local governments. The reviews seek to enhance the economic competitiveness and attractiveness of the metropolitan areas and their contribution to national growth objectives; assess their environmental performance; evaluate and improve the policies put in place to strengthen social inclusion; and identify obstacles to competitiveness and social and sustainable development within the spheres of governance and local finance, as well as ways to overcome them. The reviews follow a consistent methodology that features cross-national comparisons and recommendations on the integration of sectoral policies into urban development policy, planning and programmes. The *OECD Territorial Review of the Valle de México* focuses on the following critical urban development challenges that need to be addressed to ensure sustainability and boost competitiveness: urban regeneration and housing, inclusive mobility strategies, environmental protection and effective metropolitan governance arrangements. The success of the Valle de México in becoming a more functional urban area will have enormous implications for the well-being of its residents, and, given its size, for the country as a whole.

# *Acknowledgements*

The *OECD Territorial Review of the Valle de México* is part of a series of Territorial Reviews produced by the OECD Public Governance and Territorial Development Directorate under the leadership of Rolf Alter and its Regional Development Policy Division, led by Joaquim Oliveira Martins. This report was made possible through the support of the National Workers' Housing Institute (INFONAVIT). It was developed in collaboration with the Ministry of Environment of the Federal District (SEDEMA), as representative of the government of the Federal District.

This report was co-ordinated by Oscar Huerta Melchor under the overall supervision of Rüdiger Ahrend, Head of the Urban Development Programme. It was drafted by Aimée Aguilar Jaber, Marissa Plouin, Alexander Lembcke and Oscar Huerta Melchor. The review also draws on key contributions from Catherine Paquette (Research Development Institute, IRD).

The OECD Secretariat is grateful for the co-operation and support of the numerous officials, experts and private sector representatives in Mexico who contributed to the background report prepared for the study, met with the OECD team preparing the review (more than 60 meetings were held) and in other ways participated in the review process. Special thanks to Director General Alejandro Murat Hinojosa and the co-ordinating team at INFONAVIT led by Vicente Mendoza Téllez, with the great support from Fausto Gurrea Martínez, Gerardo Bazán Morante, Luis Octavio Flores Calvillo, Ignacio Riva Palacio y Huidobro and José Carlos González López. The Secretariat is also grateful to Minister Tanya Müller García at SEDEMA and the international relations team led by Patricia Narváez García and Paulina Chávez Cantoral for their active support throughout the process. The OECD Secretariat is also thankful for the continuous support of the Mexican Permanent Delegation to the OECD, notably Ambassador Dionisio Pérez-Jácome Friscione, and Maya Camacho Dávalos.

The report also benefited from the active engagement of two peer reviewers: Matthew Yates, Head of Transport Planning and Projects at Transport for London in the United Kingdom, and Claudia Monterrosa, Director of Public Policy at the Los Angeles Housing and Community Investment Department in the United States. Valuable input was provided by Monica Brezzi (OECD), and Maximo Martinez and Laurens Versluis (Space Syntax). Useful comments on drafts of the review were provided by Karen Maguire, William Tompson, Stephen Perkins, Alain Lumbroso, Soo-Jin Kim, Daniela Glocker, Tadashi Matsumoto, Aziza Akhmouch, Andrea Uhrhammer, Loïc Daudey, Jacobo García Villarreal, Isabelle Chatry and Maria Varinia Michalun. The draft was edited by Vicky Elliott. Jennifer Allain, in co-ordination with Ulrike Chaplar and Jennifer Kilbourne, prepared the review for publication.

# *Table of contents*

## Tables



## Figures

# Acronyms and abbreviations

| | |
|---|---|
| **ADES** | Economic and social development area (formerly ZODES)<br>*Área de desarrollo económico y social* |
| **AEP** | Public Space Authority<br>*Autoridad del Espacio Público* |
| **AGE** | Strategic management area<br>*Área de gestión estratégica* |
| **AGEB** | Basic geographical statistical area<br>*Área geoestadística básica* |
| **ALDF** | Legislative Assembly of the Federal District<br>*Asamblea Legislativa del Distrito Federal* |
| **AMB** | Barcelona Metropolitan Area<br>*Ãrea Metropolitana de Barcelona* |
| **ANZSOG** | Australia and New Zealand School of Government |
| **BANOBRAS** | National Bank of Public Works and Services<br>*Banco Nacional de Obras y Servicios Públicos* |
| **BRC** | Bus rapid corridor |
| **BRS** | Bus rapid service |
| **BRT** | Bus rapid transit |
| **CADAM** | Metropolitan Commission for Water and Sewage<br>*Comisión de Agua y Drenaje del Área Metropolitana* |
| **CAEM** | Water Commission of the State of México<br>*Comisión del Agua del Estado de México* |
| **CAF** | Spanish train construction and rail operation firm<br>*Construcciones y Auxiliar de Ferrocarriles* |
| **CAM** | Metropolitan Environment Commission<br>*Comisión Ambiental Metropolitana* |
| **CAMe** | Environmental Commission for the Megalopolis<br>*Comisión Ambiental para la Megalópolis* |
| **CANADEVI** | National Chamber of the Industry of Development and Promotion of Housing<br>*Cámara Nacional de la Industria de Desarrollo y Promoción de Vivienda* |
| **CBD** | Central business district |
| **CDM** | Metropolitan Development Council of the Valle de México<br>*Consejo para el Desarrollo Metropolitano del Valle de México* |

| | |
|---|---|
| **CECM** | Executive Commission for Metropolitan Co-ordination<br>*Comisión Ejecutiva de Coordinación Metropolitana* |
| **CEMDA** | Mexican Centre for Environmental Law<br>*Centro Mexicano de Derecho Ambiental* |
| **CEPACs** | Certificates of Additional Construction Potential<br>*Certificados de Potencial Adicional de Construção* (Brazil) |
| **CETRAM** | Modal transfer centre<br>*Centro de transferencia modal* |
| **CIDE** | Centre for Economic Research and Teaching<br>*Centro de Investigación y Docencia Económicas* |
| **CISA** | *Corredor Insurgentes* |
| **CNG** | Compressed natural gas |
| **CO** | Carbon monoxide |
| **COMEPROC** | Metropolitan Commission for Civil Protection<br>*Comisión Metropolitana de Protección Civil* |
| **COMETAH** | Metropolitan Commission for Human Settlements<br>*Comisión Metropolitana de Asentamientos Humanos* |
| **COMETRAVI** | Metropolitan Commission for Transport and Roads<br>*Comisión Metropolitana de Transporte y Vialidad* |
| **COMSPJ** | Metropolitan Commission for Public Security and Justice<br>*Comisión Nacional de Seguridad Pública y Procuración de Justicia* |
| **CONACYT** | National Council for Science and Technology<br>*Consejo Nacional de Ciencia y Tecnologia* |
| **CONAFOR** | National Forestry Commission<br>*Comisión Nacional Forestal* |
| **CONAGO** | National Conference of Governors<br>*Conferencia Nacional de Gobernadores* |
| **CONAGUA** | National Water Commission<br>*Comisión Nacional del Agua* |
| **CONAMM** | National Conference of Municipalities of Mexico<br>*Conferencia Nacional de Municipios de Mexico* |
| **CONANP** | National Commission for Protected Natural Areas<br>*Comisión Nacional de Áreas Naturales Protegidas* |
| **CONAPO** | National Population Council<br>*Consejo Nacional de Población* |
| **CONAVI** | National Housing Commission<br>*Comisión Nacional de Vivienda* |
| **COPLADE** | State Development Planning Committee<br>*Comité de Planeación del Desarrollo Estatal* |
| **COPLADEM** | Planning Committee for Municipal Development<br>*Comité de Planeación para el Desarrollo Municipal* |
| **DF** | Federal District<br>*Distrito Federal* |

| | |
|---|---|
| **EDS** | Economic Development Strategy (London, United Kingdom) |
| **EMUS** | National Sustainable Urban Mobility Strategy<br>*Estrategia de Movilidad Urbana Sustentable* |
| **ENIGH** | National Survey of Mexican Household Income and Expenditures<br>*Encuesta Nacional de Ingresos y Gastos de los Hogares* |
| **EPA** | Environmental Protection Agency (United States) |
| **EU** | European Union |
| **FM** | Metropolitan Fund<br>*Fondo Metropolitano* |
| **FOVISSSTE** | Housing Fund of the State's Employees' Social Security and Social Services Institute<br>*Fondo de la Vivienda del Instituto de Securidad y Servicios Sociales de los Trabajadores del Estado* |
| **FTA** | Federal Transport Authority (United States) |
| **FUA** | Functional urban area |
| **GACM** | Airport Group of Mexico City<br>*Grupo Aeroportuario de la Ciudad de México* |
| **GDP** | Gross domestic product |
| **GHG** | Greenhouse gas |
| **GLA** | Greater London Authority |
| **GPS** | Global Positioning System |
| **GTF** | Gas Tax Fund |
| **HAM** | Highway Assignment Model (United Kingdom) |
| **HOPE VI** | Housing Opportunities for People Everywhere (United States) |
| **IAU** | Institute for Urban Planning and Development of the Ile-de-France Region<br>*Institut d'Aménagement et d'Urbanisme d'Île-de-France* |
| **ICT** | Information and communications technology |
| **IMCO** | Mexican Institute of Competitiveness<br>*Instituto Mexicano para la Competitividad* |
| **IMEPLAN** | Metropolitan Planning Institute of the Metropolitan Area of Guadalajara<br>*Instituto Metropolitano de Planeación del Área Metropolitana de Guadalajara* |
| **IMTA** | Mexican Institute of Water Technology<br>*Instituto Mexicano de Tecnología del Agua* |
| **INECC** | National Ecology and Climate Change Institute<br>*Instituto Nacional de Ecología y Cambio Climático* |
| **INEGI** | National Institute of Statistics and Geography<br>*Instituto Nacional de Estadística y Geografía* |
| **INFONAVIT** | National Workers' Housing Fund Institute<br>*Instituto del Fondo Nacional de la Vivienda para los Trabajadores* |

| | |
|---|---|
| **INVI** | Housing Institute of the Federal District<br>*Instituto de Vivienda del Distrito Federal* |
| **IPUCC** | Urban Development Authority (Brazil) |
| **IPUMS** | Integrated Public Use Microdata Series |
| **IT** | Information technology |
| **ITDP** | Institute for Transport and Development Policy<br>*Instituto de Políticas para el Transporte y el Desarrollo* |
| **JnNURM** | Jawaharlal Nehru National Urban Renewal Mission (India) |
| **LEED** | Leadership in Energy and Environmental Design |
| **LGAH** | General Law for Human Settlements<br>*Ley General de Asentamientos Humanos* |
| **LGEEPA** | General Law on Ecological Equilibrium and Environmental Protection<br>*Ley General de Equilibrio Ecológico y la Protección al Ambiente* |
| **LMDF** | Mobility Law<br>*Ley de Movilidad* |
| **LoRDM** | London Regional Demand Model (United Kingdom) |
| **LP** | Planning Law<br>*Ley de Planeación* |
| **LTA** | Land Transport Authority (Singapore) |
| **LTyV** | Law for Transport and Roads<br>*Ley de Transporte y Vialidad* |
| **MINVU** | Ministry of Housing and Urban Development (Chile)<br>*Ministerio de Vivienda y Urbanismo* |
| **MPO** | Municipal Planning Organization (Los Angeles, United States) |
| **MSW** | Municipal solid waste |
| **MXN** | Mexican peso |
| **NAICM** | New Mexico City International Airport<br>*Nuevo Aeropuerto Internacional de la Ciudad de México* |
| **NAMA** | Nationally appropriate mitigation actions |
| **$NO_2$** | Nitrogen dioxide |
| **$NO_x$** | Nitrous oxide |
| **NOM** | Mexican Official Norm<br>*Norma Oficial Mexicana* |
| **ONZUS** | National Observatory of Sensitive Urban Zones (France)<br>*Observatoire national des zones urbaines sensibles* |
| **ORT** | Regulatory Body for Transport<br>*Órgano Regulador de Transporte* |
| **PACCM** | Mexico City's Climate Action Programme 2014-20<br>*Programa de Acción Climática del Ciudad de México 2014-20* |
| **PDU** | Urban Mobility Plan (France)<br>*Plan de déplacements urbains* |

| | |
|---|---|
| **PICCA** | Comprehensive Programme against Air Pollution<br>*Programa Integral Contra la Contaminación Ambiental* |
| **PIM** | Integral Mobility Programme<br>*Programa Integral de Movilidad* |
| **PIMUS** | Programme to Promote Sustainable Urban Mobility<br>*Programa de Impulso a la Movilidad Urbana Sustentable* |
| **PITV** | Integral Programme for Transport and Roads<br>*Programa Integral de Transporte y Vialidad* |
| **$PM/PM_{2.5}/PM_{10}$** | Particulate matter (2.5 nm-10 nm); fine airborne particles |
| **PND** | National Development Plan<br>*Plan Nacional de Desarrollo* |
| **PNRU** | Programme National de Rénovation Urbaine (France)<br>*Programme national de rénovation urbaine* |
| **POZMVM** | Spatial Urban Planning Programme for the Metropolitan Zone of the Valle de México<br>*Programa de Ordenación de la Zona Metropolitana del Valle de México* |
| **PPP** | Public-private partnership |
| **PREP** | Rescue of Public Spaces Programme<br>*Programa Rescate de Espacios Públicos* |
| **PROFEPA** | Federal Attorney for Environmental Protection<br>*Procuraduría Federal de Protección al Ambiente* |
| **PRONAPRED** | Programme for the Social Prevention of Violence and Delinquency<br>*Programa Nacional para la Prevención Social de la Violencia y la Delincuencia* |
| **PROTRAM** | Federal Programme for Supporting Urban Mass Transport<br>*Programa Federal de Apoyo al Transporte Masivo* |
| **PTC** | Public Transport Authority (Singapore) |
| **PUEC** | University Programme on City Studies<br>*Programa Universitario de Estudios sobre la Ciudad* |
| **R&D** | Research and development |
| **RIT** | Integrated Transport Network (Brazil)<br>*Rede Integrada de Transporte* |
| **RTP** | Passenger Transport Network<br>*Red de Transporte de Pasajeros* |
| **RUV** | National Housing Registry<br>*Registro Único de Vivienda* |
| **SABESP** | Basic Sanitation Company of the State of São Paulo<br>*Companhia de Saneamento Básico do Estado de São Paulo* |
| **SACMEX** | Water Utilities of Mexico City<br>*Sistema de Aguas de la Ciudad de México* |
| **SCT** | Ministry of Communications and Transport<br>*Secretaría de Comunicaciones y Transporte* |

| | |
|---|---|
| **SEDATU** | Ministry of Agrarian, Territorial and Urban Development<br>*Secretaría de Desarollo Agrario, Territorial y Urbano* |
| **SEDECO** | Ministry of Economic Development of the Federal District<br>*Secretaría de Desarollo Económico del Distrito Federal* |
| **SEDEMA** | Ministry of the Environment of the Federal District<br>*Secretaría de Medio Ambiente del Distrito Federal* |
| **SEDESOL** | Ministry of Social Development<br>*Secretaría de Desarrollo Social* |
| **SEDUVI** | Ministry of Urban Development and Housing of the Federal District<br>*Secretaría de Desarrollo Urbano y Vivienda del Distrito Federal* |
| **SEGOB** | Ministry of the Interior<br>*Secretaria en Gobernación* |
| **SEMARNAT** | Ministry of Environment and Natural Resources<br>*Secretaría del Medio Ambiente y Recursos Naturales* |
| **SEMOVI** | Ministry of Mobility of the Federal District<br>*Secretaría de Movilidad del Distrito Federal* |
| **SETRAVI** | Ministry of Transport and Roads of the Federal District<br>*Secretaría de Transportes y Vialidad del Distrito Federal* |
| **SHCP** | Ministry of Finance and Public Credit<br>*Secretaría de Hacienda y Crédito Público* |
| **SHF** | Federal Mortgage Corporation<br>*Sociedad Hipotecaria Federal* |
| **SIMAT** | Atmospheric Monitoring System<br>*Red de Monitoreo Atmosférico* |
| **SIMBAD** | State and Municipal Database System<br>*Sistema Estatal y Municipal de Bases de Datos* |
| **SISBEN** | National System for Selection of Beneficiaries (Colombia)<br>*Sistema de Identificacion de Potenciales Beneficiarios de Programas Sociales* |
| **SMA** | Ministry of Environment of the State of México<br>*Secretaría del Medio Ambiente del Estado de México* |
| **SME** | Small and medium-sized enterprise |
| **$SO_2$** | Sulphur dioxide |
| **SOBSE** | Ministry of Public Works of the Federal District<br>*Secretaría de Obras y Servicios del Distrito Federal* |
| **STC** | Collective System of Transport (underground)<br>*Sistema de Transporte Colectivo (metro)* |
| **STE** | Electric Transport Service<br>*Servicio de Transportes Eléctricos* |
| **STIF** | Transport union of the Ile-de-France<br>*Syndicat des transports d'Île-de-France* |
| **TfL** | Transport for London (United Kingdom) |
| **TOD** | Transport-oriented development |

| | |
|---|---|
| UAEM | Autonomous University of the State of México<br>*Universidad Autónoma del Estado de Morelos* |
| UITP | International Union of Public Transport<br>*Union Internationale des Transports Publics* |
| UNAM | National Autonomous University of Mexico<br>*Universidad Nacional Autónoma de México* |
| UNFCCC | United Nations Framework Convention on Climate Change |
| URBS | Urban Transport Planning Authority of Curitiba (Brazil)<br>*Urbanização de Curitiba* |
| URD | Urban Revitalization Demonstration |
| VOC | Volatile organic compound |
| VUF | Viet Nam Urban Forum |
| WHO | World Health Organization |
| YLL | Years of life lost |
| ZMVM | Metropolitan Zone of the Valle de México<br>*Zona Metropolitana del Valle de México* |
| ZMVT | Metropolitan Zone of the Valle de Toluca<br>*Zona Metropolitana del Valle de Toluca* |

# Executive summary

## Key urban dynamics facts

- **The Metropolitan Zone of the Valle de México (Zona Metropolitana del Valle de México, ZMVM) is the economic, financial, political and cultural centre of Mexico and thus has profound impacts on national performance.** It is home to 17% of the national population and contributes almost a fourth (23%) of national GDP.
- **With over 20 million inhabitants, the Valle de México is the third most populous metropolitan area within the OECD and the largest outside Asia.** National projects anticipate a further population increase of 13% between 2010 and 2030. After decades of rapid growth, the rate of population growth has slowed to about 1.2% annually over the last decade. The urbanised area has expanded significantly, but less than half of the population lives in Mexico City. The high rate of growth in the commuting zone is fairly exceptional among OECD metropolitan areas.
- **The Valle de México does not generate enough agglomeration benefits relative to its size.** GDP growth of late has mainly been driven by population growth. Annual per capita economic growth averaged 0.5% in the period 2003-10. Labour productivity (GDP per worker) in the metropolitan area (per the OECD definition) is about average among the 33 Mexican metropolitan areas. Its performance is well below the potential of a vibrant agglomeration of this size in an emerging economy, and places the ZMVM in the mid-range of OECD metro zones.
- **Based on Mexican standards, the Valle de México has kept marginalisation to low levels, however inequalities remain.** Nearly half of the municipalities and all but one *delegación* (borough) in the metropolitan area are considered to have a very low degree of marginalisation. Even so, inequalities within the metro zone can be high. In some neighbourhoods, more than 40% of homes lack at least electricity, water or drainage. Like most OECD metropolitan areas, the Valle de México has high levels of income inequality.
- **There is a mismatch between the location of jobs and that of quality housing.** More than 40% of the Valle de México's residents commute across a municipal-level boundary to go to work or school. This puts an enormous strain on the transport network as the public transport fleet represents only 8% of the vehicles in the ZMVM and covers two-thirds of the transport needs.
- **Challenges with the quality of governance and the lack of a metropolitan vision detract from agglomeration benefits and resident well-being.** Weak arrangements for inter-governmental co-ordination are in place to tackle the needs

of a region that spans the 16 *delegaciones* of Mexico City, 59 municipalities from the State of Mexico and 1 municipality from the state of Hidalgo.

## Key assessment and recommendations

- **More integrated urban regeneration initiatives can improve well-being in distressed neighbourhoods.** Investments in public space, housing rehabilitation and infrastructure upgrades have helped revitalise the once declining historic centre of the Federal District. Further regeneration efforts should be linked to mass transport investments, particularly the development of bus-rapid transit (BRT) corridors. Social housing also requires improvements. Many older, centrally located social housing blocks suffer from ageing infrastructure, poor maintenance and overcrowding. Newer social housing in distant suburbs also faces rapid deterioration, and has in some cases led to a problem of housing vacancy and abandonment. Poor location, coupled with the absence of proximate employment opportunities, access to public transport and public service deficiencies, contribute to this phenomenon. A range of interventions to improve well-being in existing social housing will be needed, including efforts to address housing and the urban environment, in addition to education, employment and social issues.
- **To guide future urban development in the Valle de México, three "smart growth" strategies could be advanced in parallel:** 1) facilitate affordable housing development in central areas; 2) remove barriers to the development of the rental market as a means to offer housing that is more affordable to low-income households; and 3) plan for – rather than restrict – growth in strategic peripheral areas. Experience suggests that failed containment policies can be much worse than planned urban expansion.
- **The Valle de México should continue to transition from a policy focused on road management to an approach that favours multi-modal access.** Car-oriented policies in the past brought about congestion, pollution, decreased productivity and low levels of well-being. Recent mobility initiatives are intended to improve air quality and facilitate access to services and more harmonious urban development. The introduction of the BRT system, the suburban train and a public bike-sharing system signal increasing prioritisation of non-motorised and public transport modes. However, further work is needed to build a coherent policy framework to ensure greater mobility and accessibility.
- **An efficient and high-quality mobility system in the Valle de México requires effective organisational arrangements and policy tools.** Greater co-ordination among state-level mobility and urban planning agencies and with private stakeholders is needed to build expertise for designing mobility projects with a metropolitan vision. Mobility policy needs to be more proactive, with a long-term view that requires financial resources, better data sets and *ex post* assessments. Reforming the bus sector demands specialised technical staff, clear rules for granting concessions and setting tariffs, and a tendering process for granting bus concessions to ensure better value for money. Financial capacity for public transport requires regular, planned and small public transport fare adjustments, targeted subsidy schemes and differentiated fares.

- **Overcoming the Valle de México's environmental challenges calls for better urban planning consistent with environmental priorities.** Water provision, air quality, solid waste management and protection of conservation land are critical environmental concerns for the metro zone. Insufficient, ageing and inadequate infrastructure for water provision and solid waste management exacerbate environmental sustainability problems. Unplanned urban growth, car-oriented policies, a focus on road construction and non-compliance with environmental standards reduce air quality. Strategic urban planning can help resolve the underlying development and infrastructure deficits that are reducing environmental quality.
- **Addressing the Valle de México's urban development challenges requires the right metropolitan governance arrangements, possibly a metropolitan-level development agency.** The problem with the current governance arrangements is not the lack of institutions, but how they operate. Moving away from sectoral to metropolitan planning while ensuring that government and non-government stakeholders work together to define and pursue long-term goals would be positive step.

# Assessment and recommendations

The 2015 *OECD Urban Policy Review of Mexico* concluded that, as a highly urbanised nation, Mexico's performance is closely tied to the functioning of its major cities and thereby to the quality of their governance. This study of the Valle de México also concludes that there is a need for major reform of metropolitan governance, to address the challenges in planning and urban development faced by the country's largest metropolitan area.

The Valle de México has complex, fragmented and often haphazard governance arrangements. Like in other metropolitan zones in Mexico and other OECD countries, in the Valle de México there seems to be an absence of clear and effective institutional arrangements for urban development and the co-ordination of urban services, including its infrastructure. This context is eroding economic productivity, environmental sustainability and more generally, the liveability of the region.

The main message of this review is that serious urban governance failings are inhibiting adequate responses to critical urban development priorities – urban regeneration, access to adequate housing, reliable and safe public transport, and environmental protection. Several technical tools and reform initiatives are currently being implemented in the Valle de México to reshape the metropolitan area. These tools and reforms will not, however, produce the desired solutions to urban problems in the absence of metropolitan thinking and action, strategic regional planning, and improved intergovernmental co-ordination and collaboration. Addressing the Valle de México's governance deficits would not only help the metropolitan area, but would have a significant impact on inclusive and sustainable growth on a national scale.

## The Valle de México is one of the world's largest metropolises, but it is not as prosperous as it could be

*The Valle de México is the third-largest OECD metropolis*

The Metropolitan Zone of the Valle de México (Zona Metropolitana del Valle de México, henceforth ZMVM or the Valle de México) is the economic, financial, political and cultural centre of Mexico. In terms of its population, it is the third-largest metropolitan area within the OECD and the largest in the world outside Asia. According to the most commonly used Mexican delimitations, the ZMVM covers approximately 7 866 $km^2$ (almost 5 times the size of the Greater London region and 3 times the size of Luxembourg), spanning the 16 *delegaciones* (boroughs) of the Federal District, 59 municipalities from the State of Mexico and 1 municipality from the state of Hidalgo. The Federal District is not a state in itself, though it is granted many state-level responsibilities and powers. Its *delegaciones* are territorial and political-administrative divisions similar to the municipalities, but with juridical and administrative differences. The municipalities and *delegaciones* are both led by publicly elected authorities, but in contrast to municipalities, *delegaciones* cannot collect their own taxes or control local police. The Federal District – also called Mexico City – is the seat of the federal government and the urban core of the metropolitan zone.

*The population of the ZMVM is still growing, mainly in the commuting zone*

Today, the Valle de México has over 20 million inhabitants, which corresponds to 17% of the national population. Somewhat less than half of the metropolitan area's population lives in the Federal District. Even though population growth has slowed markedly, it continued to average 1.2% per year over the last decade, with the commuting areas growing much more rapidly than in the urban core. This has added to the expansion of the urban area, increasing the need for more and better urban infrastructure. Fortunately, this urban expansion has not been accompanied by a decrease in urban density. Compared to European or other Latin American cities, the Valle de México remains fairly densely populated, with 13 500 residents per square kilometre.

*The ZMVM is a major contributor to the national economy, but productivity is low by comparison with other OECD cities'*

The Valle de México produces almost a quarter of the Mexican national gross domestic product (GDP). Under the internationally comparable metropolitan area definition used by the OECD, the Valle de México accounts for 17% of Mexico's residents and 18% of the country's employees, who produce 23% of the country's GDP. However, OECD metro areas with a comparable population share, such as London and Paris, produce around 30% of the national GDP. Economic growth in the ZMVM has not been up to expectations. The GDP of the Valle de México grew by 1.7% annually between 2003 and 2010, mainly driven by the population increase. Per capita annual economic growth, however, averaged only 0.5%, in the mid-range among OECD metropolitan areas but well below the economic growth potential of a similar agglomeration in an emerging economy. As a result, of all 275 OECD metropolitan areas, the Valle de México remains among the 10% with the lowest GDP per capita. In 2010, the average GDP per capita in the Valle de México was USD 16 060, masking stark variations between the levels in Mexico City (USD 26 550) and the municipalities of the State of Mexico (USD 7 140).

The Valle de México's industrial structure is concentrated in high value-added services, especially financial services and insurance, with transport and communications, real estate and business services accounting for a relatively high share of employment. For a capital city, the total share of employees in high value-added service sectors remains low, at approximately 25% of all employees. Although the opportunities available in the Valle de México attract a relatively high share of well-educated workers, skills development policies need to respond better to the demands of emerging sectors, for example, those related to a green economy.

*Fragmented governance structures prevent the metropolitan zone from realising its economic potential*

The Valle de México has a highly fragmented governance structure, which negatively affects its productivity levels. Compared to other Mexican metropolitan zones, economic productivity in the Valle de México is only slightly above average. OECD analysis suggests that this is lower than would be expected, given its size and the composition of its population. According to OECD research, larger metropolitan areas tend to have higher productivity, but the Valle de México has aggregate levels of labour productivity similar to that of other Mexican metropolitan areas with smaller populations, such as Guadalajara. One possible explanation is the mismatch between the actual socio-economic area in which its businesses and residents live and work and the administrative boundaries of jurisdictions in the metropolitan area. A larger number of stakeholders increases the degree of complexity in designing and implementing policies that require co-ordination, which can put a drag on the productivity of urban agglomerations. The problem is exacerbated by the lack of strategic regional planning frameworks at the metropolitan scale that have sufficient financial backing; ambiguous constitutional definitions of the "metropolitan zones"; and weak co-ordination and collaboration among state- and municipal-level governments for urban development.

*Although levels of "marginalisation" are low, the Valle de México remains highly unequal*

Nearly half of the municipalities and all but one of the Federal District *delegaciones* are considered to have a very low degree of "marginalisation", meaning that in these areas, most households have access to basic services according to Mexican standards. Nonetheless, the basic services in some neighbourhoods, in both the centre and the periphery, are poor, leaving more than 40% of homes with gaps in electricity, piped water or drainage. Neighbourhoods with high levels of public service coverage can be directly adjacent to deprived neighbourhoods. Both well-off and less affluent areas show high levels of income inequality, which affects social cohesion. High value-added services drive higher levels of income in some areas, but also contribute to inequality. Although unemployment in the metropolitan zone is relatively low (4.8% on average), it varies widely, ranging from less than 1% in the northeast to 7.5% in the southeast.

In terms of the distribution of the educated population, Mexico City and the municipalities to its north have a high concentration of the highly educated (in terms of upper secondary and tertiary education), typically earning comparatively high incomes. By contrast, in many peripheral neighbourhoods, the average level of schooling is below the minimum school leaving age (12-15 years old). Although the percentage of children between 12 and 15 who are in the labour force rather than in school fell from 7.4% in 2000 to 4.5% in 2010, serious concerns remain about equality of opportunity.

*Low-cost housing has expanded in peripheral areas, but jobs are concentrated in the metropolitan core*

The transport system has not been able to match the rapid urban development. Housing and population growth have largely moved outside the Federal District, where land regulations and their enforcement tend to be less restrictive and housing is often more affordable. This process has contributed to urban expansion. However, employment remains concentrated in the metropolitan core: the four central *delegaciones* of the Federal District account for one-third of the jobs and 43% of the service sector jobs. As a result, in the ZMVM, over 40% of residents cross at least one municipal boundary to get to work. The growing distance between housing and employment centres has resulted in longer commuting distances and travel times.

Although public mass transport is gaining momentum, low capacity and poor quality modes are by far the most common mode of transport. In consequence, the use of private vehicles is growing fast. Between 2010 and 2013, the numbers of cars registered grew 8.5% annually. Road traffic congestion in the metropolitan zone ranks among the highest in the world. According to the Institute for Transportation and Development Policy (Instituto de Políticas para el Transporte y el Desarrollo, ITDP), congestion causes an annual loss of 3.1% of GDP in the ZMVM. Mass transport continues to expand, but the provision of reliable public transport, particularly in peripheral areas of the urban agglomeration, remains a challenge. Despite heavy investment in mass transport in Mexico City, only 25% of the population lives within one kilometre of a station or a stop. Moreover, both the underground and the new bus rapid transit (BRT) system are already operating above capacity.

## Addressing critical urban development challenges

*Integrated urban regeneration could improve well-being in distressed areas throughout the Valle de México*

Improving the living conditions within the existing housing stock should be a priority for policy makers. The Valle de México has many demographically declining or distressed neighbourhoods, although the roots of the problem tend to be distinct in different parts of the metropolitan zone. The central area of the Federal District, for instance, has faced several decades of depopulation and deterioration, while many of the older social housing blocks (*unidades habitacionales*) built in and around the Federal District since the 1950s present problems of ageing infrastructure, poor maintenance and overcrowding. At the same time, newer social housing developments in the suburbs face rapid deterioration. The most visible manifestation of the crisis is the large percentage of unoccupied, and in some cases abandoned, homes on the metropolitan periphery. Among the reasons for this phenomenon are their remote location, the absence of employment centres within a reasonable distance, costly public transport and deficiencies in basic public services.

Urban regeneration efforts targeting the historic district and ageing social housing stock in Mexico City have had some success in recent decades, and are an important building block for further regeneration initiatives in the metropolitan zone. A promising new development is the emergence of an urban mobility approach to regeneration, which is designed to link urban revitalisation to investment in public transport. At the same time, two parallel initiatives to upgrade portions of the extensive social housing stock in Mexico City are under way, one led by the Federal District and the other by the National Workers' Housing Fund Institute (Instituto del Fondo Nacional de la Vivienda para los Trabajadores, INFONAVIT). While progress has been made, challenges remain. First, there is no co-ordination between the two programmes, even though they share similar objectives and are operating in the same territory. Second, renovation of the older social housing in the municipalities of the State of Mexico is not being addressed.

The 2015 *OECD Urban Policy Review of Mexico* concluded that Mexico should build cities, not just houses. Capitalising on recent pilot programmes, the Mexican authorities could now look to develop a clear, comprehensive national public policy and corresponding implementation programme for urban regeneration. Two critical elements of international experience in this field are especially relevant for Mexico: 1) a cross-sectoral, comprehensive approach to urban regeneration through multi-dimensional initiatives that cover education, employment, culture, safety, public services and social cohesion; and 2) the development of national plans to support locally driven initiatives to regenerate distressed neighbourhoods. A national urban regeneration strategy could be incorporated into the framework of national programmes for urban development and housing, led by the Ministry of Agrarian, Territorial and Urban Development (Secretaría de Desarollo Agrario, Territorial y Urbano, SEDATU) and the National Housing Commission (Comisión Nacional de Vivienda, CONAVI). Such a strategy would need to broaden its focus from housing abandonment to a larger conception of urban regeneration that includes housing and the surrounding environment, access to jobs and services, and efficient public transport links. Another important component of housing regeneration strategies in other OECD countries has been the pursuit of a range of measures – including demolishing housing in the most severely distressed housing settlements – to improve inhabitants' living conditions.

*To guide future housing and urban development, three strategies could be followed*

As the population of the Valle de México is projected to grow by 13% between 2010 and 2030 according to the National Population Council (Consejo Nacional de Población, CONAPO), three "smart growth" strategies to guide new developments could be pursued simultaneously:

1. **Facilitate development in central areas** to make it easier to develop new, affordable housing in the metropolitan core. This can be achieved by reducing the barriers to development and densification in central areas (e.g. modifying existing parking regulations and design guidelines); and reintroducing an inclusionary zoning policy. This could include policies to allow for higher density development, in exchange for affordable housing. However, policies that promote higher densities are not appropriate everywhere and should be accompanied by upgrading and extension of infrastructure. Finally, introducing an affordable housing subsidy, provided by national housing institutions, could also be considered in some cases to increase housing affordability in the city centre for low-income households, but it cannot be a general solution to the housing problem.

2. **Remove barriers to the development of the rental market** as a means of offering housing that is more affordable to low-income households and, in many cases, of higher quality than owner-occupied units targeting this income group. The development of additional rental housing could also increase labour mobility in the metropolitan zone. The provision of rental housing in central, accessible neighbourhoods may be a more appropriate strategy than some current efforts that seek to concentrate rental housing programmes in peripheral areas. As in most other parts of Mexico, the majority of homes are owned by their residents. The home ownership rate in the ZMVM is among the highest across Latin American metropolitan zones, even though it is slightly below the Mexican national average of 76%. The home rental market remains underdeveloped.

3. **Planning for smart growth in peripheral areas** to foster a more sustainable form of housing. Rather than restrict growth in peripheral areas, policy makers should develop strategies to anticipate growth in more peripheral areas,

prioritising development around strategic infrastructure investments. Experience suggests that failed containment policies can have worse consequences than planned urban expansion. The development of the New Mexico City International Airport (Nuevo Aeropuerto Internacional de la Ciudad de México, NAICM) and the Mexico City-Toluca train line constitute critical opportunities for well-planned new development and urban regeneration initiatives. More generally, these developments should allow for easy and faster commutes by public transport to the centres of employment, such as in the Federal District or the new international airport.

*Despite progress towards inclusive and sustainable metropolitan mobility, major obstacles remain*

Recent mobility initiatives in the Valle de México have begun the transition from a policy focused on road management to an approach that favours multimodal access. This is a positive development, since car-oriented policies in the past have led to congestion, pollution, lesser productivity and lower levels of well-being. Mobility initiatives in the Valle de México are intended not only to improve air quality but also to facilitate access to services and more harmonious urban development. One of the emblematic initiatives has been the introduction of the Bus Rapid Transit (BRT) system in Mexico City (Metrobús) and, more recently, in some municipalities of the State of Mexico (Mexibús). Other improvements include the suburban train and the introduction of buses with higher environmental and safety standards. The introduction of a public bike-sharing system (ECOBICI) and the expansion of bike road infrastructure is evidence of the increasing prioritisation of non-motorised transport modes.

The enactmentof the Mobility Law of the Federal District has helped to transform the mobility policy framework. It defines mobility as a citizen's right, standardises the criteria for allocating road space and financial resources according to a new user hierarchy (pedestrians, cyclists, users of public transport, service providers of passenger public transport, service providers of cargo and distribution goods, and private automobile users), and sets out principles to guide policy formulation towards greater sustainability and inclusiveness. Although these initiatives are steps in the right direction, more progress is needed to build a coherent policy framework for improvements in mobility and accessibility. At least two major issues need to be addressed: the limited metropolitan co-ordination on mobility and spatial planning; and the lack of solid planning, regulatory and financial capacity at local government level.

*Putting mobility on the right track requires effective organisational arrangements ...*

To achieve an efficient and high-quality mobility system, co-ordinated metropolitan planning is needed. Restoring and improving the Metropolitan Commission of Transport and Roads (Comisión Metropolitana de Transporte y Vialidad, COMETRAVI) may be instrumental in harmonising the legal framework and developing a long-term mobility master plan. To operate effectively, the COMETRAVI will require permanent staff and financial resources. It should also pursue close co-operation with other metropolitan commissions. Moreover, the federal government could evaluate how well project proposals intended to be funded by existing financial instruments (the Metropolitan Fund and the Federal Programme for Supporting Urban Mass Transport) align with the priorities of master mobility plans. A common framework for mobility project implementation could also be useful for building a metropolitan-wide integrated transport network. Harmonising vehicle regulation and enforcement procedures across the metropolitan area could also contribute to sustainable and inclusive mobility goals.

Improved co-ordination among a wide range of public and private agents in the transport sector is a basic requirement for success. For example, greater co-ordination between state-level agencies responsible for transport modes as well as with private stakeholders is essential to: 1) build expertise for designing mobility projects; 2) synchronise routes, schedules and information; and 3) integrate fares for multimodal and multi-segment trips. Better co-ordination among mobility, urban and housing authorities is critical for implementing transit-oriented initiatives, such as the mobility impact assessment of the Federal District. Authorities will need to co-ordinate public transport improvements with transport demand management strategies, such as pricing and regulation of parking. Guidelines for an optimal amount of parking spaces in different areas of the metropolitan zone need to be set by state-level governments. Parking prices should not only reflect infrastructure and operational costs, but also the opportunity costs of allocating scarce public space to parking. Finally, minimum parking requirements in new construction developments need to be eliminated. The NAICM is an opportunity to reorganise public transport in the metropolitan zone, but it requires a multimodal surface transport access plan.

### *... and efficient policy instruments*

Mobility policy for the Valle de México needs to be more proactive, with a long-term perspective. The current six-year mobility programmes should be just the first steps of a 20- to 25-year mobility strategy for the metropolitan zone and for each of the state-level governments. Assigning resources for improving data collection and modelling expertise within mobility agencies is required for developing a long-term, solid mobility strategy. *Ex post* assessments are needed to plan and monitor progress.

Reforming the bus sector requires specialised staff who can progressively acquire technical expertise to regulate the sector. Lessons from the BRT experiences (Metrobús and Mexibús) can help in developing adequate regulation and sustainable financial mechanisms for a new bus system. Moreover, the bus sector needs clear rules for granting concessions and setting tariffs, both to provide more certainty for operators and to allocate resources to other projects. Establishing a tendering process for granting bus concessions would ensure better value for money. Incentives for incumbent operators to raise their level of competitiveness, i.e. a transition period while they consolidate into professionally run companies, may be considered.

Financial capacity to improve public transport can be achieved through: 1) regular, planned and modest public transport fare adjustments; and 2) targeted subsidy schemes and differentiated fares for lower income and vulnerable groups. The use of "betterment charges" to fundpublic and non-motorised transport projects in the Federal District is a positive step for strengthening financial capacity. The State of Mexico and the state of Hidalgo could also consider making use of this financial tool. Removing the generalised subsidy for the vehicle ownership tax should also generate substantial resources for sustainable and inclusive mobility projects.

*Environmental challenges and organisational bottlenecks affect the sustainability of the ZMVM*

Water, air quality and solid waste management issues seriously endanger the sustainability and green growth objectives of the Valle de México.

- The metropolitan zone has a dual water challenge: there is too little potable water to satisfy current and future demand and, at the same time, the torrential rainfall during the rainy season results in frequent flooding. Unsatisfactory water quality, water wasted through leakage, insufficient water treatment and failure to collect rainwater are adding to the water problem.
- Despite the progress made in recent decades, improving air quality remains a critical challenge. Car-oriented policies, a focus on road construction, unplanned urban growth and non-compliance with environmental standards have contributed to reduced air quality.
- Poor management of solid waste is threatening land, water and air quality. Insufficient infrastructure, as well as low supervision of compliance with the norms in waste treatment, are part of the problem. There are no robust policy instruments to encourage waste reduction and recycling at metropolitan level. Moreover, the lack of planning is putting conservation land at risk, due to the spread of irregular settlements, uncontrolled landfills and deforestation.

Local authorities are working to control urban sprawl in rural areas and in particular, irregular settlements in conservation land, through ecological management and urban development programmes, but results have been limited so far. A lack of planning, conflicting goals and weak municipal capacity are obstacles to sustainability initiatives. Both national and sub-national stakeholders need to be involved, as no single entity has enough influence to implement a comprehensive sustainability policy. The limited institutional capacity of the Environmental Commission for the Megalopolis (Comisión Ambiental para la Megalópolis, CAMe) reflected in its inadequate funding, insufficient staffing and lack of enforcement capacity, further obstructs informed decision making and co-ordinated action in environmental matters. Moreover, environmental and development goals seem to be in conflict, as there appears to be an absence of information and understanding of how environmental protection can contribute to economic development. Municipal governments, in many cases, lack the technical expertise, infrastructure and financial resources to design, implement and monitor sustainable development policies. In addition, many residents do not have environmental information and education, and often resist conforming to environmentally sound practices.

*Urban development strategies should be consistent with environmental sustainability goals*

Integrating environmental considerations in urban policy and planning can reduce the impact of the urban area on the environment while improving residents' quality of life. This implies introducing environmental guidelines, standards and norms in land-use planning, mobility, urban regeneration, housing and urban infrastructure. As previously noted, effective mass public and non-motorised transport systems can be an important means of reducing emissions from transport. Architectural and urban design approaches that reduce energy consumption (and cost) through the use of eco-technologies can also contribute to environmental sustainability. An adequate waste management system that focuses on waste reduction measures could prevent groundwater contamination, soil pollution, generation of greenhouse gas emissions and health hazards. Moreover, authorities in the Valle de México could consider building a metropolitan resilience framework to minimise the impact of future water scarcity or flooding. Mexico City's recent experience in developing a resilience strategy to mitigate the risks of climate change could be a starting point. Adapting the Valle de México to climate change can best be achieved by addressing underlying development and infrastructure deficits. Integrating climate change mitigation and adaptation into urban planning and management would be an important step in enhancing resilience in the entire metropolitan area.

To foster environmental protection, the environment should be regarded as an economic asset. Thus, sustainability policies should be underpinned by pro-growth factors. Ensuring a workforce with the right skills and competencies for a green economy, giving an environmental orientation to investments in physical infrastructure and overcoming the barriers to innovation will be essential for shifting towards green growth. In addition, making more extensive use of market incentives for environmental policy could lead to more efficient use of natural resources and lower pollution. The federal and local governments could also promote environmentally friendly goods and activities through taxes that directly incorporate the cost of environmental damage into market prices. Fiscal incentives to encourage a greener economy and urban development such as carbon pricing, fuel taxes, parking charges, land development taxes and road user charges should be explored. Further action is needed to reduce water demand, repair leaks, raise awareness and the availability of water, allow for the refilling of aquifers, and ensure high standards of water quality. Adjusting the price of water so that households pay for their actual consumption (including investment and operation costs) and improving the collection of tariffs are possible ways to address the water challenge. To increase the availability of water, the increased use of non-freshwater sources and the collection of rainwater are encouraged.

## Transforming the Valle de México into a well-functioning urban area

Transforming the Valle de México into a well-functioning area will require comprehensive planning for both the central city (Mexico City) and its suburbs (*municipios conurbados*) in concert. Development plans should be regional, integrated and long-term, and their design and implementation co-ordinated among and across levels of governments.

*The Valle de México needs to think and act from a metropolitan perspective*

One of the biggest challenges in addressing sprawl and the social and environmental issues raised by growth is the plethora of jurisdictions – some of which are administratively independent – that complicate regional/metropolitan thinking and planning. The Valle de México is a socially divided, politically fragmented metropolis, with governance deficits and large and increasing differences in the coverage and quality of public services. While such a situation may not be uncharacteristic of other parts of the country, it imposes a particular penalty on a large metropolis with global ambitions like the Valle de México. Economic, land-use and transport patterns have evolved, and the political boundaries dividing the metropolitan zone are now ill-adapted to the needs of citizens as well as economic and social activities. Many land-use decisions are taken at the municipal level, creating contradictions, conflicts and competition that prevent co-operation and collaboration in other urban policy areas. Issues such as urban renewal, housing, public transport, environment, groundwater management and quality of life in the region all require action under a metropolitan logic. This does not necessarily imply a uniform approach, since the challenges and contexts of different parts of the metropolitan zone are distinct and diverse.

Given that the population of the metropolitan zone is projected to continue to grow, albeit at a slower pace, strategic regional planning could assist in deciding where and how new growth should be accommodated and what it should look like. Regional/metropolitan planning could be instrumental in ensuring affordable housing that allows middle-income residents to live reasonably close to their workplaces. Regional planning could help build a metropolitan mobility framework to facilitate the physical, operational and financial integration of transport modes and the introduction of metropolitan-wide mobility projects. Planning housing, urban renewal and mobility from a regional perspective would put the authorities in a better position to achieve environmental goals such as improving air quality and ensuring the sustainable management of water.

*The Valle de México needs to modernise its planning governance*

The Valle de México needs to shift from the traditional unidimensional and sectoral planning to a cross-cutting, integrated policy-making approach. Since urban development and transport infrastructure are not jointly planned, new transport projects do not fully correspond to the metropolitan area's demand for accessibility. Urban policies are still largely defined based on sectoral needs and priorities, in a reactive manner. The problem is exacerbated given that: 1) certain sectors, such as housing, transport and water delivery, are also administratively fragmented; and 2) there is no long-term shared vision for the Valle de México. Moreover, the hierarchical system in which planning is framed does not allow for much participation by municipal governments. There are also few mechanisms, instruments and organisms to assess the results and impact of the urban development plans and projects in the medium and long term. A large number of sectoral plans, sponsored by different bodies on different geographical scales and timelines, attempt to shape metropolitan development with limited reference to one another. Most of these plans seem to be obsolete and poorly linked to the political/decision-making channels through which public investment choices and budget allocations are taken. Even when the plans themselves are articulated in a horizontal/integrated manner, their implementation is still carried out by generally uncoordinated sectoral departments.

Authorities may wish to establish a Metropolitan Development Agency that implements development plans in full collaboration with both national and sub-national government authorities. Such a body can help galvanise support for a long-term vision for metropolitan development. This body should have clear responsibility for the issues and places of metropolitan significance. It could prepare long-term plans, provide technical assistance for urban services and advise the different metropolitan commissions on investments of high priority for the metropolitan area. Meanwhile, it could prepare metropolitan development projects, support municipal-level governments on urban development and develop mechanisms for municipal evaluation.

*The Valle de México needs governance mechanisms that encourage co-ordination and collaboration*

The importance of co-ordination for the ZMVM is reflected in the plethora of co-ordinating and planning bodies, commissions, committees and councils between the states of Mexico and Hidalgo, the Federal District and the federal government, intended to strengthen collaboration in areas of common interest. The problem does not seem to be the lack of institutions, but how these institutions operate. There are several reasons for these operational challenges. First, they are single-sector bodies and tend to be reactive to specific issues or problems. Second, these institutions do not act under a common metropolitan vision that guides how actions should be implemented, co-ordinated and monitored. Third, the regulatory framework for metropolitan co-ordination is vague in its definition of the metropolitan area. Fourth, the different actors in the metropolitan zone are subject to widely varying financial constraints. Fifth, there is poor follow-up to decisions and agreements reached, and a lack of rigorous outcome assessments. Finally, competition among states, the fiscal regime and lack of a co-operative culture also limit metropolitan co-ordination and collaboration. As in the rest of the country, institutional fragmentation leads to responsibility overlaps and confusion about who is responsible for what and accountable to whom.

To improve co-ordination and collaboration, the Valle de México could capitalise on the existing metropolitan commissions. The revival of the Executive Commission for Metropolitan Co-ordination (Comisión Ejecutiva de Coordinación Metropolitana, CECM), with the integration of the federal government and the state of Hidalgo, and the creation of the CAMe are positive steps towards better metropolitan governance. However, it is essential that: 1) the commissions be seen to have a mandate independent of the state-level governments, albeit based on subsidiarity; 2) all decisions reached at the interior of the commissions are legally binding on all governments and agents; and 3) the commissions have the authority to monitor, assess and establish some form of sanctions for poor performance or under-delivery of urban development projects. Ensuring that all metropolitan commissions have a permanent technical secretariat, led by professional staff, and are guaranteed the financial means to conduct their work is essential. It is important that the commissions guarantee openness and transparency in their decision making and in the implementation of the investment projects.

Inter-municipal institutional arrangements are another means to encourage co-ordination and manage the impact of administrative fragmentation. These are based on obligatory and/or voluntary co-operation among municipalities comprising the functional urban area. Their success, however, requires effective horizontal and vertical networks among urban actors that can take the form of metropolitan-wide or single-purpose bodies. Setting up special-function councils or inter-municipal institutional arrangements to encourage collaboration in metropolitan areas could be a starting point. The current discussions of reform in connection with the General Law on Human Settlements (Ley General de Asentamientos Humanos, LGAH) could include reference to setting metropolitan-wide joint authorities that allow local jurisdictions to work together for certain common services or investments.

*The political reform of the Federal District and the New Mexico City International Airport could stimulate metropolitan co-ordination*

The ongoing discussions regarding the transformation of the Federal District into a federal state called Ciudad de México could formalise the blueprint for a long-term vision for the metropolitan zone. The reform could be critical in: 1) giving municipal-level governments more incentives to engage more actively in, and be accountable for, urban planning and development; 2) making co-ordination and consultation with other levels of government and peer governments mandatory rather than voluntary; 3) ensuring a clear and consistent definition of responsibilities and resources for each level of government; 4) adopting mechanisms for the election, appointment and removal of key elected and appointed officials; 5) ensuring accountability for service delivery; 6) redefining the responsibilities of the mayor (municipal president), who would assume a more strategic role that involves thinking beyond the municipal borders; 7) adopting provisions for the installation of a council of *delegados* chaired by Mexico City's Mayor to discuss territorial and administrative policies; and 8) establishing mechanisms that galvanise citizens' participation.

The NAICM can potentially boost economic development and urban regeneration, improve urban mobility and position Mexico City as an international destination hub. It can also act as a catalyst for better inter-governmental co-operation in the Valle de México. The key question for the federal government is how to work with sub-national governments, the private sector and civil society organisations on building the airport and capitalising on this project for the economic and social benefit of the metropolitan zone. The federal government should be more inclusive, and more willing to draw more broadly on the knowledge, experience and perspectives of non-government actors and society as a whole. Transparency and accountability will need to be ensured. Networks of relevant ministries, local authorities and external actors could be formed to pool practical knowledge, identify and anticipate policy issues and practical problems, and come together to develop a consensus. A Metropolitan Co-ordination Council for the NAICM – chaired by the Ministry of Communication and Transport (Secretaría de Comunicaciones y Transporte, SCT) and the Ministry of Agrarian, Territorial and Urban Development – could be established to co-ordinate and monitor the master plan of the airport and the activities of the state and municipal development plans that have an impact on the airport.

*The Valle de México requires municipal-level governments with sufficient capacity and capability*

The complexity of the fiscal system in the Valle de México is a major barrier for urban development. State-level governments receive a large share of their income from federal transfers, which fluctuate every year, limiting long-term planning. Authorities in the Valle de México should ensure that no urban regeneration or mobility strategy is launched without the tools to recover part of the public investment, so that other projects can be viable in the future. The Metropolitan Fund, a federal subsidy to finance urban development projects, requires adjusting its operational rules under a metropolitan framework and an integrated vision for urban development. It could give priority to mass transport systems and non-motorised transport programmes, integrated treatment of water, environmental improvements and growth-enhancing infrastructure.

Authorities in the Valle de México need to invest in the skills, leadership and management capacity of the public service. Professionalising the public service and planning for the workforce strategically is a way to minimise the disruption due to changes in government. It can also protect capacity, ensure continuity of service and avoid eroding citizens' trust in government. A critical issue for national and local authorities in the Valle de México is to ensure high levels of ethical behaviour among public officials. Meanwhile, planning and monitoring tools also need to be improved, for which gathering quality data on housing, mobility and environmental issues is a priority. A common, comprehensive knowledge database could be built to inform policy making on a wide range of areas related to urban development. Adequate data collection and modelling, as well as detailed documentation of *ex post* assessments, will be essential for carrying out long-term planning.

## In conclusion

The Valle de México is well-positioned to improve its governance architecture. It has the foundations and the critical mass to establish a much-needed metropolitan governance framework. Ensuring success can take time, will require some experimentation and will depend on governments' capacity and willingness to work with each other. All parties involved in urban issues will need to sharpen their strategic focus, and identify ways to combine successful project-based sectoral initiatives with long-term, cross-sectoral strategic programming. Investing in better-quality metropolitan governance would enhance urban development and improve residents' quality of life in the region, as well as improve national economic performance.

# *Chapter 1.*

# Urban trends and challenges of the Valle de México

*This chapter provides an overview of characteristics of the Metropolitan Zone of the Valle de México. It begins by outlining the extent of the metropolitan zone, which includes the Federal District and municipalities of the State of Mexico and the state of Hidalgo and the administrations involved in its governance. It then focuses on the metropolitan area's demographic and economic development and discusses the social and distributional characteristics. In line with the focus of this study, two sections consider housing and transport and environmental aspects in depth.*

## The Valle de México metropolitan zone

### *The Metropolitan Zone of the Valle de México: More than Mexico City*

The Metropolitan Zone of the Valle de México (Zona Metropolitana del Valle de Toluca, ZMVM) is located inland in the central part of Mexico. It is the largest urban agglomeration in Mexico and among the largest worldwide. While its size can be an advantage, creating agglomeration benefits and the possibility for the provision of public amenities, it also creates significant challenges in providing public services and adequate opportunities for future development. The metropolitan zone contains Mexico City (Federal District) at its core, the seat of the federal government. While initially confined to the Federal District and the surrounding municipalities of the State of Mexico, the metropolitan zone has experienced a significant expansion of its built-up area, alongside rapid population growth. The expansion beyond the borders of the Federal District started in the 1950s, and today, the ZMVM covers 7 866 km$^2$ and extends from the Federal District into two states, the State of Mexico and the state of Hidalgo. As of 2015, less than half of the metropolitan zone's population lives inside the Federal District.[1]

### *The metropolitan zone continues to grow in population and extent*

The boundaries of the Metropolitan Zone of the Valle de México have seen significant changes over the decades. In 2000, the Ministry of Social Development (Secretaría de Desarrollo Social, SEDESOL), the National Population Council (Consejo Nacional de Población, CONAPO) and the National Institute of Statistics and Geography (Instituto Nacional de Estadística y Geografía, INEGI) published the official delineations for metropolitan zones across Mexico. The ZMVM combines the Federal District, with municipalities from 2 states, 59 from the State of Mexico and 1 from Hidalgo (Figure 1.1, left panel). The Federal District is not a state itself, though it exercises many state-level powers and responsibilities, overseen by the federal government. This status also has implications for the municipal-level governments in the Federal District. Instead of municipalities, it consists of 16 *delegaciones* (boroughs), municipal-level administrations without the power to collect their own taxes.

Figure 1.1. **The Metropolitan Zone of the Valle de México, 2010**

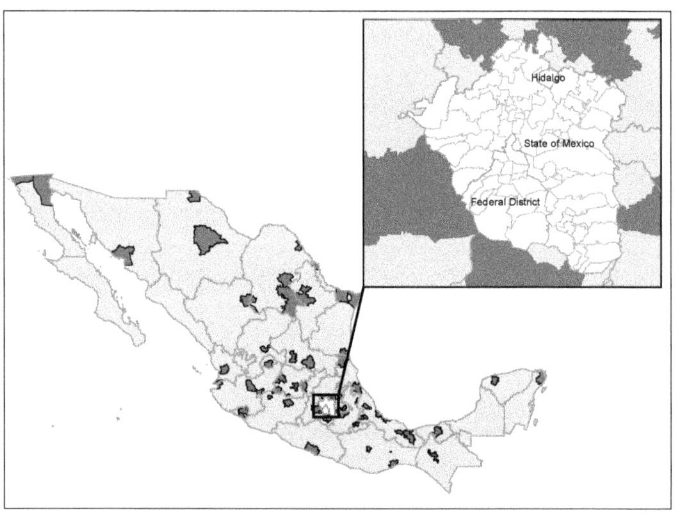


*Source*: SEDESOL-CONAPO-INEGI (2015a), "Delimitación de las zonas metropolitanas de México 2010", Consejo Nacional de Población, www.conapo.gob.mx/es/CONAPO/Zonas_metropolitanas_2010 (accessed 1 June 2015).

In 2010, the Valle de México was home to 20.1 million inhabitants, 1.7 million more than in 2000. The metropolitan zone is a major contributor to Mexico's economy. Its economic output, the gross domestic product (GDP), accounts for nearly 23% of the country's total GDP. But the economic strength is not evenly distributed within the metropolitan zone. Even though less than half of the metropolitan zone's population lives in the Federal District – 8.9 million people in 2010 – the historical centre remains the Valle de México's centre of economic activity. More than 70% of the GDP produced in the Valle de México comes from the Federal District.[2] Concentrating economic activity has the potential to create agglomeration benefits, but requires that agglomeration costs be addressed. Daily commuting flows put significant pressure on the metropolitan zone's transport infrastructure. Congestion is high, and air pollution – while it has improved in the last 15 years – remains above international standards.

Most of the analysis in this review relies on the SEDESOL-CONAPO-INEGI definition of metropolitan zones. For international comparisons, the OECD uses an internationally comparable functional definition of cities, which was developed in co-operation with the European Union (EU). The EU-OECD definition has been applied to 30 OECD member countries and results in 1 175 functional urban areas (FUAs) with 50 000 or more inhabitants and among them 275 metropolitan areas with at least 500 000 inhabitants.[3] To distinguish between the SEDESOL-CONAPO-INEGI and the EU-OECD definition, "metropolitan zones" will be used for the former and "metropolitan areas" for the latter, and explicit reference will be made to the EU-OECD definition when it is employed (see Box 1.1 for details).

## Demography and economy

### *The Valle de México is among the largest OECD metropolitan areas, but growth has slowed*

With 20 million inhabitants, the Valle de México is the third-largest metropolitan area within the OECD (using the internationally comparable EU-OECD definition of metropolitan areas) and the largest outside Asia (Figure 1.2). Comparisons outside the OECD are difficult as definitions of metropolitan areas are not unified, but the Valle de México is certainly among the 3 largest in the Americas and among the 15 largest worldwide. Moreover, it is likely to continue to grow. Between 2000 and 2012, the population of the Valle de México metropolitan area grew annually by about 1.2%.[4]

Figure 1.2. **The largest OECD metropolitan areas, 2012**

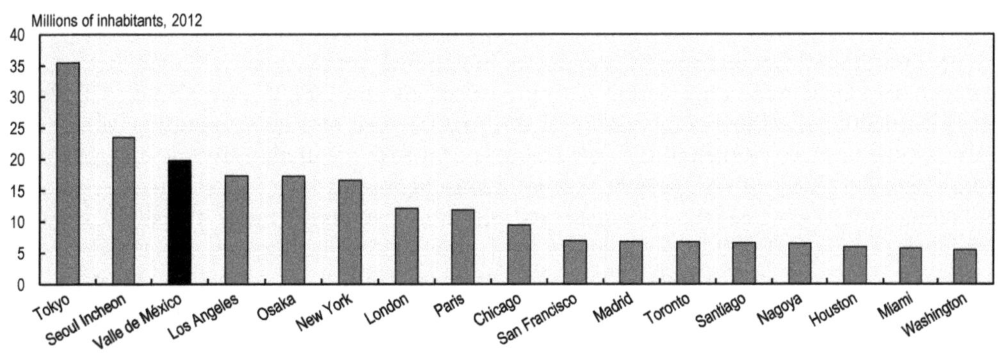


*Note:* Data for the Valle de México refers to the OECD metropolitan area definition.

*Source*: OECD (2015a), "Metropolitan areas", *OECD Regional Statistics* (database), http://dx.doi.org/10.1787/data-00531-en (accessed 13 March 2015).

## Box 1.1. Defining the extent of a metropolis

For Mexico, the Ministry of Social Development (SEDESOL), the National Population Council (CONAPO) and the National Institute of Statistics and Geography (INEGI) determine the extent of metropolitan zones (*zonas metropolitanas*). Their definition considers municipalities with an urban centre of at least 1 million inhabitants or urban centres of at least 50 000 inhabitants that (spatially or functionally) link at least 2 municipalities. These urban centres are combined with surrounding, less densely populated, municipalities based on two aspects: first, if they are functionally linked (measured by accessibility via highway and commuting flows) and exhibit a functional urban industrial structure (non-agricultural employment share); and second, if municipalities are considered in sub-national or national metropolitan planning.

Figure 1.3. **Reasons for inclusion of municipalities or *delegaciones* in the Metropolitan Zone of the Valle de México, 2010**

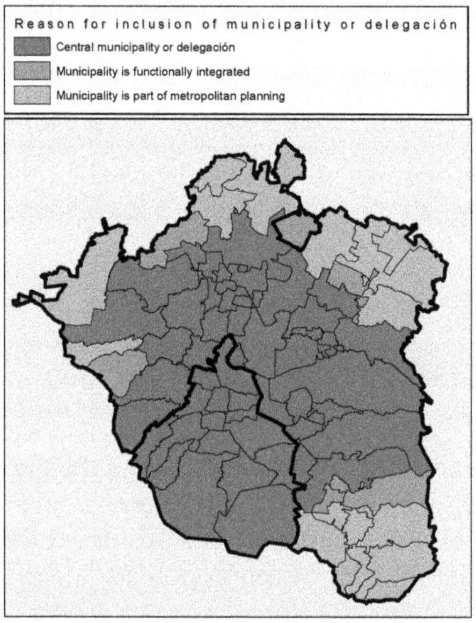


*Note:* This document and any map included herein are without prejudice to the status of or sovereignty over any territory, to the delimitation of international frontiers and boundaries and to the name of any territory, city or area.

*Sources*: SEDESOL-CONAPO-INEGI (2015a); INEGI (2014).

The OECD defines metropolitan areas as functional urban areas (FUAs) with at least 500 000 inhabitants. According to the definition used by the OECD (see OECD [2012a], for details), a functional urban area consists of an urban centre and its commuting zone. A city consists of one or more municipalities, the majority of whose population lives in an urban centre. Urban centres are defined as areas with contiguous high-density grid cells with a minimum population of 50 000 (100 000 for Japan and Korea). The high-density threshold is at least 1 500 inhabitants/km² (1 000 for Canada and the United States). An area outside the city belongs to a functional urban area if at least 15% of the employed residents commute into the city.

The differences between the two definitions arise mainly in the spatial extent. The EU-OECD definition includes 39 municipalities in the State of Mexico and does not extend into Hidalgo. While the two definitions differ in their area, the definition used by the OECD captures most of the population living in the ZMVM under the SEDESOL-CONAPO-INEGI definition.

## Box 1.1. Defining the extent of a metropolis (*continued*)

### Figure 1.4. Comparison of delineations of the Valle de México

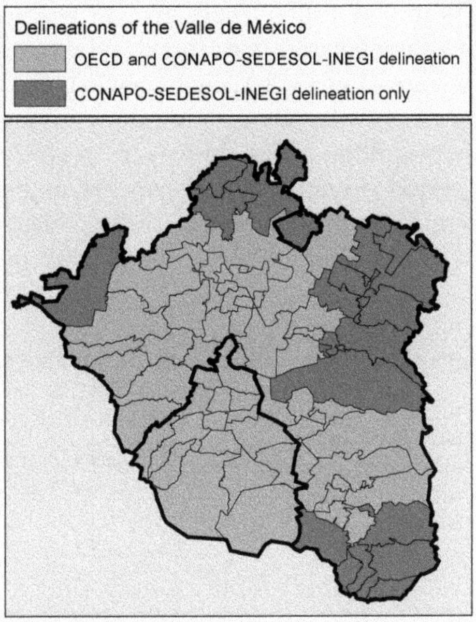


*Note:* This document and any map included herein are without prejudice to the status of or sovereignty over any territory, to the delimitation of international frontiers and boundaries and to the name of any territory, city or area.

*Source*: SEDESOL-CONAPO-INEGI (2015a); OECD (2012a).

The extent of the Valle de México is far from established, and is subject to further change. While most (suggested) delineations consider the Federal District and the 59 municipalities of the State of Mexico as part of the metropolitan area, the number of municipalities included from the state of Hidalgo varies significantly. The 2010 delineation established by SEDESOL-CONAPO-INEGI includes a single municipality from Hidalgo, which has been part of the Valle de México since 2000. Other authors recommend including much of the southern part of Hidalgo, which implies that the metropolitan zones of Tula (northwest of the Valle de México) and Pachuca (to the northeast, and the seat of the state's government) would also be incorporated into the ZMVM. In this context, the inclusion of either 21 or 29 municipalities has been suggested.[1]

*Note:* 1. The Consejo para el Desarrollo Metropolitano del Valle de México (2012) considers 21 municipalities, the Comisión Ejecutiva de Coordinación Metropolitana (2008) includes 29.

*Sources*: SEDESOL-CONAPO-INEGI (2015a), "Delimitación de las zonas metropolitanas de México 2010", Consejo Nacional de Población, www.conapo.gob.mx/es/CONAPO/Zonas_metropolitanas_2010 (accessed 1 June 2015); OECD (2012a), *Redefining "Urban": A New Way to Measure Metropolitan Areas*, OECD Publishing, Paris, http://dx.doi.org/10.1787/9789264174108-en; Consejo para el Desarrollo Metropolitano del Valle de México (2012), *Programa de Ordenación de la Zona Metropolitana del Valle de México: Actualización 2012*, available at: www.economia.unam.mx/cedrus/descargas/pozmvm_digital.pdf; Comisión Ejecutiva de Coordinación Metropolitana (2008), referenced in Gobierno del Estado de México (2009), *Conformación de las Zonas Metropolitanas: Panorama Demográfico*; INEGI (2014), *Marco Geoestadístico Nacional 2014*, Instituto Nacional de Estadística y Geografía, Aguascalientes, Mexico, www.inegi.org.mx/geo/contenidos/geoestadistica/M_Geoestadistico.aspx (accessed 15 May 2015).

While the Valle de México continues to grow, population growth in the ZMVM has slowed. The slowdown comes at the end of several decades of rapid expansion. In 1950, the ZMVM (using the contemporaneous SEDESOL-CONAPO-INEGI delineation) was home to less than 5 million residents; by 2010 the number had quadrupled. The strongest growth occurred between 1950 and 1980, where growth was exponential. Between 1980 and 1990, the metropolitan zone changed very little, and expansion continued from 1990 onwards, albeit at a slower rate (Figure 1.5, right panel). Between 2000 and 2012, the Valle de México's growth rate was the same as Mexico's overall population growth rate. The majority of OECD metropolitan areas, however, grew faster than their respective countries during the same period (Figure 1.5, left panel) Compared to other OECD metro areas, the Valle de México ranks in the lower half of the table, both when compared to all 275 metropolitan areas and in the small subset of very large metro areas with more than 5 million inhabitants.

Figure 1.5. **Demographic trends of the Valle de México and other OECD metropolitan areas, 2000-12**

Population growth gap in metropolitan areas (difference between the metropolitan area's and the country's population growth rate) by initial city size, 2000-12

Population in the Metropolitan Zone of the Valle de México, 1950-2010

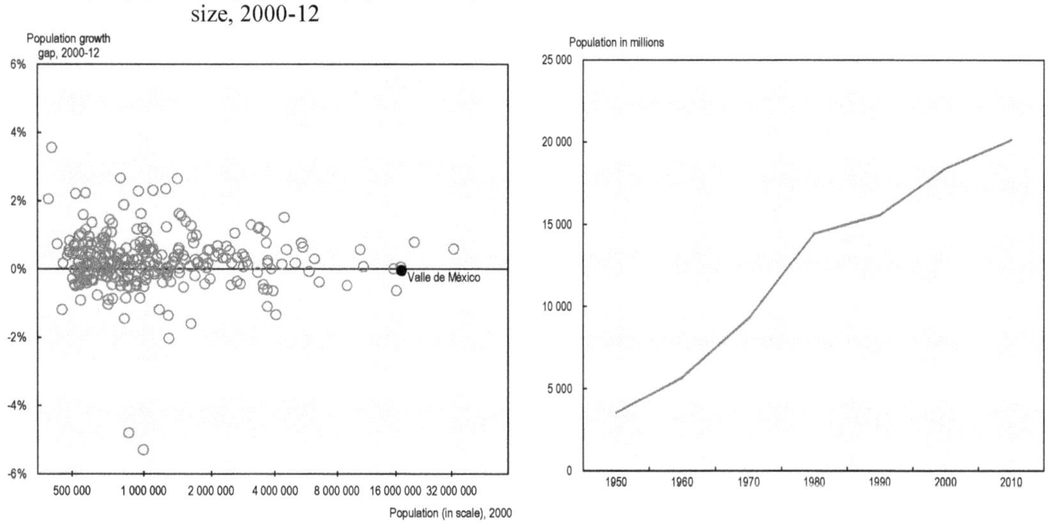


*Sources*: OECD calculations based on OECD (2015a), "Metropolitan areas", *OECD Regional Statistics* (database), http://dx.doi.org/10.1787/data-00531-en (accessed 13 March 2015); for population data from 1950-70: Comisión Ejecutiva de Coordinación Metropolitana (2008), referenced in Gobierno del Estado de México (2009), Conformación de las Zonas Metropolitanas: Panorama Demográfico; SEDESOL-CONAPO-INEGI (2015b), "Delimitación de las zonas metropolitanas de México 2000", Consejo Nacional de Población, www.conapo.gob.mx/es/CONAPO/Zonas_metropolitanas_2000 (accessed 1 June 2015); and for 1990-2010: SEDESOL-CONAPO-INEGI (2015a), "Delimitación de las zonas metropolitanas de México 2010", Consejo Nacional de Población, www.conapo.gob.mx/es/CONAPO/Zonas_metropolitanas_2010 (accessed 1 June 2015).

A slowdown in growth is to be expected as countries become more urbanised and inflows from outside urban areas decline. Additionally, high costs of living and opportunity costs in cities are likely to reduce fertility and further limit growth. Within Mexico, the ZMVM is not alone in its decline in growth. Growth rates declined in all large Mexican metropolitan zones from the 1990s to the 2000s, with the sole exception of La Laguna, where growth rates increased (Figure 1.6). While growth has slowed universally, the ZVZM, with 1.3% annual population growth, was the slowest-growing large metropolitan zone between 1990 and 2010.

Figure 1.6. **Population growth in Mexican metropolitan zones with more than 500 000 inhabitants, 1990-2010**

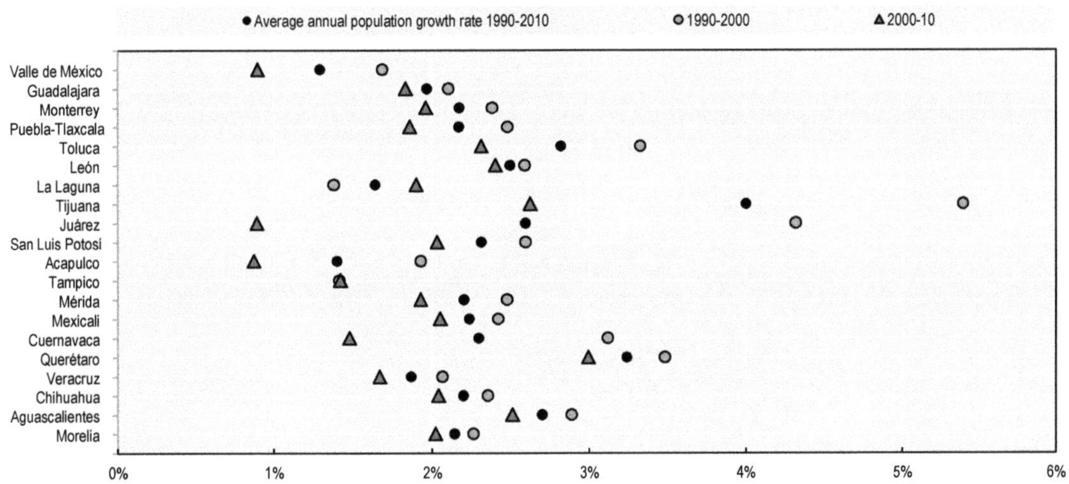


*Note:* Metropolitan zones with at least 500 000 inhabitants in 1990, ordered by their 1990 population size.

*Source*: SEDESOL-CONAPO-INEGI (2015a), "Delimitación de las zonas metropolitanas de México 2010", Consejo Nacional de Población, www.conapo.gob.mx/es/CONAPO/Zonas_metropolitanas_2010 (accessed 1 June 2015).

## *The ageing of its population is set to become a key challenge for the Valle de México*

Demographic change will be one of the key challenges for OECD cities in the coming decades and will become increasingly important for the Valle de México. In 2011, 13.9% of residents of OECD metropolitan areas were "older people", people who are 65 years and older. Across the OECD, the share of older people increased by 14% compared to 2001.[5] Mexican metropolitan areas[6] are still relatively young compared to other metros across the OECD. In 2011, 6% of the residents of the Valle de México were 65 years and older; less than half the OECD average. But while the current share is among the lowest across OECD metropolitan areas, the older population is among the fastest-growing. Between 2001 and 2011, the number of older residents increased by more than 4% annually, compared to a total population growth rate of about 1.2% (Figure 1.7). If both growth rates remain constant, the share of older people will double by 2035 and quadruple before 2060.

Ageing of metropolitan areas creates a range of challenges. They include the need to redesign infrastructure and urban development patterns to help combat social isolation, and help enhance both accessibility within the metro area and the affordability of adequate housing. The governments within the Valle de México will have to address these challenges within the constraints of local revenues, which will be affected by the ageing of the labour force and additional pressure from increases in public spending for health and social care. But unlike other potential challenges the metro area faces, ageing trends and their impact can be fairly predictable. Actions can therefore be taken to prepare for the change and might even create opportunities, such as new developments in technology and innovation, market approaches to retrofitting the housing stock that allow older people to maintain or regain their autonomy, and the organisation of services for older people by other older people in voluntary networks (OECD, 2015b).

Figure 1.7. **Annual average growth rate of older and total population in selected OECD metropolitan areas, 2001-11**

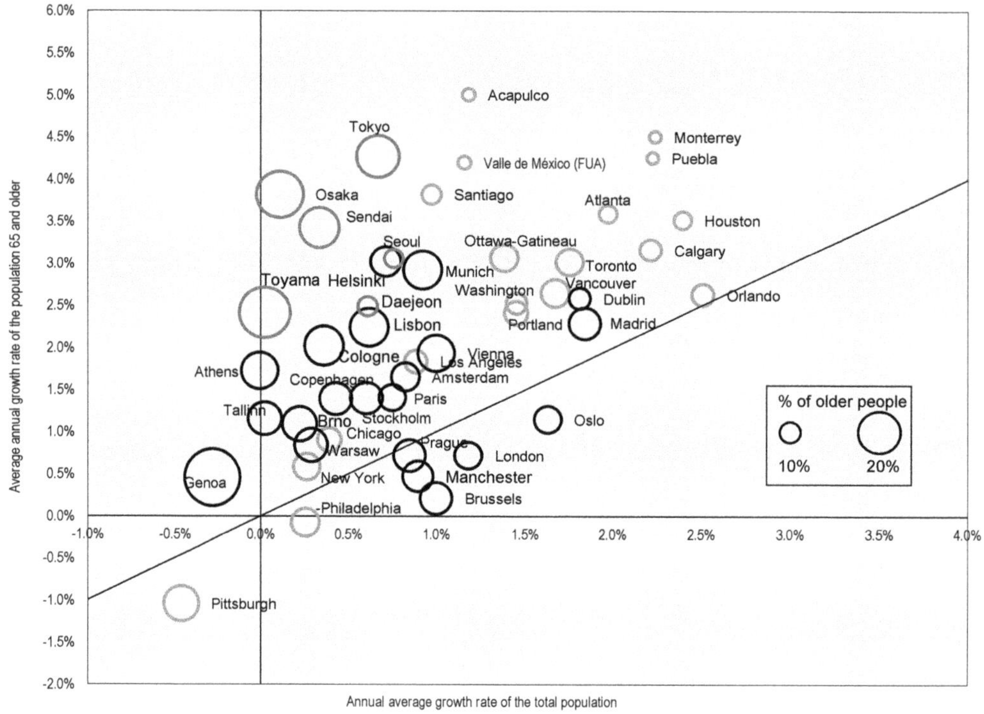


*Source*: OECD (2015b), *Ageing in Cities*, OECD Publishing, Paris, http://dx.doi.org/10.1787/9789264231160-en.

## *Most of the Valle de México's population lives in the urban centre, but growth is stronger in the commuting zone*

Most of the Valle de México's residents live in its urban centre, the dense contiguously built-up area expanding from the Federal District north and east into the State of Mexico. The EU-OECD definition of metropolitan areas distinguishes between the densely populated urban centre and the less densely populated commuting zone. In 2012, 95% of the metropolitan area's residents were concentrated in the urban centre. This is a large percentage in its own right, and also in international comparison. Among the 275 OECD metropolitan areas, the degree of concentration varies significantly, with the (less densely populated) commuting zone accounting for more than half of the population in some metropolitan areas. But the Valle de México does follow the general pattern that a larger percentage of the population of larger metropolitan areas is concentrated in the urban centre (Figure 1.8).

The aggregate population growth rate of the Valle de México masks a growth differential between the urban centre and the commuting zone. Typically, the urban centre is more attractive, as it offers a wider variety of employment opportunities and consumption amenities, but the cost of land and housing is substantially higher than in the periphery of a metropolitan area. Which part of a metropolitan area grows depends on local characteristics, e.g. transport infrastructure, land planning or urban development policies, and on residents' preferences and affluence. Across the OECD, urban centres tend to grow faster than their commuting zones, but with substantial variation. For the Valle de México, the urban centre grew less than the national population, but the less densely populated areas in the commuting zone exceeded national growth by more than 3 percentage points annually between 2000 and 2012. The high growth in the commuting zone is unusual among OECD metropolitan areas, but it has occurred in all three of the largest three Mexican metropolitan areas (Figure 1.9).

Figure 1.8. **Percentage of population in OECD metropolitan areas living in the urban centre, 2012**

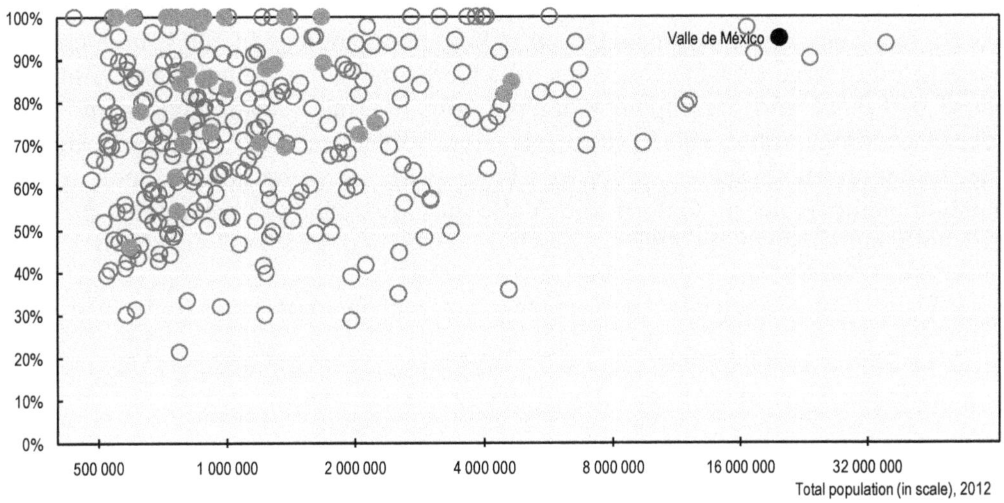


*Notes:* Percentage of the population in the 275 OECD metropolitan areas living in the urban centre. Mexican metropolitan areas are highlighted in grey.

*Source*: OECD calculations based on OECD (2015a), "Metropolitan areas", *OECD Regional Statistics* (database), http://dx.doi.org/10.1787/data-00531-en (accessed 13 March 2015).

Figure 1.9. **Population growth gap in the urban centre and commuting zone of OECD metropolitan areas, 2000-12**

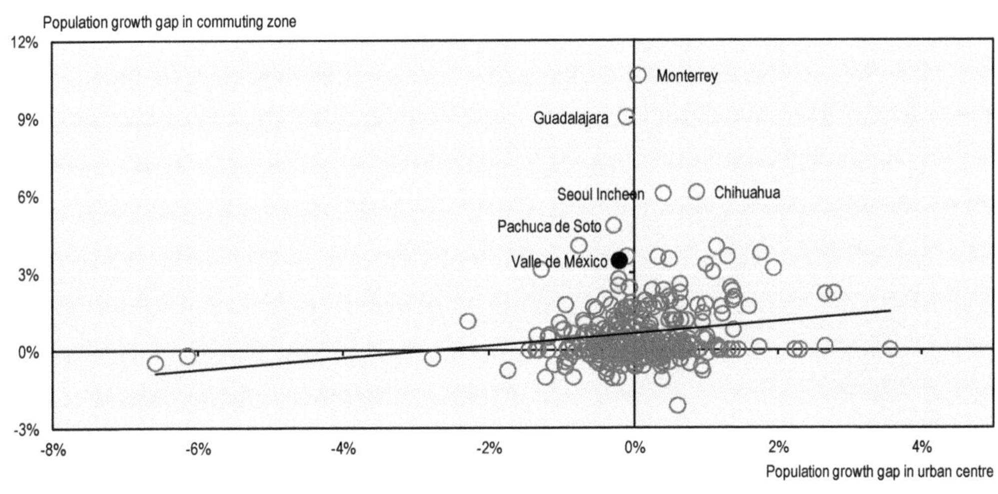


*Note:* Population growth gap is the difference between the metropolitan area's growth rate and the national population growth rate.

*Source*: OECD calculations based on OECD (2015a), "Metropolitan areas", *OECD Regional Statistics* (database), http://dx.doi.org/10.1787/data-00531-en (accessed 13 March 2015).

### *The Valle de México is a major contributor to Mexico's wealth, but retains significant potential for economic growth*

Given its size, it is not surprising that the Valle de México not only concentrates a significant percentage of Mexico's population, but also a high share of the country's economic activity. Under the internationally comparable EU-OECD metropolitan area definition, the Valle de México accounts for 17% of Mexico's residents and 18% of Mexico's employees, who, as previously mentioned, produce 23% of the country's GDP (Figure 1.10). This degree of concentration of both population and GDP is high compared to those of other large OECD economies, like Germany or the United States, and similar to those of France and the United Kingdom. But it is also lower than in most small European countries and comparable to the Asian OECD member countries, Japan and Korea. It is worth noting that London and Paris share a concentration of their country's population comparable to that of the Valle de México, but manage to produce a significantly higher share of GDP.

Figure 1.10. **Largest city's percentage of national population and GDP, 2010**

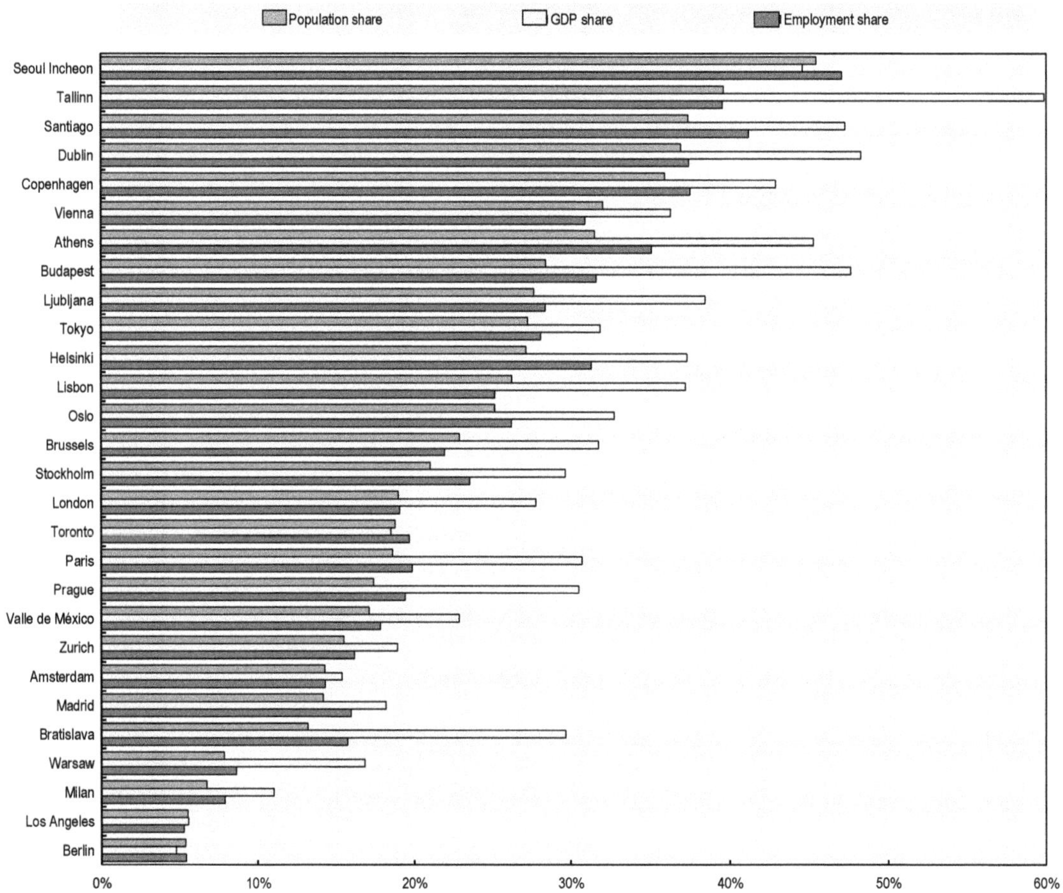


*Source*: OECD (2015a), "Metropolitan areas", *OECD Regional Statistics* (database), http://dx.doi.org/10.1787/data-00531-en (accessed 13 March 2015).

Compared to the 275 OECD metro areas, the Valle de México ranks among the bottom 10% in terms of per capita GDP. Outside Latin America, only Lublin in Poland has lower per capita GDP (Figure 1.11, upper left panel). This suggests that there is significant catching-up potential, i.e. opportunities for growth based on the ability to import technical, managerial and other innovations from the more advanced economies and by adopting best practices from firms operating at the productivity frontier. Most of the catching up is likely to be driven by international links. Per capita GDP in the metropolitan area exceeds the national average by 34% (Figure 1.11, lower left panel). The economy of the Valle de México, measured in terms of GDP, grew by 1.7% annually between 2003 and 2010. The growth was mainly driven by the city's expansion, i.e. the growth in resident population. In per capita terms – a measure of the wealth in the metropolitan area – the annual growth averaged 0.5%, which leaves Valle de México in the midfield of OECD metropolitan areas (Figure 11, upper right panel).[7] The relatively low growth is surprising, given the significant catching-up potential of the Valle de México. Lublin, which is in a similar position, had one of the highest growth rates, both in absolute and in per capita terms, among OECD metropolitan areas between 2003 and 2010. In part, the low growth reflects the experience of most of Mexico and its metropolitan areas during that period. Per capita GDP in Mexico grew by about 1%, and most Mexican metro areas experienced even lower growth (Figure 1.11, lower right panel).

Figure 1.11. **OECD metropolitan areas ranked by GDP and per capita GDP growth, 2003-10**

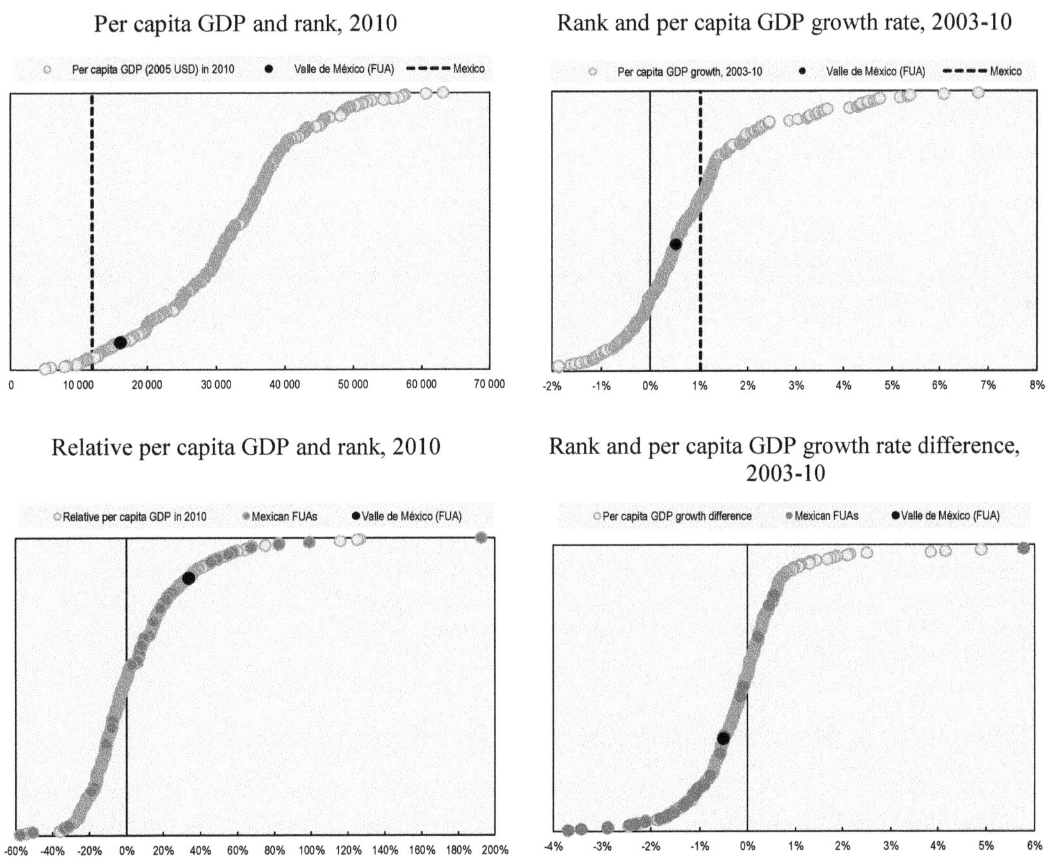


*Notes:* Figures in the upper row depict the per capita GDP and growth rate in absolute terms; the lower row depicts the two indicators relative to the metropolitan areas' national values. The left figures depict metro area per capita GDP relative to the national average. The right figures depict the difference between metro area per capita GDP growth and the national per capita GDP growth rate.

*Source*: OECD (2015a), "Metropolitan areas", *OECD Regional Statistics* (database), http://dx.doi.org/10.1787/data-00531-en (accessed 13 March 2015).

It is crucial to consider the production of the metropolitan area as a whole, rather than focusing only on a part of the Valle de México. Employees move around within a metropolitan zone, and place of residence and place of work often do not coincide. This means that the whole metropolitan area needs to be taken into account in considering the output and size of the agglomeration (in terms of population or labour force). Within the metropolitan area (using the EU-OECD metropolitan area definition), per capita GDP in 2010 was USD 16 060 (in 2005 prices). This average masks a deep split between the production by firms in the Federal District, at the core of the urban centre, and surrounding municipalities (Figure 1.12). In the Federal District, per capita GDP was nearly two-thirds higher than the metropolitan average, USD 26 550, whereas the average per capita GDP in the 39 municipalities of the State of Mexico was less than half (USD 7 140). The difference partly arises from economic links within the metropolitan zone. Employees who live in the surrounding municipalities and commute into the Federal District raise the GDP in the Federal District, but "reduce" the per capita GDP at their place of residence. Considering labour productivity measured as the GDP per employee corrects for the flows, the gap between the Federal District and the rest of the Valle de México is only slightly attenuated.

Figure 1.12. **Per capita GDP and labour productivity in the Valle de México, 2010**

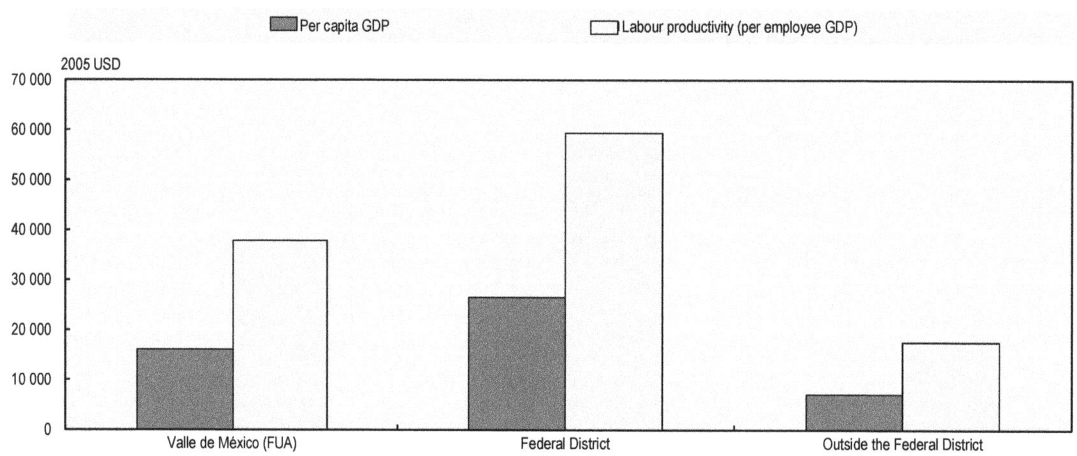


*Note:* GDP measured in 2005 USD.

*Sources*: OECD calculations based on OECD (2015a), "Metropolitan areas", *OECD Regional Statistics* (database), http://dx.doi.org/10.1787/data-00531-en (accessed 13 March 2015) and OECD (2015c), "Large Regions (TL2)", *OECD Regional Statistics* (database), http://dx.doi.org/10.1787/region-tl2-data-en (accessed 13 March 2015).

## *Employment in high value-added services is concentrated in the Valle de México*

The industrial structure in the metropolitan zone is relatively concentrated in high value-added services. Employment in financial services and insurance in particular is clustered in the Valle de México. The percentage of employees in this sector is more than 50% higher than in other Mexican metropolitan zones and more than 75% higher than in the country overall (Figure 1.13, upper panel). Similarly high concentrations can be found in transport and communications, and real estate and business services. Urban centres are typically the focal point for service industries, with land-intensive production moving towards the metropolitan commuting zones or rural areas. The concentration in services is partially driven by the expansion of the service sector in general and partially by the relocation of industries. After the North American Free Trade Agreement, a rapid expansion of manufacturing in northern Mexico and a decline of the manufacturing belt around the Valle de México have been observed (Hanson, 1998).

Figure 1.13. **Concentration of employment by industry in the Valle de México, 2010**

Relative concentration of employment compared to other metropolitan zones and the national average

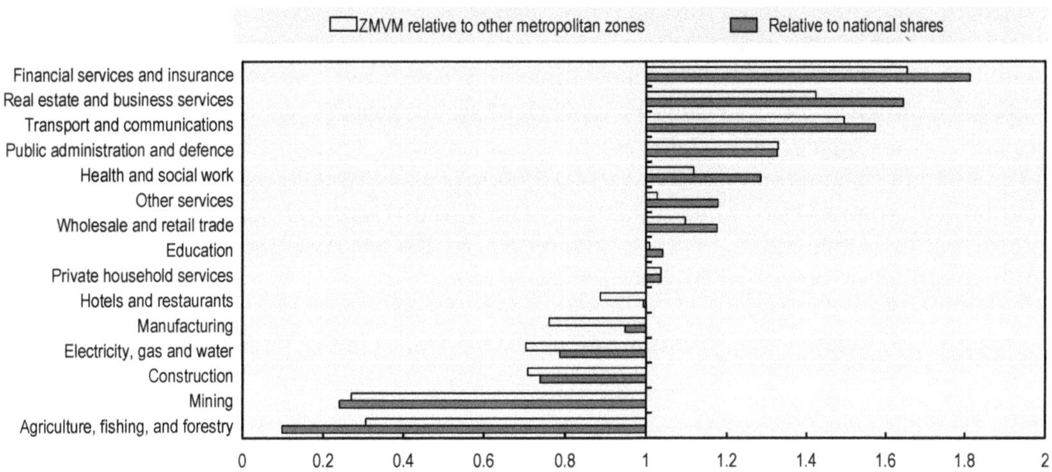


Cumulative share of employees and relative concentration of employment compared to other metropolitan zones

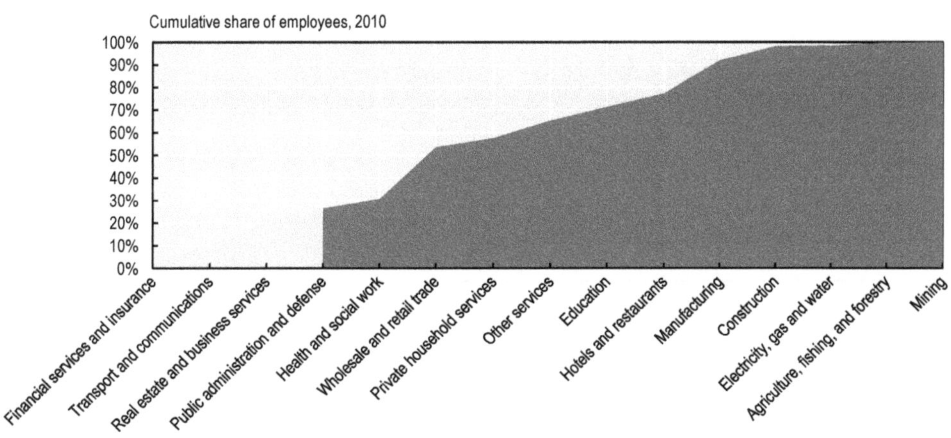


*Note:* Ratio of the employment share in different industries in the Valle de México compared to employment shares in other Mexican metropolitan zones and the overall industry employment shares in Mexico.

*Source*: IPUMS (2014), *Mexico: 2010 Population and Housing Census*, raw data provided by INEGI, IPUMS is provided by the Minnesota Population Center. Integrated Public Use Microdata Series, International: Version 6.3 [machine-readable database], University of Minnesota, Minneapolis, Minnesota.

While the Valle de México has higher employment in high value-added services than other metropolitan zones, the total percentage of employees in these sectors remains low. About one-fourth of employees work in the four industries with the highest relative employment shares (Figure 1.13, lower panel). Research shows that high value-added industries can create significant spillovers, in terms of employment and productivity in other sectors, within a metropolitan zone (Moretti, 2013). But realising spillovers requires working links between local industries and the capacity of workers to adjust to an evolving demand from a changing industrial structure. The high output within the urban centre indicates that not all parts of the Valle de México can capitalise on the relative concentration in high value-added services.

For those employees who work in high value-added industries, the benefits are significant. The industries in which the metropolitan zone is relatively specialised are associated with high labour productivity. These sectors typically also employ highly skilled and highly educated workers. Measured in employees' median earnings, a clear positive relationship between specialisation and compensation emerges (Figure 1.14). Median earnings in the four sectors with the highest relative concentration – financial services and insurance, real estate and business services, transport and communications, and public administration and defence – all significantly exceed median earnings in the metropolitan zone (MXN 4 268 in 2010). The ZMVM attracts service industries with high levels of remuneration, which in turn makes the metropolitan zone attractive for highly qualified workers specialising in these sectors.

Figure 1.14. **Relative specialisation and median earnings in the Valle de México, 2010**

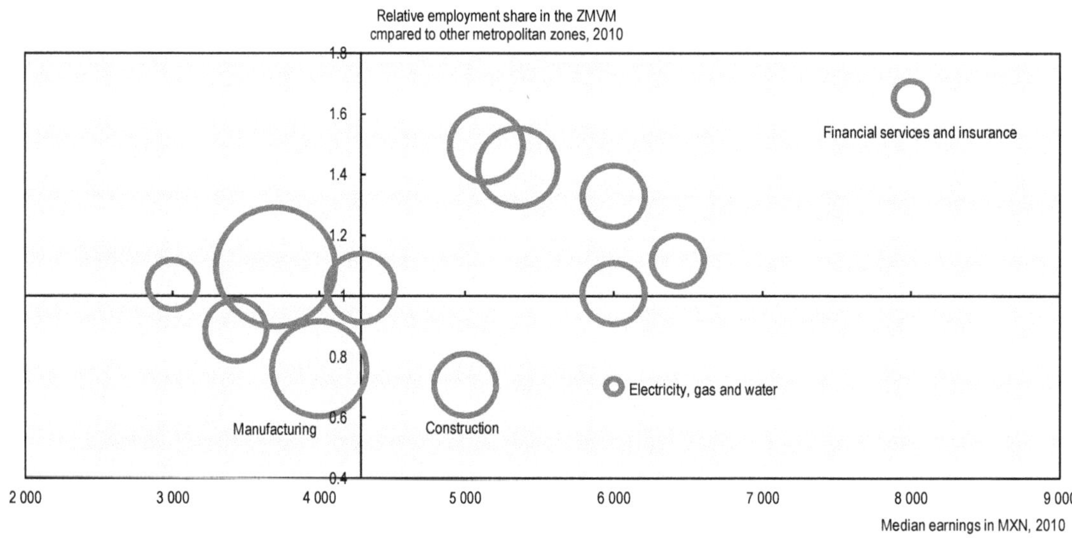


*Notes:* The graph depicts the percentage of employment by industry in the Metropolitan Zone of the Valle de México (ZMVM) relative to the employment percentage across all other Mexican metropolitan zones on the vertical axis. The horizontal axis shows the median earnings in the industries in the Valle de México, i.e. 50% of employees in the industry report earnings above and below the median value. The size of the bubbles indicates the employment share of the industry.

*Source*: OECD calculations based on IPUMS (2014), *Mexico: 2010 Population and Housing Census*, raw data provided by INEGI, IPUMS is provided by the Minnesota Population Center. Integrated Public Use Microdata Series, International: Version 6.3 [machine-readable database], University of Minnesota, Minneapolis, Minnesota.

## *Opportunities in the Valle de México have helped to upgrade skills*

The opportunities created in the Valle de México attract a relatively high percentage of well-educated workers. About 50% of residents in the Valle de México who moved across state-level borders between 2005 and 2010, e.g. from the State of Mexico to the Federal District or from Puebla to the State of Mexico, had some form of upper secondary or tertiary education. Across Mexico, the percentage is 40%. The Federal District in particular attracts the highly educated. About 40% of new residents had a tertiary education and another 20% at least an upper secondary education (Figure 1.15, left panel).

Crucially, the inflow into the Valle de México elevates the skill level in the metropolitan area. The percentage of highly educated workers among the new residents is higher than among residents who lived in the same area in 2005. For example, in 2010, the percentage of university graduates among residents who had moved into the Valle de México after 2005 is 25% higher than among those who were already living in the Valle de México in 2005 (Figure 1.15, right panel). While the percentage of highly educated workers among the new residents within the Federal District exceeded the percentage for the municipalities from the State of Mexico and Hidalgo, the influx of the new residents who located to areas outside the Federal District increased the level of skills in those areas. However, the relatively stronger appeal of the Federal District for the highly educated reinforces the existing gaps within the metropolitan zone. In addition, the low growth experienced in the metropolitan zone suggests that the potential for growth created by increasing skill levels within the metropolitan zone is not fully utilised.

Figure 1.15. **Educational attainment among new residents, 2010**

Educational attainment of new residents in 2010 who had moved across state borders since 2005

Relative educational attainment of new residents and residents who were living in the area in 2005

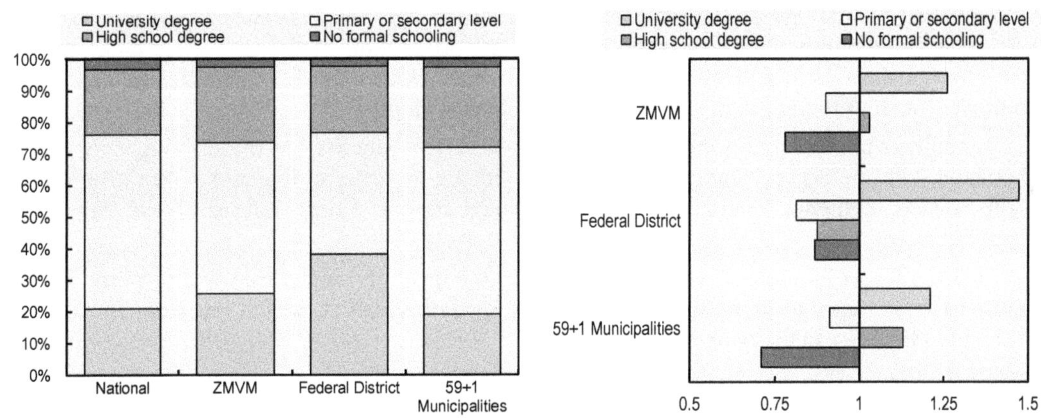


*Note:* Population 12 and older in 2010 who were not residing in the same federal state in 2005. Percentages are rescaled to account for missing information on education; "59+1 municipalities" refers to the 59 municipalities of the State of Mexico and 1 municipality from Hidalgo that are part of the ZMVM.

*Source*: OECD calculations based on INEGI (2010a), *Censo de Población y Vivienda 2010*, Instituto Nacional de Estadística y Geografía, Aguascalientes, Mexico.

Cities can create benefits beyond the skill distribution of their residents. A highly skilled worker will be highly productive in a variety of places, but some cities can create additional benefits. These benefits can arise from different factors, for example a high percentage of highly educated workers can create positive externalities for workers of both low and high educational attainment. In the United States, for a 10 percentage point increase in the percentage of university educated population, the productivity of non-university educated residents rises by 5-6% (Moretti, 2004). Moreover, the size of a city and the associated opportunities for workers and firms to interact can create significant "agglomeration" benefits. Larger local markets mean lower transport costs for firms, an incentive for greater specialisation and – crucially for modern production – greater opportunity for knowledge spillovers (Box 1.2).

Box 1.2. **Bigger is better? Sources of agglomeration benefits**

The mechanisms that create agglomeration benefits can be broadly split into three groups: sharing, matching and learning. The outline below follows Duranton and Puga's contribution to the *Handbook of Regional and Urban Economics* (2004) and builds on a long history of research, with early discussion of the concept of agglomeration benefits ranging back to the 19th-century economist Alfred Marshall and his *Principles of Economics* (Duranton and Puga, 2004; Marshall, 2009).

Sharing of facilities or inputs by a large number of firms is one way of creating critical mass, which is necessary to provide certain goods or facilities. For example, diverting a river to provide a constant stream of fresh water for an industrial site involves large fixed costs that are only worth paying if there are enough firms benefiting from this investment. A similar argument applies to the provision of specialised goods and services. Specialisation creates gains, but also requires sufficient demand to sustain the business model.

Larger labour markets result in better matches between employers and employees. A better match means that the person who is hired for a job is better suited for his or her position and hence more productive. Most people tend to look for jobs primarily within their city. In larger cities, they have more choice between different potential employers and are more likely to find a matching one.

So-called technology spillovers are also relevant in this respect. Businesses tend to learn from other neighbouring businesses about the latest production methods. Larger cities tend to have more businesses in a given field, offering the businesses more opportunities to learn about the most efficient production methods and to adapt accordingly.

In addition to these main mechanisms, agglomeration benefits are often thought to also be associated with the higher "connectivity" of individuals in larger cities, and potentially to arise in the context of higher levels of "knowledge-based capital" (intangible assets) in enterprises located in larger cities.

Lastly, a larger number of businesses increases the level of competition within a city. Fiercer competition ensures that unproductive businesses leave the market, which increases the average level of productivity in a city and raises its GDP.

*Sources*: OECD (2015d), *The Metropolitan Century: Understanding Urbanisation and its Consequences*, OECD Publishing, Paris, p.47, http://dx.doi.org/10.1787/9789264228733-en, based on Duranton, G. and D. Puga (2004), "Micro-foundations of urban agglomeration economies", in: Henderson, J.V. and J.F. Thisse (eds.), *Handbook of Regional and Urban Economics*, Vol. 4, Ch. 48, pp. 2 063-2 117, Elsevier; Marshall, A. (2009), *Principles of Economics*, unabridged eighth edition, Cosimo, Inc, New York.

### *Agglomeration benefits in the metropolitan area are below their potential*

Labour productivity in the Valle de México metropolitan area (according to the EU-OECD definition) is about average among the 33 Mexican metropolitan areas. As for per capita GDP, the Federal District far exceeds the metropolitan average (Figure 1.16). Only the resource-rich metropolitan area of Centro has higher labour productivity. The question is, how much of the productivity observed across the metropolitan areas can be attributed to the skill and knowledge of the individual worker and how much to the spillovers created within the metro area? In other words, what would happen to the productivity of a worker if the worker moved to another metro area? To answer this question, the productivity needs to be decomposed into different elements: those that depend on workers' characteristics – their human capital – and those that are determined by the characteristics of the metro area, the spillovers and agglomeration benefits.

Figure 1.16. **Labour productivity in Mexican metropolitan areas and the Federal District, 2010**

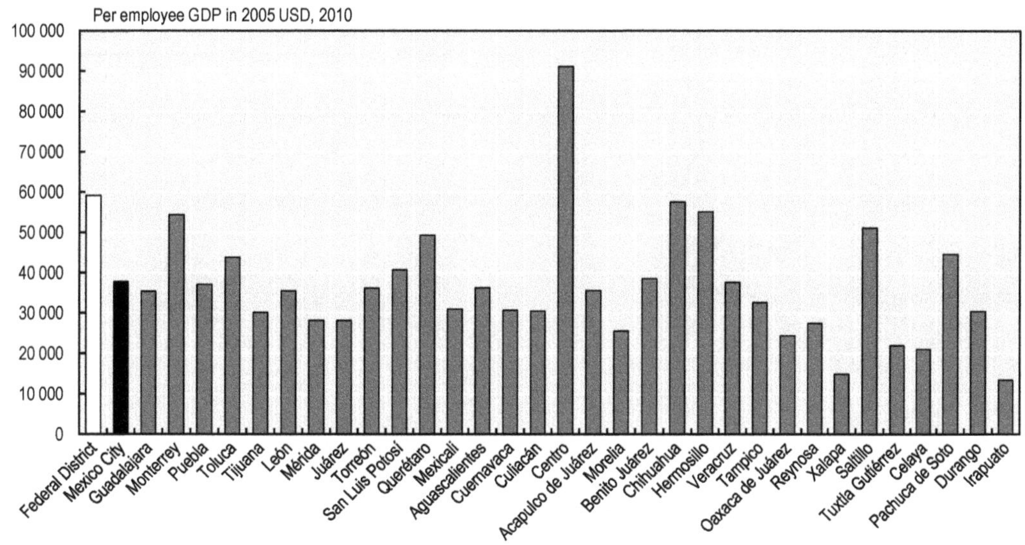


*Sources*: OECD calculations based on OECD (2015a), "Metropolitan areas", *OECD Regional Statistics* (database), http://dx.doi.org/10.1787/data-00531-en (accessed 13 March 2015) and OECD (2015c), "Large Regions (TL2)", *OECD Regional Statistics* (database), http://dx.doi.org/10.1787/region-tl2-data-en (accessed 13 March 2015).

Evidence from five OECD countries, including Mexico, suggests that the Valle de México metropolitan area produces a lower benefit than might be expected given its size (Ahrend et al., 2014). Once the characteristics of the workforce are taken into account, estimates for all five countries show that larger metro areas tend to raise the productivity of their workers. These agglomeration benefits are around 2-5%, i.e. a doubling in population is associated with 2-5% higher productivity (Figure 1.17, left panel). For Mexico, the pattern clearly holds, but the Valle de México does not follow the aggregate trend (Figure 1.17, right panel). The opposite is the case in Guadalajara, the second-largest metropolitan area in Mexico. The aggregate levels of labour productivity in the Valle de México and Guadalajara are similar. They are slightly lower in Guadalajara, but agglomeration benefits there are estimated to be among the highest in Mexico.

A variety of factors might explain this result. OECD evidence suggests that part of the impact arises from a mismatch between the functional reality of the city and its administrative boundaries. A large number of stakeholders increases the degree of complexity in designing and implementing policies that require co-ordination, which can limit the productivity of urban agglomerations. Furthermore, local governmental units may fail to take into account the positive externalities associated with the public goods relevant at the metropolitan level. Thus administrative fragmentation can, for example, obstruct transport infrastructure investments and effective land-use planning, thereby increasing congestion and reducing a city's attractiveness to individuals and businesses (Ahrend, Gamper and Schumann, 2014). Fragmentation may also pose problems in the area of business and environmental regulation, if the additional bureaucracy associated with fragmented governance impedes growth through its effect on the ease of doing business.

Figure 1.17. **Productivity and city size, 2007**

Productivity differentials (five countries pooled)

Productivity differentials (Mexico)

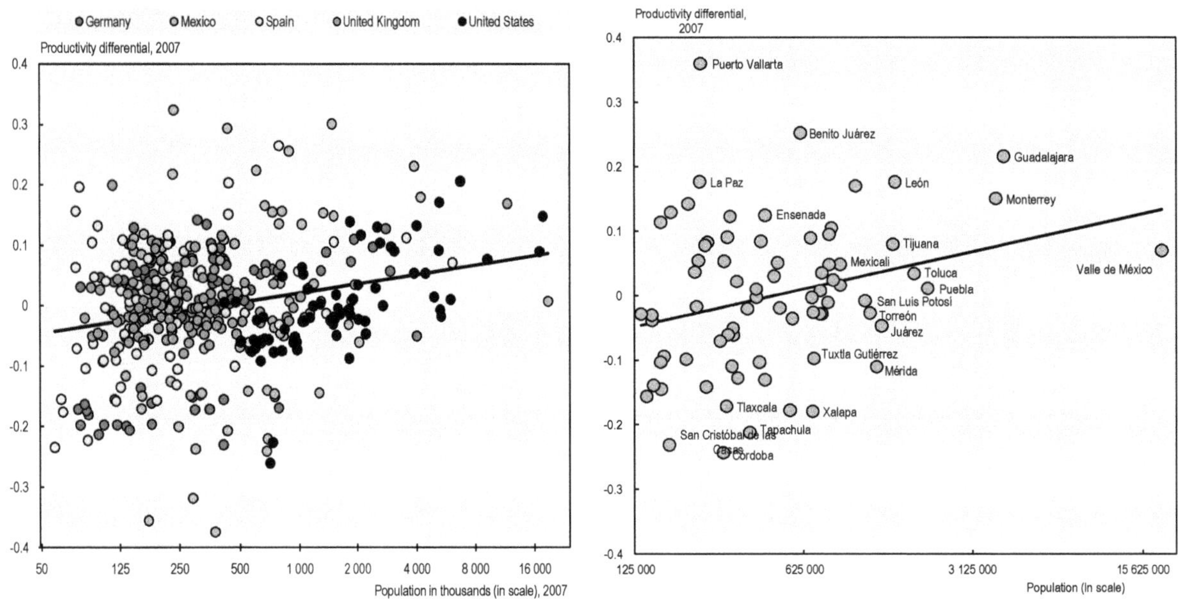


*Notes:* Productivity differentials are estimated from individual earnings data using multivariate regressions. The estimates account for individual characteristics associated with productivity (e.g. education, occupation or age). The productivity differentials therefore capture the externalities of functional urban areas that affect employees' earnings. Productivity differentials in the right panel account for "northing", which controls for the impact of distance to the US border.

*Source*: OECD calculations based on Ahrend, R. et al. (2014), "What makes cities more productive? Evidence on the role of urban governance from five OECD countries", *OECD Regional Development Working Papers*, No. 2014/05, OECD Publishing, Paris, http://dx.doi.org/10.1787/5jz432cf2d8p-en.

Empirical evidence suggests that administrative fragmentation can indeed create significant negative effects on productivity (Box 1.3). Ahrend et al. (2014) find that productivity is reduced by 6% if the number of local governments is doubled in a given metropolitan area. The authors also find that half of this penalty is reduced by the presence of a governance body.[8] This result holds on average. The impact of a governance body is, however, likely to depend on its strength and its effectiveness, with highly effective bodies possibly achieving full mitigation and less effective ones having little positive impact. Given the variety of governance structures and in their quality, it is likely that the presence of an effective governance body can be even stronger.

## Box 1.3. The price of administrative fragmentation

Metropolitan areas frequently contain more than 100 local governments. This degree of administrative fragmentation can result in positive outcomes. Competition among local administrations may help to improve the services they provide, or reduce the fiscal burden on citizens by resulting in lower local taxes. But administrative fragmentation also adds complexity to the design and implementation of policies that require co-ordination, and this can limit the productivity of urban agglomerations. Fields that require co-ordination at the metropolitan scale, such as land-use or transport planning, or economic policies that create externalities across administrative borders, are adversely affected by administrative fragmentation and result in a burden on metropolitan areas if their administrative boundaries do not coincide with their economic realities.

Ahrend et al. (2014) quantify the impact of administrative fragmentation. Using a two-step estimation procedure, they first estimate the relative productivity of functional urban areas (FUAs) from micro-data on employees' earnings. These differentials indicate how much more (or less) a worker with the same attributes earns in different FUAs. Assuming that labour markets are competitive, these capture how much productivity differs across FUAs. In a second step, the productivity differentials are explained by characteristics of FUAs that influence the productivity of the workforce. These characteristics include the FUA's size (to capture agglomeration benefits), its industrial structure and degree of specialisation, and an indicator for capital cities and port cities, Crucially, Ahrend et al. (2014) also control for the degree of administrative fragmentation and the presence of a metropolitan governance body.

Ahrend et al. (2014) find a strong negative impact of administrative fragmentation on productivity. Their results also show that metropolitan governance bodies, which are present in many OECD metropolitan areas, can help alleviate the burden. The empirical results indicate that in comparing two metropolitan areas of similar size and population composition (in terms of observable characteristics), the productivity of the one with twice the number of municipalities is about 6% lower. Governance bodies are estimated to reduce the penalty by about half.

Figure 1.18. **Administrative fragmentation and productivity**

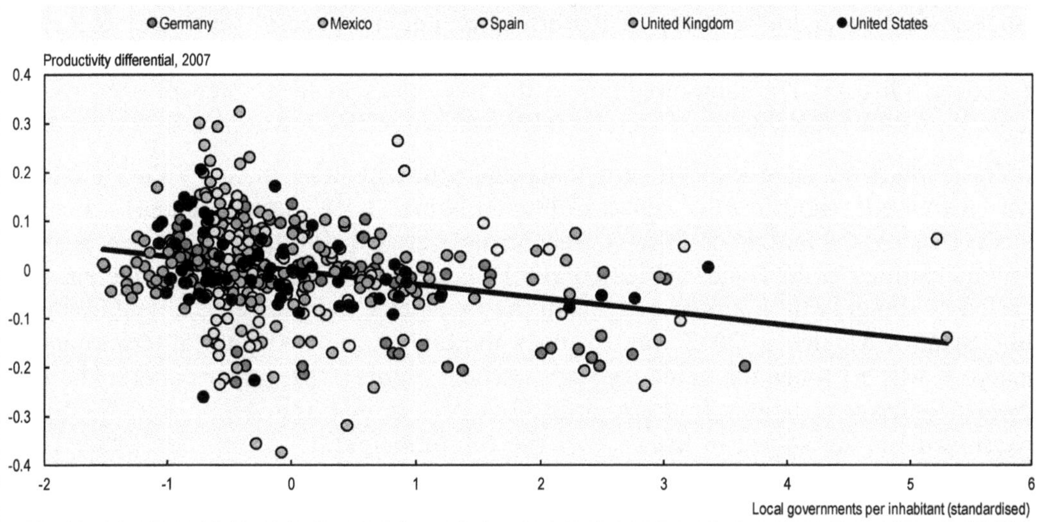


*Source*: Ahrend, R. et al. (2014), "What makes cities more productive? Evidence on the role of urban governance from five OECD countries", *OECD Regional Development Working Papers*, No. 2014/05, OECD Publishing, Paris, http://dx.doi.org/10.1787/5jz432cf2d8p-en.

### *The ZMVM is both vertically and horizontally fragmented*

The size of the Valle de México and the number of political actors make co-ordination of policies a challenge. As outlined above, the metropolitan zone combines entities from two states with the Federal District. The Federal District – as of July 2015 – does not have the status of a federal state, but a political reform is currently under discussion (see Chapter 5). This means that the government of the Federal District does not have the same responsibilities and powers as the state governments. For example, the Federal District's budget must be approved by the federal government. It also means that some of the duties typically carried out by municipalities are provided by the Federal District. In general, public service delivery of water and sanitation services are the responsibility of the municipalities, but they are pooled in the Water Utilities of Mexico City (Sistema de Aguas de la Ciudad de México, SACMEX) in the Federal District.

### *Public budgets have grown significantly in the ZMVM, with most of the increase at the state level*

Metropolitan-level governance arrangements involve co-ordination between the governments of the Federal District and the two states. Integration of the metropolitan area is supported by a dedicated federal fund for metropolitan areas, the Metropolitan Fund (see Chapter 5). Projects in the Valle de México received MXN 1 billion (USD 95 million) in 2006, from the predecessor fund – the Fondo Metropolitano de Proyectos de Impacto Ambiental en el Valle de México, and MXN 3.3 billion-MXN 3.6 billion (USD 260 million-USD 320 million) between 2007 and 2012.[9] The majority of resources is dedicated to road infrastructure, and in practice, little co-operation is achieved across state boundaries.[10]

For the state-level governments inside the Valle de México, the Metropolitan Fund accounts for only a small fraction of the total budget. In the Federal District, for example, in 2012 it accounted for less than 1.2% of the total budget.[11] The majority of funds come from transfers from higher tiers of government, i.e. the federal level and the states. In 2013, transfers accounted for 87% in Hidalgo, 70% in the State of Mexico and 57% in the Federal District. The municipalities in the two states in turn received 68% of their budget from either their state or federal transfers (Figure 1.19, lower panel).[12]

The budgets of state-level governments and municipalities in the Valle de México have increased significantly since 1990 (Figure 1.19, upper panel). For the Federal District, the budget doubled (in real terms) between 1990 and 2013, while for the 60 municipalities in the State of Mexico and Hidalgo, it quadrupled. These increases are dwarfed by the growth in public budgets in the two states themselves. The public budget in the State of Mexico in 2013 was 10 times the budget in 1990 (in real terms) and for Hidalgo it was 13 times the value 23 years earlier (Figure 1.19, upper panel). The rapid increase in budgets comes both from local revenues and transfers from the federal government (or the states, in the case of the 60 municipalities from the 2 states). The share of direct transfers from higher tiers of government has been fairly stable in Hidalgo since 1990, which means that both transfers and local revenues increased in tandem. Locally raised revenue has become slightly more important for the State of Mexico since 2004 and for the Federal District since 2008.

Figure 1.19. **Public budgets of the state-level governments and municipalities in the Metropolitan Zone of the Valle de México, 1990-2013**

Growth in real public budget of the Federal District, the State of Mexico and Hidalgo and the 59+1 municipalities of the ZMVM, 1990-2013 (1990=100)

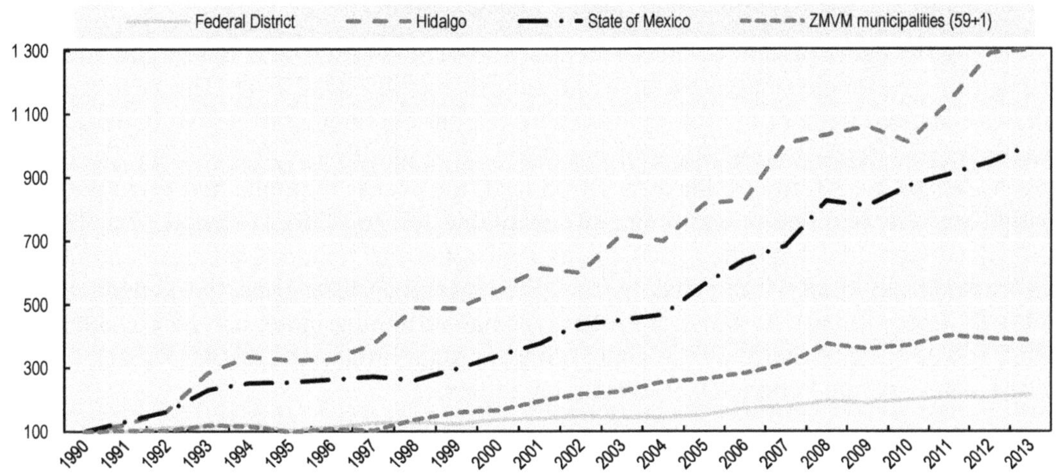


Percentage of public budget from federal (or state) contributions

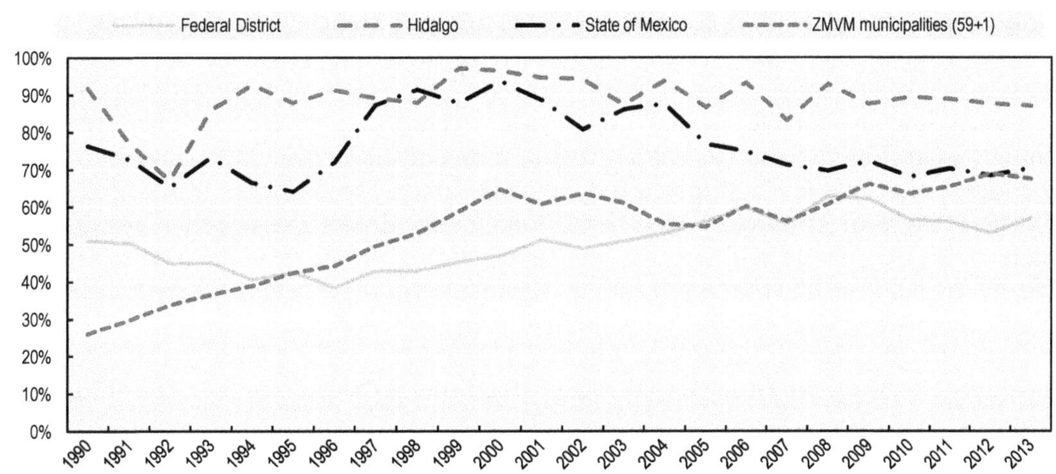


*Notes:* Contributions from national or state-level governments are *aportaciones federales y estatales* and *participaciones federales* for municipalities and *aportaciones federales* and *participaciones federales* for state-level governments. Budgets are deflated using consumer prices.

*Source*: INEGI (2015a), *Sistema Estatal y Municipal de Bases de Datos (SIMBAD)*, Version 2.0, Instituto Nacional de Estadística y Geografía, Aguascalientes, Mexico, http://sc.inegi.org.mx/cobdem/index.jsp?recargar=false (accessed 22 June 2015).

## Inclusiveness and well-being

Economic prosperity is only one among several pillars that support a person's well-being and quality of life. To capture the broad concept of "well-being", the OECD considers a multi-dimensional measure that rests on 11 distinct pillars (OECD, 2013). In addition to income, the measure includes aspects that relate to the professional, social, public and private lives of individuals. Among the professional measures are education and skills in the population, the availability of high-quality jobs, as well as the work-life balance among the employed. The social and public aspects of well-being are captured by social connections, civic engagement and trust, personal safety and subjective overall life satisfaction. The private sphere includes measures that capture the quality of housing, health status and the environmental quality in each country.

Using the national indicators as a stepping stone, the OECD has developed a regional measure of well-being based on 8 of the 11 pillars (OECD, 2014). The regional focus allows the measurement of well-being where people experience it; it also highlights that access to resources and opportunities is not the same in all parts of a country. To capture this accessibility, a further pillar was introduced, the access to public and private services within regions. Results on well-being are available for 362 OECD regions. For Mexico, INEGI collaborated with the OECD to expand upon the regional database and collated information along all 12 dimensions for all 31 Mexican states and the Federal District (OECD, forthcoming). Some of the pillars of the well-being index can be considered for the Valle de México metropolitan zone; however, data limitations restrict the calculations to the states and the Federal District for most pillars.

Well-being in the Federal District exceeds the national average in five dimensions and lags behind it in four. The State of Mexico provides average levels of well-being in most dimensions, but in five dimensions the aggregates show significant catching-up potential. Income, high-quality housing with access to public and private services and a relatively educated workforce raise the level of well-being compared to the national average in the Federal District. Three pillars stand out at the opposite end of the scale. In both state-level entities, the composite indicators for safety and work-life balance are relatively low and for the Federal District also overall life satisfaction. For safety, both entities scores' are among the bottom five in terms of their crime rates, levels of trust in the local police and levels of perceived personal safety. For residents' work-life balance, the percentage of employees who work long hours drives the negative result in the State of Mexico, while self-reported low satisfaction with the time devoted to leisure is the main factor in the Federal District. Residents of the Federal District also report relatively low levels of satisfaction with their lives in general.

Figure 1.20. **Multi-dimensional well-being in the Federal District and the State of Mexico**

Federal District | State of Mexico

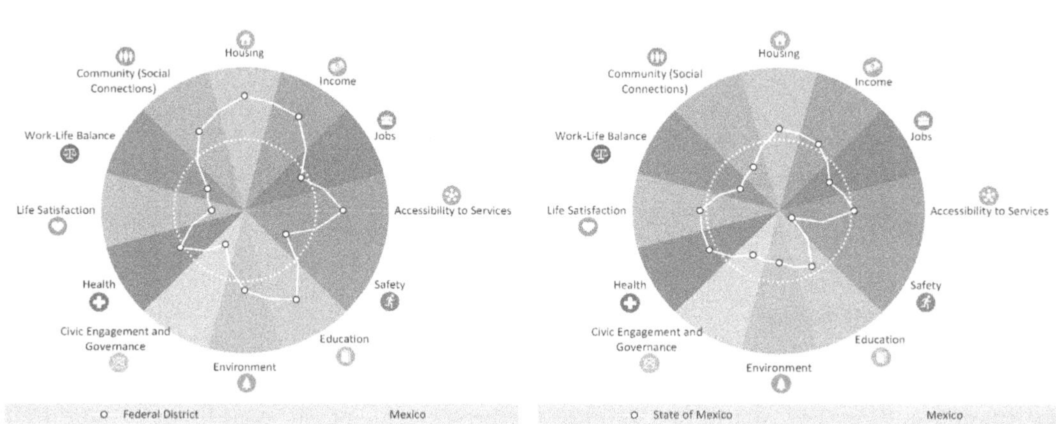


*Note:* Data for 2014 or latest year available.

*Source*: OECD (forthcoming), *Measuring Well-being in Mexican States*, OECD Publishing, Paris.

### *Marginalisation in most of the metropolitan zone is low, although the fringes show intermediate levels*

Despite the challenges it faces in providing and co-ordinating service delivery, the Valle de México has succeeded in creating low levels of marginalisation inside its boundaries. CONAPO provides a census data-based summary of social marginalisation at the municipal level for the whole of Mexico. The index is a combination of nine indicators that capture local social and economic characteristics and local households' access to public services. Specifically, social characteristics are the percentages of illiterate residents and residents without primary education, the percentage of small settlements (of less than 5 000 inhabitants) within the municipality, and the percentages of overcrowded homes and homes with earthen floors. Economic marginalisation is captured by the percentage of working residents who earn less than twice the minimum wage. Access to public services is measured by the percentages of homes without access to drainage or sanitary facilities, without electricity and without piped water.[13]

Nearly half of the municipalities, 29 to be exact, and all but one *delegación* in the Valle de México, are considered to have a very low degree of marginalisation. Another 26 are classified as having low levels of marginalisation. Only municipalities in the fringes of the metropolitan zone are classified as having intermediate levels of marginalisation. The core areas of concern across Mexico are mainly clustered in the rural areas in the south and northwest of the country.

Figure 1.21. **Marginalisation in Mexico and the Valle de México, 2010**

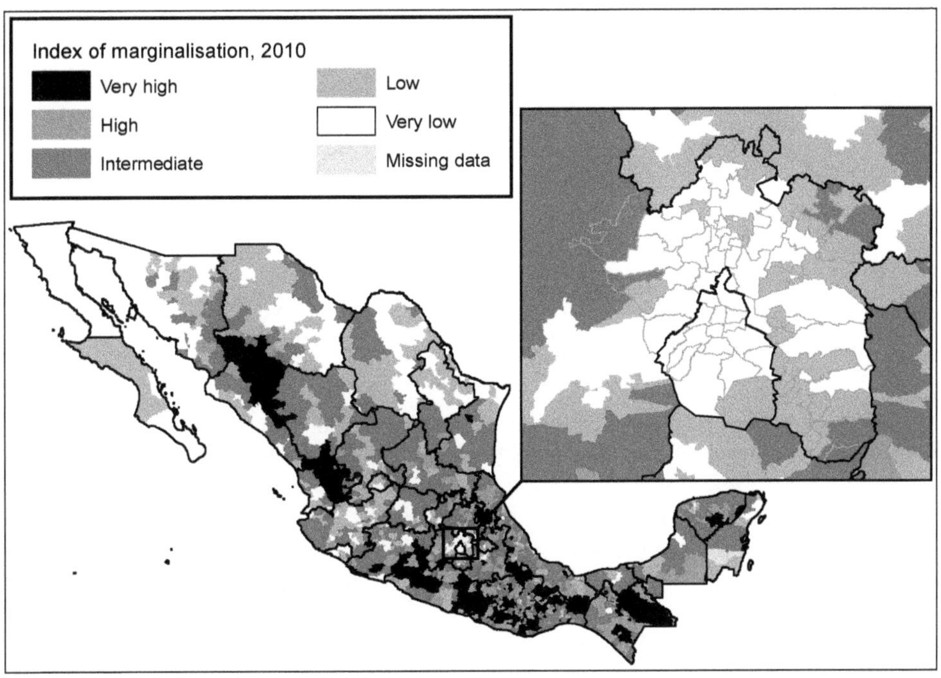


*Note:* This document and any map included herein are without prejudice to the status of or sovereignty over any territory, to the delimitation of international frontiers and boundaries and to the name of any territory, city or area.

*Source*: CONAPO (2015a), *Índice de Marginación por Entidad Federativa y Municipio 2010*, Consejo Nacional de Población, www.conapo.gob.mx/es/CONAPO/Indices_de_Marginacion_2010_por_entidad_federativa_y_municipio (accessed 2 April 2015).

### *Most households have access to basic services, but some neighbourhoods show significant deprivation*

But the homogenous picture painted at the municipal and *delegación* levels masks strong divides within the Valle de México. While coverage with basic services, i.e. access to electricity, piped water and drainage, is almost universal in some parts of the Valle de México, some neighbourhoods have more than 40% of homes without at least one of these services. And areas with low levels of basic services are located not only on the fringes of the metropolitan area, but spread across the centre and the periphery.

While neighbourhoods in the periphery of the Valle de México show the highest percentages of homes missing basic services, even central *delegaciones* in the Federal District include neighbourhoods where 20-40% of homes are not connected to the water, drainage or electricity network. Another striking feature is that neighbourhoods with a high level of public service coverage can be directly adjacent to deprived neighbourhoods, in some cases even encompassing them.

Figure 1.22. **Distribution of homes without access to basic services in the Valle de México's urban neighbourhoods, 2010**

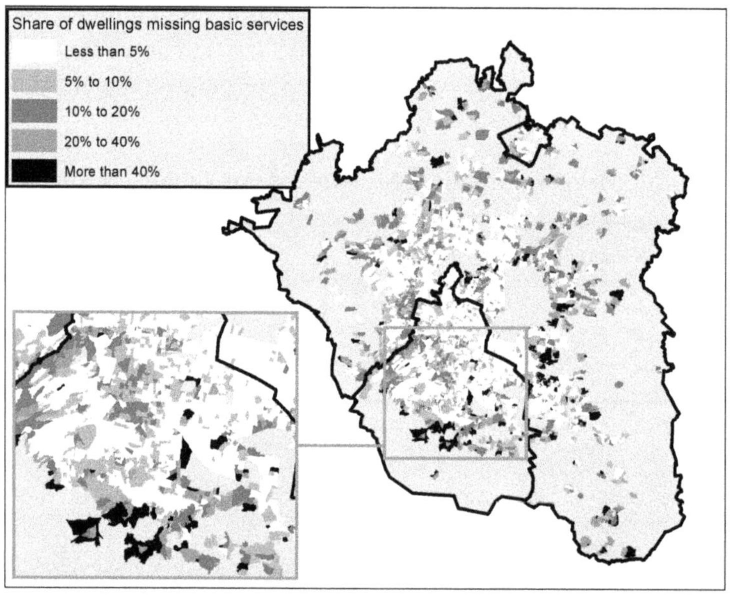


*Note:* This document and any map included herein are without prejudice to the status of or sovereignty over any territory, to the delimitation of international frontiers and boundaries and to the name of any territory, city or area.

*Sources*: OECD (2015e), *OECD Urban Policy Reviews: Mexico 2015: Transforming Urban Policy and Housing Finance*, OECD Publishing, Paris, http://dx.doi.org/10.1787/9789264227293-en based on INEGI (2010a), *Censo de Población y Vivienda 2010*, Instituto Nacional de Estadística y Geografía, Aguascalientes, Mexico.

### *The highly educated and high earners live mainly in the Federal District and municipalities to its north*

Within the Valle de México, the highly educated population is clustered around the Federal District and the municipalities around its northern border with the State of Mexico (Figure 1.23). Given the strong association between education and earnings, the distribution of education can be taken as indicative of the economic affluence of the residents. The differential in average levels of schooling between the core and the periphery is striking, amounting to more than four years of formal schooling between neighbourhoods whose residents have the highest average levels of educational attainment and those with the lowest levels. Many peripheral neighbourhoods have an average level of schooling below the current – albeit recently increased – minimum school leaving age, i.e. less than nine years of formal education. Local clusters of relatively highly educated residents (11-12 years on average) are surrounded by neighbourhoods with declining levels of average years of schooling (9-11 in the adjacent neighbourhoods and less than 9 further away from these clusters).

Figure 1.23. **Average years of schooling in the Valle de México's urban neighbourhoods, 2010**

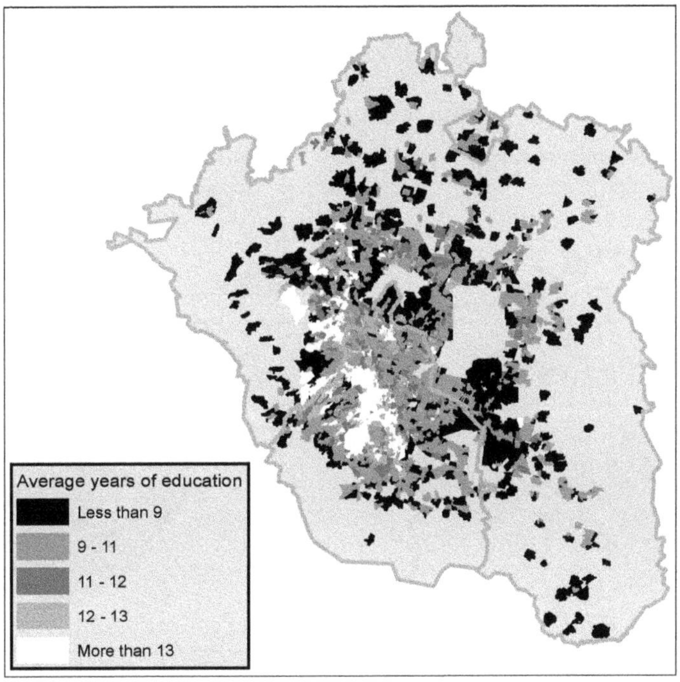


*Note:* This document and any map included herein are without prejudice to the status of or sovereignty over any territory, to the delimitation of international frontiers and boundaries and to the name of any territory, city or area.

*Sources*: OECD (2015e), *OECD Urban Policy Reviews: Mexico 2015: Transforming Urban Policy and Housing Finance*, OECD Publishing, Paris, http://dx.doi.org/10.1787/9789264227293-en based on INEGI (2010a), *Censo de Población y Vivienda 2010*, Instituto Nacional de Estadística y Geografía, Aguascalientes, Mexico.

The highest-earning employees in the Valle de México tend to live around the northern part of the Federal District. As earnings rise with educational attainment, the distribution of median earnings follows the pattern set out by the average years of schooling. The median earnings denote the level of monthly income that evenly splits the working population, i.e. 50% of workers earn less and 50% earn more than the median.[14] Across the Valle de México, median earnings in 2010 are MXN 4 286. However, median earnings in the majority of municipalities fall below this level (Figure 1.24, left panel).[15] The most affluent municipalities and *delegaciones* are again clustered around the urban centre, extending north and south. The inequality across the metropolitan zone is significant. Median earnings in the most affluent *delegación* are more than double the median earnings across the metropolitan area.

## *Income inequality varies across the metropolitan zone and its industries*

Despite the concentration of high levels of median earnings, income inequality varies throughout the Valle de México. One measure of income inequality is the ratio of 75th percentile earnings to 25th percentile earnings. The measure indicates the relative difference between the level that demarcates the 25% highest-earning residents and the level below which the 25% lowest earners fall. The *delegaciones* with the highest median earnings are also among the most unequal, but less affluent municipalities exhibit similar and even higher levels of income inequality. The highest ratios found across the metropolitan zone are 4.5-5, indicating that the 25% of high earners have an income that is at least 4.5-5 times the income of a person that is among the 25% of lowest income earners in the municipality or *delegación* (Figure 1.24, right panel).

Figure 1.24. **Median income and income inequality in the Valle de México, 2010**

Median income | Income inequality: 75th/25th percentile ratio

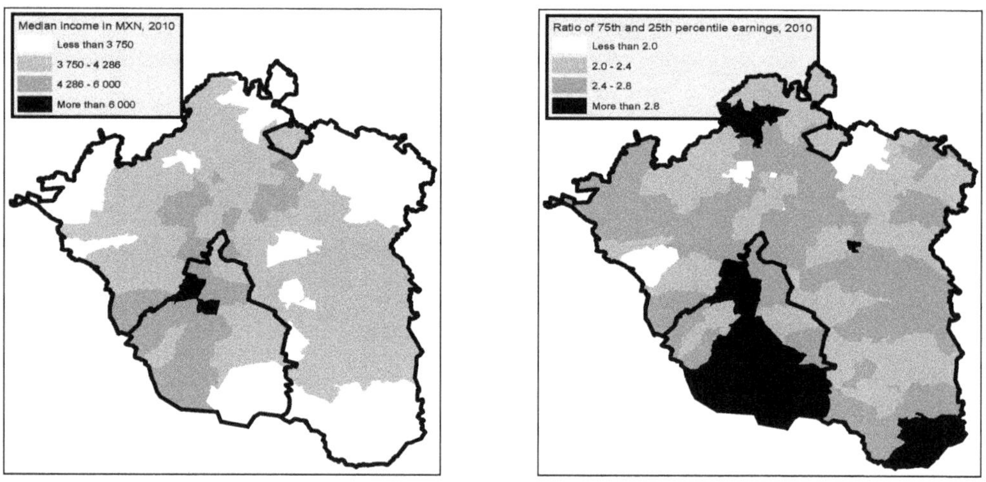


*Note:* This document and any map included herein are without prejudice to the status of or sovereignty over any territory, to the delimitation of international frontiers and boundaries and to the name of any territory, city or area.

*Source*: OECD calculations based on IPUMS (2014), *Mexico: 2010 Population and Housing Census*, raw data provided by INEGI, IPUMS is provided by the Minnesota Population Center. Integrated Public Use Microdata Series, International: Version 6.3 [machine-readable database], University of Minnesota, Minneapolis, Minnesota.

High median earnings in the centre are likely to be driven by high value-added services, but these services also show high levels of income inequality. The gap between high (75th percentile) and low (25th percentile) earners within an industry in the Valle de México is wide. The six highest-paying industries have earnings gaps of at least 100% (Figure 1.25, left panel). This is comparable to other Mexican metropolitan zones (Figure 1.25, right panel). What differs significantly is the level of earnings within the Valle de México compared to those of other metropolitan zones. The ZMVM offers the highest returns for highly skilled individuals, which can help explain why such a high percentage of highly educated workers choose to move to the metropolitan zone from abroad. The Valle de México does offer relatively high returns at the upper end of the income distribution. Median earnings in the metropolitan zone tend to be higher than the

75th percentile earnings in other metropolitan zones. Earnings at the 75th percentile in the Valle de México are nearly double those at the 75th percentile in other metropolitan zones.

Figure 1.25. **Distribution of earnings by industry in the Valle de México and other Mexican metropolitan zones, 2010**

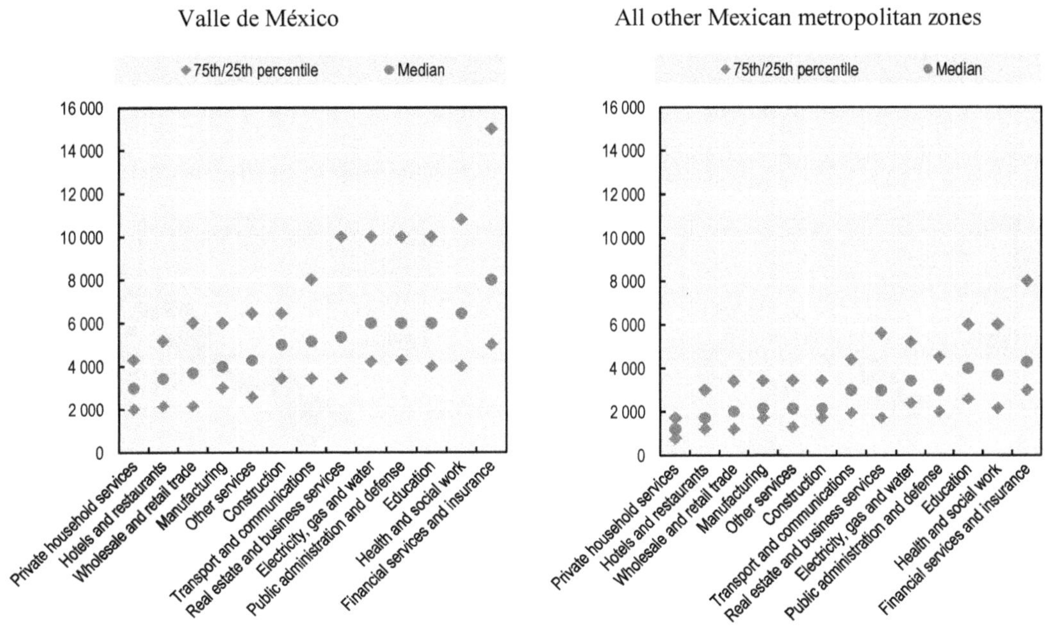


*Note:* Distribution of monthly earnings in 2010 MXN.

*Source*: OECD calculations based on IPUMS (2014), *Mexico: 2010 Population and Housing Census*, raw data provided by INEGI, IPUMS is provided by the Minnesota Population Center. Integrated Public Use Microdata Series, International: Version 6.3 [machine-readable database], University of Minnesota, Minneapolis, Minnesota.

While income inequality can threaten social cohesion, it is important to create an appealing environment that offers competitive employment to highly skilled workers. A major concern in Mexico is the "brain drain" of high-skilled Mexicans. There is evidence to suggest that Mexico may be failing to retain its high-skilled population. While the Valle de México tends to attract a large percentage of highly educated workers, a significant percentage might find more lucrative opportunities outside the country. According to Lowell and Findlay (2001), in 1990 Mexico was the world's third-largest exporter of college-educated migrants, with approximately 30% of its scientific and engineering graduates living abroad.

### *Residents of the Valle de México move towards the centre, newcomers relatively more towards the periphery*

Residents who move within the Valle de México tend to move from municipalities around the urban centre into the Federal District and to municipalities around its northern limits. Conversely, new residents who arrive from outside the metropolitan area tend to cluster in the periphery of the metropolitan zone, the southern and western part of the Federal District and the western and northern municipalities in the State of Mexico.

Residential flows of prior residents can help to assess the attractiveness of different areas within a metropolis. Typically, those with a history in the area have had time to establish themselves and choose a residential location ideal for both their professional and private lives. Within the Valle de México, the most attractive areas are clustered around the urban centre. Municipalities and *delegaciones* around the north-eastern border between the Federal District and the State of Mexico experienced a net gain in excess of 50 000 residents between 2005 and 2010, with the municipalities just north and east of this area experiencing the highest net losses (Figure 1.26, left panel).

Figure 1.26. **Location of mobile residents from within and outside the Valle de México, 2010**

Net change in the number of residents who lived in the Valle de México in 2005 and moved between 2005 and 2010

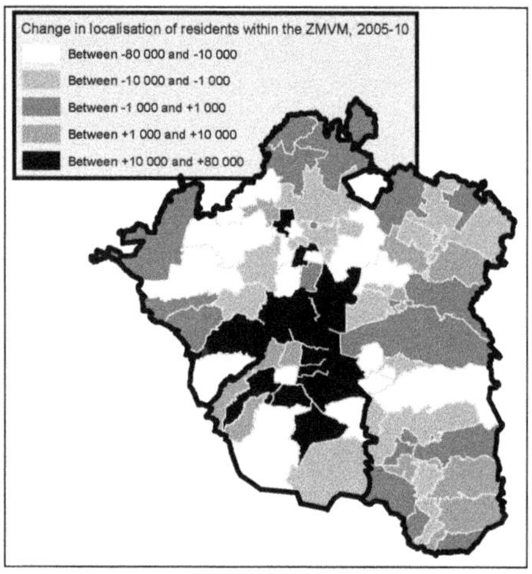


Ratio of the percentage of external to internal movers

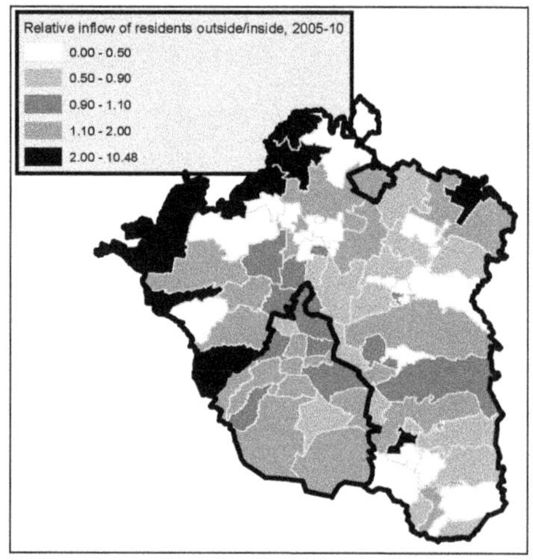


*Notes:* The left panel plots the difference between the number of residents who moved into and out of a municipality/*delegación* between 2005 and 2010, but remained within the Valle de México (internal movers). The right panel plots the ratio between two percentages. The denominator is the percentage of internal movers who choose a municipality or *delegación* among all internal movers. The numerator is the same percentage, but for residents in the Valle de México in 2010 who lived outside the metropolitan zone in 2005.

This document and any map included herein are without prejudice to the status of or sovereignty over any territory, to the delimitation of international frontiers and boundaries and to the name of any territory, city or area.

*Source*: CONAPO (2015b), "Matriz de movilidad laboral 2010" [Municipal labour mobility matrix 2010], Consejo Nacional de Población, www.conapo.gob.mx/work/models/CONAPO/Migracion_Interna/Descargas/Matriz_movilidad_laboral_2010.xlsx (accessed 25 March 2015).

Compared to similar residents who relocate within a metropolis, new arrivals from outside tend to find housing in less attractive areas. Searching for accommodation is always costly, but more so if a person moves over long distances. Additionally, movers who are attracted by the potential employment opportunities in the metropolitan zone might not have the financial capacity to find housing in more sought-after – and therefore more expensive – neighbourhoods. To consider the relative distribution of movers from within the metropolitan zone and those who came from outside, Figure 1.26 shows the ratio between internal and external movers of the percentage who chose a particular municipality or *delegación*. Within the Valle de México, the percentage of new residents in some municipalities in the periphery is more than double the percentage of internal movers. On the other hand, the central *delegaciones* and municipalities attract about as high a percentage of external movers as internal movers (Figure 1.26, right panel).

### *Unemployment is relatively low, but rose through the 2000s*

Unemployment in the metropolitan area of the Valle de México (following the EU-OECD definition) started rising in the mid-2000s, peaking in 2009 (Figure 1.27). The increase can in part be attributed to the global financial crisis, given that the steep increase in unemployment in the Valle de México after 2008 was also seen in other OECD metropolitan areas. However, the rise in unemployment in the mid-2000s in the Valle de México is less evident for other OECD countries. Unemployment in the Federal District closely mirrors the experience in the metropolitan area as a whole. If the developments in the Federal District are taken as a proxy for the metropolitan area, reductions in unemployment remain moderate and volatile even after 2009.

Figure 1.27. **Unemployment rate in the Valle de México, the Federal District and OECD metropolitan areas, 2000-13**

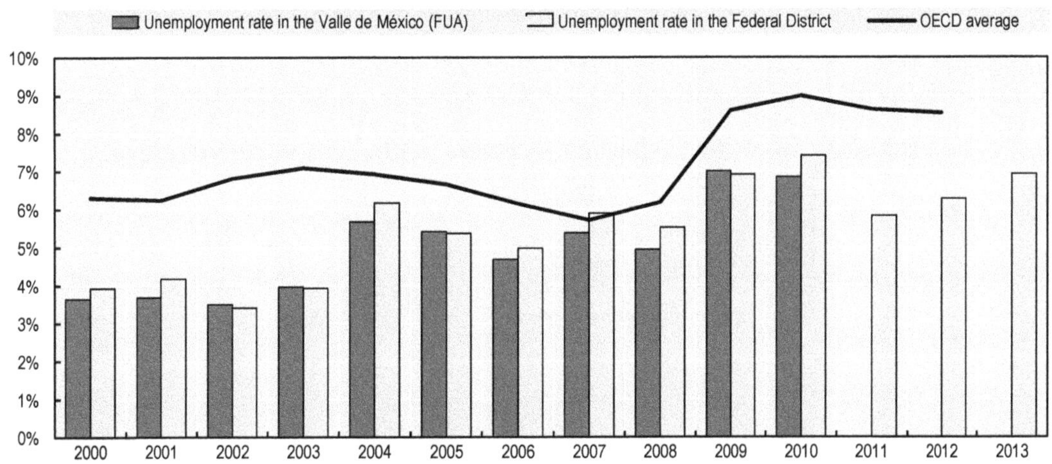


*Note:* The OECD average is calculated based on the number of employees and the size of the labour force for 200 OECD metropolitan areas. Excluded are metros from Denmark, Finland, Japan, Mexico, Slovenia and Switzerland, which are missing data for at least one of the years between 2000 and 2012.

*Sources*: OECD (2015a), "Metropolitan areas", *OECD Regional Statistics* (database), http://dx.doi.org/10.1787/data-00531-en (accessed 13 March 2015); OECD (2015c), "Large regions (TL2)", *OECD Regional Statistics* (database), http://dx.doi.org/10.1787/region-tl2-data-en (accessed 13 March 2015).

Adequate employment is essential for a person's well-being. Beyond the direct impact earnings have on living conditions, jobs can increase life satisfaction. But future prospects are severely diminished if children are not given the opportunity to attain sufficient levels of education, which can give them access to high-quality jobs. In 2010, 4.5% of 12- to 15-year-olds, i.e. children below the current school leaving age, were reported not to be in school but were either employed or unemployed. While this is a marked reduction compared to the 7.4% in 2000 and lower than the percentage in other metropolitan zones (6.4%) or in more rural communities (8.3%), it raises serious concerns about equality of opportunity for all residents.

The opportunities provided to children differ significantly across the metropolitan zone. Schools are clustered around the urban centre, with municipalities in the periphery offering significantly less educational choice. Most schools in the Valle de México do not significantly deviate from the average across the metropolitan zone. Individual schools with above-average performance exist both in the central and the more peripheral parts of the metropolitan zone. Clusters of excellence, i.e. clusters of schools that perform (statistically) significantly above the metropolitan average are, however, almost exclusively found in the Federal District and the municipalities to the north-west of it. Conversely, the eastern part of the Federal District and the State of Mexico's municipalities at the Federal District's eastern limit show a high concentration of schools that underperform by comparison with the metropolitan average. Unsurprisingly, these areas coincide with strong net outflows of internal migrants.

Table 1.1. **Percentage of 12-15 year olds in the labour force, 2000 and 2010**

| | 2000 | 2010 |
|---|---|---|
| Valle de México | 7.4% | 4.5% |
| Other Mexican metropolitan zones | 11.1% | 6.4% |
| Rural municipalities | 14.2% | 8.3% |

*Source*: OECD calculations based on IPUMS (2014), *Mexico: 2010 Population and Housing Census*, raw data provided by INEGI, IPUMS is provided by the Minnesota Population Center. Integrated Public Use Microdata Series, International: Version 6.3 [machine-readable database], University of Minnesota, Minneapolis, Minnesota.

Figure 1.28. **Secondary school performance in the Valle de México, 2013**

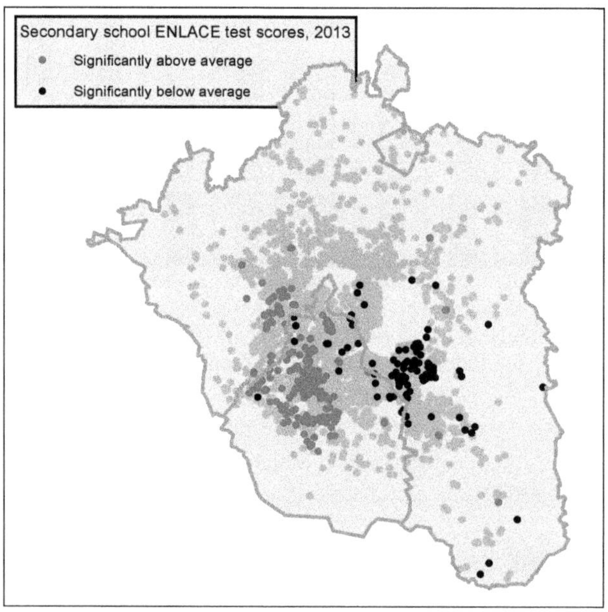


*Note:* This document and any map included herein are without prejudice to the status of or sovereignty over any territory, to the delimitation of international frontiers and boundaries and to the name of any territory, city or area.

*Source*: OECD calculations based on Mejora tu Escuela (n.d.), Organisation website, www.mejoratuescuela.org (accessed 20 May 2015).

## Housing and transport

### *After a period of declining urban density, sprawl in the Valle de México did not significantly change between 2000 and 2010*

A main concern for urban development is sprawl. Cities have a tendency to expand outwards, while population density decreases. This presents challenges for public service delivery, increases the cost of providing public and private transport and may significantly increase the environmental cost of cities.[16] Considering only the urban built-up area, the Valle de México tends to be fairly densely populated compared to other Latin American metropolitan zones. For example, population density in Buenos Aires' built-up urban area was only slightly more than half (7 400 residents per km$^2$) the density in the Valle de México (13 500 residents per km$^2$) in 2000. Density is high compared to large metropolitan zones in Europe or the United States, and only megacities in Asia of comparable size exceed the Valle de México's density (Angel et al., 2010). In 2010, density in the Valle de México was highest inside a 30-kilometre radius around the historical centre. Outside that area, urban neighbourhoods tend to develop with lower densities (Figure 1.29).

Figure 1.29. **Population density in the Valle de México, 2010**

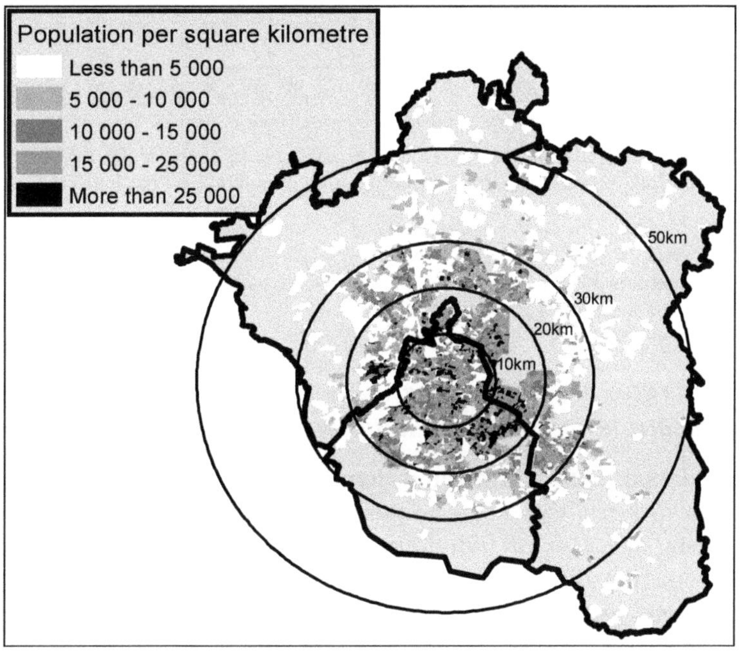


*Note:* This document and any map included herein are without prejudice to the status of or sovereignty over any territory, to the delimitation of international frontiers and boundaries and to the name of any territory, city or area.

*Source*: OECD calculations based on INEGI (2010a), *Censo de Población y Vivienda 2010*, Instituto Nacional de Estadística y Geografía, Aguascalientes, Mexico.

Between 2000 and 2010 density in the Valle de México did not change significantly. The levelling out in this period ended a long period of sprawling development. Estimates of the urban density of the Valle de México for the last 200 years show a significant decline in the density of the built-up area from the turn of the last century – after the proliferation of motorised transport – until 2010 (Figure 1.30). While density was stable from the 1930s until the 1970s, it halved in the next 30 years. On aggregate, Mexico's metropolitan zones showed a tendency towards urban sprawl and more multi-hub, i.e. polycentric, development between 2001 and 2011 (OECD, 2015e). The slowing of sprawled development in the Valle de México between 2000 and 2010 appears to be common among metropolitan zones that went through rapid urban expansion in the years before 2000 (OECD, 2015e).

Figure 1.30. **Population density, 1807-2010**

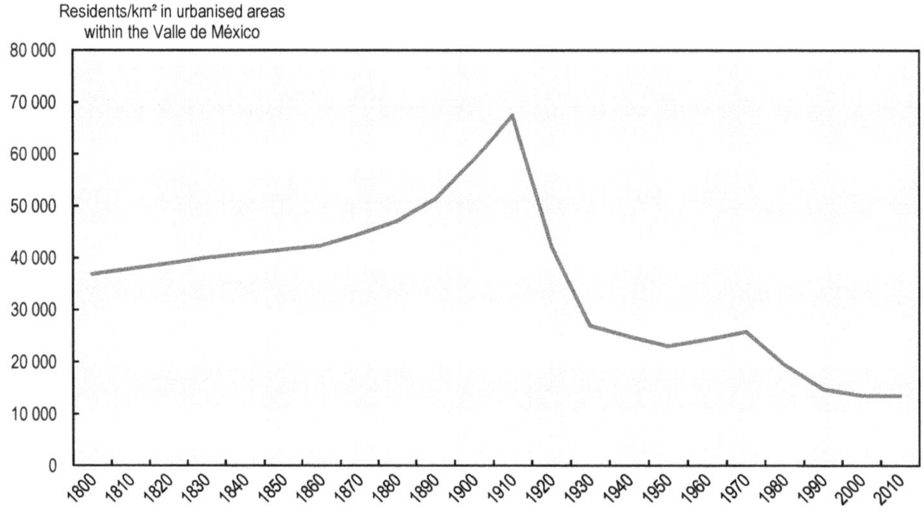


*Note:* The graph depicts the population density in the urbanised area of the Valle de México. Boundaries are contemporaneous and defined based on the built-up urban area in and around the Federal District.

*Sources*: For 1800-2000: Angel, S. et al. (2010), *Atlas of Urban Expansion*, Lincoln Institute of Land Policy, Cambridge, Massachusetts, www.lincolninst.edu/subcenters/atlas-urban-expansion (accessed 20 May 2015); for 2010: OECD calculations based on INEGI (2010a), *Censo de Población y Vivienda 2010*, Instituto Nacional de Estadística y Geografía, Aguascalientes, Mexico.

## *Home ownership rates are high in the Valle de México, with a significant percentage of vacant homes in some neighbourhoods*

An underdeveloped rental market and therefore high home ownership rates can be a contributing factor to urban expansion in peripheral areas. Land outside the central areas is cheaper, reducing the cost of individual homes, which may be the only affordable solution for low-income or first-time buyers. In 2010, the majority of homes in the Federal District were owned by their residents. This has not always been the case. Between 1950 and 2000, home ownership rates in the metropolitan zone grew by 45 percentage points (Figure 1.31). The ownership rate is among the highest across Latin American metropolitan zones, but slightly lower than the Mexican average of 76.4% (OECD, 2015e). Moreover, among the low percentage of non-owner tenants, the formal rental market is underdeveloped. In 2009, the most recent year with comparable data, less than 15% of dwellings in Mexico were formally rented, putting Mexico just behind Poland and Chile and ahead of only six member countries (OECD, 2012c).

A relatively large percentage of homes in the Valle de México are vacant. Vacancy in itself is not a problem, occurring naturally as new homes are built and not immediately occupied or as existing housing stock is being remodelled. Sales or changes in tenants also result in periods of vacancy. Excess vacancies, however, constitute a problem, reducing the economic productivity of urban areas while space is underutilised. This constitutes a misallocation of resources and, moreover, creates negative environmental impacts associated with urban sprawl (OECD, 2015e). In the northern and southern parts of the Federal District, most neighbourhoods have very low vacancy rates, but among the central *delegaciones*, neighbourhoods with more than 10% of homes vacant are common, some exceeding even one-fifth (Figure 1.32).[17] Compared to the Mexican average (approximately 14% of vacant homes), this might not seem excessive, but typically, economically dense areas are characterised by lower vacancy rates than their country average. In Spain, for example, vacancy rates in 2011 were 13.7% in the country, but 9% in Madrid, the country's capital and largest metropolis.

Figure 1.31. **Home ownership in selected Latin American cities, 1950s-2010s**

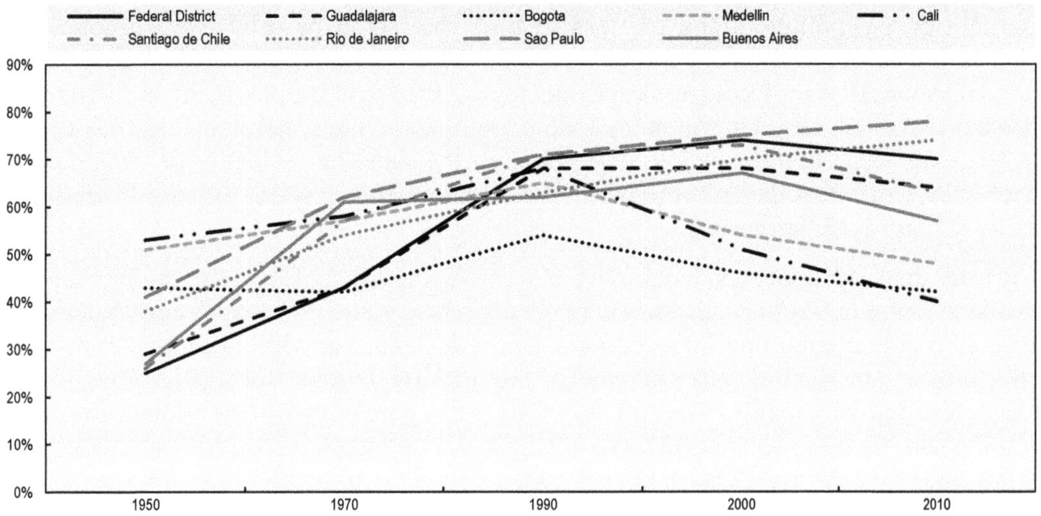


*Sources*: OECD (2015e), *OECD Urban Policy Reviews: Mexico 2015: Transforming Urban Policy and Housing Finance*, OECD Publishing, Paris, http://dx.doi.org/10.1787/9789264227293-en, adapted from Blanco, A.G., V. Fretes Cibils and A.F. Muñoz (2014), *Rental Housing Wanted: Policy Options for Latin America and the Caribbean*, Inter-American Development Bank, available at: www10.iadb.org/intal/intalcdi/PE/2014/13900en.pthe Federal District.

Figure 1.32. **Percentage of vacant housing in the Valle de México, 2010**

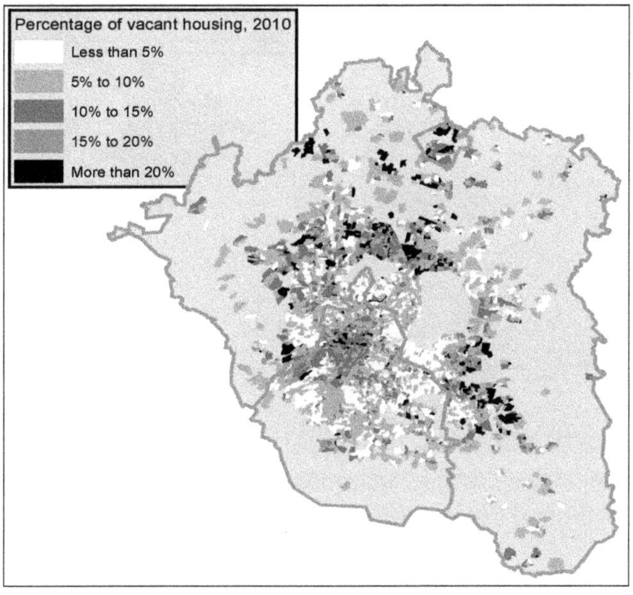


*Note:* This document and any map included herein are without prejudice to the status of or sovereignty over any territory, to the delimitation of international frontiers and boundaries and to the name of any territory, city or area.

*Source*: INEGI (2010a), *Censo de Población y Vivienda 2010*, Instituto Nacional de Estadística y Geografía, Aguascalientes, Mexico.

## *More than 40% of Valle de México's residents commute across a municipal-level boundary*

In stylised models of cities, the urban centre is considered to be the "central business district" (CBD) that workers commute to daily. This creates strain on public infrastructure, congestion on roads and in public transport, but also environmental externalities, i.e. pollution, and the loss of time that could be used more productively, either at work – for economic benefits – or for leisure – to enhance well-being. In reality, the CBD models are of course simplified representations. Employment is available in different parts of a city, but the models do capture some core characteristics of cities. In the Valle de México, most people (57%) live in the same municipality or *delegación* in which they work. Residents in the peripheral municipalities especially tend to find work locally (Figure 1.33, left panel).

More than 40% of residents of the ZMVM cross at least one municipal-level boundary to get to work. The distance residents in the Valle de México commute can be substantial. The commuting flows show a clear CBD pattern, with more than 50% of the employees in the central *delegaciones* in the Federal District travelling from another *delegación* or municipality. Around this CBD, the percentage of non-local employees declines with distance to the CBD. An exception is the municipality of Cuautitlán, north of the Federal District. Cuautitlán and its surrounding municipalities form a smaller, secondary, focal point for employees. Taken together, this evidence suggests high demand for transport infrastructure that connects both *delegaciones* and municipalities in and around the urban centre and allows access from more peripheral municipalities.

Figure 1.33. **Place of employment and place of residence in the Valle de México, 2010**

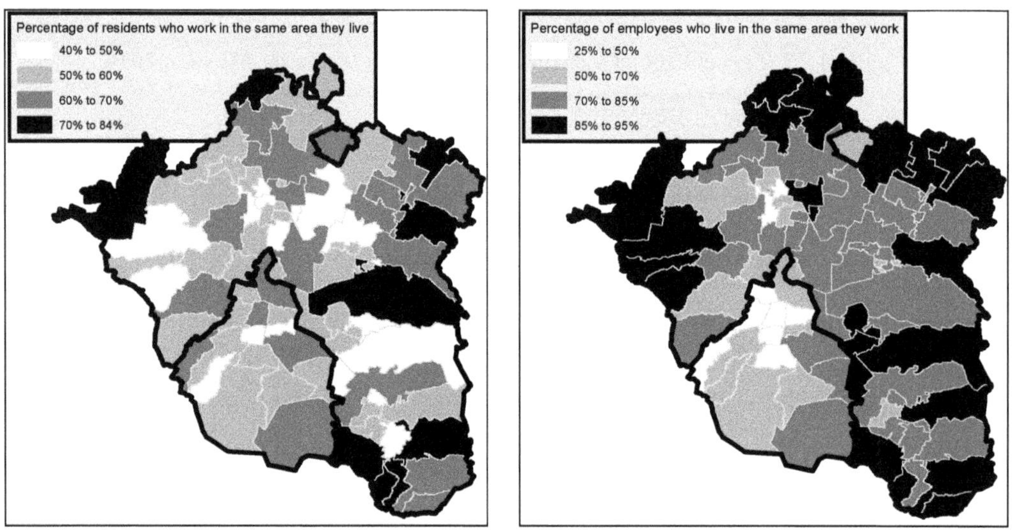


*Note:* This document and any map included herein are without prejudice to the status of or sovereignty over any territory, to the delimitation of international frontiers and boundaries and to the name of any territory, city or area.

*Source*: CONAPO (2015b), "Matriz de movilidad laboral 2010" [Municipal labour mobility matrix 2010], Consejo Nacional de Población, www.conapo.gob.mx/work/models/CONAPO/Migracion_Interna/Descargas/Matriz_movilidad_laboral_2010.xlsx (accessed 25 March 2015).

## *The "space syntax" of the Valle de México*

The social, economic and environmental performance of places – from the scale of the entire city to the scale of the individual street and building – is measurably affected by the interaction of two key properties of urban areas: the geometry of its street network and the location, size and type of different land uses. "Space syntax" is a set of techniques that allow for the analysis of these properties and how they affect human activity within the urban area (Box 1.4). For the analysis, the street network of the Valle de México is divided into 301 470 individual segments, with each segment being the part of a street between two intersections. The analysis considers the space syntax of these segments – and the space they create – at two scales of accessibility: metro-wide and local.

### Box 1.4. Space syntax: Understanding how space influences the city

Space syntax is a set of techniques for analysing spatial layouts and human activity patterns in buildings and urban areas. It is also a set of theories linking space and society. Space syntax addresses where people are, how they move, how they adapt, how they develop and how they talk about it. It uses a unique space-based modelling approach building on extensive theoretical and empirical research that identifies important regularities in human behaviour and links them to the spatial layout of cities with measurable outcomes, like the movement of people through the city, land use, social segregation and crime. These outcomes do not depend on the properties of individual places, but on the configuration of the whole network at the metro-wide scale, as captured by space syntax analysis.

For urban agglomerations, the approach works by transforming the road network into a network "graph". The graph consists of the paths formed by the road network and the space in between, the urban land that the network connects. For the analysis, the road network is divided into individual "segments", a segment being the street or path between two intersections. Each segment, depicting a place, is evaluated using a mathematical algorithm to calculate its inter-accessibility within the wider network. Two types of accessibility can be distinguished: "to movement", which measures how relatively easy or difficult it is to reach a segment from all other segments, and "through movement", which captures how central a segment is for mobility within the city. "Through movement" is measured by the likelihood that movement between different parts of the network passes through a segment. Key to the success of this approach is the discovery that movement in cities often follows a "least angle" path between origins and destinations, i.e. people are willing to travel longer routes that require fewer (sharp) turns.

Space syntax analysis is conducted at different scales, distinguishing between short- and long-distance journeys. Both can be simultaneously evaluated and show how different parts of the same network are used differently, depending on the scale of journey. Frequently, the same parts of the network are used on short- and long-distance journeys. Land-use analysis shows that these multi-scale places are typically successful commercial locations, thus demonstrating the importance of careful spatial layout design in creating multi-scale opportunities for shops to trade to more than one scale of movement.

*Source*: Space Syntax (2015), "Spatial layout analysis of Valle de México", report for the OECD.

At the metro-wide scale, the space syntax of the Valle de México generally follows a "deformed wheel" structure. This is a structure that can be found in other large metros, for example in London (Figure 1.34). In London, the spokes are the radials emerging outward from the city centre, and the continuous structure of the M25 motorway forms the encompassing rim. In the ZMVM, however, rapid urbanisation and the constraints of the topography have resulted in less continuity in the spokes, and an elongated and distorted rim.

Figure 1.34. **Metro-wide accessibility of London**

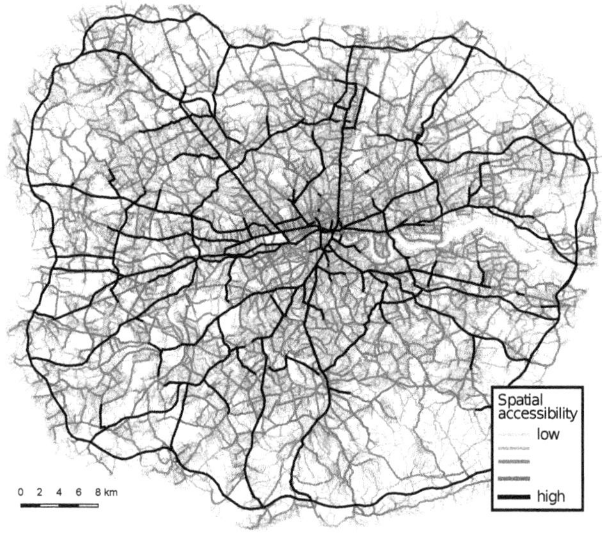


*Source*: Space Syntax (2015), "Spatial layout analysis of Valle de México", report for the OECD.

The ZMVM consists of multiple centres, which, as a result of a rapid expansion and the topography of the Valle de México, are often only weakly connected through metro-wide routes. Within the metro-wide network, the space syntax of the Valle de México consists of three dominant urban typologies: a central core, a peripheral structured grid and linear segregated development (Figure 1.35). The central core is mostly contained within the Federal District, approximately corresponding to the size of the metropolitan zone in the 1950s. Outside the centre, areas of peripheral structured development create neighbourhoods with a high degree of local accessibility, but little connectivity to the remainder of the metropolitan zone. Linear segregated development is found where urban development meets the various hills and volcanoes in the Valle de México and where the topography of the neighbourhoods limits the possible access routes.

The ZMVM maintains a clear, well-connected central core, which combines metro-wide connections with a block structure that has the potential to support pedestrian movement over vehicle-oriented transport (Figure 1.36). The central core has a grid-like pattern dominated by north-east routes, with a network of shorter east-west routes. The primary grid of main road connections supports a dense network of secondary streets that have a high degree of local accessibility. Streets on the secondary grid are sometimes slightly offset due to the rapid expansion of the central core through residential developments. There are few interruptions to the grid, notably Bosque de Chapultepec, Mexico City Airport and the industrial area of Azcapotzalco. The intense grid at the core of the metropolitan zone is typical for large agglomerations. As cities grow, their central areas tend to intensify accessibility through a process of plot subdivision.

The second typology is also a highly structured grid and is represented by larger regeneration projects such as Ciudad Nezahualcóyotl (Figure 1.37). Built in the 1960s, the development was aimed to accommodate the rapid population growth, and within 10 years of its inception, it had grown to 580 000 inhabitants. The planned structured grid in the periphery provides, at first sight, a homogenous intelligible street pattern. It consists of a vast regular grid made out of an array of superblock structures, which can be read as individual neighbourhood units, each of these units covers approximately 1 km². These neighbourhood centres are locally accessible but, in contrast to the ZMVM's central core, offer little accessibility at the metro-wide scale. This disjuncture limits the integration of the neighbourhood into the rest of the metropolitan zone.

Figure 1.35. **Metro-wide spatial accessibility in the Valle de México**

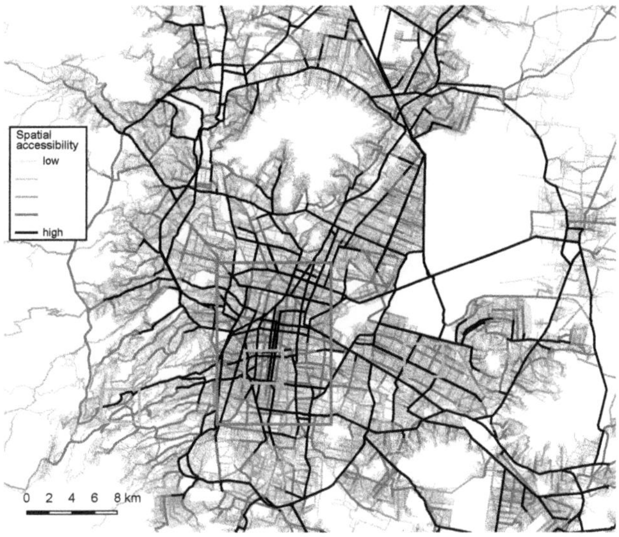


*Note:* The dark blue rectangle shows the approximate extent of the central core. Light blue rectangles highlight examples of the three topologies of the spatial layout of the Valle de México. From left to right: linear segregated development, central core and peripheral structured grid.

*Source*: Space Syntax (2015), "Spatial layout analysis of Valle de México", report for the OECD.

Figure 1.36. **Metropolitan Zone of the Valle de México space syntax: Structure of the central core**

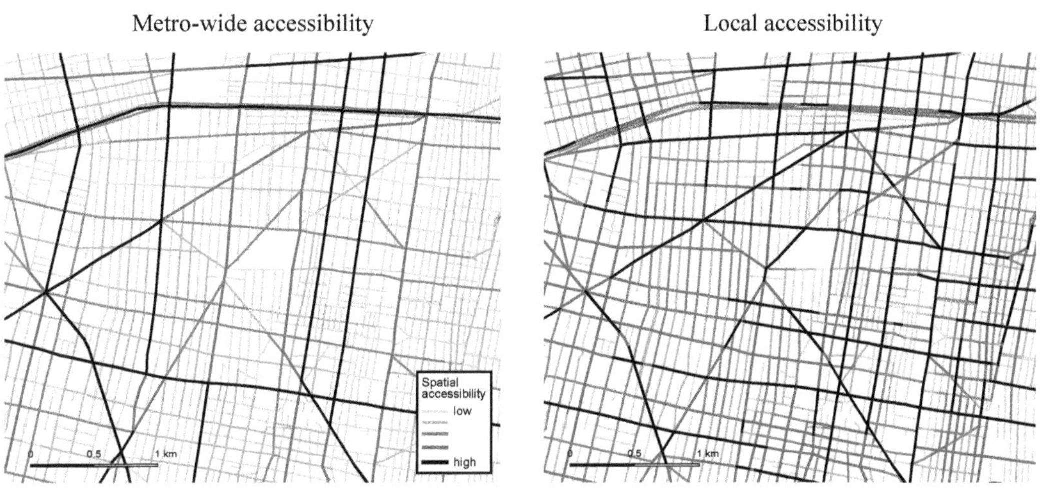


*Source*: Space Syntax (2015), "Spatial layout analysis of Valle de México", report for the OECD.

The least-connected parts of the city have linear segregated development that focuses on access via few, sometimes even single, trunk routes. The dominant land use in this spatial typology is a combination of formal and informal residential developments and is typically found where natural barriers limit expansion. As the topography impedes connectivity, the dominant routes become linear along the possible pathways, connecting neighbourhoods with short perpendicular streets or paths, resulting in linear segregated development. The resilience of a grid, where alternative secondary routes can be used, is replaced by a single trunk route that needs to carry the majority of movement. This results in an urban network with low levels of spatial accessibility, less movement capacity and increased vehicular traffic.

Figure 1.37. **Metropolitan Zone of the Valle de México space syntax: Peripheral structured grid in Nezahualcóyotl**

*Source*: Space Syntax (2015), "Spatial layout analysis of Valle de México", report for the OECD.

Santa Fe, a key commercial and retail district in the Valle de México, gives an idea of the challenges arising from linear segregated development (Figure 1.38). It also shows that it is not only informal settlements that create this spatial typology. In Santa Fe, the spatial segregation is compounded by the lack of a background road network and low levels of residential use. The metro-wide routes were designed as urban motorways, without active frontages and with poor provision for pedestrians and cyclists. Although attempts have been made to improve the connectivity of the area by the introduction of the Supervia Poniente, a north-south urban motorway, the spatial accessibility of southwest periphery of the ZMVM is low. This has the potential to adversely affect the long-term viability of the area.

Combined, the space syntax of the ZMVM shows that despite its rapid extension, the metropolitan zone has a clear and well-connected central core. The core has strong global connections and a block structure that permits pedestrian movement rather than vehicle-oriented transport. But the spatial core of the city has a relatively low density. With the exception of Ciudad Nezahualcóyotl, the most densely populated areas are located at the periphery of the Valle de México, in the spatially segregated zones of the metropolitan zone. Resilience and performance of the ZMVM can benefit from integrating these peripheral centres, based on a strategy that continues to expand public transport and shifts away from urban motorways, to enhance the appeal for non-motorised transport and to retain local accessibility. A possible strategy is a focus on a "boulevard" approach, i.e. on streets designed with pedestrians and cyclists as a priority, which combine frequent pedestrian crossings with a capacity for high vehicular flows. This approach can benefit both long-distance movement and local connectivity.

Figure 1.38. **Metropolitan Zone of the Valle de México space syntax: Linear segregated development in Santa Fe**

*Source*: Space Syntax (2015), "Spatial layout analysis of Valle de México", report for the OECD.

## *Most travel relies on small-scale motorised transport, but public mass transport gathered momentum*

Small motorised vehicles are by far the most common mode of transport for trips in the metropolitan zone. In 2010, 45% of non-pedestrian travel relied on minibuses, another 20% on private cars and 6% on taxis.[18] The number of vehicles in use in the Valle de México has steadily risen since 1986. Between 1986 and 2014, the total stock more than tripled, from 1.6 million to 5.3 million vehicles (Figure 1.39). Between 1990 and 2010, the number of registered vehicles grew on average by 4.4% annually, compared to a 1.3% population growth rate. The expansion of the vehicle fleet was driven by vehicles registered outside the Federal District, which is not surprising, given the demographic trends of stronger population growth outside the Federal District. Trends observed in countries that exceed Mexico's level of economic development suggest that the growth in the number of private cars is likely to be maintained. Demand for cars increases with economic development. While this trend often slows down when high income levels are reached, the Valle de México remains significantly below motorisation rates in wealthier countries in Europe or the United States, which have an average of more than 600 four-wheelers per 1 000 inhabitants.[19] An increase in wealth need not necessarily equate with a larger vehicle fleet. Provision of appealing alternative modes of transport can reduce reliance on small motorised vehicles. Singapore, for example, has a per capita GDP more than double that of the Valle de México, but had only 120 cars per 1 000 inhabitants in 2011 (compared to 198 in the Valle de México).[20]

Mass transport has expanded in the ZMVM, but has significant potential for further growth. The Federal District has both a metro and a bus rapid transit (BRT) system, and the State of Mexico has a separate BRT system. The BRT systems were introduced starting in 2005 (2010 in the State of Mexico) and are being expanded. New routes in both the Federal District and the State of Mexico are opening in 2015. Even with the expansion, only 38% of the urban population in the Valle de México lives within 1 kilometre of a station or stop. The Federal District's mass transport covers 25% of the population, and the State of Mexico's BRT another 13% (Figure 1.40). Even given such a low degree of coverage, the metro in the Federal District is already one of the busiest in the world. With 1.6 billion annual passenger trips, it ranks in eighth place worldwide, between the metro systems of New York City and Paris (UITP, 2014). However, the area of both New York and Paris is significantly smaller than that of the Valle de México. Part of the shortfall is compensated by BRTs. In New York and Paris, the BRT accounts for 200 000 and 90 000 daily passengers respectively, while the Federal District's Metrobús serves 900 000 passengers across its 5 routes, and one of the three routes of the State of Mexico's Mexibús serves another 140 000.[21]

Figure 1.39. **Number of motorised vehicles in the Valle de México, 1986-2014**

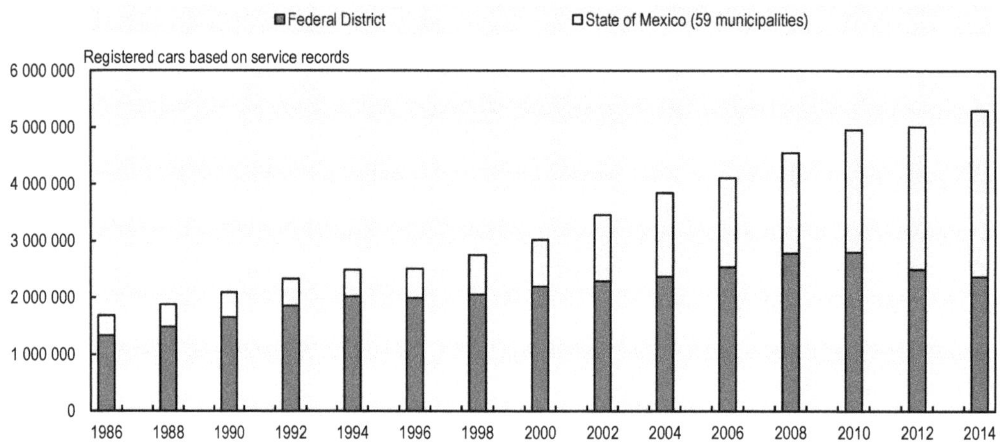


*Notes:* Data include personal (cars, SUVs and motorcycles), freight transport (below and above 3.8 tonnes, pick-ups) and passenger transport (buses and taxis) vehicles. Data refer to active four- and two-wheelers rather than registered vehicles. For private vehicles, the number of active cars is estimated based on the mandatory *Programa de Verificación Vehicular Obligatoria.*

*Source*: SEDEMA (2015), "Proaire 2011-2020", presentation to the OECD delegation on 20 April 2015 in Mexico City, Secretaría de Medio Ambiente del Distrito Federal.

## *Road traffic congestion in the Valle de México ranks among the highest in the world*

Despite the expansion of public mass transport, congestion in the Valle de México is among the worst in the world. Estimates based on travel data from GPS navigation systems show that for a daily 30-minute commute, an additional 29 minutes are lost due to delays in traffic (Table 1.2). With an overall congestion level of 55%, which indicates that travel times increase by 55% due to congestion, the Valle de México ranks as the 2nd most congested among 146 worldwide cities, outranked only by Istanbul in Turkey. The economic cost associated with delays due to congestion is significant. Estimates for the Valle de México amount to an annual loss of MXN 82 billion, or 3.1% of the metropolitan zone's GDP (ITDP, 2012a). This estimate accounts for the direct economic cost of congestion, the detrimental impact on residents' overall well-being is even higher.

Figure 1.40. **Urban neighbourhoods in the Valle de México within 1 kilometre of a bus rapid transit, *suburbano* or metro station**

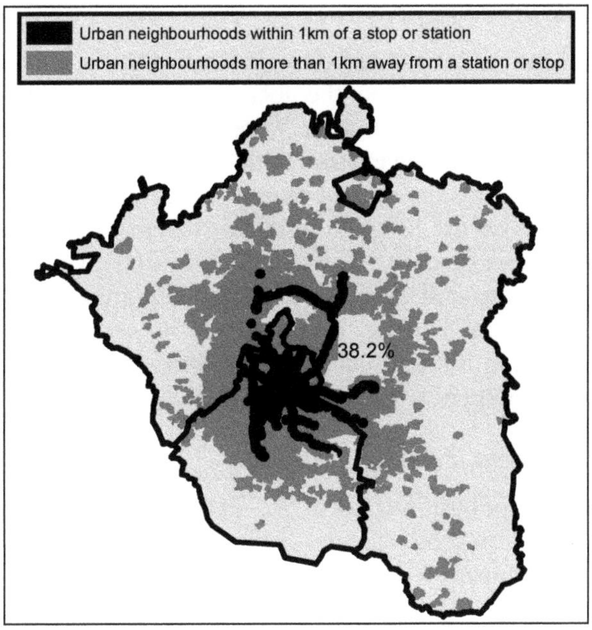


*Notes:* Stops of a commuter train connecting the Federal District and the State of Mexico (*suburbano*), the underground (metro) and bus rapid transit systems of the Federal District (Metrobús) and the State of Mexico (Mexibús) are included in the figure. The population covered includes residents who live in neighbourhoods (census tracts: *AGEB*) within 1 kilometre of a stop or station. The public transport system is current as of June 2015; population figures are taken from the 2010 census.

This document and any map included herein are without prejudice to the status of or sovereignty over any territory, to the delimitation of international frontiers and boundaries and to the name of any territory, city or area.

*Source*: OECD calculations based on INEGI (2010a), *Censo de Población y Vivienda 2010*, Instituto Nacional de Estadística y Geografía, Aguascalientes, Mexico and public transport shapefiles provided by SEMOVI and ITDP.

Table 1.2. **Most congested metropolitan areas, 2014**

| Rank | Metropolitan area | Congestion level | Minutes lost per day with 30 minutes commute |
|---|---|---|---|
| 1 | Istanbul, Turkey | 58% | 29 |
| 2 | Valle de México, Mexico | 55% | 29 |
| 3 | Rio de Janeiro, Brazil | 51% | 26 |
| 4 | Moscow, Russian Federation | 50% | 29 |
| 5 | Salvador, Brazil | 46% | 24 |
| 6 | Recife, Brazil | 45% | 27 |
| 7 | St. Petersburg, Russian Federation | 44% | 27 |
| 8 | Bucharest, Romania | 41% | 27 |
| 9 | Warsaw, Poland | 40% | 25 |
| 10 | Los Angeles, United States | 39% | 25 |

*Source:* TomTom (2015), "TomTom Traffic Index", TomTom International BV, www.tomtom.com/en_gb/trafficindex/# (accessed 30 March 2015).

## Environment

### *Environmental challenges are pressing*

The expansion of the Valle de México, its industrial development and increased prosperity have taken a heavy toll on the local environment. In the early 1990s, the metropolitan zone's levels of air pollution were considered among the highest in the world. Of a sample of 20 megacities with at least 10 million inhabitants, the Valle de México scored among the most polluted cities in 5 out of 6 indicators.[22] Both greenhouse gas emissions that are linked to climate change and fine airborne particles that cause health problems were severely elevated. In addition to a legacy of air pollution, climate change and the associated extreme weather phenomena pose a serious hazard to the metropolitan area's future. During the rainy season, heavy rains and storms, which regularly cause flooding and disruptions in traffic, have been severe enough to warrant declarations of states of emergency.[23]

### *Air pollution has improved, but remains high*

Particulate matter air pollution affects the health of a sizeable percentage of the population. Globally, 8% of lung cancer deaths, 5% of cardiopulmonary deaths and around 3% of respiratory infection deaths can be attributed to exposure to fine particulate matter only (WHO, 2009). Particles of fine diameter, $PM_{10}$ and $PM_{2.5}$, which are small enough to penetrate the lungs, are the cause of most concern.[24] Pollution is likely to have long-lasting effects on residents' health, particularly because of its impact on children, who are more susceptible to air pollution than adults. Children breathe more than adults relative to their body weight, and have smaller airways and lungs and immature host defence mechanisms. Children also have different rates of toxification and detoxification, and are more exposed to pollutants, because they spend more time outdoors and ventilate more, due to play and exercise (OECD, 2012d).

Since the early 1990s, air quality has markedly improved in the Valle de México. Four air measuring stations have provided uninterrupted data on the volume of $PM_{10}$ in the ambient air from 1980 until the present.[25] All stations show strong seasonal variation in pollution levels, but they also measured a strong declining trend in daily $PM_{10}$ volumes. Pollution levels in excess of 100 $\mu g/m^3$ were a common occurrence in the 1990s, but became rarer in the 2000s and 2010s (Figure 1.41). Annual average levels were 283 (XAL), 137 (TLA), 129 (MER) and 82 (PED) in 1990, and by 2014 declined to 64, 51, 45 and 31, respectively. While significant progress has been achieved, the current levels are still significantly above guideline values set by the World Health Organization (WHO). WHO considers 50 $\mu g/m^3$ per day excessive and suggests an annual average of no higher than 20 $\mu g/m^3$ as a guideline value.

Estimates suggest that transport contributes more than 45% of the current air pollution. Another 20% is contributed by direct emissions and energy consumption from private homes and industrial production, respectively (Figure 1.42, left panel). Across the Valle de México, the majority of emissions arise outside the Federal District. About two-thirds of greenhouse gas emissions and 80% of particulate matter pollution come from outside the Federal District (Figure 1.42, right panel). Given the concentration of economic activity and the daily flows of workers into the CBD in the Federal District, this is not surprising. This means that solutions to cut emissions need to come from combined efforts across the metropolitan zone. These efforts need to address mobility within the whole metropolitan area and support mobility that relies on transport modes with low levels of emission. The source of air pollution also masks the relative impact.

Particulate matter does not stop at administrative boundaries, and greenhouse gas emissions affect not only the Valle de México, but the metropolitan area and beyond.

Figure 1.41. **Air pollution ($PM_{10}$) in the Valle de México's urban centre, 1989-2015**

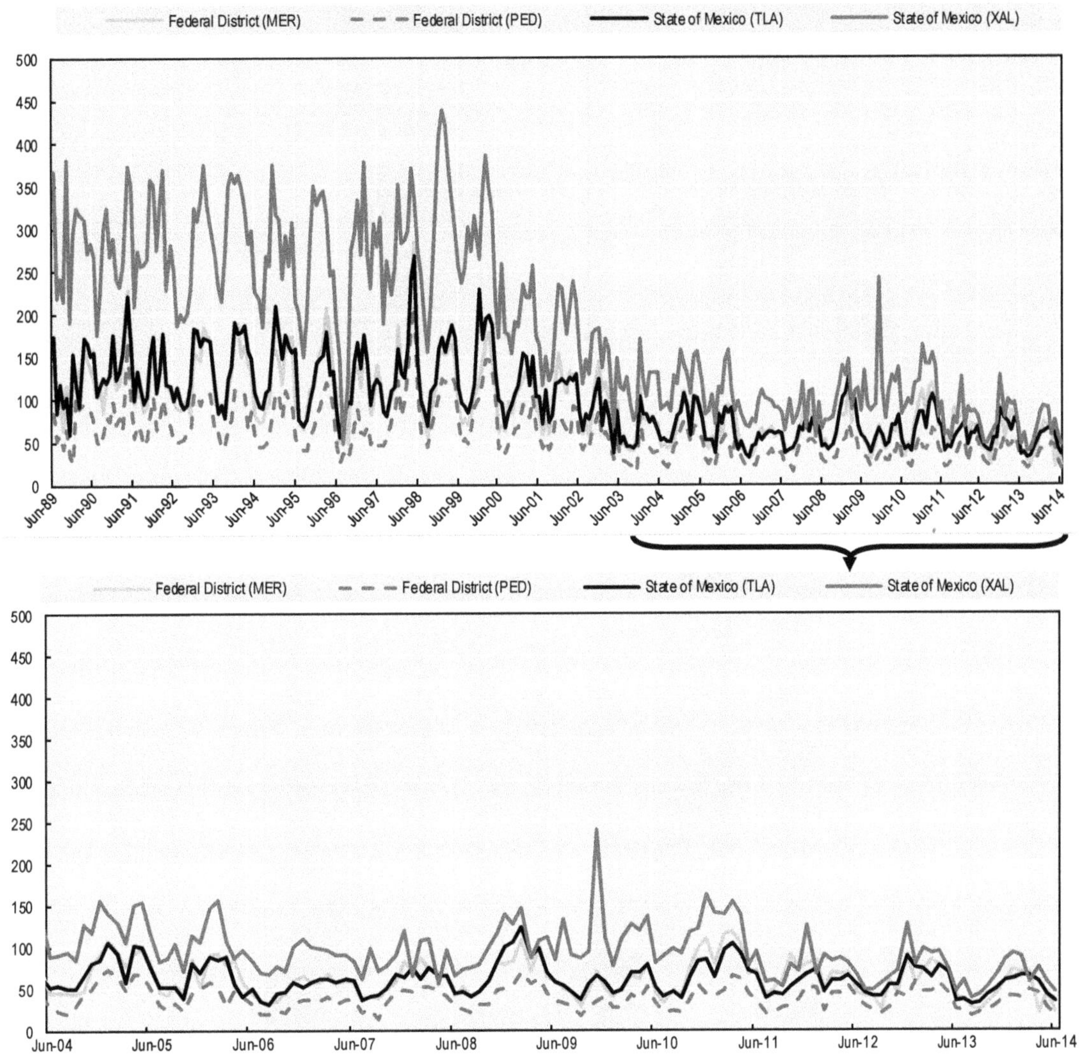


*Note:* Average monthly $PM_{10}$ levels.

*Source*: Secretaría del Medio Ambiente del Distrito Federal (2015), "Calidad del aire" website, http://www.aire.df.gob.mx/default.php (accessed 3 June 2015).

The topography of the Valle de México amplifies environmental challenges. The Valle de México – as the name suggests – is located in a valley, surrounded by mountains on three sides (Figure 1.43). The plateau, upon which it rests, is situated more than 2 000 metres above sea level. The result is that air pollution can be trapped inside the metropolitan zone. Meanwhile, the provision of potable water in the area relies on local aquifers, with little available soil to allow for natural refill. At the other end of the water spectrum, drainage relies on artificial canals that use gravity to move wastewater from the urban centre north into the adjacent Tula Valley. Due to soil subsidence, gravity alone no longer suffices, and pumps, as well as deep drainage tunnels, have to be constructed to support the flows.

Figure 1.42. **Sources of air pollution in the Valle de México**

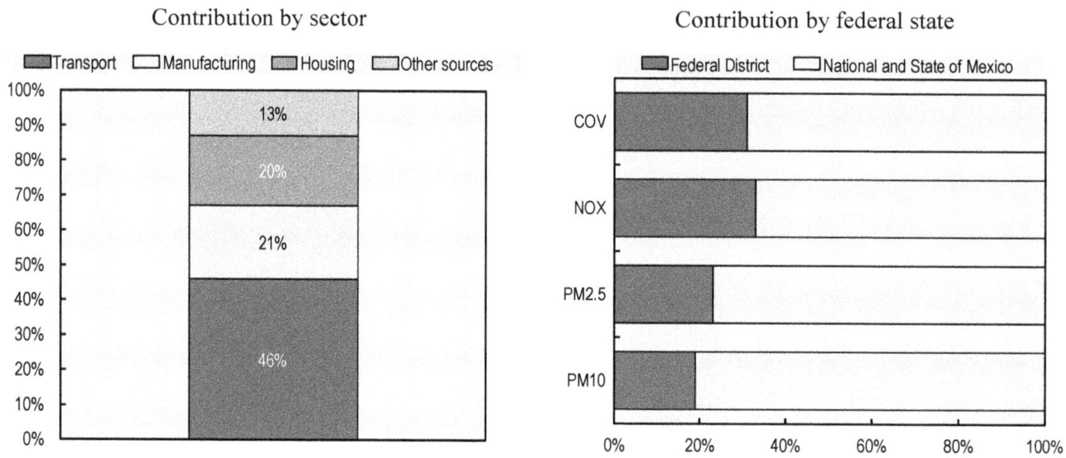


*Source*: Secretaría del Medio Ambiente del Distrito Federal (2015), "Calidad del aire" website, http://www.aire.df.gob.mx/default.php (accessed 27 May 2015).

Figure 1.43. **Elevation of the Metropolitan Zone of the Valle de México**

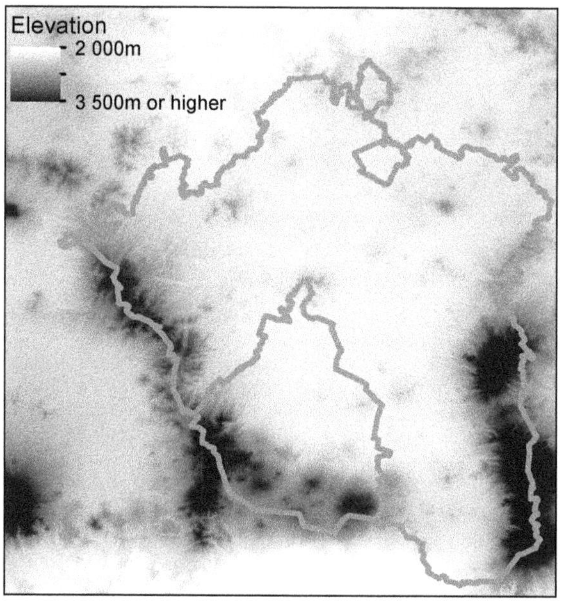


*Source*: INEGI (2015b), *Continuo de Elevaciones Mexicano 3.0*, Instituto Nacional de Estadística y Geografía, Aguascalientes, Mexico, www.inegi.org.mx/geo/contenidos/datosrelieve/continental/descarga.aspx (accessed 10 March 2015).

## *Potable water resources in the Valle de México are strained*

The rapid growth of the Valle de México has imposed a severe strain on local resources. Demand for potable water has been met by drawing from local aquifers, whose natural refill lags significantly behind the daily demand. As a result, nearly all aquifers in the Valle de México are considered overexploited and are slowly being drained (Figure 1.44). Since the 1940s, additional water has been pumped into the Valle de México from reservoirs around the Lerma River, and since the 1970s, from the

Cutzamala River. Water from these sources not only travels distances of more than 100 kilometres but has to be pumped up to the height of the Valle de México. Only small reservoirs of surface water remain, after centuries of draining local wetlands. The largest body of water is the artificially created lake Nabor Carrillo, which accounts for 10 of the remaining 15 km$^2$ of permanent bodies of water.

Figure 1.44. **Overexploited aquifers, 2012**

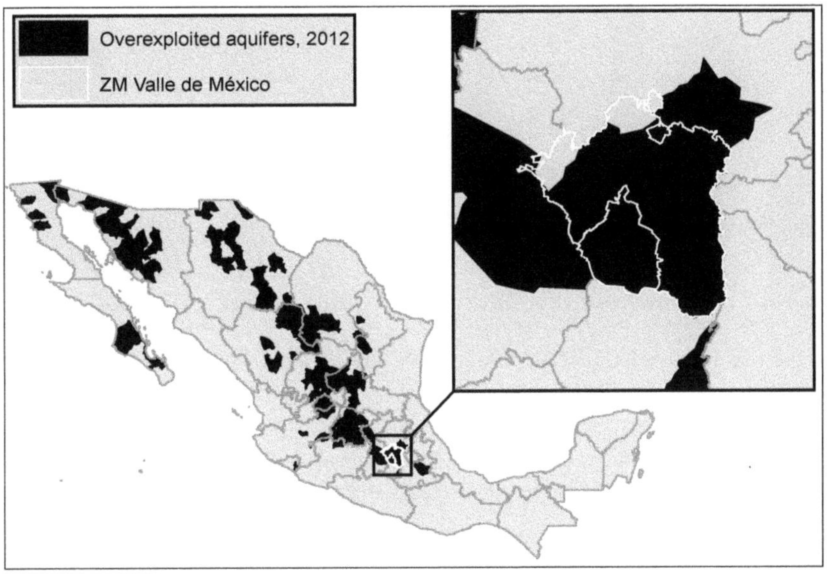


*Note:* This document and any map included herein are without prejudice to the status of or sovereignty over any territory, to the delimitation of international frontiers and boundaries and to the name of any territory, city or area.

*Source*: OECD (2015e), *OECD Urban Policy Reviews: Mexico 2015: Transforming Urban Policy and Housing Finance*, OECD Publishing, Paris, http://dx.doi.org/10.1787/9789264227293-en.

Several factors contribute to the high demand for water in the Valle de México. The size alone of the metropolitan zone is a major contributing factor, but per capita consumption and losses within the water delivery system contribute to a significant degree. In the Federal District, individual consumption in 2010 was 178 litres per day (Figure 1.45, left panel), but the total supply of potable water (for public use) is significantly higher. In 2013, the average daily per capita water supply was 336 litres.[26] A significant percentage is lost along the supply chain. Leakage in 2010 accounted for 37% of losses in the Federal District (Figure 1.45, right panel). For both consumption and leakage, the Federal District ranks around the average among large Latin American agglomerations.

### *Designated conservation land in the Federal District does not extend across its borders*

Protected green space in the Valle de México is concentrated in the Federal District and along the State of Mexico's eastern border with Puebla. In addition to protected land, the government of the Federal District considers most of the southern *delegaciones* as conservation land (*suelo de conservación*). These areas consist of less densely populated settlements and green space. However, urban settlements are encroaching on the conservation land and protected areas. Partly these are informal settlements, but partly this is due to a mismatch in conservation land across state-level boundaries. The designated conservation land is not matched in the adjacent municipalities in the State of Mexico, and urban development has been taking place along the north-eastern part of the conservation area.

Figure 1.45. **Water consumption and system leakage in Latin America**

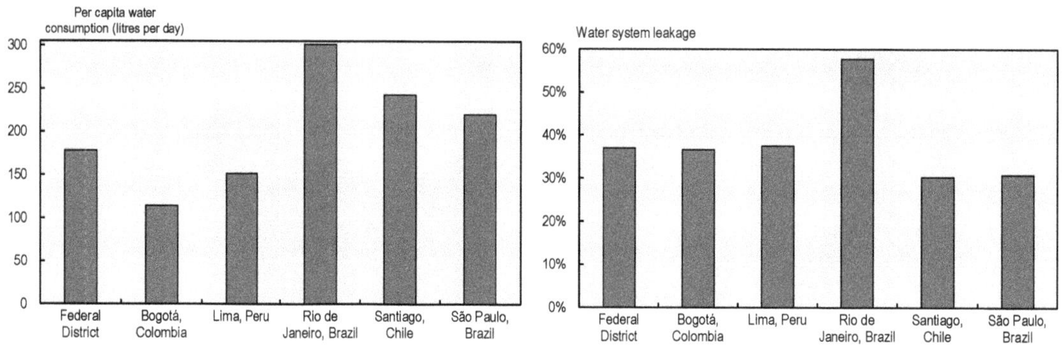


*Note:* Data for the Federal District for 2010, Bogotá for 2009, Rio de Janeiro for 2008, São Paulo for 2007, Lima and Santiago 2009 for water consumption and 2008 for leakage.

*Source*: Economist Intelligence Unit (2010), "Latin American Green City Index: Assessing the environmental performance of Latin America's major cities", Siemens AG, Munich, Germany, available at: www.siemens.com/entry/cc/features/greencityindex_international/br/en/pdf/report_latam_en.pdf.

The green belt in the south of the Federal District is considered essential for environmental sustainability, as it not only provides a natural filter for air quality, but also supports infiltration of rainwater into the aquifer. The soil in the south of the Federal District is more permeable than in other areas, where the clay soil of the former lakebed is relatively impermeable. Sufficient infiltration into the local aquifers is essential for ensuring sustainability of the local water supply and to help combat soil subsidence. Reductions in groundwater levels have led to a densification of the soil in the Valle de México, leading to subsidence of up to 30 centimetres per year.[27] The permeability of the soil in the conservation land increases the environmental risk posed by informal or inadequately serviced settlements. Unfiltered sewage can potentially seep into the aquifer, contaminating the already strained resources.

## Key challenges for the Valle de México

Rapid population growth has made the Valle de México one of the largest megacities in the world. The appeal of the metropolitan zone has also led to continuous increases in agglomeration costs. Economic growth around the time of the global economic crisis was sluggish, even though the metropolitan zone has more high value-added employment than other Mexican metropolitan zones and though new residents have tended to increase skills in the metropolitan zone. Inequality, both in terms of income and of living conditions, remains persistent. Most residents have access to basic services, but the quality of the services varies across the metropolitan zone, and a high quality of life requires more than the most basic amenities. Environmental concerns are at the forefront of the Valle de México's challenges, and while air quality has significantly improved since the late 1990s, pollution levels remain high. Public transport has been expanded and improved accessibility, congestion and pollution, but the network covers only a minority of residents and offers very few direct links across state-level borders.

Figure 1.46. **Protected areas and conservation land in the Valle de México**

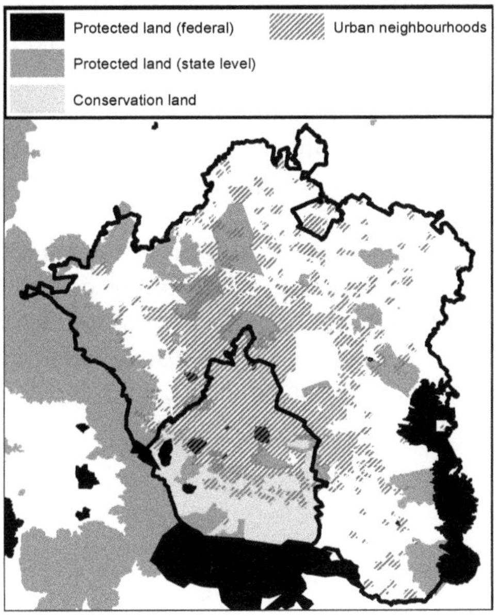


*Note:* This document and any map included herein are without prejudice to the status of or sovereignty over any territory, to the delimitation of international frontiers and boundaries and to the name of any territory, city or area.

*Sources*: CONANP (2015), "Areas naturales protegidas", Comisión Nacional de Areas Naturales Protegidas, available at: www.conabio.gob.mx/informacion/gis (accessed 3 June 2015); and PAOT (2015a), "Zonificacion conservacion", Procuraduría Ambiental y del Ordenamiento Territorial del Distrito Federal, www.paot.org.mx/index.php/mapoteca (accessed 17 August 2015).

Figure 1.47. **Infiltration capacity of conservation land in the Federal District**

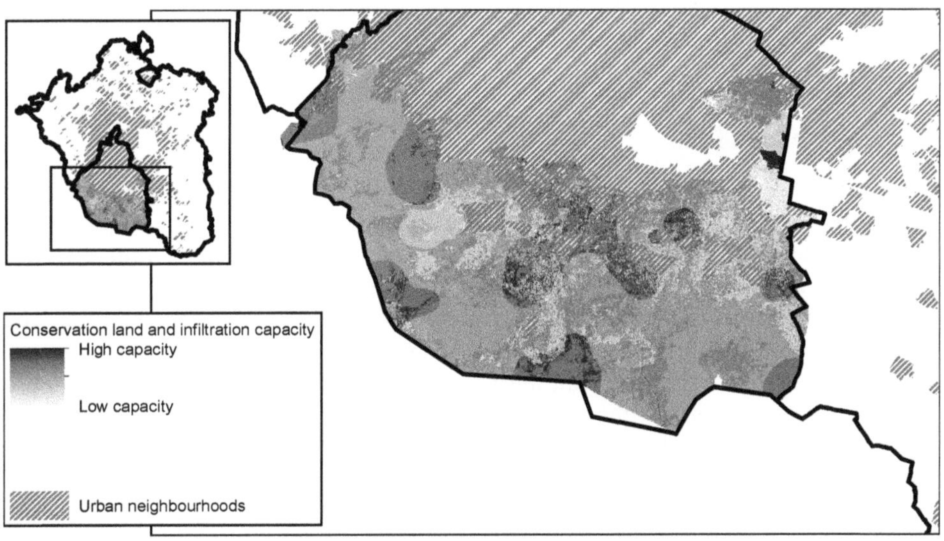


*Note:* This document and any map included herein are without prejudice to the status of or sovereignty over any territory, to the delimitation of international frontiers and boundaries and to the name of any territory, city or area.

*Source*: PAOT (2015b), "Aptitud infiltración", Procuraduría Ambiental y del Ordenamiento Territorial del Distrito Federal, www.paot.org.mx/index.php/mapoteca (accessed 17 August 2015).

While new residents tend to locate both in the centre and the periphery of the metropolitan zone, the densest developments and the strongest population increases are in the periphery. Development in central areas, however, is likely to keep down costs for public service provision and result in better environmental outcomes. Building on the existing infrastructure, integrated urban regeneration strategies can help improve quality of life and well-being in existing neighbourhoods and support distressed neighbourhoods throughout the metropolitan zone. On the periphery, urban development has built areas with highly structured blocks that require better integration with the metro-wide network, to increase attractiveness for both residents and firms. A combination of local and global accessibility is key to the development of thriving commercial centres. No single government in the Valle de México can hope to address all challenges on its own. Neither economic, traffic nor environmental linkages respect administrative boundaries, and tackling the challenges requires co-ordinated effort.

## Notes

1. See SEDESOL-CONAPO-INEGI (2015a) for details.
2. Data for 2010 from OECD (2015a; 2015b).
3. See OECD (2012a) for details.
4. Within the boundaries set by SEDESOL-CONAPO-INEGI, the population of the Metropolitan Zone of the Valle de México grew even less rapidly, by less than 1% annually, between 2000 and 2010.
5. See OECD (2015c) for details.
6. Using the EU-OECD definition of metropolitan areas. See OECD (2012a) for details.
7. At No. 144 out of 263.
8. Governance bodies are organisations intended to help with the governance of metropolitan areas. These organisations differ widely in their scope, powers and effectiveness across and within countries. The OECD requires four criteria to be satisfied for an organisation to be considered a "metropolitan governance body": 1) the organisation must cover the central city and a large percentage of the remaining parts of the metropolitan area. If its geographical scope extends beyond the metropolitan area, the metropolitan area must constitute the predominant part of its sphere of responsibility (geographical scope); 2) national or sub-national governments must be dominant actors within the organisation or, alternatively, the organisation itself must have the status of a sub-national government (involved actors); 3) the organisation must primarily deal with issues that are directly and predominantly relevant to metropolitan area governance (thematic focus); 4) an organisation must have a mandate that allows it to work on more than one issue related to metropolitan area governance (thematic width).

9. MXN 3.3 billion in 2007 and 2010, MXN 3.5 billion in 2011 and 2012 and MXN 3.6 billion in 2008 and 2009 (Fondo Metropolitano del Valle de México, available at: http://fmvm.edomex.gob.mx/catalogo_obras, accessed 1 June 2015).

10. See ITDP (2012a) and OECD (2015e) for details.

11. Expenditures from the Metropolitan Fund in the Federal District in 2012 were MXN 1 681 million (Fondo Metropolitano del Valle de México, n.d.), in a total budget of MXN 146 billion (INEGI, 2015a).

12. The reported percentages refer to the classification used by INEGI (2015a). The percentages reported by the government of the Federal District deviate from the figures reported by INEGI. According to the *Cuenta Pública del Distrito Federal* (Government of the Federal District, 2014; 2015), federal transfers accounted for 53.4% and 51.4% of the budget of the Federal District's government in 2013 and 2014 respectively.

13. See CONAPO (2011) for a detailed description of the constructed index.

14. Earnings in the IPUMS (2014) data are right censored, i.e. the reported earnings are set to a maximum value if they exceed a certain threshold. Using the median avoids biasing the statistic downwards.

15. Reported earnings tend to exhibit a tendency to cluster around certain "round" numbers, typically multiples of 100 or 1 000. In the Mexican census data, mass points arise at those multiples but also for less obvious values, e.g. 4 286 or 2 143. These are likely to represent multiples of the daily minimum wage at the time of the interview.

16. See OECD (2012b) for details.

17. OECD (2015d) includes a discussion of different definitions of vacancy. The definition of "vacancy" used here is census based. INEGI defines "uninhabited housing" (*vivienda deshabitada*) as individual homes that are fully constructed and immediately inhabitable, but in which no one is living at the time of the census, or using for commercial activities or as a secondary home. "Uninhabited homes" includes housing that has previously been inhabited as well as housing that has never been inhabited. INEGI distinguishes "uninhabited housing" from "housing for seasonal, recreational or occasional use" (*vivienda de uso temporal*); "seasonal homes" are defined as those that are fully constructed and immediately inhabitable but that at the time of the census are used for holiday or recreational use for several days, weeks or months (in other words, they are not used as a residence year-round).

    The process by which INEGI determines whether housing is inhabited, uninhabited or for seasonal, recreational or occasional use is described in detail in INEGI (2010b). In summary: municipal census analysts made a preliminary classification of inhabited, uninhabited or seasonal-use homes. Subsequently, for the 2010 census, a specialised operational unit was created and trained to verify the initial findings of the municipal analysts. For homes judged to be uninhabited or for seasonal use, members of the specialised unit were required to confirm the occupation status of the home with at least six neighbours" OECD (2015e: 130).

18. See Government of Mexico City (2012) for details.

19. See OECD/ITF (2015) for details.

20. Data for Singapore from Ghate and Sundar (2014), for the Valle de México from SEDEMA (2015). Cars in the Valle de México combines two categories, *autos particulares* and SUVs, which make up 75% of all registered vehicles.

21. Data: http://brtdata.org (Version 3.2, 6 May, 2015, accessed 2 June 2015). Only data for one of the three BRT corridors in the State of Mexico are available (Linea I: Ciudad Azteca-Ojo de Agua).

22. See WHO/UNEP (1992) for details.

23. Rainfall-related disasters between 2009 and 2013 occurred in September and October 2009; February 2010; and July, August and September 2011; with states of emergency declared in February 2010 and July 2011 (Sistema del Atlas Nacional de Riesgos, 2015).

24. $PM_{10}$ and $PM_{2.5}$ refer to the size of the particulate matter, 10 and 2.5 μm respectively.

25. Two of the stations are located in the Federal District, one in a residential area close to a street (MER), another in a less densely populated part of town surrounded by green space (PED). The other two stations are in the State of Mexico, one next to a school (TLA), the other in a neighbourhood mainly used for production, storage and commerce (XAL).

    MER: www.aire.df.gob.mx/entornos/entorno_detalle.php?est=fneC

    PED: www.aire.df.gob.mx/entornos/entorno_detalle.php?est=gXd0

    TLA: www.aire.df.gob.mx/entornos/entorno_detalle.php?est=hX5x

    XAL: www.aire.df.gob.mx/entornos/entorno_detalle.php?est=iXN8.

26. Total public water supply was 1 089.6 cubic hectometres in 2013 for 8 893 742 inhabitants (CONAGUA, 2014).

27. See: www.esa.int/spaeinimages/Images/2014/12/Mexico_City_subsidence for a recent assessment.

# Bibliography

Ahrend, R., C. Gamper and A. Schumann (2014), "The OECD Metropolitan Governance Survey: A quantitative description of governance structures in large urban agglomerations", *OECD Regional Development Working Papers*, No. 2014/04, OECD Publishing, Paris, http://dx.doi.org/10.1787/5jz43zldh08p-en.

Ahrend, R. et al. (2014), "What makes cities more productive? Evidence on the role of urban governance from five OECD countries", *OECD Regional Development Working Papers*, No. 2014/05, OECD Publishing, Paris, http://dx.doi.org/10.1787/5jz432cf2d8p-en.

Angel, S. et al. (2010), *Atlas of Urban Expansion*, Lincoln Institute of Land Policy, Cambridge, Massachusetts, www.lincolninst.edu/subcenters/atlas-urban-expansion (accessed 20 May 2015).

Blanco, A.G., V. Fretes Cibils and A.F. Muñoz (2014), *Rental Housing Wanted: Policy Options for Latin America and the Caribbean*, Inter-American Development Bank, www10.iadb.org/intal/intalcdi/PE/2014/13900en.pthe Federal District (accessed 20 May 2015).

Comisión Ejecutiva de Coordinación Metropolitana (2008), referenced in Gobierno del Estado de México (2009), *Conformación de las Zonas Metropolitanas: Panorama Demográfico*.

CONAGUA (2014), "Estadícas del agua en México: Edición 2014", Comisión Nacional del Agua, available at: www.conagua.gob.mx/CONAGUA07/Publicaciones/Publicaciones/EAM2014.pdf.

CONANP (2015), "Areas naturales protegidas", Comisión Nacional de Areas Naturales Protegidas, www.conabio.gob.mx/informacion/gis (accessed 3 June 2015).

CONAPO (2015a), *Índice de Marginación por Entidad Federativa y Municipio 2010*, Consejo Nacional de Población, www.conapo.gob.mx/es/CONAPO/Indices_de_Marginacion_2010_por_entidad_federativa_y_municipio (accessed 2 April 2015).

CONAPO (2015b), "Matriz de movilidad laboral 2010" [Municipal labour mobility matrix 2010], Consejo Nacional de Población, www.conapo.gob.mx/work/models/CONAPO/Migracion_Interna/Descargas/Matriz_movilidad_laboral_2010.xlsx (accessed 25 March 2015).

CONAPO (2011), *Índice de Marginación por Entidad Federativa y Municipio: 2010*, Consejo Nacional de Población, available at: www.conapo.gob.mx/work/models/CONAPO/indices_margina/mf2010/CapitulosPDF/1_4.pdf.

Consejo para el Desarrollo Metropolitano del Valle de México (2012), *Programa de Ordenación de la Zona Metropolitana del Valle de México: Actualización 2012: Síntesis Ejectiva*, www.economia.unam.mx/cedrus/descargas/pozmvm_digital.pdf (accessed 1 June 2015).

Duranton, G. and D. Puga (2004), "Micro-foundations of urban agglomeration economies", in: Henderson, J.V. and J.F. Thisse (eds.), *Handbook of Regional and Urban Economics*, Vol. 4, Ch. 48, pp. 2 063-2 117, Elsevier.

Economist Intelligence Unit (2010), "Latin American Green City Index: Assessing the environmental performance of Latin America's major cities", Siemens AG, Munich, Germany, available at: www.siemens.com/entry/cc/features/greencityindex_international/br/en/pdf/report_latam_en.pdf.

Fondo Metropolitano del Valle de México (n.d.), "Catálogo de obras", Government of the State of Mexico, http://fmvm.edomex.gob.mx/catalogo_obras (accessed 1 June 2015).

Ghate, A.T. and S. Sundar (2014), "Proliferation of cars in Indian cities: Let us not ape the west", policy brief, The Energy and Resources Institute, New Dehli, June, available at: www.teriin.org/policybrief/docs/cars.pdf.

Government of the Federal District (2015), *Cuenta Pública del Distrito Federal 2014*, Secretaría de Finanzas, www.finanzas.df.gob.mx/egresos/cp2014/index.html (accessed 21 August 2015).

Government of the Federal District (2014), *Cuenta Pública del Distrito Federal 2013*, Secretaría de Finanzas, www.finanzas.df.gob.mx/egresos/cp2013/index.html (accessed 21 August 2015).

Hanson, G.H. (1998), "North American economic integration and industry location", *Oxford Review of Economic Policy*, Vol. 14, No. 2, pp. 30-44, http://dx.doi.org/10.1093/oxrep/14.2.30.

INEGI (2015a), *Sistema Estatal y Municipal de Bases de Datos (SIMBAD)*, Version 2.0, Instituto Nacional de Estadística y Geografía, Aguascalientes, Mexico, http://sc.inegi.org.mx/cobdem/index.jsp?recargar=false (accessed 22 June 2015).

INEGI (2015b), *Continuo de Elevaciones Mexicano 3.0*, Instituto Nacional de Estadística y Geografía, Aguascalientes, Mexico, www.inegi.org.mx/geo/contenidos/datosrelieve/continental/descarga.aspx (accessed 10 March 2015).

INEGI (2014), *Marco Geoestadistico Nacional 2014*, Instituto Nacional de Estadística y Geografía, Aguascalientes, Mexico, www.inegi.org.mx/geo/contenidos/geoestadistica/M_Geoestadistico.aspx (accessed 15 May 2015).

INEGI (2010a), *Censo de Población y Vivienda 2010*, Instituto Nacional de Estadística y Geografía, Aguascalientes, Mexico.

INEGI (2010b), *Resultados de la Encuesta de Verificación de Viviendas Deshabitadas y de Uso Temporal del Censo de Población y Vivienda 2010*, Instituto Nacional de Estadística y Geografía, Aguascalientes, Mexico.

INEGI (2000), *XII Censo General de Población y Vivienda 2000*, Instituto Nacional de Estadística y Geografía, Aguascalientes, Mexico.

IPUMS (2014), *Mexico: 2010 Population and Housing Census*, raw data provided by INEGI, IPUMS is provided by the Minnesota Population Center. Integrated Public Use Microdata Series, International: Version 6.3 [machine-readable database], University of Minnesota, Minneapolis, Minnesota.

ITDP (2012a), *Transforming Urban Mobility in Mexico: Towards Accessible Cities Less Reliant on Cars*, Institute for Transport and Development Policy.

ITDP (2012b), "Gasto federal para la movilidad urbana: Reporte del Fondo Metropolitano 2012", Institute for Transport and Development Policy, Mexico, http://mexico.itdp.org/documentos/reporte-fondo-metropolitano-2012 (accessed 1 June 2015).

Lowell, L.B. and A.M. Findlay (2001), "Migration of highly skilled persons from developing countries: Impact and policy responses", draft synthesis report, International Labour Office, Geneva.

Marshall, A. (2009), *Principles of Economics*, unabridged eighth edition, Cosimo, Inc, New York.

Mejora tu Escuela (n.d.), Organisation website, www.mejoratuescuela.org (accessed 13 May 2015).

Moretti, E. (2013), *The New Geography of Jobs*, Mariner Books, Chicago.

Moretti, E. (2004), "Workers' education, spillovers, and productivity: Evidence from plant-level production functions", *American Economic Review*, Vol. 94, No. 3, pp. 656-690.

OECD (forthcoming), *Measuring Well-being in Mexican States*, OECD Publishing, Paris, forthcoming.

OECD (2015a), "Metropolitan areas", *OECD Regional Statistics (database)*, http://dx.doi.org/10.1787/data-00531-en (accessed 13 March 2015).

OECD (2015b), *Ageing in Cities*, OECD Publishing, Paris, http://dx.doi.org/10.1787/9789264231160-en.

OECD (2015c), "Large regions (TL2)", *OECD Regional Statistics* (database), http://dx.doi.org/10.1787/region-tl2-data-en (accessed 13 March 2015).

OECD (2015d), *The Metropolitan Century: Understanding Urbanisation and its Consequences*, OECD Publishing, Paris, http://dx.doi.org/10.1787/9789264228733-en.

OECD (2015e), *OECD Urban Policy Reviews: Mexico 2015: Transforming Urban Policy and Housing Finance*, OECD Publishing, Paris, http://dx.doi.org/10.1787/9789264227293-en.

OECD (2014), *How's Life in Your Region?*, OECD Publishing, Paris, http://dx.doi.org/10.1787/9789264217416-en.

OECD (2013), *How's Life? 2013: Measuring Well-being*, OECD Publishing, Paris, http://dx.doi.org/10.1787/9789264201392-en.

OECD (2012a), *Redefining "Urban": A New Way to Measure Metropolitan Areas*, OECD Publishing, Paris, http://dx.doi.org/10.1787/9789264174108-en.

OECD (2012b), *Compact City Policies: A Comparative Assessment*, OECD Green Growth Studies, OECD Publishing, Paris, http://dx.doi.org/10.1787/9789264167865-en.

OECD (2012c), *OECD Economic Surveys: Chile 2012*, OECD Publishing, Paris, http://dx.doi.org/10.1787/eco_surveys-chl-2012-en.

OECD (2012d), *OECD Environmental Outlook to 2050*, OECD Publishing, Paris, http://dx.doi.org/10.1787/9789264122246-en.

OECD/ITF (2015), *ITF Transport Outlook 2015*, OECD Publishing/ITF, Paris, http://dx.doi.org/10.1787/9789282107782-en.

PAOT (2015a), "Zonificacion conservacion", Procuraduría Ambiental y del Ordenamiento Territorial del Distrito Federal, www.paot.org.mx/index.php/mapoteca (accessed 17 August 2015).

PAOT (2015b), "Aptitud infiltración", Procuraduría Ambiental y del Ordenamiento Territorial del Distrito Federal, www.paot.org.mx/index.php/mapoteca (accessed 17 August 2015).

Secretaría del Medio Ambiente del Distrito Federal (2015), "Calidad del aire" website, www.aire.df.gob.mx/default.php (accessed 3 June 2015).

SEDEMA (2015), "Proaire 2011-2020", presentation to the OECD delegation on 20 April 2015 in Mexico City, Secretaría de Medio Ambiente del Distrito Federal.

SEDESOL-CONAPO-INEGI (2015a), "Delimitación de las zonas metropolitanas de México 2010", Consejo Nacional de Población, www.conapo.gob.mx/es/CONAPO/Zonas_metropolitanas_2010 (accessed 1 June 2015).

SEDESOL-CONAPO-INEGI (2015b), "Delimitación de las zonas metropolitanas de México 2000", Consejo Nacional de Población, www.conapo.gob.mx/es/CONAPO/Zonas_metropolitanas_2000 (accessed 1 June 2015).

Sistema del Atlas Nacional de Riesgos (2015), *Base de Datos Sobre Declaratorias de Emergencia, Desastre y Contingencia Climatológica*, July, available at: www.atlasnacionalderiesgos.gob.mx/index.php/biblioteca/category/24-herramientas?download=65:declaratorias (accessed 15 May 2015).

Space Syntax (2015), "Spatial layout analysis of Valle de México", report for the OECD.

TomTom (2015), "TomTom Traffic Index", TomTom International BV, available at: www.tomtom.com/en_gb/trafficindex/#.

UITP (2014), "Statistics brief: World metro figures, October 2014", International Association of Public Transport, Brussels, available at: www.uitp.org/sites/default/files/cck-focus-papers-files/Metro%20report%20Stat%20brief-web_oct2014.pdf.

WHO (2009), *Global Health Risks: Mortality and Burden of Disease Attributable to Selected Major Risks*, World Health Organization, Geneva, available at: www.who.int/healthinfo/global_burden_disease/GlobalHealthRisks_report_full.pdf.

WHO/UNEP (1992), *Urban Air Pollution in Megacities of the World*, World Health Organization, United Nations Environment Programme, Blackwell, Oxford, United Kingdom.

# *Chapter 2.*

# Housing and urban regeneration policies for the Valle de México

*This chapter assesses the most pressing housing and urban development challenges in the Valle de México: rapid urban expansion, infrastructure gaps, limited affordable housing in the centre and a large quantity of abandoned housing in peripheral areas. It then proposes two strategies to improve housing and urban development in the metropolitan zone. The first strategy is to improve quality of life and well-being in existing neighbourhoods through integrated urban regeneration strategies. The second is to guide future housing and urban development through a more co-ordinated metropolitan approach. Such an approach could include: 1) facilitating development in the city centre; 2) placing a stronger emphasis on rental housing to relieve affordable housing pressures; and 3) planning for – rather than restricting – growth in strategic peripheral areas.*

While many of the most pressing challenges and opportunities for housing and urban development in the Valle de México[1] are shared by many other Mexican cities, the scale of the metropolitan zone and its complex institutional landscape put it in a class of its own. With roughly 17% of the country's population and housing stock, and 23% of its gross domestic product (GDP), the Valle de México is by far the most important urban centre in Mexico. It is home to over 20 million inhabitants, making it one of the world's largest cities. As in many Mexican cities, policy makers in the Valle de México must grapple with rapid urban expansion at the expense of a depopulating city centre, a lack of centrally located affordable housing, and a large – if hard to quantify – stock of unoccupied housing, which includes a large percentage of abandoned homes among the recently built social housing settlements. A range of other urban challenges must also be dealt with, such as high levels of congestion, air and water pollution, water scarcity and social inequality.[2] The institutional landscape does little to remedy the situation: more than 75 sub-national entities are responsible for governing the metropolitan area. Meanwhile, the institutional toolbox to guide urban planning and development has typically had a limited – or even undesirable – impact on urban outcomes and is fragmented across different administrations. In some cases, the absence of a co-ordinated, metropolitan approach to housing and urban development has resulted in policies that exacerbated the urban challenges they set out to solve.

The Federal District, along with other municipalities in the Valle de México, has made impressive progress in recent decades toward an ambitious sustainable urban development agenda.[3] These locally driven efforts are now in a position to be reinforced by a recent shift in housing and urban policies at the national level. The federal government's new approach aims to encourage more sustainable housing and urban development in all Mexican cities. The transition stems from increasing concern over the high costs of the previous urban growth model, which had positioned Mexico as the third most rapidly sprawling country in the OECD in the last decade (OECD, 2015). Previous housing policies, driven by the rapid expansion of housing finance led by the National Workers' Housing Fund Institute (Instituto del Fondo Nacional de la Vivienda para los Trabajadores, INFONAVIT),[4] the country's largest provident housing fund, helped reduce the country's quantitative housing deficit and make home ownership more accessible to all income levels. However, this housing model came with high qualitative costs, facilitating the development of mass-produced homes throughout the country on inexpensive, peri-urban land far from job opportunities, city centres and urban services. The recent shift in national housing and urban development policies is especially important given the continued weight of the federal government in the housing development process. A closer alignment of policies across all levels of government could help significantly to advance a more sustainable and inclusive housing and urban development model in the Valle de México.

This chapter will first discuss some of the main housing and urban development challenges facing policy makers in the Valle de México. It will then focus on two overarching strategies for improving housing and urban outcomes in the metropolitan zone. The first is to improve quality of life and well-being in existing neighbourhoods through integrated urban regeneration strategies. The second is to guide future housing and urban development through a more co-ordinated metropolitan approach. Such an approach could include: 1) facilitating affordable housing development in the city centre; 2) placing stronger emphasis on rental housing to relieve affordable housing pressures; and 3) planning for – rather than restricting – growth in strategic peripheral areas.

## Primary housing and urban development challenges in the Valle de México

This chapter will discuss some of the core challenges for housing and urban development in the Valle de México: urban expansion, infrastructure gaps, declining neighbourhoods and abandoned housing.

### *Rapid urban expansion, significant infrastructure gaps*

In the last three decades, despite a clear slowdown in the overall growth of the Valle de México, the urbanised area of the metropolitan zone has expanded significantly (Figure 2.1; see also Chapter 1). The trend toward urban expansion is nevertheless consistent with the experience of most Mexican urban areas, as well as global trends in spatial development in recent years. In a sample of 120 global cities and metropolitan areas, Angel et al. (2010a) find that between 1990 and 2000, the average built-up area densities declined by 2% annually and that in many cities, urban land cover grew at more than twice the rate of population.

Figure 2.1. **Urban expansion in the Valle de México, 1800-2010**

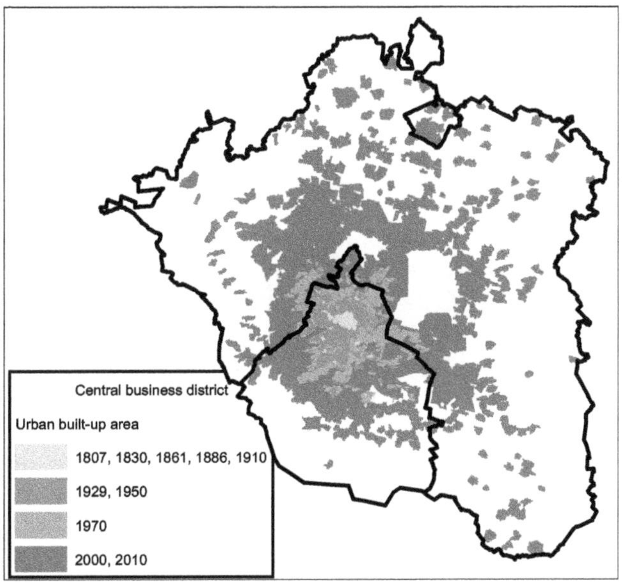


*Note:* This document and any map included herein are without prejudice to the status of or sovereignty over any territory, to the delimitation of international frontiers and boundaries and to the name of any territory, city or area.

*Sources*: Adapted from Angel, S. et al. (2010a), *Atlas of Urban Expansion*, Lincoln Institute of Land Policy, Cambridge Massachusetts, www.lincolninst.edu/subcenters/atlas-urban-expansion (accessed 25 May 2015) for data on urban expansion for all years prior to 2000; data for 2000 and 2010 are based on INEGI (2000), *XII Censo General de Población y Vivienda 2000*, Instituto Nacional de Estadística y Geografía, Aguascalientes, Mexico and INEGI (2010a), *Censo de Población y Vivienda 2010*, Instituto Nacional de Estadística y Geografía, Aguascalientes, Mexico.

### *Housing and population growth have shifted to the metropolitan periphery …*

In the Valle de México, most population and housing growth in recent decades has occurred outside the Federal District, in peripheral municipalities within the State of Mexico (Table 2.1). Between 1990 and 2010, the population in the Federal District increased by just 7%, compared to an increase of 53% in the 59 municipalities of the

State of Mexico that are part of the Valle de México (the population of Tizayuca, in the state of Hidalgo, more than tripled during this period, although its percentage of the metropolitan population – 0.5% – is small). Meanwhile, in terms of new housing construction, the municipalities outside the Federal District experienced much more housing growth during these two decades: the number of dwellings in the 59 municipalities in the State of Mexico increased by 106% (double the population growth) and by 295% in Tizayuca, compared to just 33% in the Federal District. In 1990, the Federal District still housed the majority of both population and dwellings in the Valle de México. By 2010, however, more than half of the metropolitan population (56%) and the metropolitan housing stock (54%) could be found **outside** the Federal District, in the State of Mexico and Hidalgo. Moreover, housing growth significantly outpaced population growth during this period, more than double in the State of Mexico and more than triple in the Federal District.

Table 2.1. **Growth in population and housing in the Valle de México, 1990-2010**

| | Population | | | | Dwellings | | | |
|---|---|---|---|---|---|---|---|---|
| | 1990 | 2000 | 2010 | % change, 1990-2010 | 1990 | 2000 | 2010 | % change, 1990-2010 |
| Federal District | 8 253 744 | 8 605 239 | 8 851 080 | 7% | 1 789 171 | 2 103 752 | 2 386 605 | 33% |
| State of Mexico (59 municipalities) | 7 297 758 | 9 745 094 | 11 168 301 | 53% | 1 352 460 | 2 097 410 | 2 780 236 | 106% |
| State of Hidalgo (1 municipality) | 30 293 | 46 344 | 97 461 | 222% | 6 132 | 10 541 | 24 213 | 295% |
| Total Valle de México | 15 581 795 | 18 396 677 | 20 116 842 | 29% | 3 147 763 | 4 211 703 | 5 191 054 | 65% |

*Sources*: INEGI (1990), *XI Censo General de Población y Vivienda 1990*, Instituto Nacional de Estadística y Geografía, Aguascalientes, Mexico; INEGI (2000), *XII Censo General de Población y Vivienda 2000*, Instituto Nacional de Estadística y Geografía, Aguascalientes, Mexico; INEGI (2010a), *Censo de Población y Vivienda 2010*, Instituto Nacional de Estadística y Geografía, Aguascalientes, Mexico.

Public policies at different levels of government contributed to the concentration of demographic and housing growth in outer municipalities. On the one hand, national policies aimed to boost the supply of new housing, often in peripheral areas (OECD, 2015). On the other hand, as will be discussed later in this chapter, increased pressure for commercial activities in the centre has resulted in the replacement of residential land uses by commercial uses (Suárez and Delgado, 2007). Meanwhile, local land-use regulations and zoning codes have restricted development and densification in central areas (Marron Institute, 2013, 2014; Fundación Idea/Cámara de Senadores/SIMO Consulting, 2014). Relative to the Federal District, regulations and their enforcement have tended to be less restrictive in the State of Mexico and Hidalgo. Thus, in constraining the development potential of the central area, pressures for commercial development and the relatively restrictive land-use regulations of the Federal District have inadvertently reduced housing affordability (pushing low-income households into more affordable areas in the periphery) and contributed to urban expansion (pushing new development to areas with less-restrictive regulations – also in the periphery). Strategies to facilitate development in the Federal District and improve planning for new development in peripheral areas will be discussed later in this chapter.

### *... while jobs remain highly concentrated in the metropolitan core*

While both population and housing may have left for peripheral neighbourhoods in recent decades, employment has remained largely centralised in the metropolitan core. The four central *delegaciones* of the Federal District account for one-third of metropolitan employment and 43% of jobs in the service sector (INEGI, 2009). In a survey of economic data of the 16 *delegaciones* in the Federal District and 43 municipalities in the State of Mexico, Aguilar and Alvarado (2004) found that almost 70% of metropolitan employment was located in the first and second rings of the metropolitan zone. Most employment was concentrated in 35 "sub-centres" located in or near the core of the metro zone. More recent studies (see Muñiz, Sánchez and Garcia-López, 2015; Aguilar and Hernandez, 2011; Suárez and Delgado, 2009; Aguilar and Alvarado, 2004; and Graizbord and Acuña, 2005) confirm that employment is more centralised and more geographically concentrated than the population in the Valle de México. Although the past 15 years have seen a decentralisation of employment gradually emerge, an important percentage of jobs remains in the metropolitan core, because the Valle de México still retains a "strong monocentric inertia" (Muñiz, Sánchez and Garcia-López, 2015).

The growing distance between housing and employment centres resulted in longer commuting distances and travel times on both public and private transport. Between 1994 and 2007, rising levels of congestion led to a drop in the average speed of public transport trips and private vehicle trips by 3.6% and 9.0%, respectively (Guerra, 2013; INEGI, 2007). The average daily travel time for residents of the State of Mexico commuting by public transport is 73 minutes, compared to 47 minutes for inner-city residents traveling by private vehicle. The result, while not surprising, is due both to longer trip distances and the stronger likelihood that residents will travel by public transport from outer areas rather than private vehicle, which can be slower. Indeed, buses and collective taxis (*colectivos*) have become the most convenient form of public transport in peripheral areas. It should also be mentioned that the concentration of employment within the central metropolis places a considerable burden on the public infrastructure networks of the Federal District and those of neighbouring municipalities in the State of Mexico. In these areas, authorities must manage, in addition to their own residential populations, the 10 million workers who travel to (and through) their territory on a daily basis, adding to already congested transport networks and high levels of pollution, and affecting overall quality of life.

### *Transport challenges and basic infrastructure gaps throughout the Valle de México*

There are multiple causes for the mismatch between the location of housing and employment; one significant factor is a systematic lack of co-ordination within and across policy fields. Cross-sectoral planning and investment for urban infrastructure has remained a significant challenge throughout Mexican cities. The provision of urban transport infrastructure, particularly in more peripheral areas of the metropolitan zone, is difficult. As will be discussed, the new public transport networks in peripheral areas have not always been well connected to existing lines; further, in some new housing developments, promised transport infrastructure investments that would have made distant housing developments more accessible to job centres never materialised, leaving residents with long and expensive commutes (Box 2.1).

Moreover, gaps remain in the provision of basic services (water, electricity) throughout the Valle de México, despite notable progress in recent decades. Between 1990 and 2010, the percentage of dwellings equipped with piped water increased from 62% to 80% in the Valle de México (Minnesota Population Center, 2013). Nevertheless, as discussed in Chapter 1, there are important deficiencies throughout the metropolitan zone (see Figure 1.22 in Chapter 1). For instance, some neighbourhoods within central *delegaciones* in the Federal District register between 20% and 40% of dwellings that lack connections to water, drainage or electricity networks, while basic service coverage can also be deficient in some newer developments located in peripheral municipalities. The case of Zumpango is an extreme example, with electricity provided by generators that do not run for a full 24 hours a day, and extremely polluted water sources (based on OECD interviews with representatives of the municipality of Zumpango, 2015). In addition to water quality challenges, water scarcity is another critical issue in the Valle de México, as will be discussed in greater detail in Chapter 4.

### *Social inclusion and income inequality*

As discussed in Chapter 1, the Valle de México shows evidence of spatial segregation. Both highly educated and high-earning workers tend to be clustered around the Federal District and the municipalities to its northern border with the State of Mexico. Moreover, significant differences in education levels exist between the metropolitan core and the periphery. Years of schooling in many peripheral neighbourhoods fall below the national minimum standard. In terms of income inequality, the *delegaciones* in the Federal District with the highest median earnings are also among the most unequal, with percentages of both very high and very low earners (see Figure 1.24 in Chapter 1).

## ***Declining and distressed neighbourhoods throughout the metropolitan zone***

Demographically declining or distressed urban neighbourhoods are a problem in different parts of the Valle de México, although the causes – and potential solutions – tend to be distinct. The challenge affects many different parts of the metropolitan zone. The central area of the metropolitan zone has faced several decades of depopulation and deterioration. Yet it is not the only area that faces challenges: an estimated half of all high-rise social housing developments built since the 1950s in the Federal District and inner rings of the metropolitan zone are poorly maintained, overcrowded and/or in need of major upgrading (Procuraduría Social del Distrito Federal, 2015). Finally, and somewhat paradoxically, the most recently developed peripheral areas, urbanised since the mid-1990s, have also rapidly deteriorated and in some cases face a worrisome problem of abandoned housing.

### *Pronounced needs for urban regeneration in the historic centre and surrounding areas*

Between the mid-1970s and 2000s, the central *delegaciones* of the Federal District and several neighbouring municipalities progressively lost population. Initially, depopulation was a problem confined to four central *delegaciones* of the Federal District (Cuauhtémoc, Venustiano Carranza, Miguel Hidalgo and Benito Juárez), as the area lost around 1.2 million inhabitants between 1970 and 2000 (INEGI, 1970; 2000). From 1990 onwards, the *delegación* of Coyoacán and Nezahualcóyotl, a municipality in the State of Mexico, also began to depopulate. In subsequent years, Naucalpan and Tlalnepantla, neighbouring municipalities in the State of Mexico, joined Coyoacán and Nezahualcóyotl and also began to lose inhabitants. Tlalnepantla was especially affected, losing more than 50 000 residents in a decade (INEGI, 2000; 2010a). Moreover, depopulation of the historic centre of the Federal District, a 10 $km^2$ territory belonging to the World Heritage List since 1987, has been even more acute than those of the larger city centre. The so-called "A Perimeter", which corresponds to the very centre of the city in which urban and historic heritage is concentrated, lost 67% of its population

(65 000 residents) between 1970 and 2005. The trend appears to have reversed slightly in the past few years, since the historic centre gained 2 500 inhabitants between 2005 and 2010 (INEGI, 2005; 2010a).

The roots of the depopulation process in the central area of the metropolitan zone are complex and have changed over time. Poorly maintained and ageing urban infrastructure (streets, buildings, etc.), land-use changes from residential to commercial uses, the growing number of home ownership opportunities (whether formal or not) outside the central city in new urban peripheries, and the 1985 earthquake, which led to significant migration to the suburbs, were all contributing factors. As previously noted, mass housing construction, facilitated by public policies at national and state levels, has also drawn households away from central areas toward new developments in peripheral areas (OECD, 2015; Paquette and Delaunay, 2009). Traffic, pollution, crime and poor environmental conditions have also been cited as contributing to a shift of residents from the city centre toward outer areas (Paquette and Delaunay, 2009).

Although the depopulation of the centre has subsided recently, the quality of housing and the living environment in the central area remains a challenge. Improving the quality of life of residents in the central metropolis through urban regeneration initiatives should be a priority for policy makers.

### *Deterioration of older social housing neighbourhoods in the central city*

Given the large number of ageing social housing units in the total housing stock of the Federal District and the severity of their deterioration in many areas, social housing blocks (*unidades habitacionales*) are also a significant challenge for urban regeneration in the central part of the metropolitan zone. Since the beginning of the 1950s, many social housing blocks have been built in the Federal District and in neighbouring municipalities in the State of Mexico. Unlike the massive social housing production of the 2000s, which consisted of small, individual houses, the older social housing stock in the city centre consists primarily of multistory collective housing blocks. The nearly 2 000 *unidades habitacionales* in the Federal District consist of 430 000 housing units and house 1.6 million inhabitants, or 19% of the Federal District's population (Procuraduría Social del Distrito Federal, 2015). Around 7% of the stock was built in the 1940s and 1950s; 39% by or under the aegis of INFONAVIT in the 1970s and 1980s, before the reform of the institute (see OECD, 2015); and around half by private developers in the last 20 years.

Living conditions within and around these *unidades habitacionales* are in some cases quite poor. Currently, according to the Federal District government, 60% of the social housing blocks in the Federal District require replacement (Procuraduría Social del Distrito Federal, 2015). The challenges are varied: ageing structures and infrastructure, poor maintenance (particularly for the oldest units, which were built without specific condominium regulations) and overcrowding (it is not rare for 10 or 12 people to share a single-family apartment). Overcrowding may, by extension, lead to unauthorised extensions of units that considerably damage or weaken the building structure (Esquivel, 2007). In some cases, safety concerns are also a critical challenge of these developments. Some of the units, such as the Unidad El Rosario in Azcapotzalco, the biggest *unidad habitacional* ever built in the Federal District, whose construction was begun in 1972, is known as one of the least safe. Covering an area of 350 hectares, the *unidad* contains 6 734 apartments and around 80 000 inhabitants. The problems of the *unidades habitacionales* in the Federal District are relatively well-documented; meanwhile, social housing in several neighbouring municipalities in the State of Mexico (principally

Cuautitlán Izcalli, Coacalco and Tlalnepantla) are widely thought to be similar, though no data are available on this stock.

## *Social housing neighbourhoods built in the distant suburbs over the past two decades are a concern*

A much more recent, worrisome phenomenon concerns, paradoxically, new housing developments in the peripheral areas of the Valle de México constructed since the mid-1990s, which are facing rapid deterioration. In contrast to earlier decades, when peripheral urban development consisted primarily of irregular settlements, since the 1990s and especially the 2000s, new development in the Valle de México and other Mexican cities has been driven by national housing policies designed to reduce the housing deficit (see OECD, 2015). These federal policies resulted in the construction of massive social housing neighbourhoods (*conjuntos habitacionales*) by private homebuilders, often on inexpensive peripheral land. Mass housing construction has been especially evident on the eastern and northern periphery of the Valle de México. Between 2006 and 2013, 70% of new housing development in the Valle de México registered in the Single Housing Registry (*Registro Único de Vivienda*, RUV) was concentrated in the outer areas of the metropolitan zone, compared to just 9% in central areas (Figure 2.2). These new developments were often not part of the initial municipal development plans; in some cases, development was conducted in the absence of a municipal plan, or municipal plans were modified – often by the developers themselves – to accommodate the construction of new housing. The result is that the living conditions of some of these newer peripheral social housing settlements require urgent action to improve the quality of life and well-being of inhabitants (including long and expensive commutes, lack of basic services and security concerns).

Figure 2.2. **Location of new development within Mexican metro zones, 2006-13**

Housing that has been completed or remodelled, by size of Mexican metro zone

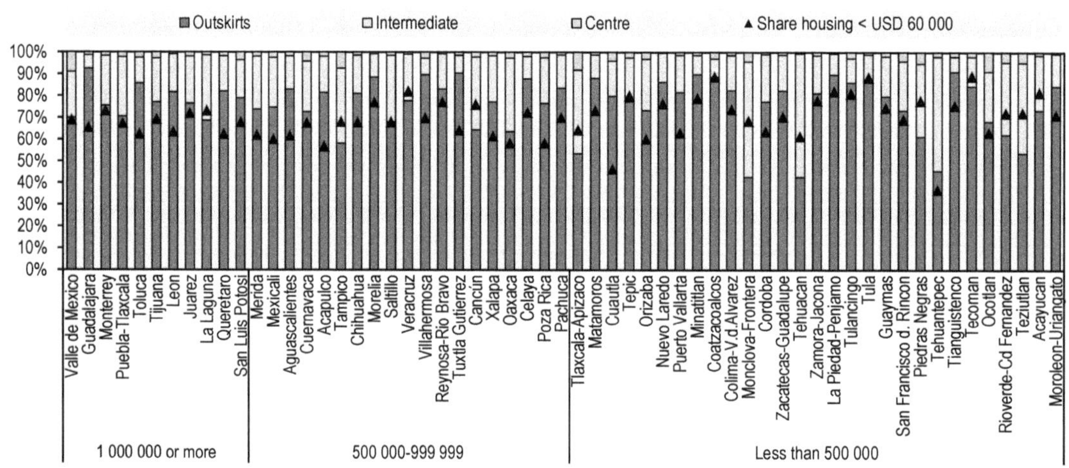


*Notes:* Data aggregated for all years. The category "outskirts" combines the two categories in the Single Housing Registry (*Registro Único de Vivienda*, RUV) "periphery" and "outskirts". Although not all housing constructed after 2005 is accounted for in this registry, the findings provide interesting insights into recent trends in housing location.

*Source:* SHF Housing Statistics (n.d.) (data series: total number of properties valued by year of completion of the work or remodelling), https://www.shf.gob.mx/avaluos/extranet?service=direct/0/Home/$DirectLink, (accessed 15 April 2015).

No comprehensive statistics are available on the overall number of social housing units that have been built in the Valle de México. Partial existing data on housing construction have only recently become available: the RUV only began to require developers to submit statistics on new housing development in 2005. In the absence of comprehensive data on social housing construction, it is thus necessary to rely on studies of specific projects or territories.[5] For instance, a rough estimate, based on building permit data from the State of Mexico, indicates that approximately 500 000 housing units were built in the Valle de México in the early 2000s (Duhau and Jacquin, 2008).

### *Housing lies vacant and abandoned throughout the metropolitan zone*

A large percentage of uninhabited and/or abandoned homes is the most visible manifestation of the crisis faced by some recently built large social housing neighbourhoods in the metropolitan periphery. Although data on this issue are not comprehensive,[6] several recent studies provide an overview of the issue (see, for instance, OECD, 2015; Monkkonen, 2014; INFONAVIT, 2015a, 2013; Sánchez and Salazar, 2011). Among the causes attributed to the phenomenon are the lack of employment centres within a reasonable distance and the high cost of public transport; the small size of new homes; and basic service deficiencies. Meanwhile, the economic crisis has made it more difficult for some households to continue to pay their mortgage (see INFONAVIT, 2014).

Within the Valle de México, several municipalities have been seriously affected by housing vacancies and abandonment. According to the National Institute of Statistics and Geography (Instituto Nacional de Estadística y Geografíai, INEGI) in the Population and Housing Census,[7] the Federal District has a very low vacancy rate (8%, six points below the national mean). Meanwhile, two Valle de México municipalities within the State of Mexico registered some of the highest percentages of unoccupied housing in 2010: Huehuetoca (44.7%) and Zumpango (39.7%; INEGI, 2010a). Both municipalities have a large number of recent social housing developments, and, according to INFONAVIT (2015c), the highest number of abandoned homes in the metro zone. The municipality of Tizayuca in the state of Hidalgo also reports that 45% of housing is vacant.[8] The case of Zumpango, located about 60 kilometres from the Federal District, is particularly extreme (Box 2.1). Zumpango does not necessarily reflect the norm, but it is not uncommon for some of the newer housing developments to continue to lack urban services, such as uninterrupted water and electricity, schools or parks, years after houses have been built (based on OECD interviews with authorities from the municipality of Zumpango, 2015). Moreover, it is often the location of the developments that is most problematic for residents, as the large housing tracts are far from jobs and city centres, and only accessible at great time and cost on the existing public transport network. In a 2012 survey of 309 INFONAVIT affiliates in 6 metropolitan zones (including the Valle de México),[9] a primary reason many households cited for leaving their INFONAVIT-financed home was the location of the housing, far from work, the city centre and/or schools (INFONAVIT, 2012). As noted earlier, one of the main challenges of residential suburbanisation in the Valle de México is that jobs have not yet followed the most recent residential patterns.

Vacant or abandoned social housing is problematic for several reasons. Vacancy that is in excess of the structural vacancy rate – that is, the percentage of housing that is necessarily vacant in a healthy housing market (Rosen and Smith, 1983) – can reduce the economic productivity of urban areas, waste investment in consumption rather than productive sectors, generate negative environmental impacts associated with urban sprawl and weaken homeowners' financial assets and the fiscal health of lending institutions like INFONAVIT as a result of unpaid mortgages. Excess vacancies can also lead to inefficient use of public subsidies (since social housing receives grants), in addition to urban and social deterioration due to vandalism and insecurity. Migrants have also recently been reported to have occupied vacant houses in the north of the Valle de México because they are located close the freight train line to the US border.[10]

### Box 2.1. Urban challenges in the municipality of Zumpango (State of Mexico)

The housing stock of Zumpango, a small agricultural town of just over 50 000 inhabitants in 1980, tripled between 1990 and 2010 (INEGI, 1980, 1990, 2010a), due in part to public policies that facilitated a wave of new residential construction developed by some of the country's largest developers. A majority of the new homes were purchased with INFONAVIT-issued mortgages.

Despite a veritable construction boom – over 100 000 permits were delivered between 1994 and 2013, the bulk of which were authorised between 2006 and 2012 – urban service provision for water, sewerage and electricity, as well as schools, often fell well short of developers' deliverables (Municipality of Zumpango, 2015). The population of the municipality more than doubled between 1990 and 2010, from around 71 000 inhabitants to 160 000 (INEGI, 1990; 2010a). As a result partly but not only of the global financial crisis, many of the largest construction firms faced significant financial difficulties after 2008, leading to the suspension of housing and infrastructure construction (Torres, 2013; see also, OECD, 2015). At the same time, the limited supply of local jobs (since agriculture has disappeared and industry is nonexistent) means that only 9% of the active population works within the municipality (INEGI, 2010a). New residents are thus subjected to long, costly commutes in traveling to work (Paquette and Negrete, 2013). Although there is some public transport, it is very expensive, and new transport routes and stations are not always well integrated with the existing network.[1] Security concerns have also risen significantly.

Many residents have since abandoned their homes in Zumpango. As of 2015, the municipality accounts for 40% of the total percentage of abandoned houses recorded by INFONAVIT in the Valle de México, as indicated by the borrowers' irregularities in payment; abandoned houses make up around 13% of the municipality's social housing stock (INFONAVIT, 2015c). Residents of the city have demonstrated to protest the poor living conditions, but the municipal administration does not have the fiscal resources to complete the unfinished infrastructure or provide basic urban services.

*Note:* 1. The development of the Mexibús Line 4 and the suburban train is illuminating in this respect. The Mexibús terminal was built one mile from the existing Lecheria suburban train station, rather than connected to it, which could have facilitated transport connections for users and generated more riders, and by extension, more profit.

*Sources*: INEGI (1980, 1990, 2010a); Torres (2013); OECD (2015); INFONAVIT (2015c); Municipality of Zumpango (2015); Paquette and Negrete (2013); Jones and Ward (1998); Eibenschultz Hartman and Benlliure (2009).

The large social housing neighbourhoods on the periphery of the Valle de México have become one of the most pressing issues facing policy makers, particularly in light of their rising security concerns. The next section will consider the range of policy options for social and urban regeneration throughout the Valle de México – including, in some cases, the demolition of some housing developments.

## Improving well-being through integrated urban regeneration

Although much remains to be done to improve living conditions in the existing housing stock in the Valle de México, much has been achieved in the past ten years. Urban regeneration is now considered an important means of improving quality of life and well-being in distressed neighbourhoods throughout the metropolitan zone. While concerns about the historic centre of the Federal District remain, local authorities have slowed depopulation and proposed strategic investment, as in the San Pablo District project.[11] Local and national authorities are investing in upgrading the Federal District's ageing social housing stock. More recently, proposals for urban regeneration have also emerged outside the Federal District in neighbouring municipalities in the State of Mexico. Meanwhile, the situation in more recent developments of the metropolitan periphery has become an increasingly urgent concern.

A growing number of stakeholders at all levels of government, as well as in the private sector, are making urban regeneration a priority, setting the stage for targeted policy efforts. This is the case both in the centre of the metropolitan zone and in peripheral areas, where distressed social housing neighbourhoods are, as noted, increasingly common. Better co-ordination of urban regeneration initiatives among different actors and levels of government; more involvement from the Ministry of Agrarian, Territorial and Urban Development (Secretaría de Desarollo Agrario, Territorial y Urbano, SEDATU), policy makers in the State of Mexico and local housing agencies; and the development of appropriate tools – and adjustments to some existing instruments – will be critical. These issues are discussed in detail in the next section.

### *Building on urban regeneration efforts in the central metropolis*

#### *Repopulation strategies and urban mobility investments have benefited the metropolitan core*

Efforts to revitalise the Historic District of Mexico City are not new. Beginning in the 1990s, with the creation of the Historic Centre Trust (Fideicomiso para el Centro Histórico), numerous initiatives have been implemented to repopulate and revitalise the heart of the metropolitan zone. In 2007, the Federal District created the Historic Centre Authority (Autoridad del Centro Histórico), which is charged with co-ordinating the more than 20 institutions and stakeholders involved in revitalisation efforts in the city centre. Guided by the Integrated Management Plan of the Historic District, 2011-2016 (*Plan Integral de Manejo del Centro Histórico, 2011-2016*), the Historic District Authority aims to rehabilitate older buildings and services and, more recently, facilitate the development of large urban areas, complete with new housing construction and the provision of related services and infrastructure. Its interventions include public space renewal, non-motorised mobility investments, risk prevention, heritage conservation, economic revitalisation, housing rehabilitation and integral infrastructure renewal. Since its creation, marked improvements have been evident in basic infrastructure networks (water, energy, communications), which were completely upgraded, and in public spaces.[12] The authority has also begun to work with both SEDUVI (the Federal District's urban development and housing department) and the National Housing Commission (Comisión Nacional de Vivienda, CONAVI) to build partnerships with private actors. The private sector has also become increasingly involved in the rehabilitation process. Even so, the many initiatives launched in the past two decades often remained discrete, one-time efforts concentrated on the touristic centre of the historic district.

Meanwhile, in the central part of the Federal District, other significant efforts have been undertaken. In the 2000s, thanks in large part to a repopulation and densification policy implemented by the Federal District authorities, the depopulation trend was halted in all but one *delegación* (Venustiano Carranza), and the area's population began to grow. One contributing factor was the *Bando Dos* policy, introduced in 2001. *Bando Dos* aimed to attract people to the central *delegaciones* and contain urban expansion in the peripheral *delegaciones* of the Federal District, where most new development had occurred in previous years. While relatively successful in limiting expansion in the outer *delegaciones*, *Bando Dos* nevertheless had a number of unintended (and undesirable) outcomes (Box 2.2).

### Box 2.2. **The mixed results of the *Bando Dos* policy**

Introduced by the government of the Federal District in December 2000, the *Bando Dos* regulation aimed to repopulate and increase the density of the centre of the Federal District, concentrating growth in four central *delegaciones,*[1] and restricting urban expansion in more peripheral *delegaciones.*[2] It was also seen as a way of encouraging more affordable housing in the city centre. Local authorities offered incentives (such as expedited permitting and licences) to developers for central city construction projects, while halting the issue of building permits in outer *delegaciones*.

On the one hand, the *Bando Dos* policy generated a real estate boom, helped repopulate the city centre and limited expansion in outer *delegaciones* (Paquette and Yescas, 2009). On the other hand, it has also had a number of unintended consequences. Some have argued that the policy "ended up intensifying some of the problems it set out to solve" (Ortega-Alcazar, 2006), leading to far higher real estate prices in the central city (and making the area even less affordable to lower income households) and contributing to leapfrog development in areas outside the Federal District in the State of Mexico, where the policy did not apply. These negative outcomes were partly the result of the absence of a metropolitan approach to urban planning and development. Ultimately, strong public opposition contributed to the suspension of the *Bando Dos* policy in 2007 (De Alba, 2009).

*Notes:* 1. Benito Juárez, Cuauhtémoc, Miguel Hidalgo and Venustiano Carranza. 2. Álvaro Obregón, Coyoacán, Cuajimalpa de Morelos, Iztapalapa, Magdalena Contreras, Milpa Alta, Tláhuac, Tlalpan and Xochimilco.

*Sources:* Paquette, C, and M. Yescas (2009), "Producción masiva de vivienda en la Ciudad de México: Dos políticas en debate", *Centro H,* 2009, No. 3, pp. 15-26; Ortega-Alcazar, I. (2006), "Mexico City: Housing and neighbourhoods", *LSE Cities*, February, London School of Economics and Political Science, https://lsecities.net/media/objects/articles/mexico-city-housing-and-neighbourhoods/en-gb (accessed 20 April 2015); De Alba, M. (2009), "Representaciones y prácticas sociales entorno a políticas urbanas: La movilización Nimby frente a la redensificación de las zonas centrales de la Ciudad de México", *Cultura y Representaciones Sociales*, No. 6, pp. 43-72.

## *Transport-oriented development as the way forward*

As will be discussed in Chapter 3, urban mobility strategies have evolved dramatically in the Valle de México – and especially in the Federal District – since the inauguration of the first Metrobús line in 2005. The implementation of this bus rapid transit (BRT) line was the first step in a series of measures to improve the city's urban transport network. Today, eight BRT lines are operating in the Valle de México. More are being developed as bus rapid corridors (BRC). As in many other Latin American cities, the introduction of the BRT system in the Valle of México has in some cases been rapidly followed with investments in public space and non-motorised mobility (incentivising cycling and, more recently, walking) (see Paquette, 2014, and Chapter 3).

The urban mobility approach to regeneration is a critical new development. Indeed, when the *Bando Dos* policy was implemented during the first half of the 2000s, urban development and mobility were issues managed separately by the local authorities. Thus, although the Metrobús Line 1 was operating throughout the area with the intention of redensifying the zone, few links were made between the urban densification policy and the existing BRT network (Paquette, 2008). This has now changed dramatically, and nearly all stakeholders (federal and local governments in addition to private developers) are aware of the importance of linking planning and investment for urban development and transport, in line with a national trend toward transport-oriented development (TOD). Most public and private stakeholders agree that urban density should be increased in proximity to public transport, and in particular along transport corridors (Metrobús, Mexibús, BRC, metro lines, etc.). The Integrated Mobility Programme of the Federal District (*Programa Integral de Movilidad*) identifies specific objectives for TOD. In addition, the proposal for a "Sustainable Housing Programme for the Federal District" (*Programa de Vivienda Sustentable para el Distrito Federal*) recently prepared by a group of private developers who are members of the CANADEVI (National Chamber of the Industry of Development and Promotion of Housing, Valle de México chapter) is an example of how TOD approaches are being promoted by a wide range of actors. The development of this proposal was led by the developers in an effort to persuade the federal and local governments to create specific financial mechanisms to boost the construction of affordable housing in the Federal District. It was directly inspired by the successful Chilean *Programa de Repoblamiento*, discussed later in this chapter.

Anchoring regeneration in strategic investments in urban mobility is a promising way to revitalise neighbourhoods, especially given the increasing number of transport corridors developed in the Valle de México over the last decade. The municipality of Ecatepec, for instance, is in the process of defining an urban regeneration strategy to take advantage of the Mexibús Line 1, which has successfully been developed by the government of the State of Mexico with good results in the municipalities (Box 2.3). The municipality is also updating its municipal development plan, which will include a 20-year vision – one of the first municipal plans to include a regional vision – and will cover issues including mobility, water, conservation land and environmental protection.[13]

### *Regeneration of ageing social housing has been led by the Federal District and, recently, INFONAVIT*

Two parallel initiatives – one that has been operated by the Federal District since 1989 and another more recent programme led by INFONAVIT – aim to renovate the large, ageing social housing stock (*unidades habitacionales*) in the Federal District. The programme, managed by the Federal District, which operates only in the common areas of units that are more than five years old, focuses on several issues: repair of water and electrical systems, rehabilitation of public space, and in some cases, new construction (such as the development of small meeting halls for inhabitants). The programme is competitive, as residents of social housing units must formally organise themselves and then compete for programme funds. Initiatives financed through this programme are in some cases linked to other social programmes to improve neighbourhood communal living that specifically target women, children and seniors. One of the primary limitations of the programme is its small budget: only MXN 900 (EUR 56) is granted per housing unit – which, in the case of a 500-unit housing complex, totals EUR 28 000. The demand for programme funds far exceeds supply: of the 2 000 annual applications, only 400-500 are ultimately funded, with fairly modest interventions. Even so, in many cases, this has had an important impact on residents' quality of life, and especially on their capacity to further organise to improve the neighbourhood.

### Box 2.3. A new approach to urban regeneration and mobility in Ecatepec

Located on the northeastern border of the Federal District, Ecatepec, with 1.66 million inhabitants in 2010, is the largest municipality in the Valle de México and one of the largest in the country. Most inhabitants are of low- and middle-low income. Ecatepec developed rapidly in the 20th century, but its population has grown very little in recent decades (Bassols and Espinosa, 2011).

The first Mexibús line in the Valle de México located outside the Federal District was built in Ecatepec in 2010. Five years later, this public transport corridor has had an important impact, both on inhabitants' quality of life (given the improved urban connectivity and above all, more security in the corresponding urban area) and on the local authorities in charge of urban affairs. As in the Federal District, the State of Mexico's first public transport corridor has improved public space management and mobility, as well as urban densification. Municipal authorities are working on density along the main urban corridor, Avenida Morelos, where vertical housing (ten-story residential buildings) has recently been authorised. The municipality, which now has two Mexibús lines and a third (Mexibús Line 4) expected soon, will also develop a Metrocable line to bring service to marginal settlements on high ground in the Sierra de Guadalupe, a small mountain in the municipal territory. The cable will connect to Mexibús Line 1 along the main avenue. Ecatepec is also developing cycling paths and improving pedestrian mobility and public spaces. These mobility strategies are closely linked to efforts to retain the numerous firms and industries in the municipality, and attract new ones, so that inhabitants can live close to their work.

*Source*: Bassols, M. and M. Espinosa (2011), "Construcción social del espacio urbano: Ecatepec y Netzahualcóyotl. Dos gigantes del oriente", *Polis*, Vol. 7, No. 2, January.

In 2013, INFONAVIT introduced its own rehabilitation programme, *Mejorando la Unidad* (Improving the Housing Unit), which focuses on the social housing stock in the Federal District built by the institute before its reform in the early 1990s. This programme includes repairs and improvements to public spaces, the creation of community murals[14] and the organisation of participatory workshops. Since the programme was launched, ten social housing units have benefited.[15] One of the key features of the programme is the participation of prominent Mexican architects in the implementation of rehabilitation projects. Finally, another federal programme, the Restoration and Rehabilitation of Social Housing Units (*Programa de Reordenamiento y Rescate de Unidades Habitacionales*) aims to improve the common areas of social housing units.

The programmes operated by the Federal District and INFONAVIT have had a positive effect on the quality of life in some of the older social housing stock, but they have two primary limitations. First, although both programmes generally have the same objectives and concentrate on the same territory (the Federal District), there is no co-ordination between them. Moreover, confining the target area to the Federal District means that the older social housing stock in the State of Mexico is not eligible for these upgrading programmes, despite its importance. Many large social housing developments have been built or financed by INFONAVIT in the State of Mexico since the 1970s; they now also require repairs and upgrades, which the current framework does not address.

## *An ambitious urban and housing regeneration programme for central Valle de México*

Moving forward, the Mexican authorities could consider launching an ambitious housing and urban regeneration programme for the historic centre of Mexico City. They could draw on the experience of Santiago de Chile, which faced similar challenges in recent decades.[16] Like the central area of the Valle de México, the centre of Santiago municipality suffered a huge population decline during the second half of the 20th century, its population falling by more than half between 1940 and 2002 (Contreras, 2011; Paquette, 2005). In the beginning of the 1980s, this municipality had one of the least active housing markets in the country and an increasing number of underutilised areas and decaying buildings. In the early 1990s, municipal authorities launched an ambitious repopulation programme (*Programa de Repoblamiento*) managed by a semi-public corporation, the Santiago Development Corporation (*Corporación para el Desarrollo de Santiago*). The primary task of the corporation was to work with private developers and landowners to mobilise land for new development. These efforts were largely successful: many high-density buildings were constructed (many of more than 20 stories) transforming the urban landscape. The programme has helped repopulate the area, from 200 000 inhabitants in 2002 to 308 000 in 2012. In 2013, almost 31% of housing sales in the metropolitan area were concentrated in the central municipality (Cámara Chilena de la Construcción, 2014).

Central Santiago de Chile's regeneration can be attributed to a combination of factors and a strong coalition. One important factor was a grant for first-time homeowners awarded by Chile's Ministry of Housing and Urban Development (Ministerio de Vivienda y Urbanismo, MINVU), which applied to specific urban areas defined as "renewal areas" (Rojas, 2004). Investment in transport in the central area included the extension of several Metro lines and the development of new metro stations. These, from the perspective of developers, were a strong selling point to draw young, middle-class households to the area. Meanwhile, the municipality undertook several important urban projects to improve the central area (such as the relocation of the prison) and negotiated with private firms to build supermarkets and local services in the centre.

Lessons of the Santiago de Chile experience that seem especially relevant for the Valle de México include:

- A comprehensive approach to urban rehabilitation. Santiago de Chile pursued a comprehensive urban regeneration agenda that combined investment in housing, mobility, basic services, public spaces, public safety and green areas. The authorities in the Valle de México are proposing to move in this direction.
- Co-ordinated investments in housing and mobility. The Santiago de Chile experience also demonstrated the importance of prioritising proximity to public transport to guide urban and housing investments, and vice versa. In the Valle de México, authorities are willing to pursue densification and renewal efforts along new mass transport corridors. These efforts could be combined with the development of urban intensification around the new multimodal stations (modal transfer centres, CETRAMs; Chapter 3).
- The reliance on a special subsidy for the construction of affordable housing in the central city. In Santiago de Chile, this subsidy has helped to ensure more inclusive repopulation of the central area and opened the redeveloped area, so that it is not only accessible to middle-high and high-income groups (which has been the case

in the Valle de México in the New Polanco development in the Miguel Hidalgo *delegación*). According to private developers in the Valle de México, a housing unit sold for MXN 800 000 (the lowest viable price, given the current land values in the Federal District) is still not affordable for low-income households without a specific grant. Such subsidies have been proposed by members of the Valle de México chapter of the CANADEVI, for instance. Recent evidence suggests that policies to facilitate mixed-income levels within neighbourhoods may yield significant benefits, especially to young children, over the long term (Box 2.4).

- The leadership of a multi-stakeholder public-private entity. In the Valle de México, it is particularly important for the leadership to include representatives from the Federal District, in addition to municipalities in the State of Mexico, which have hitherto been absent from the discussions on central urban regeneration. Moreover, co-ordinated actions of local and national actors – as in Santiago – would also be needed. Policies designed to repopulate the central area (e.g. *Bando Dos*) have failed in some respects for lack of a co-ordinated approach among local authorities (the Federal District and municipalities in the State of Mexico) and across levels of government (the redensification effort by the Federal District and massive housing construction facilitated by federal policies and programmes).

### Box 2.4. **Improving social mobility across generations: The potential long-term benefits of mixed-income neighbourhoods**

Can public policies reduce the weight of parents' socio-economic background on the future educational and economic opportunities of their children? The link between socio-economic background and social mobility – that is, individuals' ability to move up the social ladder as compared to their parents (OECD, 2010a) – has long been a topic of interest to both researchers and policy makers. OECD (2010a) found that in all countries for which data was available, the socio-economic background into which an individual is born influences his or her educational attainment, career prospects and lifetime earnings, if to varying degrees.

On the one hand, in many countries, public policies, whether implicitly or explicitly, have reinforced the effects of socio-economic background by facilitating the clustering of income groups. For instance, housing and urban planning policies have led to the concentration of disadvantaged or low-income households in certain neighbourhoods. Spatial segregation of households by income level is often coupled with segregation within the education system, since many students attend schools in or near their neighbourhood. Nevertheless, the strength of the relationship between school performance and students' socio-economic background varies across school systems. Education can either "reinforce economic advantages across generations or help improve social and economic mobility from one generation to another", depending on different aspects of the education system (OECD, 2010b: 52).

On the other hand, a range of policies has attempted to sever the link between socio-economic background and social mobility by encouraging the development of mixed-income neighbourhoods. These include: inclusionary zoning, requiring developers to build a specified percentage of affordable housing units in otherwise market-rate residential developments (as discussed later in this chapter), and voucher programmes that allow lower income households to move to higher income neighbourhoods or better schools. Causa and Chapuis (2009: 195) find that increasing the social mix of students in schools can lead to improvements in the relative performance of disadvantaged students. In other words, "education, housing and urban planning policies that encourage social mix within neighbourhoods could play a role in mitigating educational socio-economic inequalities and raise social mobility".

Box 2.4. **Improving social mobility across generations: The potential long-term benefits of mixed-income neighbourhoods** (*continued*)

Recent evidence suggests that some policies that encourage social mix may have particularly strong benefits for young children. The Moving to Opportunity initiative in the United States, which offered randomly selected households living in high-poverty housing projects housing vouchers to move to neighbourhoods with less poverty, is a case in point. Preliminary evidence found that the programme did not affect adults' short-term economic outcomes but did have some positive benefits on their physical and mental health (Ludwig et al., 2008; see Orr et al., 2003; Kling, Liebman and Katz, 2007; Ludwig et al., 2013). However, more recent evidence suggests that the most significant long-term impact of such policies is for the children in disadvantaged households who move to a lower poverty neighbourhood at a young age. Chetty, Hendren and Katz (2015) find that children who moved before the age of 13 are more likely to attend college and have on average 31% higher earnings as adults. Moreover, as adults, the children often live in better neighbourhoods and are less likely to become single parents, suggesting that benefits of such social mobility policies can persist across generations. The long-term effects of the programme on older children, by contrast, tend to be negative, perhaps due to the disruption and the reduced likelihood of benefiting from the short time in a lower poverty environment. Such findings suggest that the potential benefits of moving to low-poverty neighbourhoods depend on the age when children move; this is consistent with recent evidence that the duration of exposure to a better environment during childhood is a key determinant of the long-term outcome on an individual (Chetty, Hendren and Katz, 2015). However, more research is needed, given that outcomes of such interventions are not always as successful (Oreopoulos, 2003; 2008).

*Sources*: OECD (2010a), OECD *Economic Policy Reforms 2010: Going for Growth*, OECD Publishing, Paris, http://dx.doi.org/10.1787/growth-2010-en; OECD (2010b), *PISA 2009 Results: Overcoming Social Background: Equity in Learning Opportunities and Outcomes (Volume II)*, PISA, OECD Publishing, Paris, http://dx.doi.org/10.1787/9789264091504-en; Causa, O. and C. Chapuis (2009), "Equity in student achievement across OECD countries: An investigation of the role of policies", *OECD Economics Department Working Papers*, No. 708, OECD Publishing, Paris, http://dx.doi.org/10.1787/223056645650; Ludwig, J. et al. (2008), "What can we learn about neighborhood effects from the Moving to Opportunity experiment?", *American Journal of Sociology*, Vol. 114, No. 1, July, pp. 144-88, The University of Chicago, available at: http://home.uchicago.edu/ludwigj/papers/AJS-Ludwig-2008.pdf; Orr, L. et al. (2003), "Moving to opportunity interim impacts evaluation", US Department of Housing and Urban Development, Office of Policy Development and Research, June, Washington, DC, available at: www.abtassociates.com/reports/2003302754569_71451.pdf; Ludwig, J. et al. (2013), "Long-term neighborhood effects on low-income families: Evidence from Moving to Opportunity", *American Economic Review: Papers and Proceedings 2013*, Vol. 103, No. 3, pp. 226-31, http://dx.doi.org/10.1257/aer.103.3.226; Kling, J., J. Liebman and L. Katz (2007), "Experimental analysis of neighborhood effects", *Econometrica*, Vol. 75, Issue 1, pp. 83-119, January; Chetty R., N. Hendren and L. Katz (2015), "The effects of exposure to better neighbourhoods on children: New evidence from the Moving to Opportunity experiment", National Bureau of Economic Research, *NBER Working Papers*, No. 21 156, http://dx.doi.org/10.3386/w21156; Oreopoulos, P. (2008), "Neighbourhood effects in Canada: A critique", *Canadian Public Policy – Analyse de politiques*, Vol. 34, No. 2, pp. 237-58, June, University of Toronto Press, available at: http://oreopoulos.faculty.economics.utoronto.ca/wp-content/uploads/2014/08/Neighbourhood_Effects_in_Canada.pdf; Oreopoulos, P. (2003), "The long-run consequences of living in a poor neighborhood", *The Quarterly Journal of Economics*, MIT Press, Vol. 118, No. 4, pp. 1533-1575, November, http://dx.doi.org/10.1162/003355303322552865.

## *Regenerating distressed social housing neighbourhoods on the metropolitan periphery*

### *INFONAVIT has made significant progress*

Since 2010, concerns over the living conditions in the most recent social housing developments in the metropolitan peripheries throughout Mexico – and including those in the Valle de México – have become a central concern of INFONAVIT. These newly developed, distressed areas represent a real financial risk for both the institute and the households taking on loans, in the cases where homes are abandoned and credits unpaid (*cartera vencida*). The challenge is more than a financial one, affecting the well-being and financial situation of thousands of workers in Mexican cities.

INFONAVIT's initial efforts to address the issue, focused on remarketing the troubled housing stock (or "moving the inventory"), were soon extended to include a comprehensive approach to the social and urban regeneration of the neighbourhoods. Initially, the institute organised housing lot auctions (*macro subastas*) for private homebuilders. These private developers (generally those who had initially built the houses or others specialised in mass social housing production) would buy, repair and resell the so-called "recovered houses" (*viviendas recuperadas*) to INFONAVIT-lending beneficiaries. At the beginning of 2015, INFONAVIT had auctioned off a total of 21 000 houses, of which only 300 were located in the Valle of México.[17] In a second phase, the institute began to incorporate a more comprehensive approach to regeneration. Its recently developed Urban and Social Regeneration Programme (*Regeneración Urbana y Social*), the first initiative to target the peripheral distressed housing stock in Mexico, is the result of an extensive exploratory process carried out over the last three years. Based on an in-depth examination of 36 social housing developments across the country (3 of the 36 developments are located in the Valle de México),[18] the programme defines a consistent methodology for urban and social regeneration. A master plan for each of the 36 developments will be established, identifying the precise steps for upgrading physical and social dimensions. The framework of the *macro subastas* will be maintained, but home builders that purchase the housing lots will now be obliged to contribute up to 10% of the value of the homes toward rehabilitation measures specified in the master plan. Moreover, extensive consultation and collaboration with the existing community will be managed throughout the process by a non-profit organisation, Fundación Hogares, developed in the late 2000s with funding from INFONAVIT.[19] Under the new plan, Fundación Hogares receives 4% of the amount dedicated to regeneration actions to be used for investment in social rehabilitation.

In addition to its Urban and Social Regeneration Programme, INFONAVIT has initiated other efforts in the past three years to address the challenges associated with the peripheral housing stock. The institute's Urban Development Unit (Gerencia de Desarrollo Urbano) has launched several projects to prevent deterioration in social housing units by improving public spaces and increasing community involvement.[20]

### *Increasing co-ordination among the main players*

Other housing agencies are joining the efforts to tackle the high levels of vacancy and abandonment in the most recently built social housing stock. In late 2014, an inter-institutional working group was created on social housing regeneration and urban environment (Mesa de Trabajo Interinstitucional de Regeneración de Vivienda y Entorno Urbano). Its goal is to draw up an integrated public policy strategy to prevent the abandonment of social housing and help provide an adequate allocation of housing subsidies. Under the leadership of CONAVI, the technical arm of SEDATU specialised in housing that is responsible for preparing the National Housing Programme and operating housing subsidies, the working group gathers the national housing institutions (INFONAVIT, FOVISSSTE) and key stakeholders, such as commercial banks, financial intermediaries and the Fundación Hogares. INFONAVIT plays a central role in this working group, assuming the technical secretariat. The group will build on the diagnosis and methodology recently carried out by INFONAVIT with respect to the 36 social housing developments to implement urban and social regeneration projects. In a first phase, the working group will concentrate on 4 of the 36 developments (none of which are in the Valle de México), for which the National Housing Commission will dedicate a fund of MXN 250 million to finance the development of master plans and the implementation of regeneration measures, as defined in INFONAVIT's Urban and Social Regeneration Programme.

Although the creation of this working group is a crucial step toward the creation of a clear strategy for the regeneration of distressed social housing, the very minor role allocated to local housing institutions and local powers (states and municipalities) could limit its efficacy. In some respects, the limited role of local agencies is not surprising, since housing issues in Mexico are largely managed by federal institutions, despite the existence of regional housing organisations at state level and the urban development responsibilities of local governments. However, as will be seen, one particular strength of regeneration programmes in other OECD countries (France, the United States) has been the anchoring of national plans in locally driven strategies. To this end, state-level public housing agencies (Organismos Estatales de Vivienda, OREVIs) in the Valle de México, including the Housing Institute of the Federal District (Instituto de Vivienda del Distrito Federal, INVI), should be strengthened and involved in the discussion. Moreover, the government of the State of Mexico should be much more involved in these efforts – particularly in light of the pressing needs of some municipalities that are part of the metropolitan zone. One main challenge is that while urban regeneration appears to be a key priority of the Federal District government, it is not for the State of Mexico government. The risk is that urban regeneration in the Valle de México will proceed at different speeds and quite possibly in different directions.

Moreover, while the participatory approach to the regeneration process is relatively well-developed, more needs to be done to link urban regeneration efforts to broader urban revitalisation. Greater involvement from SEDATU could be helpful in moving beyond a housing-centred approach toward a more comprehensive urban strategy. Mexico has a long history of involving community and social groups in social development projects. This began with the regularisation of informal settlements and is now being used for formal social housing regeneration.[21] This approach could be very useful to other countries facing similar problems of social housing deterioration. However, while progress has been made to broaden the approach to addressing vacant and abandoned housing, more attention could be paid to the larger urban issues associated with these challenges, such as the location of new housing developments and their links to centres of employment and services.

### *Developing a common, comprehensive evidence base on the extent and conditions of social housing*

INFONAVIT has recently been setting up an Urban Development and Housing Observatory and an *Atlas of Abandoned Housing*. The observatory is a geographical information system currently under development, with information available from INFONAVIT and other stakeholders (concerning, among other things, crime prevention and marginal urban settlements). Both of these information systems should be available to all public stakeholders to help formulate better public policies.

Nevertheless, more needs to be done to improve the knowledge base on social housing, including information on the quantity, location and current conditions of social housing throughout Mexico. Recent initiatives like the Single Housing Registry (*Registro Único de Vivienda*, or RUV) and the *Abandoned Housing Atlas* are positive steps in this direction. However, no comprehensive database exists to map the number or conditions of social housing units built in the Valle de México in recent decades, apart from partial coverage made possible by the RUV and national censuses and surveys that provide statistics on different aspects of the issue.[22] Most existing knowledge about the issue is based on empirical studies of discrete neighbourhoods at a given moment in time. Other data that could be used as a proxy refer to the number of loans and grants that have been issued; however, while instructive, such figures do not allow for a reliable estimate of the number of houses that were actually built. These gaps are an obstacle in formulating a national strategy that can adequately address urban regeneration issues.

Given the amount of data to be collected, an important next step could be to develop a typology to help identify and target priority regeneration areas across the country. INFONAVIT has begun to create a series of indicators of social and physical decay, which could serve as the basis for this research (see INFONAVIT, 2015a). One possibility could be to partner with the National Council for Science and Technology (Consejo Nacional de Ciencia y Tecnologia, CONACYT). CONACYT, which already operates a common call for projects with CONAVI, could invite researchers to contribute to the knowledge base on distressed social housing neighbourhoods. Such indicators could become the basis for urban and social observatory of social housing developments, which could also be used to monitor the impact of public policies and programmes. The French Observatory of Sensitive Urban Zones (ONZUS)[23] could be a useful reference for Mexico. Created in 2003 to accompany the implementation of the National Programme for Urban Renovation, it produces an in-depth diagnosis and monitoring of investment in priority urban development zones. The ONZUS publishes an annual report that has become an important national reference for stakeholders involved in reviving distressed social housing.[24] Chile has a similar instrument, if less developed than France's, to analyse its social housing stock (MINVU, 2014). The Urban Development and Housing Observatory now under construction at INFONAVIT is a good starting point, but it will need to be formally shared with other public, private and voluntary sector institutions.

### *From pilot programmes to the implementation of a national public policy*

Building on recent pilot programmes and with greater involvement from SEDATU, the Mexican authorities could develop a clear, comprehensive national public policy and corresponding programme for urban regeneration. Two countries, France and the United States, have developed ambitious national policies in this area. Despite some fundamental differences (in France, social housing is owned by public institutions and rented to occupants; in the United States, public housing has been developed on a much smaller scale), these experiences could be instructive for Mexico (Box 2.5).

Two features of the French and American programmes should be of particular interest to Mexican policy makers:

- A cross-sectoral, comprehensive approach to urban regeneration. Both the French and American approaches simultaneously address a range of issues related to well-being, including education, employment, culture, safety, urban services and social cohesion. In other words, these programmes manage to focus simultaneously on housing, people and neighbourhoods. Efforts have also been made to link the regeneration programmes to other national initiatives, to concentrate public resources more effectively on distressed areas. In the United States, preference is given to Choice Neighborhood grant applicants, designated "Promise Neighbourhoods" by the US Department of Education.

Box 2.5. **National urban regeneration programmes in France and the United States**

**France's National Urban Regeneration Programmes**

The regeneration of France's post-World War II social housing stock has, for several decades, been a national priority for French policy makers.[1] The first National Urban Regeneration Programme (*Programme National de Rénovation Urbaine*, PNRU) was launched in 2003 with the aim of regenerating 500 distressed neighbourhoods. The programme resulted in an unprecedented public mobilisation effort. A national public agency (Agence Nationale de Rénovation Urbaine, ANRU) was established to operate the programme as a "one-stop shop" to simplify funding procedures. The regeneration framework mobilised a wide range of national and local actors over more than ten years, including the majority of the professionals on urban and social issues as well as part of civil society (Kirzbaum, 2009; Merlin, 2012). The PNRU, which was subject to some criticism (see Donzelot, 2012), was replaced in 2014 by a new ten-year national urban regeneration programme (*Nouveau Programme National de Renouvellement Urbain*, NPNRU).

**The United States' HOPE VI programme**

The United States has also led a comprehensive and sustained public effort to renew distressed social housing neighbourhoods. Although the proportion of social housing ("public housing") complexes is much smaller than in France and Mexico, the United States implemented a national policy that marked a turning point in urban regeneration.[2] HOPE VI (Housing Opportunities for People Everywhere), originally known as the Urban Revitalization Demonstration (URD), resulted from recommendations by the National Commission on Severely Distressed Public Housing, charged with proposing a national plan to eradicate severely distressed public housing. HOPE VI consisted of a large grant programme to public housing authorities, which began operating in 1993, ten years before the French PNRU (which it in fact inspired; see Kirzbaum, 2009). HOPE VI was followed in 2010 by the creation of the Choice Neighborhoods, which currently operates in a limited number of cities (Kirzbaum, 2013).

*Notes:* 1. See Merlin (2012) for the historical context of France's social housing developments. 2. As mentioned in Kirzbaum (2013), it is not easy to estimate the proportion of housing or households that benefit from public grants in the United States. Research using several data sources suggests a rough estimate of 7% of the total stock (approximately 110 million housing units) have benefited from public grants. This proportion is far less than in Europe or Mexico.

*Sources*: Kirzbaum, T. (2009), *Rénovation urbaine: Les leçons américaines*, Presses Universitaires de France, Paris; Merlin, P. (2012), *Des grands ensembles aux cités*: *L'avenir d'une utopie*, Ellipses, Paris; Donzelot, J. (2012), *A quoi sert la rénovation urbaine?*, Presses Universitaires de France, Paris; Kirzbaum, T. (2013), "Rénovation urbaine et équité sociale: Choice Neighborhoods aux États-Unis" (in French), working paper for the Commissariat général à la stratégie et à la prospective et le Secrétariat général du Comité interministériel des villes, Paris.

- National plans supporting locally driven initiatives. The comprehensive vision of the two programmes is also reflected in the range of stakeholders involved. Authorities at several levels of government, private agencies (including philanthropic institutions and associations), and local communities take part in the regeneration process. Moreover, although they are based on visions and mechanisms designed at the national level (national plans), the French and American approaches both fundamentally support locally driven strategies to address distressed neighbourhoods. In the context of the PNRU 2003-2014, the French National Agency for Urban Regeneration financed projects developed and submitted by local authorities, with the help of the national agency. The recent NPRU 2014-2024 goes one step further, requiring the creation of "city contracts" (*contrats de ville*), which gather all local stakeholders and define precisely a list of the measures needed to start the regeneration of the distressed neighbourhoods. The level of financial commitment of each stakeholder is also incorporated into the contract, to ensure that the entire community has a clear understanding of the obligations.

A national strategy for urban regeneration should be a priority for Mexican policy makers, in light of the extent and, in some cases, the severity of distressed social housing. The new strategy could be easily incorporated into the current policies established by SEDATU and CONAVI in the framework of the national programmes for urban development and housing. Moreover, the strategy should broaden its focus from housing abandonment – the expression and the most severe symptom of urban and social deterioration – to a broad conception of urban regeneration that includes housing and the surrounding environment, access to jobs and services, and strong transport links. This can help to anticipate and avoid housing abandonment in the future. As recommended in OECD (2015), SEDATU could take a much more active role in ensuring that this broader perspective is taken into account: the aim is now to build **cities**, not just houses. Finally, the diversity and complexity of social housing neighbourhoods across the country render the involvement of local and municipal governments essential. Urban regeneration strategies could be integrated into municipal development plans, for instance.

### *A global strategy of urban regeneration may include the demolition of some housing*

Another important component of housing regeneration strategies in other OECD countries has been the pursuit of an array of measures – including housing demolitions – to improve distressed social housing developments. In Chile, France and the United States, authorities have implemented a trio of solutions, depending on the specific conditions, ranging from housing rehabilitation, new development and, in the case of some of the most problematic units, demolition. Such demolitions were seen as an opportunity to restructure and redevelop the most distressed neighbourhoods.

Demolitions have been especially numerous in the context of France's National Urban Regeneration Programme. They have been systematically combined with new construction, often in excess of the units demolished. In many cases, regeneration projects have been seen at the local level as an important development opportunity. In France between 2003 and 2014, 145 000 social housing units were demolished and rebuilt, 300 000 were rehabilitated and 85 000 new housing units were produced (Ministry of Cities, Youth and Sports, 2014).

In a different context – more analogous to the situation in Mexico – Chile also employed demolition as an experimental solution for its most distressed social housing neighbourhoods. As the first Latin American country to carry out a housing policy based on mass production, Chile invented the framework that Mexico adopted a decade later, in which private developers assume the construction of housing, while the central government provides homebuyers with loans and grants. To reduce its significant housing deficit, Chile launched a massive housing production policy in the late 1980s that peaked in the 1990s. Around 200 000 social housing units were built in Santiago de Chile, providing a home for 1 million inhabitants – one-fifth of the metropolitan population (Rodriguez and Sugranyes, 2010). The mass-produced housing stock rapidly began to deteriorate, becoming a new urban problem. Since the mid-2000s, Chile has experimented with several programmes to address the issue, namely the Improved Neighbourhoods (*Recuperación de Barrios*) programme that began in 2006. This programme, which focuses not only on social housing developments but can apply to other neighbourhoods facing problems of social vulnerability and segregation, addresses the physical deterioration of buildings, public spaces and urban infrastructure, guided by an action plan drawn up in partnership with the community.

In 2013, Chile bolstered these efforts with the launch of a pilot programme of partial demolitions of social housing developments. The Recovery of Social Housing Communities Programme – Second Chance (*Programa de Recuperación de Condominios Sociales – Segunda Oportunidad*) is not explicitly presented as a demolition programme for political reasons. Nevertheless, demolition is a core element of the programme, in which the government purchases apartments in buildings that are considered to be irreparable – and which households have agreed to leave – and then demolishes them. Apartment owners receive a special grant from the government to purchase another house; rental occupants receive a grant to help pay several months of future rent. Additionally, all families receive a grant to cover their moving cost. Despite widespread criticism, this pilot project is still in high demand: in 2013, 828 households benefited from it; the target for 2014 was around 1 400 (MINVU, 2015). The redevelopment of the demolished areas is expected to follow an Urban Regeneration Plan, under the aegis of MINVU.

In sum, demolitions of distressed social housing developments should be considered one component of a global strategy for urban regeneration. The Chilean experience is of particular relevance for Mexican authorities, given the parallels with privately built social housing that is primarily owner-occupied. Demolition may be relevant for some of the most critical cases in Mexico, when other urban regeneration efforts are not likely to improve the neighbourhood. Before determining the best course of action, the neighbourhood's long-term viability should be analysed in depth.

### *Make urban regeneration happen: Planning tools and financing strategies*

While urban regeneration has become a shared priority among many stakeholders, the means to accomplish it are not yet clear. New tools and adjusting the existing instruments will be necessary. Authorities will also need to overcome the financial obstacles to the often costly process of urban regeneration. This section discusses planning tools and financing strategies for urban regeneration.

#### *Urban planning tools to support housing regeneration*

Planning tools should be reinforced to support urban regeneration. In the Federal District, the Urban Development Programme (*Programa de Desarrollo Urbano*) was last updated in 2003 and no longer reflects the aims of the current administration. Several attempts to update the planning framework have been undertaken since 2006, but many issues around urban management in the Federal District are politically charged (e.g. Norma 26,[25] discussed below), often stalling progress. Authorities in the State of Mexico have made progress toward making all municipal plans publicly accessible on the state's website. In addition, in 2007-08, the state dramatically revised and simplified its administrative code, to ease the administrative burden of different development procedures. Capacity challenges nevertheless remain in terms of urban planning and development.

Meanwhile, the metropolitan area suffers from a lack of co-ordinated urban planning. The recently updated Regional and Urban Planning Programme for the Valle de México (*Programa de Ordenación de la Zona Metropolitana del Valle de México*, POZMVM), which uses the larger definition of the Valle de México, is not legally binding. As the *Bando Dos* experience clearly demonstrates, the absence of a coherent urban strategy at the metropolitan scale can lead to the failure of well-intentioned redensification policies for specific sub-areas (Tamayo, 2007). Moreover, different parts of the metropolitan zone tend to move at different speeds and, at times, to different ends, as in the case of urban regeneration strategies mentioned earlier. One obstacle to more co-ordinated metropolitan planning is that existing tools and terminology are inconsistent and fragmented across different administrations. For instance, the definition of mixed-use development is not the same in the Federal District and the State of Mexico; regulations (and their level of enforcement) also tend to be different across administrative boundaries. Land-use regulations and terminology across the Valle de México could be harmonised. The development of a metropolitan approach to housing and urban development, and a more "metropolitan" toolbox, should be made a priority; components of such a strategy are discussed later in this chapter.

While harmonising terms and regulations is needed, a metropolitan approach should not, however, imply a uniform approach to these issues, as the challenges and contexts of different parts of the metropolitan zone are both distinct and diverse. Certainly, it is important that metropolitan stakeholders agree on the general principles and vision for future housing and urban development in the Valle de México. However, the specific tools may differ in different parts of the metropolitan zone. For instance, in the case of vacant and abandoned housing, new instruments need to be created to expedite the urban regeneration process and mobilise land more effectively in the central area. According to the Historic District Authority, the mobilisation of land is the main barrier to implementation of the San Pablo District project mentioned earlier. Several current projects in the Federal District are testing the waters in this respect, such as the "Health City" initiative (*Ciudad de la Salud*) and CETRAM projects (Chapter 3). Strategic management areas (*áreas de gestión estratégicas*, AGE) and economic and social development areas (*áreas de desarrollo economico y social*, ADES; formerly ZODES) are also under development.[26] While the redevelopment of vacant housing in the historic core of the Federal District might need to focus on instruments to reduce the cost of regeneration in these more expensive central locations, different tools will be required to address abandoned housing in peripheral municipalities (e.g. a greater focus on developing transport links or improving access to jobs, and in the most severe cases, considering the demolition of some social housing developments). Finally, in addition to improving the co-ordination of policies for housing and urban development across administrative borders, policy makers must also continue to make policies across relevant urban sectors, in particular, housing, mobility and economic development, more coherent.

### *Financing the regeneration of distressed social housing*

Financing the revitalisation of distressed social housing neighbourhoods is undoubtedly one of the most significant challenges that the Mexican authorities will have to face in developing their regeneration agenda. Regeneration is expensive because it often involves building new infrastructure and major structural adjustments; demolition, moreover, is very costly. The French and the American experiences show that regeneration of distressed social housing neighbourhoods is a long-term challenge that requires significant investment and financing. The French PNRU 2003-2014, for instance, involved a EUR 11 billion investment in public subsidies; the current PNRU has a budget of EUR 5 billion. In the United States, USD 7 billion has been allocated to the Hope VI programme. And Chile's Second Opportunity and the Improved Neighbourhoods programme are also based on a large volume and variety of subsidies: in 2013, the

Second Opportunity programme had a budget of EUR 14.6 million; the Improved Neighbourhoods programme operated with a budget of EUR 47.7 million.

**Levy betterment charges to capture the benefits of urban investment.** One important opportunity to finance urban regeneration and investment is land value capture, notably in the form of a betterment charge (see Chapters 3 and 5). A betterment charge [or special assessment] is a "compulsory charge imposed by a government on the owners of a selected group of properties to defray, in whole or in part, the cost of a specific improvement or services that is presumed to be of general benefit to the public and of special benefit to the owners of such properties" (IAAO, 2013). Such charges are already imposed under the financial code of the Federal District (the charge is levied at completion of the improvement in question), but have only recently been put to use; they have also been used in the past in the State of Mexico. Since 2014, after a change in the Federal District fiscal code, some urban transport improvements (e.g. public transport, bicycle lanes and CETRAMs) have been eligible to be financed through betterment charges; this is not, however, the case in the State of Mexico and Hidalgo (as discussed in detail in Chapter 3). Given the continued focus on transport-oriented development and transport corridors for future development in the Valle de México, this kind of tool should be considered an essential means of boosting public resources and contributing to regeneration efforts. The potential gains of a betterment charge are, moreover, aligned with the recent efforts of the Federal District to boost fiscal resources through improved tax collection. In Latin America, Colombia (where it is known as *Participación de Plusvalía*) and Brazil (where a related tool, *certificados de potencial adicional de construção*, CEPACs, has been implemented in areas of some cities) both have experience of land-value capture that could be relevant for the Valle de México. In short, no urban regeneration strategy should be undertaken without the tools for recovering part of the public investment, so that other projects in the future can be viable.

**Social housing settlements could receive funds from existing social welfare programmes.** Another possibility would be to modify the regulations of several existing social welfare subsidy programmes so that the funds could also be applied to distressed social housing. In some cases, the rules governing these programmes preclude their application (e.g. the allocation of subsidies) to existing social housing developments; such rules could be modified and co-ordinated to include existing social housing developments among the eligible beneficiaries. For instance, the Hábitat programme, launched by SEDESOL in the early 2000s and now operated by SEDATU, is well known and often used by local governments. The programme offers subsidies for urban improvements in target areas. Nevertheless, formal housing settlements are not eligible to receive these funds; the funds are intended for marginal settlements that have generally been developed through informal development. The rules governing other federal programmes that offer subsidies for crime and violence prevention and public space renewal could also be modified to help regenerate distressed social housing developments, by allowing their use in existing social housing:

- The National Programme for Social Prevention of Violence and Crime (*Programa Nacional para la Prevención Social de la Violencia y la Delincuencia*, PRONAPRED), operated by the Ministry of the Interior (Secretaría en Gobernación, SEGOB): the objective is to prevent violence and crime and encourage social cohesion.
- Rescue of Public Spaces Programme (*Programa Rescate de Espacios Públicos*, PREP), operated by SEDATU: the aim is to improve quality of life and safety of inhabitants in marginal zones through investment in public spaces.

- Hábitat Programme III: Preventative interventions (*Programa Hábitat, Vertiente III "Intervenciones preventivas"*), operated by SEDATU: the aim is to improve living and social conditions of inhabitants of target areas, through subsidies for urban renewal and community development.

**Reform the constraints of the property status of social housing.** One of the primary financing constraints on urban regeneration efforts in Mexico is the property regime of social housing units. Social housing units are owner-occupied, but public funds cannot be applied to the improvement or transformation of private property. This is why many regeneration programmes have hitherto limited their intervention to public spaces and common areas, even though it is recognised that in many cases the homes and apartments themselves require upgrades. Chile overcame this obstacle with its Second Opportunity programme, by purchasing housing from the owners. Mexico could also consider this approach to help finance urban regeneration, and in the case of the most distressed areas, demolition. Alternatively, the financing barrier could be overcome by channelling a portion of CONAVI's national housing subsidy to distressed social housing neighbourhoods, to be used for housing improvements in priority urban regeneration areas – in other words, setting aside a larger percentage of CONAVI subsidies for existing ("used") housing, relative to new housing construction. A percentage of these funds could also be used for used housing to the particular case of recovering abandoned housing. These options, which both require public subsidies and are conditional on their availability over time, would appear to be the only way that public funds could be used for housing regeneration.

Some innovative approaches to regeneration finance have also been introduced through market-based schemes from private actors with a significant component of community participation. Such approaches, which have so far been used largely in the northern part of the country, could be adapted to the Valle de México and scaled up (Box 2.6).

Box 2.6. **Innovating urban regeneration in Mexico: The private-sector approach led by Provive**

Provive, a private company devoted to buying, repairing and selling abandoned social housing, works within the *macro subastas* scheme established by INFONAVIT (auctions of abandoned social housing recovered by the institute and resold to private developers), but adds a crucial dimension: participatory community engagement throughout the process to improve the neighbourhood physically and socially. While Provive manages the purchase, repair and resale of the units, a separate foundation, *Tú y Yo*, manages the community engagement aspect, with a contribution from Provive equivalent to 5% of the home sale value. The *Tú y Yo* foundation works with inhabitants to develop social cohesion. Provive and the *Tú y Yo* foundation is working in three cities in northern Mexico (Tijuana, Mexicali and Ciudad Júarez), and has refurbished and resold 2 000 homes and helped to improve neighbourhoods.

This model's economic viability is particularly promising. One limitation, however, is that the approach has primarily been used in neighbourhoods without major infrastructure deficiencies. Social housing neighbourhoods with severe transport issues, as in the northern periphery of the Valle de México, would require another type of intervention. Their regeneration can only be achieved by a significant investment in public transport, improvements in accessibility and job creation in the area.

**Seek greater involvement from private developers in the regeneration process.** Finally, given the significance of the construction industry in the Mexican economy, the involvement of private developers in urban regeneration should also be strongly encouraged. A new strand of the housing industry based on regeneration issues – concentrating not only on social housing neighbourhoods but on urban regeneration needs more broadly – could make an important contribution to the economy. The positive economic repercussions of a successful national urban regeneration programme can be significant: in France, the numerous projects implemented since the launch of the first national programme have generated strong economic activity for the entire urban and housing sector. The programme is even considered to have played an important role in sustaining the economy when the 2008 crisis hit, particularly for small construction firms.[27] If well managed, urban regeneration could help Mexico transform the current economic and social risks of distressed social housing into an opportunity to improve the well-being of inhabitants across Mexican cities.

## Guiding future housing and urban development from a metropolitan perspective

The population of the Valle de México is projected to continue to grow in the coming decades – by 13% between 2010 and 2030 – albeit at a slower pace than many other Mexican cities and metropolitan zones (CONAPO, 2010). Where should this growth occur, and what should it look like? Three strategies to guide new development could be advanced:

- The first strategy could be to facilitate new development in central areas to make it easier (and, by extension, cheaper) for developers to construct new, affordable housing in the metropolitan core. This could be done by: 1) reducing the regulatory barriers to development and densification in the central areas of the metropolitan zone (especially parking requirements); 2) reintroducing an inclusionary zoning policy (e.g. offering incentives to developers to produce a percentage of affordable housing in market-rate developments) in the Federal District; and 3) if required and only in certain cases, providing an affordable housing subsidy (for example through CONAVI) that could be applied in strategic areas.
- A second strategy could be to remove barriers to the development of the rental market as a means of offering housing that is both more affordable to low-income households and, in many cases, of higher quality than owner-occupied units targeting this income group. A larger rental market could also help increase labour mobility in the metropolitan zone.
- A third strategy could be to encourage a more sustainable form of housing development in the metropolitan periphery by planning for smart growth in peripheral areas. Rather than highly restrictive urban containment policies, like those that have been attempted at various points in the Valle de México's history, policy makers should plan for growth in peripheral areas, prioritising new development and urban regeneration initiatives in areas linked to strategic infrastructure investments. The two major infrastructure projects on the horizon in the Valle de México – the New Mexico City International Airport (Nuevo Aeropuerto Internacional de la Ciudad de México, NAICM) in the northeast and the Mexico City-Toluca rail line that would link the Federal District to Toluca to the west – offer critical opportunities.[28] Failed containment policies can be much worse than planned urban expansion.

Together, these strategies could constitute a new, metropolitan approach to urban planning in the Valle de México, in which policies for housing and urban development are well aligned across administrative borders and levels of government.

### *Facilitate affordable development in the central metropolis*

One factor driving households toward peripheral areas is that formal housing in the city centre is unaffordable to many low-income households. CONAVI reported that in June 2014, only 7 of the 95 397 housing subsidies for low-income households that it had issued nationwide had been used in the Federal District. The primary cause for this is that the types of social and economic housing eligible for the subsidy are not available in the Federal District due, among other factors, to high land costs (Santa Rita, 2014). Based on data from Sociedad Hipotecaria Federal (SHF), between 2005 and 2011, housing prices increased in the Federal District 1.75 times the national average and 4.52 times more than those of homes in the State of Mexico (Fundación Idea/Cámara de Senadores/SIMO Consulting, 2014). Further, in the 2015 housing demand projections developed by the SHF, just 5% of all housing finance through INFONAVIT, FOVISSSTE, banks and other financial entities are expected to be issued in the Federal District, even though it accounts for 18% of the country's population and housing units (SHF, 2015; INEGI, 2010a).[29]

Why is land so expensive and, by extension, housing so unaffordable in the Federal District? First, there are important physical constraints to development. Much of the Federal District is already built up, and the remaining land is not suitable for development. Around 59% of all land in the Federal District is classified as conservation land (*suelo de conservación*), which is located primarily in the southern half of the city (Government of the Federal District, 2015). Conservation land is protected from formal development because it provides important environmental services for the city (e.g. water catchment areas), though it has over the decades been a significant source of land for informal settlements. This means that more than half of the metropolitan core is not available for formal development. In addition, topographical and climactic features are other factors restricting development in some areas.

Second, in addition to land scarcity, there are important regulatory barriers to new development and densification. Housing is under-produced in the Federal District: SEDUVI estimates that the annual housing demand (45 000-48 000) was more than twice the annual housing production in 2014 (Fundación Idea/Cámara de Senadores/SIMO Consulting, 2014; Marron Institute, 2014). Current regulations require that all new housing units built are equipped with parking, which can represent on average around 21% of the total price of an affordable housing unit (ITDP, 2014). According to the Marron Institute (2014), the city's zoning norms restrict density, increase housing costs and contribute to urban sprawl. Interviews with developers concur: one home builder specialising in dense inner-city development reported that "land-use regulations do not always facilitate the development of 'vertical' [higher density] housing."[30] One study found that the density restrictions introduced by Regulation 11 (Norma 11) in the Federal District in 2005 regarding the number of dwellings permitted and construction intensity are the most significant constraint on new development: in a simulation that applied existing land-use restrictions to 100 random lot samples, Bertaud and Rangel Smith (in: Marron Institute, 2014) found that Regulation 11 resulted in a 95% decrease in development potential. In other cases, there is unexploited development potential around mass transit (see ITDP, n.d.). Barriers include, as mentioned, minimum parking regulations and design regulations, which often make it financially unviable to develop new affordable housing or to increase density of existing development in proximity to transport stations and corridors (see ITDP, 2014; 2015).

As a result of this affordability gap, informal settlements have, for decades, been the primary means of shelter for most low-income households (see, for instance, OECD, 2015; Fernandes, 2011; Blanco, Fretes Cibils and Muñoz, 2014; Dowall and Wilk, 1989). Indeed, between 1950 and 1980, informal development accounted for approximately 65% of all housing produced in the Mexico City metro area (Dowall and Wilk, 1989), such that it made up 14% of the housing stock in 1952 and around 60% by 1990 (Blanco, Fretes Cibils and Muñoz, 2014). Another contributing factor to the continued expansion of informal settlements has been that housing assistance for low-income households has been insufficient in quantity and available for only a portion of the population: those with salaried, formal employment. Even if INFONAVIT and FOVISSSTE together provide eight out of ten mortgages in Mexico, conventional housing finance offered through these and para-public entities is largely outside the reach of at least half of the Mexican population – those working in the informal sector (Eibenschultz Hartman and Benlliure, 2009; INFONAVIT, 2013; Fernandes, 2011).

### *Reduce the most burdensome land-use regulations*

Reducing, and in some cases, eliminating some of the most burdensome land-use regulations could facilitate new housing construction in the central metropolitan zone and, by extension, help make centrally located housing more affordable. Revisions to current restrictions on lot sizes, building sizes and heights, density, parking requirements and building permits could all be considered (see ITDP, 2014, 2015; Marron Institute, 2014). In particular, establishing maximum, rather than minimum, parking requirements in new developments located in proximity to public transport stations and corridors could be one possibility, in addition to adjusting current maximum density requirements based on the capacity of public transport (see ITDP, 2015). Moreover, rather than require developers to adhere to strict development restrictions (which can in turn have negative effects on housing affordability), it may be preferable to offer incentives for developers to comply with the desired type and form of development. Schuetz, Meltzer and Been (2011) found that voluntary programmes that offer incentives to develop affordable units have, in practice, produced more affordable housing units than mandatory requirements.

### *Reintroduce an inclusionary zoning policy in the Federal District*

The reduction of restrictive land-use regulations could be pursued in parallel with revisions to the Federal District's inclusionary zoning policy[31] (Regulation 26, or Norma 26), which was suspended by the government in late 2013. Indeed, Regulation 26 is high on the current political agenda of the Federal District. Introduced in 1997 and reformed in 2010, the law was developed as an inclusionary zoning policy to facilitate the production of affordable housing in the Federal District, and was in fact one of the only laws promoting the construction of affordable housing for low-income residents in the Federal District (Adler, 2015). The regulation offered incentives to developers – namely, tax breaks and density bonuses – in exchange for the provision of a percentage of affordable housing units[32] in otherwise market-rate housing developments (mixed-income housing developments). However, numerous abuses have been reported. According to a report released by the government of the Federal District, 78% of the affordable units ("social interest housing") developed under Regulation 26 did not meet the affordability requirements (cited in Adler, 2015). Instead, developers "have used [Regulation 26] to make windfall profits … a recent investigation by city prosecutors revealed these abuses yielded gains of over MXN 2.5 billion – about USD 170 million" (Adler, 2015). Since Regulation 26 was suspended in August 2013, new regulations have been under discussion to correct for some of its main shortcomings, namely Regulations 30 and 31 (Normas 30 and 31), which are designed to promote more affordable housing. At the time of writing, these regulations are still under discussion for approval by the Legislative Assembly of the Federal District (Asamblea Legislativa del Distrito Federal, ALDF).

The revival of some form of inclusionary zoning – particularly via regulations that allow developers to build at higher densities, provided that a certain percentage of affordable housing is constructed – could indeed become one important means of promoting housing affordability in the central area of the Valle de México; it should not, however, be conceived as the only instrument in the toolbox. Moreover, policy makers should also keep in mind that densification strategies to produce new housing units are not likely to be appropriate everywhere – nor should higher densities in the central area of the Valle de México be conceived as the "silver bullet" to achieve more affordable, centrally located housing. Several considerations are important to keep in mind:

- First, given that current densities in the Federal District – and on average, across the Valle de México – are already high and, in some cases, existing service networks are already strained, the capacity of existing infrastructure and the cost of extending, upgrading or replacing these networks should be key factors in determining whether densification is appropriate in a given neighbourhood.
- Second, higher densities should be understood as one of many tools, and, critically, a means to an end, rather than an end in itself. In other words: density levels should not be the key variable in delivering more sustainable urban environments; rather, it is the quality of planning and design that matters.

Third, density comes at a cost, with both advantages and disadvantages. These trade-offs should be well understood by policy makers to ensure that the potential gains outweigh the costs (Table 2.2). Moreover, the potential benefits of density are not automatic (as can be gleaned from some of the conflicting findings in Table 2.2, for instance, regarding the links between density and crime levels); rather, careful design and planning is required in order for higher densities to deliver the potential benefits. Without good planning and design, higher densities can actually yield undesirable results.

#### *In certain cases, provide a subsidy for the development of affordable housing*

Even with the appropriate regulatory environment in place, it may nonetheless be necessary to provide targeted subsidies, via CONAVI, to assist in the development of affordable housing in central areas. As mentioned earlier in this chapter, a similar subsidy was developed by MINVU in Chile to help make central city construction more affordable for developers. Such a subsidy could operate within the framework of SEDATU's urban polygons, a series of graduated urban growth perimeters designed to limit sprawl and encourage infill development.[33] Even so, additional modifications to the definition of these zones may be desirable to ensure that they correspond to the provision (or potential provision) of public transport (see, for instance, ITDP, 2015).

### *Remove barriers to the development of rental housing*

Although the percentage of rental housing in the Valle de México (31% in 2010) is larger than in many other Mexican metro zones, it is nonetheless small by international standards.[34] Its limited size is the result of many factors: policies favouring home ownership over rental housing; a large percentage of informal settlements, which are often self-built and owner-occupied;[35] strong tenant protections; a high taxation of rental income; a burdensome regulatory framework and a judicial system that tends to favour tenants' rights over those of landlords; and underdeveloped credit markets (see OECD, 2015, for a detailed discussion). The many potential benefits of rental housing are identified in Blanco, Fretes Cibils and Muñoz (2014). Among those that would appear most relevant for the Valle de México are the capacity of rental housing to provide housing that is more affordable, more centrally located, and of higher quality than owner-occupied housing targeting low-income households; rental housing may also contribute to higher levels of labour mobility.

Table 2.2. **Higher urban densities imply trade-offs**

| | Potential advantages of higher urban densities | Potential disadvantages of higher urban densities |
|---|---|---|
| Mobility | – Reduce fossil fuel emissions/carbon footprint by decreasing the total number of vehicle trips and the number of kilometres traveled per trip<br>– Enhance accessibility, as people live closer to where they work, shop and play<br>– Make transit more economically viable and efficient<br>– Enable public health benefits from more walkable and bike-friendly environments<br>– Create efficiencies in mixed-use developments through shared parking | – Exacerbate traffic congestion, parking problems; increased traffic accidents<br>– Create pedestrian congestion and congestion in public transport<br>– In compact, monocentric cities, may only have significant positive environmental effects when a greater percentage of commuters use mass transit |
| Land/resource use | – Make better use of existing resources and infrastructure<br>– Reduce development pressure on green spaces, agriculture and industrial land<br>– Create a greater mix of land uses | – Limit recreational opportunities and reduce the availability of green/open space<br>– Reduce an area's capacity to absorb rainfall because of open space/recreational loss<br>– Exacerbate pollution, possibly because of reduced area for trees/vegetation |
| Social equity | – Reduce segregation and social exclusion<br>– Add diversity, safety, vitality and opportunities for creative and social interaction<br>– Provide access to facilities (e.g. schools, employment, shops), without the need for a (costly) private vehicle<br>– Reduce crime by increasing pedestrian activity and encouraging a 24-hour community (more "eyes on the street") | – Lead to loss of privacy and increased noise, nuisance, etc.<br>– Reinforce social inequality and social segregation<br>– Increase crime<br>– Generate cramped living environments |
| Economic development | – Enable investments in community amenities as well as better quality and more attractive building materials<br>– Promote a critical mass necessary to support local retail and service areas | – Additional cost to build and maintain high-density projects and city-centre infrastructure<br>– Higher relative prices for land, housing and many other goods and services |
| Environmental sustainability and energy | – Preserve green open spaces, clean air and water, fauna and flora systems (when higher density development occurs elsewhere)<br>– Facilitate innovative green design and district energy; reduce water and energy consumption<br>– Facilitate the technological and economic viability of certain energy technologies and transport systems | – Higher energy consumption during the construction of high-density buildings<br>– Limit some forms of ambient energy systems<br>– Increased noise |

*Sources*: Adapted from Boyko, C. and R. Cooper (2011), "Clarifying and re-conceptualising density", *Progress in Planning*, Vol. 76, No. 1, pp. 1-61, July, http://dx.doi.org/10.1016/j.progress.2011.07.001; Fundación Idea/Cámara de Senadores/SIMO Consulting (2014), "México compacto: Las condiciones para la densificación urbana inteligente en México", Fundación Idea, Cámara de Senadores and SIMO Consulting, Federal District, Mexico, available at: http://fundacionidea.org.mx/assets/files/MexicoCompacto_Senado_IDEA_SIMO.pdf; Gaigné, C., S. Riou and J.-F. Thisse (2012), "Are compact cities environmentally friendly?", *Journal of Urban Economics*, Vol. 72, Issues 2-3, pp. 123-136, September-November, http://dx.doi.org/10.1016/j.jue.2012.04.001.

OECD (2015) recommended that Mexico develop a national policy for rental housing, based on a series of broad measures targeting the fiscal, regulatory and legal framework of rental housing. Expanding the rental housing market was also identified in the National Housing Programme as an important aim moving forward, though few details were provided. Such measures could ensure more balanced treatment between rental housing and home ownership, and help provide a more conducive environment for some of the recent, *ad hoc* rental programmes introduced by INFONAVIT and CONAVI. Among the primary macro-strategies that should be envisaged by the national government to improve the environment for rental housing: 1) review the regulatory framework to ensure more balanced treatment for property owners and renters; 2) reduce the tax burden on rental properties; and 3) implement rental assistance programmes for individuals (OECD, 2015).

Some of the current proposals in the Valle de México to expand rental housing may need to be reconsidered. For instance, INFONAVIT's Arrendavit programme offers its affiliates a credit to access rental housing; the institute acts as an intermediary between lessor and lessee, withholding rental payments directly from the renter's salary. While take-up on the programme has been slow, INFONAVIT aims to target this programme to specific areas in the Valle de México, such as the Venustiano Carranza *delegación* in the Federal District and 19 municipalities in the State of Mexico, including Tecámac, Huehuetoca and Zumpango – 3 municipalities selected due to their high rate of abandoned housing. While the institute's objective to expand rental housing is on the right track, targeting rental housing in more central areas, as well as more peripheral areas that are well-connected to the public transport network, would seem to be a more appropriate strategy.

### *Plan for growth in peripheral areas, prioritising development around strategic infrastructure investments*

#### *Why urban containment policies are not the answer*

Despite many calls for an end to urban expansion in the Valle de México – and globally in cities across the developed and developing world – strict urban containment policies tend to be ill-advised (see Angel et al., 2010b). Indeed, the experience with *Bando Dos* in the Federal District (see Box 2.2) demonstrates the potential pitfalls of the pursuit of highly restrictive urban containment policies. The difficulties in successfully containing growth are not unique to Mexico: as Angel et al. (2010b) point out, urban containment strategies have failed (or hardly succeeded) in many other cities and countries and have typically come with large unintended costs. Consider that, over a three-decade period, the urban outcomes measured in terms of urban expansion, fragmentation and changes in density were not so different in Portland, Oregon (United States) – which established an urban growth boundary in 1973 – and Houston, Texas – one of the only US cities that does not have a zoning code (see Angel et al., 2010b). Moreover, in the case of Portland, researchers have found that while the urban growth boundary has generally been successful in curbing urban sprawl, urban densities decreased, housing and land prices increased, and leap-frog development occurred in areas beyond the boundary. Greenbelt policies in Korea and the United Kingdom have also had limited success (Kamal-Chaoui and Sanchez-Reaza, 2012). Like densification strategies, urban containment policies have costs.

Highly restrictive urban containment policies can be especially counter-productive in fast-growing urban areas (Angel et al., 2010b). Even though the pressure to expand in the Valle de México may not be as strong in the coming decades given its lower projected growth rates relative to other Mexican metropolitan zones (CONAPO, 2010), growth rates of different parts of the metropolitan zone have historically been extremely heterogeneous. CONAPO's projections to 2030 anticipate highly differentiated growth rates of different municipalities within the Valle de México, with many peripheral municipalities projected to grow by more than 30% or 40%. Certainly, public policies, particularly at national level, have shifted since the release of these projections and could affect the extent and speed of growth in individual municipalities. However, it is fair to assume that some parts of the metro zone will continue to grow faster than others and that some level of new development is bound to occur in outer areas. The SHF (2015) anticipates that the vast majority of demand for housing credits in the Federal District and the State of México (statistics are not available at the Valle de México level) will be for home acquisition, rather than home improvements or self-built housing (Table 2.3). In both cases, the percentage projected for home acquisition (86% for the Federal District and 71% for the State of Mexico, which includes both new and "used", or existing, housing) is much higher than the national average (53%). Some of these home acquisitions will be for newly constructed housing. For instance, in terms of INFONAVIT lending alone, the institute projects that new housing construction will make up the majority of lending for housing acquisition in the state of Hidalgo (66% of projected INFONAVIT lending in the state), compared to 39% in the State of Mexico and just 14% in the Federal District. Meanwhile, INFONAVIT lending for the purchase of existing housing is expected to range from 42% of all projected INFONAVIT lending in the Federal District to 15% in the state of Hidalgo (based on INFONAVIT, 2015b).

Table 2.3. **Projected housing credits for the entities in the Valle de México, 2015**

| | Housing acquisition | | Home improvements | | Self-built | | State total |
|---|---|---|---|---|---|---|---|
| | No. of credits | % of state total | No. of credits | % of state total | No. of credits | % of state total | No. of credits |
| Federal District | 52 016 | 86% | 8 453 | 14% | 310 | 1% | 60 779 |
| State of Mexico | 79 043 | 71% | 23 929 | 21% | 8 655 | 8% | 111 627 |
| State of Hidalgo | 11 389 | 55% | 7 763 | 37% | 1 603 | 8% | 20 755 |
| National | 615 109 | 53% | 4 443 623 | 383% | 199 748 | 17% | 1 159 480 |

*Source*: SHF (2015), "Demanda de vivienda 2015", Dirección de Estudios Económicos de la Vivienda, Sociedad Hipotecaria Federal, January, available at: www.shf.gob.mx/estadisticas/EstudiosVivienda/Documents/demanda%202015.pdf.

## *Develop strategies for anticipating sustainable growth in less urbanised areas*

Rather than try to completely restrict new urban development in the metropolitan periphery, policy makers could instead look to complement the urban regeneration and densification policies mentioned earlier in this chapter with actions that anticipate sustainable growth in less urbanised, more peripheral neighbourhoods. How, concretely, can cities plan for sustainable growth? Drawing on the work of Angel et al. (2010) and Angel (2008a), one of the most important ways to prepare for growth in less urbanised neighbourhoods is to plan out an arterial grid of roads, spaced one kilometre apart, which can eventually support public transport. Such planning helps to secure the rights of way for a future comprehensive road and infrastructure grid. Doing so can help ensure that: 1) land remains affordable; 2) urban infrastructure guides, rather than follows, urban expansion; 3) residential densities are high enough to sustain public transport; 4) environmental objectives can be attained via planning for public transport and open space; and 5) the financial burdens on municipal budgets are minimised or, at the least, spread out over time (Angel et al., 2010b). The municipality of Milagro (Ecuador) successfully undertook this strategy in the mid-2000s. Two legal tools were central to the plan's success: one regulation permitting municipalities to acquire at no cost up to 35% of any land being urbanised for public use; the other allowing the municipality to acquire at no cost up to 10% of any land parcel as a public right of way (see Angel et al., 2008b).

### *Leverage major infrastructure projects for a more co-ordinated, metropolitan future*

Two of the country's most important infrastructure investments are currently under way in and around the Valle de México: the New Mexico City International Airport (NAICM) in the northeastern part of the Valle de México and the Mexico City-Toluca train line, which will connect the capital city of the State of Mexico (which is not part of the Valle de México) to the Federal District. Both projects have the potential to transform the metropolitan zone in the coming decades and constitute a critical opportunity for policy makers to synchronise recent urban regeneration policy goals at all levels of government and smarter, more sustainable urban development. Without a co-ordinated, common and public plan for integrating transport, housing, and urban and economic development for these major infrastructure investments (at present, no such plans have been made public), these projects also present an enormous risk to the future of the metropolitan zone, if past mistakes are repeated (Box 2.7).

#### Box 2.7. **The New Mexico City International Airport and Mexico City-Toluca train present a nexus of opportunity for development and regeneration**

**The new Mexico City airport: Potential to structure new development and revitalise existing areas**

The development of the new airport in Texcoco, a largely non-urbanised area, will be a key factor in restructuring the marginal and under-equipped eastern zone of the Valle de México. This eastern periphery is composed of a number of irregular settlements built from the 1950s onward. Although these marginal settlements are now consolidated, they still lack basic infrastructure and have a high concentration of urban poverty. The municipality of Nezahualcóyotl, for instance, was originally informally developed and later regularised; it is now home to 1.1 million inhabitants. The eastern part of the metropolitan zone also contains a number of large, problematic social housing neighbourhoods built in the 1990s and 2000s, such as those in the Ixtapaluca municipality (see Vega, 2003). Finally, this eastern sector of the metro zone includes a large number of poor and marginal semi-rural settlements requiring service improvements.

SEDATU is currently working on a survey for the new airport area, including 11 municipalities of the State of Mexico and 2 *delegaciones* in the Federal District. Other studies have been conducted or are under way (IMCO/CTS EMBARQ/CEMDA, 2015). The SEDATU survey is intended to create a complete diagnosis of the area and identify urban integration and mitigation strategies. In terms of mobility (see also Chapter 3), two metro lines are planned for extension toward the eastern periphery of the metropolitan zone to serve future airport employees. Metro Line A will be extended from La Paz to Chalco, a densely populated municipality in the southeast of the metropolis, and Line 6 is to be extended 25 kilometres toward the east (see also the discussion in Chapter 3).

**The Mexico City-Toluca train line: A key opportunity for urban regeneration in the Valle de México**

The Mexico City-Toluca train line is the second-largest infrastructure project under development in the Valle de México. It is expected to be inaugurated in December 2017. It plans to extend metro Line 12 to the Observatorio station, which would become the new terminus of the train. Authorities are also pursuing a large urban regeneration project (of eight hectares) around this station, in an area that faces a range of urban challenges. The project is expected to include the construction of new multimodal stations (CETRAMs) and urban redevelopment. In addition to the redevelopment of the area surrounding the station in the Federal District, the train is also expected to generate considerable urban development on the western periphery of the Valle de México, particularly around the four new stations.

These projects are likely to generate considerable change in the eastern and western peripheries of the Valle de México. The risk is that, without effective urban planning, urbanisation in these areas could be disordered and ultimately dysfunctional. At the same time, the two projects also represent an unprecedented opportunity to restructure the metropolitan zone. With the construction of the new airport, an important new employment centre will develop. Accessibility should also improve in some areas, thanks to planned extensions of the metro network. The urban environment of the distressed social housing neighbourhoods, as well as those of the informal settlements, is thus likely to change drastically. The construction of the airport and the rail line represent a unique opportunity to improve these peripheral areas to the east and west, to reoccupy vacant social housing and to urbanise or revitalise large parts of the metropolitan zone. The redevelopment of the existing airport will be another critical redevelopment opportunity – and risk – for the Valle de México; cities across the globe have faced a similar challenge (Box 2.8).

**Box 2.8. Redeveloping former airports: A challenge faced by many cities**

The redevelopment of defunct airports is a challenge that has been faced by cities across the world (Guangzhou, People's Republic of China; Athens, Greece; Hong Kong, China; Denver, Colorado; Austin, Texas; Quito, Ecuador), as older airports become obsolete with the development of newer, larger facilities. Guangzhou, for instance, closed the original Guangzhou Baiyun International Airport in 2004 after the completion of a new, larger airport 25 kilometres away. The former site was redeveloped with residential and commercial buildings and parks. Parts of the Kai Tak airport site in Hong Kong, China, which was closed in 1998, have since been redeveloped as a cruise ship terminal and public housing estates. Athens closed the Hellenikon International Airport in 2001; the site is currently abandoned, with possible plans for redevelopment as a resort complex. In the United States, former airport sites in Austin and Denver are being planned for sustainable, mixed-use housing and commercial redevelopment. In the case of Denver, the creation of a comprehensive master plan and a dedicated development foundation to guide the redevelopment of the former airport was an instrumental step in the process. It should be well understood that the cost and complexity of airport redevelopment are considerable, given the airport infrastructure that must be deconstructed.

## Conclusion

This chapter has outlined two main strategies to address some of the most pressing housing and urban development challenges facing policy makers in the Valle de México. The first set of recommendations aims to improve the well-being and quality of life of inhabitants in existing neighbourhoods through urban regeneration initiatives. Distressed neighbourhoods exist in the central area of the metropolitan zone after decades of demographic decline that has only recently begun to recover, among the ageing social housing stock in the Federal District and its neighbouring municipalities, as well as within the newer social housing stock built on the metropolitan periphery. The urban regeneration experience of Chile, France and the United States can all be instructive for policy makers in the Valle de México.

The second set of recommendations is focused on guiding new urban development. Because the metropolitan zone will continue to grow, and because a significant undersupply of housing persists in some areas, demand for new housing development will continue in the Valle de México. A more co-ordinated approach – both across administrative borders within the metropolitan zone, as well as across policy domains, notably housing, transport and public services – is needed. First, policy makers could facilitate development in the city centre by modifying existing land-use regulations (especially parking requirements) and reintroduce an inclusionary zoning policy. Second, removing the barriers to rental housing could provide an alternative for households that have previously turned toward the more affordable, distant homes in the metropolitan periphery; such a policy shift would require regulatory, fiscal and legal reforms at the national level. Finally, rather than restrict, or completely proscribe, new development in more peripheral areas (e.g. through strict containment policies, as have been applied in various countries with mixed results), policy makers could plan for growth in strategic expansion areas. Two major infrastructure projects under way – the New Mexico City International Airport and the Mexico City-Toluca train line – could transform the Valle de México in the decades ahead and offer an opportunity to crystallise a smarter, more sustainable approach to urban development and regeneration linking housing, transport and employment.

## Notes

1. As discussed in Chapter 1, several definitions of the Valle de México metropolitan zone exist. This chapter will use the functional definition jointly developed by three federal institutions in Mexico (Ministry of Social Development [Secretaría de Desarrollo Social, SEDESOL], the National Institute of Statistics and Geography [Instituto Nacional de Estadística y Geografía, INEGI] and the National Population Council [Consejo Nacional de Población, CONAPO]) in CONAPO/INEGI/SEDESOL (2012). It defines the Valle de México as the 16 *delegaciones* of the Federal District, 59 municipalities in the State of Mexico (which account for only part of the state) and 1 municipality from the state of Hidalgo.

2. Many of the challenges faced by Mexico's urban areas were assessed in detail in OECD (2015). In addition to those mentioned in this chapter, other housing and urban development challenges exist in the Valle de México (such as a large quantity of irregular settlements and informal housing development), but will not be analysed in this report.

3. The terms "Federal District" and "Mexico City" are used interchangeably throughout this chapter.

4. INFONAVIT is a housing provident fund established in 1972. The institute presently operates under a dual mandate of providing housing finance and managing the savings of salaried, formal-sector workers. Employers contribute a 5% payroll tax to an individual account managed by INFONAVIT. Accounting for 70% of the Mexican mortgage market, INFONAVIT has become one of the most important actors in housing development in Mexico: one in four Mexicans lives in a house financed by the institute. INFONAVIT manages the assets of approximately 18.1 million currently active affiliates. An additional 31.3 million workers have an account with INFONAVIT to which they are not actively contributing, probably because they are not currently formally employed.

5. This is the case, for instance, for the municipality of Zumpango, where a recent quantitative analysis was carried out by the municipality in collaboration with INFONAVIT.

6. Uninhabited and/or abandoned social housing is a problem in many Mexican metropolitan zones, but the phenomenon is not yet statistically well documented.

7. INEGI and INFONAVIT initially developed different approaches to the definition and methodology for measuring vacant housing. INEGI defines "uninhabited housing" (*vivienda deshabitada*) as individual homes that are fully constructed and immediately inhabitable, but in which no one is living at the time of the census, or is being used for commercial activities or as a secondary home. The process by which INEGI determines whether housing is inhabited, uninhabited or for seasonal, recreational or occasional use is described in detail in INEGI (2010b). INFONAVIT categorises "unoccupied housing" (*vivienda no ocupada*) into three subgroups: "uninhabited housing" (*vivienda deshabitada*), consists of individual homes that are unfurnished and well-maintained (e.g. clean, without graffiti or with no damaged doors/windows) in which no one is currently residing; "abandoned housing" (*vivienda abandonada*) is housing that is uninhabited, unfurnished and unmaintained, with some damages (e.g. broken windows); "vandalised housing" (*vivienda vandalizada*) is housing that is uninhabited, unfurnished and unmaintained, with relevant damages in the structure (no doors, no windows, no toilets, graffiti). For more on this topic, see OECD (2015); INEGI (2010b); INFONAVIT (2015a; 2014; 2012).

8. Based on OECD interviews with municipal authorities from Tizayuca.

9. The survey consisted of interviews in six metropolitan zones (Ciudad Juárez, Guadalajara, Laguna, Puebla-Tlaxcala, Tijuana and the Valle de México) with 309 INFONAVIT affiliates who do not live in their INFONAVIT-financed homes.

10. Based on OECD interviews with INFONAVIT in April 2015.

11. The San Pablo District Project, currently a master plan for an area in the Historic District, consists of redeveloping a high-potential 17-hectare site that is currently nearly uninhabited and with few constructions. The project includes several 12-story buildings that will combine housing (4 000 units), retail, services and car parks. Its central location should allow inhabitants to walk or ride bicycles to their jobs (Autoridad del Centro Histórico, 2014).

12. From 2007 to 2014, many measures were carried out in the Historic District: comprehensive rehabilitation of 20 corridors; removal of street vendors on 238 blocks; creation of 30 ECOBICI stations; implementation of a Metrobús line that allows the removal of a large quantity of old vehicles from circulation; rehabilitation of green areas and creation of pocket parks; development of 500 affordable housing units within a total of 3 000 new units built; and rehabilitation of 6 000 existing housing units (Autoridad del Centro Histórico (2004: 111).

13. Based on OECD interviews with municipal authorities.

14. This corresponds to another initiative developed by INFONAVIT in 2013, Let's Paint Mexico (*Pintemos México*). The objective of the programme is to improve urban areas and neighbourhood identity in social housing settlements.

15. Based on OECD interviews with INFONAVIT.

16. As noted, the successful experience in Santiago de Chile served as the inspiration for the Housing Programme recently developed for the Federal District by a group of private developers associated with the Valle de México chapter of the National Chamber of the Industry of Development and Promotion of Housing (CANADEVI Valle de México).

17. The states in which most abandoned units were auctioned to developers include Chihuahua (due to an agreement with the state and its housing commission), Baja California, Jalisco and Sonora (based on OECD interviews with INFONAVIT).

18. The three social housing developments in the Valle de México that are part of the *Regeneración Urbana y Social* programme are located in the municipalities of Zumpango and Huehuetoca, which are considered to be in a critical situation. Of the limited regeneration programmes implemented thus far in Mexico, only one has targeted the Valle de México.

19. This foundation has been working for several years to develop projects to prevent social and urban deterioration in large social housing settlements (improving public spaces, for instance). It has also developed a regeneration methodology and model, which has been applied in several social housing settlements, relying on community work.

20. *Recompensa de Desarrollo Comunitario y Recuperación del Entorno* awards special grants to neighbourhood organisations for the realisation of a physical rehabilitation project that will benefit the community and increase real estate values. To benefit from this grant, neighbourhood groups must be registered in another INFONAVIT programme ("Neighbourhood Rehabilitation – My Neighbours My Community", *Rehabilitación de Barrios – Mis vecinos Mi communidad*), in operation since 2011, which aims to develop social cohesion through public space improvements. To date, 32 units have benefited from the programme, resulting in the creation and improvement of urban squares, murals, urban farms and small libraries.

21. Precise methodologies for participative urban regeneration have been developed in recent years and are being implemented in several pilot projects by the Fundación Hogares, *Tú y Yo* Foundation and other organisations. The *Tú y Yo* Foundation has been working in northern Mexico in co-ordination with Provive, a private company devoted to buying, repairing and selling abandoned social housing (see Box 2.6).

22. See, for instance, the Population and Housing Census (conducted every ten years), the Population Count (every five years) and the National Survey of Mexican Household Income and Expenditures (*Encuesta Nacional de Ingresos y Gastos de los Hogares*, ENIGH; every two years).

23. Now the Observatoire National de la Politique de la Ville.

24. The ONZUS annual report is based on the analysis of a wide range of indicators on the following issues: demography, household income, employment, housing, education, safety, health, discrimination, public services and the urban environment.

25. Norma 26 (Regulation 26) was introduced in 1997 as an inclusionary zoning policy to facilitate the production of affordable housing in the Federal District. The regulation offered incentives to developers (e.g. tax breaks and density bonuses) in exchange for the provision of a percentage of affordable housing units in mixed-income housing developments. Due to numerous abuses of the policy (e.g. the housing units produced were often sold at a higher price than initially envisaged and not necessarily to low-income families), the regulation was suspended in 2013.

26. Strategic management areas (AGE) are instruments co-ordinated by SEDUVI (the Ministry of Urban Development and Housing of the Federal District) and created by the new Federal District Urban Development Law in 2010. They are considered "fast-track" planning instruments that define land-use possibilities within a strategic urban area, with the aim of boosting the regeneration of large underutilised or distressed historic, urban or natural areas in the city. While not a financial instrument, AGEs allow authorities to change the urban regulations without having to modify the existing planning instruments, and are considered controversial by some neighbourhood associations. Economic and social development areas (ADES) were created by the Federal District Economic Development Law and are co-ordinated by the Ministry of Economic Development of the Federal District (Secretaría de Desarollo Económico del Distrito Federal, SEDECO). The objective of the ADES is to encourage economic development in designated areas through fiscal and financial incentives.

27. Based on interviews with officials from the ANRU.

28. The high-speed train between Mexico City and Querétaro, in the event that plans are reactivated, would constitute a third critical opportunity for a more comprehensive approach to urban investment in the Valle de México.

29. There are several reasons for the small share of housing demand projected for the Federal District, including the slower rate of population growth relative to other Mexican metro zones and the limited supply of land available.

30. Based on OECD interviews with home builders conducted during a study mission to the Valle de México in April 2015.

31. Inclusionary zoning policies can vary in their structure, but generally speaking, they require or encourage developers to set aside a certain percentage of housing units in new or rehabilitated projects for low- and moderate-income residents (US Department of Housing and Urban Development, 2013).

32. Affordable units were defined as those with a selling price of 20 to 30 times the annual minimum wage (see Fundación Idea/Cámara de Senadores/SIMO Consulting, 2014).

33. Three graduated urban perimeters – U1, U2 and U3 – were drawn by the federal government in 340 Mexican cities and are defined as follows: U1 areas are consolidated urban zones with high employment-to-resident ratios; U2 zones are those in the process of urban consolidation but with high (at least 75%) coverage of basic services; and U3 zones are buffers contiguous to the urban area. Housing subsidies are allocated based on a scoring system, in which location accounts for up to 400 out of 1 000 possible points. Developments approved within U1 areas are likely to receive the largest subsidies, with successively smaller subsidies for developments in U2 and U3 areas. Housing units outside the perimeters are not eligible for federal housing subsidies, except for projects that have been certified as "certified developments" (*desarrollos certificados*) and other specific cases. The guidelines for the polygons are described in detail in SEGOB (2014).

34. Rental housing makes up around half of the total housing stock in some large OECD metropolitan areas: Los Angeles (50.8%), New York (48.9%) and in the Paris/Île-de-France region (49.3%; US Census Bureau, 2013; INSEE, 2014).

35. Surveys indicate that informal settlements are often informally rented; this rental market is thus not accounted for in statistics on housing tenure (see, in particular, Gilbert, 2008).

# *Bibliography*

Adler, D. (2015), "The fight for Mexico City's future", *Latin America News Dispatch*, 2 March, http://latindispatch.com/2015/03/02/the-fight-for-mexico-citys-future (accessed 25 April 2015).

Aguilar, A.M. and C. Alvarado (2004), "La reestructuración del espacio urbano de la Ciudad de Mexico: Hacia la metropoli multinodal?", in: Aguilar, A.G. (coord.), *Procesos Metropolitanos y Grandes Ciudades: Dinamicas Recientes en Mexico y Otros Países*, Mexico the Federal District, (ed.) Miguel Angel Porrua.

Aguilar, A.G. and J. Hernández (2011), "Metropolitan transformation and polycentric structure in Mexico City. Identification of urban subcenters 1989-2009", presented at the IGU Urban Commission Meeting, Canterbury Christ Church University, Canterbury, United Kingdom, 14-20 August 2011, www.slideserve.com/milo/adrian-guillermo-aguilar-and-josefina-hern-ndez-lozano-institute-of-geography-unam (accessed 25 April 2015).

Angel, S. (2008a), "An arterial grid of dirt roads", *Cities*, Vol. 25, No. 3, pp. 146-162, June, http://dx.doi.org/10.1016/j.cities.2008.03.005.

Angel, S. (2008b), "Preparing for urban expansion: A proposed strategy for intermediate cities in Ecuador", in: Martine, G. et al. (eds.) *The New Global Frontier: Urbanization, Poverty and the Environment in the 21st Century*, Earthscan, London.

Angel, S. et al. (2010a), *Atlas of Urban Expansion*, Lincoln Institute of Land Policy, Cambridge, Massachusetts, www.lincolninst.edu/subcenters/atlas-urban-expansion (accessed 25 May 2015).

Angel, S. et al. (2010b), *Making Room for a Planet of Cities*, Lincoln Institute of Land Policy, Cambridge, Massachusetts, www.lincolninst.edu/pubs/1880_Making-Room-for-a-Planet-of-Cities-urban-expansion (accessed 25 May 2015).

Autoridad del Centro Histórico (2014), "Reporte Autoridad del Centro Histórico 2007-2014", p. 111, September, Scientika, www.autoridadcentrohistorico.df.gob.mx/index.php/reporte-2007-2014 (accessed 18 June 2015).

Bassols, M. and M. Espinosa (2011), "Construcción social del espacio urbano: Ecatepec y Netzahualcóyotl. Dos gigantes del oriente", *Polis*, Vol. 7, No. 2, January.

Blanco, A.G., V. Fretes Cibils and A.F. Muñoz (2014), *Rental Housing Wanted: Policy Options for Latin America and the Caribbean*, Inter-American Development Bank, www10.iadb.org/intal/intalcdi/PE/2014/13900en.pthe Federal District (accessed 25 May 2015).

Boyko, C. and R. Cooper (2011), "Clarifying and re-conceptualising density", *Progress in Planning*, Vol. 76, No. 1, pp. 1-61, July, http://dx.doi.org/10.1016/j.progress.2011.07.001.

Cámara Chilena de la Construcción (2014), *Renovación Urbana en Chile. Éxitos, Desafíos y Oportunidades. Segundo Encuentro Inmobiliario Chile*, Santiago, 5 July available at: www.cchc.cl/comunicaciones/noticias/56642-presentaciones-ii-encuentro-inmobiliario-chile-peru .

Causa, O. and C. Chapuis (2009), "Equity in student achievement across OECD countries: An investigation of the role of policies", *OECD Economics Department Working Papers*, No. 708, OECD Publishing, Paris, http://dx.doi.org/10.1787/223056645650.

Chetty, R., N. Hendren and L. Katz (2015), "The effects of exposure to better neighbourhoods on children: New evidence from the Moving to Opportunity experiment", National Bureau of Economic Research, *NBER Working Papers*, No. 21 156, http://dx.doi.org/10.3386/w21156.

CONAPO (2010), *Proyecciones de la Población de las Zonas Metropolitanas 2010-2030*, available at: www.conapo.gob.mx/work/models/CONAPO/Resource/1206/2/images/Proyecciones_de_Poblacion_ZM.xlsx

CONAPO/INEGI/SEDESOL (2012), *Delimitaciones de las Zonas Metropolitanas de México 2010*, Secretaría de Desarrollo Social, Consejo Nacional de Población, Instituto Nacional de Estadística y Geografía, Mexico, D.F., www.conapo.gob.mx/es/CONAPO/Zonas_metropolitanas_2010 (accessed 25 May 2015).

CONAVI (2014), *Históricos de Vivienda* (database), www.conavi.gob.mx/php/mapa_interactivo/busqueda_avanzada/historicos_viviendas/mapa_interactivo.php (accessed 25 May 2015).

Contreras, Y. (2011), "La recuperación urbana y residencial del centro de Santiago: Nuevos habitantes, cambios socioespaciales significativos", *Eure*, Vol. 37, No. 11, pp. 89-113, September, available at: www.scielo.cl/pdf/eure/v37n112/art05.pdf.

De Alba, M. (2009), "Representaciones y prácticas sociales entorno a políticas urbanas: La movilización Nimby frente a la redensificación de las zonas centrales de la Ciudad de México", *Cultura y Representaciones Sociales*, No. 6, pp. 43-72.

Donzelot, J. (2012), *A quoi sert la rénovation urbaine?*, Presses Universitaires de France, Paris.

Dowall, D. and D. Wilk (1989), "Population growth, land development, and housing in Mexico City", Working Paper No. 502, University of California at Berkeley, Institute of Urban and Regional Development.

Duhau, E. and C. Jacquin (2008), "Les ensembles de logement géants de Mexico: Nouvelles forms de l'habitat social, cadres de vie et reformulations par les habitants", *Autrepart*, No. 47, pp. 169-186, Presses de Sciences Po (PFNSP), http://dx.doi.org/10.3917/autr.047.0169.

Eibenschultz Hartman, R. and P. Benlliure (2009), "Mercado formal e informal del suelo: Analisís de ocho ciudades", available at: http://biblioteca.diputados.gob.mx/janium/bv/ce/scpd/LX/merc_for_inf.pdf.

Esquivel, M.T. (2007), “La convivencia condominial: Problematica, análisis y débil legislación”, *Metropoli 2025*, Vol. 2, No. 22, October, p. 8, available at: http://ciudadanosenred.com.mx/htm/areas/0/boletin22.pdf.

Fernandes (2011), *Regularization of Informal Settlements in Latin America,* Lincoln Institute of Land Policy Focus Report, available at: www.lincolninst.edu/pubs/dl/1906_1225_Regularization PFR Rev 2012.pdf.

Fundación Idea/Cámara de Senadores/SIMO Consulting (2014), “México compacto: Las condiciones para la densificación urbana inteligente en México”, Fundación Idea, Cámara de Senadores and SIMO Consulting, Federal District, Mexico, available at: http://fundacionidea.org.mx/assets/files/MexicoCompacto_Senado_IDEA_SIMO.pdf.

Gaigné, C., S. Riou and J.-F. Thisse (2012), “Are compact cities environmentally friendly?”, *Journal of Urban Economics*, Vol. 72, Issues 2-3, pp. 123-136, September-November, http://dx.doi.org/10.1016/j.jue.2012.04.001.

Gilbert, A. (2008), “Slums, tenants and home-ownership: On blindness to the obvious”, *International Development Planning Review*, Vol. 30, No. 2.

Gilbert, A. (1998), *The Latin American City*, LAB, London.

Government of the Federal District (2015), background report prepared for the OECD, unpublished.

Graizbord, B. and B. Acuña (2005), “La estructura polinuclear del Área Metropolitana”, in: Aguilar, A.G. (ed.), *Procesos Metropolitanos y Grandes Ciudades. Dinámicas Recientes en México y Otros Países*, Mexico, D.F., Porrua, pp. 309-328.

Guerra, E. (2013), “The new suburbs: Evolving travel behavior, the built environment, and subway investments in Mexico City”, University of California Transportation Center, UCTC Dissertation UCTC-DISS-2013-01, University of California, Berkeley, Berkeley, California, www.uctc.net/research/UCTC-DISS-2013-01 (accessed 8 September 2015)

IAAO (2013), “Glossary for property appraisal and assessment”, International Association of Assessing Officers, Chicago, Illinois, available at www.iaao.org/media/Pubs/IAAO_Glossary.pdf

IMCO (2012), *El Municipio: Una Institución Diseñada para el Fracaso. Propuestas para la Gestión Profesional de las Ciudades*, Instituto Mexicano para la Competitividad, Mexico, p. 178.

IMCO/CTS Embarq/CEMDA (2015), *Observatorio Ciudadano del Nuevo Aeropuerto de la Ciudad de México*. USAID, Cooperación Alemana Deutsche Zusammenarbeit, GIZ, CTS Embarq, CEMDA, IMCO.

INEGI (2010a), *Censo de Población y Vivienda 2010*, Instituto Nacional de Estadística y Geografía, Aguascalientes, Mexico.

INEGI (2010b), *Resultados de la Encuesta de Verificación de Viviendas Deshabitadas y de Uso Temporal del Censo de Población y Vivienda 2010*, Instituto Nacional de Estadística y Geografía, Aguascalientes, Mexico.

INEGI (2009), *Censos Económico 2009*, Instituto Nacional de Estadística y Geografía, Aguascalientes, Mexico.

INEGI (2007), *Encuesta Origin – Destino de los Viajes de los Residentes de la Zona Metropolitana del Valle de México 2007*, Instituto Nacional de Estadística y Geografía, Aguascalientes, Mexico.

INEGI (2005), *II Conteo de Población y Vivienda 2005*, Instituto Nacional de Estadística y Geografía, Aguascalientes, Mexico.

INEGI (2000), *XII Censo General de Población y Vivienda 2000*, Instituto Nacional de Estadística y Geografía, Aguascalientes, Mexico.

INEGI (1990), *XI Censo General de Población y Vivienda 1990*, Instituto Nacional de Estadística y Geografía, Aguascalientes, Mexico.

INEGI (1980), *X Censo General de Población y Vivienda 1980*, Instituto Nacional de Estadística y Geografía, Aguascalientes, Mexico.

INEGI (1970), *IX Censo General de Población 1970*, Instituto Nacional de Estadística y Geografía, Aguascalientes, Mexico.

INFONAVIT (2015a), "Índice de Deterioro de la Vivienda Social en México. Reporte general del diagnóstico de 36 conjuntos habitacionales con altos niveles de vivienda abandonada. Documento de divulgación", Mexico, p. 291.

INFONAVIT (2015b), "Plan de labores y de financiamientos 2015", Instituto del Fondo Nacional de la Vivienda para los Trabajadores, https://portal.infonavit.org.mx/wps/wcm/connect/5a5a868c-f72e-4efb-be9f-167a557ce29a/Plan_de_Labores_y_de_Financiamientos_2015.pdf?MOD=AJPERES (accessed 8 September 2015).

INFONAVIT (2015c), Communication from INFONAVIT Valle de México Regional Delegation to the OECD, dated 26 February 2015, unpublished.

INFONAVIT (2014), *Atlas del Abandono de la Vivienda*, Instituto del Fondo Nacional de la Vivienda para los Trabajadores, Mexico City, p. 122.

INFONAVIT (2013), *Proyecto de Regeneración Urbana de La Trinidad, Zumpango, Estado de México*, Instituto del Fondo Nacional de la Vivienda para los Trabajadores, Mexico.

INFONAVIT (2012), "Estudio nacional de vivienda deshabitada, Fase II: Causas de deshabitación", internal INFONAVIT document shared with the OECD.

INSEE (2014), "Chiffres clés logement", Institut national de la statistique et des études économiques, Paris, www.insee.fr/fr/themes/tableau_local.asp?ref_id=LOG&millesime=2010&typgeo=REG&codgeo=11 (accessed 8 September 2015).

Institut de Recherche pour le Développement (IRD) and Institut français d'Amérique latine (IFAL) (2014), *Aportaciones de la Co-operación Francesa sobre la Producción Masiva de Vivienda Social en México*, p. 64.

ITDP (n.d.), *Towards a Transit-oriented Development Strategy for Mexico City*, working paper, Institute for Transportation and Development Policy, Mexico City, available at: http://mexico.itdp.org/wp-content/uploads/Towards-a-TOD-Strategy-for-Mexico-City1.pdf.

ITDP (2015), "Oportunidades de desarrollo orientado al transporte y bajo en emisiones en la zona metropolitana del Valle de México", SEDATU/USAID/ITDP, Mexico City, available at: http://mexico.itdp.org/wp-content/uploads/Valle-de-Mexico.pdf.

ITDP (2014), "Menos cajones, más ciudad: El estacionamiento en la Ciudad de México", Institute for Transportation and Development Policy, Mexico, http://mexico.itdp.org/noticias/menos-cajones-mas-ciudad-el-estacionamiento-en-la-ciudad-de-mexico (accessed 18 August 2015).

Jones, G.A. and P.M. Ward (1998), "Privatising the commons: Reforming the *ejido* and urban development in Mexico", *International Journal of Urban and Regional Research*, Vol. 22, No. 1, pp. 76-93, March, http://dx.doi.org/10.1111/1468-2427.00124.

Kamal-Chaoui, L. and J. Sanchez-Reaza (2012), "Urban trends and policies in OECD countries", *OECD Regional Development Working Papers*, No. 2012/01, OECD Publishing, Paris, http://dx.doi.org/10.1787/5k9fhn1ctjr8-en.

Kirzbaum, T. (2013), "Rénovation urbaine et équité sociale: Choice Neighborhoods aux États-Unis" (in French), working paper for the Commissariat général à la stratégie et à la prospective et le Secrétariat général du Comité interministériel des villes, Paris.

Kirzbaum, T. (2009), *Rénovation urbaine: Les leçons américaines*, Presses Universitaires de France, Paris.

Kling, J., J. Liebman and L. Katz (2007), "Experimental analysis of neighborhood effects", *Econometrica*, Vol. 75, Issue 1, pp. 83-119, January.

Ludwig, J. et al. (2013), "Long-term neighborhood effects on low-income families: Evidence from Moving to Opportunity", *American Economic Review: Papers and Proceedings 2013*, Vol. 103, No. 3, pp. 226-31, http://dx.doi.org/10.1257/aer.103.3.226.

Ludwig, J. et al. (2008), "What can we learn about neighborhood effects from the Moving to Opportunity experiment?", *American Journal of Sociology*, Vol. 114, No. 1, July, pp. 144-88, The University of Chicago, available at: http://home.uchicago.edu/ludwigj/papers/AJS-Ludwig-2008.pdf.

Marron Institute (2014), "Impacts of regulation on housing affordability in Mexico City: Collaboration between the Marron Institute and Secretaria de Desarrollo Urbano y Vivienda", June.

Marron Institute (2013), *Policy Recommendations for Inclusionary Zoning Comparing Regulations in New York and Mexico City*, December.

Merlin, P. (2012), *Des grands ensembles aux cités: L'avenir d'une utopie*, Ellipses, Paris.

Ministry of Cities, Youth and Sports (France) (2014), *Le nouveau programme national de renouvellement urbain*, December, p. 56.

Minnesota Population Center (2013), *XI Censo General de Población y Vivienda 1990* and *Censo de Población y Vivienda 2010*, INEGI, Mexico City.

MINVU (2014), *Vivienda Social en Copropiedad. Catastro Nacional de Condominios Sociales*, Secretaría Ejecutiva Desarrollo de Barrios, Ministerio de Vivienda y Urbanismio, Santiago.

Monkkonen, P. (2014), "The role of housing finance in Mexico's vacancy crisis", *Ziman Center Working Paper*, No. 22, UCLA Ziman Center for Real Estate, available at: www.anderson.ucla.edu/Documents/areas/ctr/ziman/2014-22WP.pdf.

Municipality of Zumpango (2015), housing and urban development reports shared with the OECD, unpublished.

Muñiz, I., V. Sánchez and M.A. Garcia-López (2015), "Estructura espacial y densidad de población en la ZMVM 1995-2010: Evolución de un sistema urbano policéntrico", *EURE*, Santiago, Vol. 41, No. 122, pp. 75-102, http://dx.doi.org/10.4067/S0250-71612015000100004.

OECD (2015), *OECD Urban Policy Reviews: Mexico 2015: Transforming Urban Policy and Housing Finance*, OECD Publishing, Paris, http://dx.doi.org/10.1787/9789264227293-en.

OECD (2013), *OECD Territorial Reviews: Puebla-Tlaxcala, Mexico 2013*, OECD Publishing, Paris, http://dx.doi.org/10.1787/9789264203464-en.

OECD (2010a), *Economic Policy Reforms 2010: Going for Growth*, OECD Publishing, Paris, http://dx.doi.org/10.1787/growth-2010-en.

OECD (2010b), *PISA 2009 Results: Overcoming Social Background: Equity in Learning Opportunities and Outcomes (Volume II)*, PISA, OECD Publishing, Paris, http://dx.doi.org/10.1787/9789264091504-en.

Oreopoulos, P. (2008), "Neighbourhood effects in Canada: A critique", *Canadian Public Policy – Analyse de politiques*, Vol. 34, No. 2, pp. 237-58, June, University of Toronto Press, available at: http://oreopoulos.faculty.economics.utoronto.ca/wp-content/uploads/2014/08/Neighbourhood_Effects_in_Canada.pdf.

Oreopoulos, P. (2003), "The long-run consequences of living in a poor neighborhood", *The Quarterly Journal of Economics*, MIT Press, Vol. 118, No. 4, pp. 1533-1575, November, http://dx.doi.org/10.1162/003355303322552865.

Orr, L. et al. (2003), "Moving to opportunity interim impacts evaluation", US Department of Housing and Urban Development, Office of Policy Development and Research, June, Washington, DC, available at: www.abtassociates.com/reports/2003302754569_71451.pdf.

Ortega-Alcazar, I. (2006), "Mexico City: Housing and neighbourhoods", *LSE Cities*, February, London School of Economics and Political Science, https://lsecities.net/media/objects/articles/mexico-city-housing-and-neighbourhoods/en-gb (accessed 8 September 2015).

Paquette, C. (2014), "Les politiques d'investissement urbain", in: *Les enjeux du développement en Amérique latine: Dynamiques socio-économiques et politiques publiques*, AFD, Paris, pp. 185-211.

Paquette, C. (2008), "El Metrobús en el contexto de la redensificación urbana: Implicaciones y oportunidades", pp. 195-240, in: Lezama, J.L. and C. Salazar (eds.), *Construir Ciudad: Un Análisis Multidimensional para los Corredores de Transporte en la Ciudad de México*, El Colegio de México, Mexico City.

Paquette, C. (2005). "La reconquête du centre de Santiago du Chili: Un nouveau modèle pour la récupération des centres historiques d'Amérique latine?", *Cahiers des Amériques latines*, No. 47, pp. 151-165.

Paquette, C. and D. Delaunay (2009), "Movilidad residencial y política de redensificación: El área central de la Ciudad de México", *Eure*, Santiago, Vol. 35, No. 105, pp. 95-112, August.

Paquette, C. and M.E. Negrete (2013), "Transport collectif, développement urbain et inclusion sociale à Mexico: Le rôle et les limites du transport public concede", *Revue de Géographie des Transports*, No. 1-2.

Paquette, C, and M. Yescas (2009), "Producción masiva de vivienda en la Ciudad de México: Dos políticas en debate", *Centro H*, No. 3, pp. 15-26.

Procuraduría Social del Distrito Federal (2015), interview with Catherine Paquette.

Rodriguez, A. and A. Sugranyes (2010), *Los con Techo. Un Desafío para la Política de Vivienda Social en Chile*, Santiago de Chile, ediciones SUR, p. 255.

Rojas, E. (2004), "Volver al centro. La recuperación de áreas urbanas centrales", Inter-American Development Bank, Washington, DC, p. 265.

Rosen, K. and L. Smith (1983), "The price-adjustment process for rental housing and the natural vacancy rate", *The American Economic Review*, Vol. 73, No. 4, pp. 779-786.

Sánchez, L. and C. Salazar (2011), "Lo que dicen las viviendas deshabitadas sobre el censo de población 2010" [What does vacant housing tell us about the population census of 2010], *Coyuntura Demográfica*, Vol. 1, pp. 66-72.

Santa Rita, I. (2014), "DF registra rezago en subsidios a la vivienda a julio", *El Financiero*, 20 August, Sección Empresas, www.especialistas.com.mx/saiweb/viewer.aspx?file=SA6CN4vCWFEHE12iNRaokTJ1valzIcq/hI4/lKn4rr10pVmmyYOee7gQbSflwLLo&opcion=0&encrip=1 (accessed 4 September 2015)

Schuetz, J., R. Meltzer and V. Been (2011), "Silver bullet or Trojan horse? The effects of inclusionary zoning on local housing markets in the United States", *Urban Studies*, Vol. 48, No. 2, pp. 297-329.

SEGOB (2014), *Reglas de Operación del Programa de Esquemas de Financiamiento y Subsidio Federal para Vivienda, para el Ejercicio Fiscal 2014*, Secretaría de Gobernación, www.dof.gob.mx/nota_detalle_popup.php?codigo=5304701 (accessed 18 June 2015).

SHF (2015), "Demanda de vivienda 2015", Dirección de Estudios Económicos de la Vivienda, Sociedad Hipotecaria Federal, January, available at: www.shf.gob.mx/estadisticas/EstudiosVivienda/Documents/demanda%202015.pdf.

SHF Housing Statistics (n.d.) (data series: total number of properties valued by year of completion of the work or remodelling), https://www.shf.gob.mx/avaluos/extranet?service=direct/0/Home/$DirectLink, (accessed 15 April 2014).

Suárez, M. and J. Delgado (2009), "Is Mexico City polycentric? A trip attraction capacity approach", *Urban Studies*, Vol. 46, No. 10, pp. 2 187-2 211, http://dx.doi.org/10.1177/0042098009339429.

Suárez, M. and J. Delgado (2007), "La expansión urbana probable de la Ciudad de México. Un escenario pesimista y dos alternativos para el año 2020", *Estudios Demográficos y Urbanos*, Vol. 22, No. 1, January-April, pp. 101-142, available at: www.redalyc.org/pdf/312/31222105.pdf.

Tamayo, S. (2007), *Los desafíos del Bando 2: Evaluación multidimensional de las políticas habitacionales en el Distrito Federal 2000-2006*, GDF/SEDUVI/UACM, Mexico, D.F.

Torres, E. (2013), "Public housing companies: An early ending?", *Economic Watch, Mexico, BBVA Research*, 14 August, www.bbvaresearch.com/KETD/fbin/mult/130814_ObsInmobiliarioMexico_23_eng_tcm348-399184.pthe Federal District?ts=2652014 (accessed 21 May 2015).

UN-Habitat (2003), *Rental Housing: An Essential Option for the Urban Poor in Developing Countries*, United Nations Human Settlements Programme, Nairobi, Kenya.

US Census Bureau (2013), "Rental housing market condition measures: A comparison of U.S. metropolitan areas from 2009 to 2011", *American Community Survey Briefs*, ACSBR/11-07, April, US Department of Commerce, Economics and Statistics Administration, US Census Bureau, Washington DC, available at: www.census.gov/prod/2013pubs/acsbr11-07.pdf.

US Department of Housing and Urban Development (2013), "Inclusionary zoning and mixed-income communities", US Department of Housing and Urban Development, Washington, DC, www.huduser.org/portal/periodicals/em/spring13/highlight3.html (accessed 8 August 2015)

Vega, A.L. (2003), "Urbanización explosiva de la periferia", *Ciudades*, No. 57, pp. 57-61, January-March.

# *Chapter 3.*

# Getting mobility in the Valle de México on the right track

*This chapter looks at the major elements of the Valle de México's mobility policies. It begins with an exploration of the current progress towards inclusive and sustainable mobility, looking at the metropolitan framework for air quality, transport policies aimed at improving residents' well-being and recent steps towards prioritising public and non-motorised transport users. This is followed by an examination of the obstacles to improving mobility in the metropolitan zone, such as limited planning and institutional capacity weaknesses. A major section focuses on proposed actions to achieve a high-quality mobility system through improved metropolitan co-ordination, policy coherence, long-term mobility planning, and ensuring robust financial capacity. It ends with an analysis of the two major federal transport projects: a train line and the New Mexico City International Airport. Overall, the chapter emphasises the links between mobility and urban development policies and the benefits of addressing them in tandem.*

The Metropolitan Zone of the Valle de México (Zona Metropolitana del Valle de México, ZMVM) has to cope with a wide range of negative consequences from decades of automobile-oriented policies.[1] Prioritisation of road infrastructure investment and a focus on improving traffic speeds for private vehicles has resulted in a public transport service with severe capacity and quality limitations, and deteriorating conditions for walking and cycling. These two conditions negatively affect quality of life for a majority of the population. Moreover, focus on road expansion and accessibility of private vehicles has not even been effective for coping with increasing congestion and its related costs. In a context of high income inequalities, poor-quality but relatively cheap public transport has maintained a high modal share.[2] However, the accelerated growth of private vehicle travel is a clear sign that under present quality, efficiency and safety conditions, public transport use will be significantly displaced by private modes of transport as incomes continue to grow. From this perspective, the ZMVM will face increasing pressure to manage the social costs generated by rapidly growing motorisation. In addition, the population remaining as "captive users" of public transport will continue to face suboptimal travel conditions and restricted accessibility.

The authorities want to move towards a more sustainable and inclusive mobility system. With this aim, a series of projects, mostly in the Federal District, have shown a return towards public transport investment, progressive efforts to promote walking and cycling, and a change in priorities in the allocation of road space and investment in favour of non-motorised and public transport users. The principles of sustainability and inclusiveness reflected in these types of projects have also been recently introduced into legal and planning instruments linked to mobility policy in the Federal District. The State of Mexico has stated that it is making the corresponding changes to its legal framework. While these actions constitute important progress, many challenges remain.

This chapter looks at major elements of mobility policy in the Valle de México and how they could contribute to progress towards sustainable and inclusive mobility goals. It discusses recent projects and achievements in this direction, considers the challenges in building a coherent policy framework for the ZMVM and offers some recommendations based on international good practice. A final section addresses the Mexico City-Toluca train project and the New Mexico City International Airport.

The chapter emphasises that the institutional framework for mobility policy needs to be strengthened to align policies with new goals for sustainable and inclusive mobility. Central to achieving this is building a strong metropolitan co-ordination structure for mobility planning and implementation; aligning private and public actors to achieve consistency across policies and projects; moving away from reactive actions and developing long-term planning capacity; and assigning human and financial resources to generate the right technical expertise for the kind of policies that are coherent with new priorities. Projects funded and planned by the federal government will need adequate urban infrastructure and land-use strategies, to help promote public and non-motorised modes and thus support the shift towards sustainable and inclusive mobility in the ZMVM.

## Current progress towards inclusive and sustainable mobility

Car-oriented policies have accelerated car use and have had significant mobility-related social costs in the ZMVM. Between 1990 and 2009, car travel in the ZMVM had an average annual growth rate of 5.3% (ITDP, 2012). The rapid pace at which car use has been growing becomes evident given the slow growth in population and GDP per capita in the metropolitan zone. Population increased at an annual average of 1.3% between 2000 and 2010, while GDP per capita growth showed a 0.5% yearly average from 2003 to 2010.[3] By 2014, the vehicle fleet in the ZMVM had reached a total of 5.3 million vehicles (compared to 2 million in 1990), of which 3.6 million were cars and SUVs (SEDEMA, 2015a).[4] Despite the prioritisation of road infrastructure investment, the ZMVM faces severe congestion. Between 1990 and 2007, average speeds on urban roads decreased from 38.5 km/hr to 17 km/hr (Tarriba and Alarcón, 2012), and according to the Institute for Transportation and Development Policy (ITDP), the cost of congestion in the ZMVM reached MXN 82 000 million (USD 6.1 billion) in 2009 (ITDP, 2012).[5] Another important issue is road safety. Information is not available at the scale of the ZMVM. However, the Central region of Mexico, to which the ZMVM belongs, has been recognised as having the highest rate of pedestrian mortality in the country (ITDP, 2014a). In 2009, the costs generated by traffic accidents in the ZMVM were estimated at MXN 10 300 million (USD 762 million).[6]

In response to the deteriorated mobility conditions, authorities have set goals to reduce reliance on cars, promote sustainable transport modes and reduce pollution. This section analyses programmes and projects, as well as changes to the legal framework and the planning tools used. In many cases, the projects described face challenges (which are addressed in the next section of this chapter). However, their implementation highlights an important shift from a policy focused on road management to one centred on multimodal access for the population. Several new instruments and institutions have yet to be created for some of the legal changes introduced recently. This section provides an overview of these instruments and institutions and their importance to different areas of mobility policy. The following section addresses the challenges that some of them face, while the section after it provides recommendations on how they can be developed effectively.

### *A metropolitan framework for addressing air quality*

The extraordinary deterioration of air quality in the ZMVM, especially during the late 1980s, was a crucial driver for increasing regulation in the transport sector. The Metropolitan Commission for the Environment (Comisión Ambiental Metropolitana, CAM) was successful in steadily encouraging agreements between entities in the ZMVM to tackle air pollution.[7] Transport-related measures undertaken under CAM co-ordination include an inspection and maintenance scheme, the introduction of unleaded gasoline, making catalytic converters for cars compulsory, a scrapping programme to incentivise bus fleet renewal and the vehicle restriction programme *Hoy No Circula* (SEDEMA, 2015a).[8]

In 2013, the CAM became the Environmental Commission for the Megalopolis (Comisión Ambiental para la Megalópolis, CAMe), so that it could address new concerns about air quality at a more adequate scale.[9] While earlier efforts have managed to reduce sulphur dioxide, lead and carbon monoxide, other pollutants, such as ozone and $PM_{2.5}$ and $PM_{10}$, are still a problem. The recent research suggests that air quality can no longer be treated as a metropolitan problem, but needs to be considered at the scale of the megalopolis.[10] As a set of initial steps, the CAMe is focusing on expanding the air quality monitoring system to the megalopolis, standardising software and data quality, and improving its public communication strategy. A second short-term goal is to harmonise regulations and the technologies used in the inspection and maintenance programme across the states. Part of this endeavour requires co-ordination to prevent the possibility of transferring vehicle plates across state lines to avoid the fines and more stringent standards. The CAMe has also launched two pilot projects in Morelos, introducing zones where only low-emission vehicles are allowed. These pilot projects are collecting evidence with a view to implementing such zones throughout the megalopolis.

### *Relying on public transport to address well-being challenges*

Recent mobility initiatives in the Valle de México indicate a new approach to tackling environmental and health concerns and improving citizens' well-being, by reviewing public transport expansion and improvement. Measures taken during the 1990s to recover air quality focused on improving fuel quality, accelerating vehicle fleet renewal and introducing cleaner technologies. However, transport outcomes were also defined by the stagnation of mass transit and the deregulation of bus services.[11] More recent projects have resumed mass transit expansion and have introduced significant improvements in bus service.

#### *Bus rapid transit is contributing to sustainable objectives and is a first step towards bus regulation reform*

Imported from cities like Bogotá in Colombia, and Curitiba in Brazil, the bus rapid transit (BRT) offers a lower cost alternative to underground rail and thus has made it easier to advance air quality and environment goals by expanding mass transit. The BRT scheme in Mexico City is called Metrobús. In 2005, a first BRT corridor was introduced by the Federal District. The Federal District government invests in and manages the infrastructure, while private operators are in charge of operation and fleet investments. Initially, air quality benefits were the focus of the initiative, recognising the potential in substituting old microbuses with high-capacity buses in the transport corridors selected. Funds from the existing vehicle substitution programme were used to incentivise the substitution, and in many cases, the elimination, of microbuses with BRT buses by incumbent operators incorporated in the BRT corridors. Later, $CO_2$ emission mitigation became another key pillar of the project (OECD, 2012). In this way, the authorities developed a measuring, reporting and verification (MRV) methodology that was approved by the United Nations Framework Convention on Climate Change (UNFCCC), allowing Metrobús to receive funds from the Clean Development Mechanism. Metrobús has expanded to a total of 5 corridors (105 kilometres), carrying 950 000 passengers per day (Metrobús, 2015).[12] In 2010, the State of Mexico government started construction of BRT corridors in municipalities in the ZMVM. Unlike the Metrobús scheme, infrastructure construction and maintenance is also concessioned to the private sector. The scheme, called Mexibús, so far has 4 corridors (81 kilometres) and carries 564 000 passengers a day (Government of the State of Mexico, 2015).

In addition to environmental objectives, a central achievement of the BRT schemes has been to shift from a system operated by a multitude of small operators to one run by larger, more professional enterprises subject to higher quality and safety standards. Among the most important achievements of the Metrobús scheme has been the reduction of about 150 000 daily car trips, an average of 40% reductions in travel times for its users and an estimated reduction of 122 000 tonnes of $CO_2$ emissions per year (Metrobús, 2015). In addition, many elements distinguish operation rules in the new scheme from the microbus framework. Among the most relevant is the introduction of a centralised fee collection system, together with a private trust fund that collects and distributes the income generated among stakeholders. Additionally, operating companies in BRT corridors receive remuneration on the basis of the kilometres travelled, as opposed to the remuneration per passenger they received when operating microbuses on the same route.

Integrated ticketing has recently been introduced for Metrobús and the underground, although Mexibús is not included.

As in many other cities that have reformed their bus systems, renegotiation of the public-private arrangement through the implementation of BRT has been a complex process.[13] Nonetheless, the introduction of BRT has increased regulation and improved efficiency, quality and safety. In the case of Metrobús, regulation was undertaken by establishing a public agency, also called Metrobús, that has legal status as well as technical and administrative autonomy (*órgano descentralizado*). This agency is meant to carry out planning, administration and control of the corridor system (Government of Mexico City, 2005). For Mexibús, no special regulation agency has been created. Regulation is the direct responsibility of the Ministry of Communications of the State of México.[14] Bus reform has facilitated the explicit renegotiation of operational rules as well as the progressive acquisition of technical expertise. In the case of Metrobús, the documentation available on the conditions negotiated for the different bus lines show that the transport authority and regulatory agency have been able progressively to negotiate agreements more likely to allow for financial sustainability (Flores-Dewey and Zegras, 2012).

### *Other public transport services are being expanded and improved*

Apart from BRT services, other mass transit schemes have been established or expanded in the ZMVM, including the expansion of the underground system and the construction of suburban rail. In addition, corridors for trolley bus services running in a dedicated lane (zero-emission corridors) were also introduced recently. A short description of these projects is provided in Table 3.1. Several initiatives for bus service improvements have also been introduced in the Federal District (summarised in Table 3.2). Figure 3.1 (left-hand panel) shows all mass-transit and trolley bus services operating in the ZMVM. Figure 3.1 (right-hand panel) shows mass-transit and trolley bus services in combination with publicly run bus services and new BRS corridors. Despite the introduction of the suburban rail and the Méxibus, and the expansion of the underground lines, public transport services (other than *microbúses* and *combis*) are principally located inside Mexico City.

Figure 3.1. **Public transport services in the Metropolitan Zone of the Valle de México***

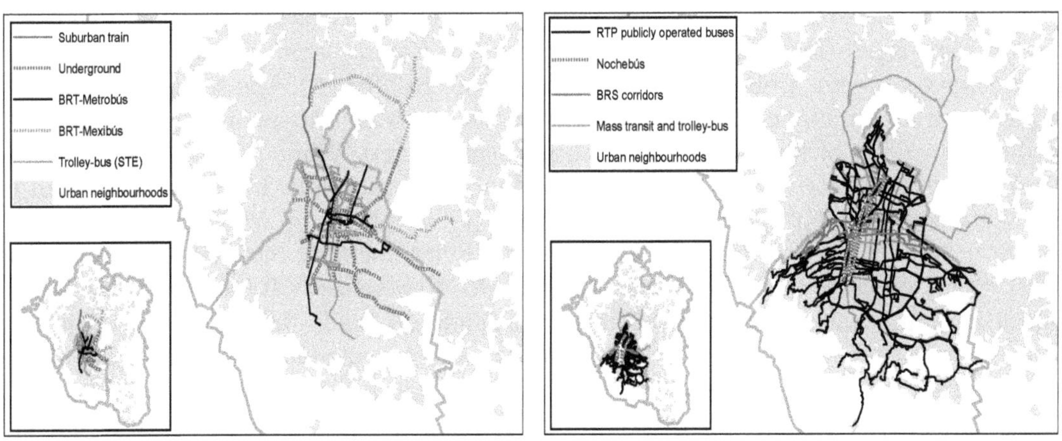


*Note:* * Except low-capacity concessioned modes and taxis.

*Source*: OECD based on data provided by SEMOVI.

Table 3.1. **Recent construction and expansion of mass transit systems (other than bus rapid transit) and other transport services using a dedicated lane in the Metropolitan Zone of the Valle de México**

| Scheme | Entity responsible | Year | Coverage | Description |
|---|---|---|---|---|
| Suburban rail | Construcciones y Auxiliar de Ferrocarriles (CAF) | 2008 | Mexico City and State of Mexico | The commuter rail connects the Federal District and the northwestern suburbs in the State of Mexico with a 27-kilometre rail infrastructure. The development of the project involved collaboration between the Federal Minister of Communications and Transport, the Governor of the State of Mexico and the Head of Government of the Federal District. The financial scheme chosen for the development of the project was a public-private partnership. Construcciones y Auxiliar de Ferrocarriles (CAF) was the winning company in the public tender. |
| Underground expansion | Sistema de Transporte Colectivo (STC) | 2012 | Mexico City and State of Mexico | After almost a decade without any expansion in the underground network, the Federal District government destined funds, complemented by funds raised through loans taken out by the city, for construction of a new underground rail line. New extensions to several lines of the network are being planned in the near future by STC. The National Plan for Infrastructure 2014-2018 also establishes the commitment of the federal government to provide funding for the extension of Line A, which connects Mexico City and the State of Mexico (to be opened by 2017). |
| Zero-emission corridors (trolley bus) | Electric Transport Service (STE) | 2009 | Mexico City | Microbuses and RTP services were replaced by trolley buses in major avenues. In contrast to the Metrobús/Mexibús scheme, operators have been relocated to other routes, rather than incorporated into the new services through the formation of new companies. Three different corridors have been implemented to date. |

*Sources:* OECD, with information from STE (n.d.), "Servicio de Transportes Eléctricos del Distrito Federal", Mexico City, www.ste.df.gob.mx (accessed 2 July 2015); Rutzen, B., N. Hutson and L. Loftus-Otway (2010), "Mexico City commuter rail: Planning and implementation of a multijurisdictional, PPP project", in: *Transportation Research Record: Journal of the Transportation Research Board*, Vol. 2 146, The National Academies of Sciences, Engineering and Medicine, Washington, DC, pp.119-126, http://trrjournalonline.trb.org/doi/abs/10.3141/2146-15 (accessed 15 June 2015); Government of Mexico (2014), *Programa Nacional de Infraestructura 2014-2018*, Presidencia de la República, http://presidencia.gob.mx/pni/consulta.php?c=1 (accessed 7 August 2015).

### *New priorities for road space allocation in favour of public and non-motorised transport users*

The introduction of a public bike-sharing system is an important reflection of changing road-space priorities in the Federal District. In addition to projects like the BRT, which already shifted road-space priority to public transport users, the introduction of ECOBICI (in 2010) has shown a commitment to give priority to bicycle users. ECOBICI has been managed from the start by the Ministry of Environment of the Federal District (Secretaría de Medio Ambiente del Distrito Federal, SEDEMA). The scheme has rapidly expanded and currently covers 42 neighbourhoods, equivalent to an area of about 35 km$^2$ in the central part of the city (Figure 3.2, left-hand panel). While still covering only the central part of Mexico City, ECOBICI is the fourth-largest public bike-sharing system in the world, after Hangzhou, London and Paris (Government of Mexico City, 2015).[15] While installing bike stations, the Ministry of Environment of the Federal District has significantly expanded road infrastructure dedicated to bike use.[16] It must be noted though that a large percentage of ECOBICI trips are made on roads that do not have bicycle infrastructure. In addition, better connections between bicycle lanes will be needed if this type of infrastructure is to develop into a useful network for bicycle users (Figure 3.2, right-hand panel). There are a growing number of bicycle parking facilities throughout the city, including in underground, Metrobús and trolley bus (zero-emission corridor) stations.

Table 3.2. **Recent improvements in bus services**

| Service | Entity in charge | Year | Coverage | Description |
|---|---|---|---|---|
| RTP express service | Public transport network (RTP) | 2009 | Mexico City | Express service covers 11 routes. The service introduced 145 new buses that make fewer, more strategic stops. Among other improvements, new buses are compliant with the EPA 04 standard, are equipped for persons with disabilities and have a satellite tracking system. |
| ECOBUS | Public transport network (RTP) | 2010 | Mexico City | The service is operated with large buses with compressed natural gas (CNG) combustion engines. The first route connects the historic centre to Santa Fe (located to the west and the site of corporate activities and various universities). In 2014, a second ECOBUS route was introduced in a recently constructed toll-road, connecting the southern area of Mexico City and Santa Fe. This ECOBUS service was implemented under the logic that, besides car access, the newly constructed road infrastructure needed to provide a high-quality public transport. While the fee for car users is MXN 80 (USD 6), the price of the ECOBUS service is MXN 5 (USD 0.4). |
| Bus rapid service (BRS) corridors | Transport Regulation Organism (ORT)[1] | 2014 | Mexico City | Bus services with preferential right of way are being introduced in various corridors in Mexico City. As in the case of BRT schemes, authorities have negotiated with incumbent operators to annul individual concessions in exchange for giving priority in granting new concessions to enterprises formed by these incumbent operators. BRS corridor services have introduced specific bus stops, centralised fee collection and GPS technologies for tracking buses. While no smart card has yet been introduced, buses acquired by concessionaires are required to be prepared for introducing this technology in the near future. The BRS corridors introduced to date are Valenciana-Tacubaya, Chapultepec-Palmas and Peñón-Panteón San Isidro. |
| Nochebús | RTP, STE and private concessionaires | December 2014 | Mexico City | These are 11 bus routes that operate between midnight and 5 a.m., 7 days a week. The price of the service is MXN 7 (USD 0.5). Nochebus routes cover 330.8 kilometres and are available in 14 of the 16 *delegaciones* of Mexico City. Priority for route design has been given to areas of employment and recreation activities. |

*Note:* 1. The ORT is a new regulatory body that has been introduced by the New Mobility Law for the Federal District, but has not yet been set up.

*Sources*: OECD with information from RTP (n.d.), www.rtp.gob.mx (accessed 5 July 2015); SEMOVI (n.d.a), www.semovi.df.gob.mx/wb/stv/nochebus.html (accessed 6 August 2015); interviews conducted with SEMOVI and RTP.

ECOBICI has achieved significant success in increasing bicycle use by residents of the Federal District and even residents of the State of Mexico. The latest survey for users (2014) showed that 14% of users are residents of the State of Mexico. Results from the survey show that 45% of trips in which ECOBICI is used are commuting trips (SEDEMA/CEMCA, 2015). Table 3.3 shows the evolution in trips, and calculated benefits from the 2010-14 period. Figure 3.2 (right-hand panel) shows flows from the top 500 most frequent daily trips. Besides high flows in the Reforma corridor, where the largest bike-segregated lane is located, frequent trips are also made on major north-south corridors. Many of these flows end at major public transport stations like Buenavista, which connect the Federal District to the northern suburbs of the ZMVM. Along with the ECOBICI system, several programmes have been introduced in Mexico City to encourage bicycle use. Among the most relevant is the conversion of several streets and avenues to bicycle and pedestrian use on Sunday mornings. The programme, called

Travel by Bike (*Muévete en Bici*), was first implemented in 2007, with a total of ten kilometres of road space being closed to motorised traffic every Sunday between 7 a.m. and 2 p.m. By 2012, road space used for the programme expanded to 24 kilometres.

Table 3.3. **Evolution of selected statistics for ECOBICI**[1]

| | 2010 | 2011 | 2012 | 2013 | 2014 |
|---|---|---|---|---|---|
| Trips | 841 079 | 2 542 963 | 2 737 917 | 6 515 328 | 7 952 247 |
| Estimated travel time reduction (expressed in days)[2] | 57 | 776 | 1 232 | 2 608 | 11 931 |
| Estimated $CO_2$ emission reduction (tonnes) | 22 | 83 | 127 | 267 | 896 |
| Estimated monetary savings (MXN)[3] | 29 776 (USD 2 356) | 404 139 (USD 32 530) | 641 496 (USD 48 710) | 1 348 275 (USD 105 564) | 6 210 885 (USD 467 249) |

*Notes:* 1. Benefits expressed in the table were provided by the Ministry of Environment and are based on a study developed by the Centre for Sustainable Transport EMBARQ Mexico in 2013: *Estudio de la Reducción de Emisiones y los Co-Beneficios generados por la Implementación del Programa ECOBICI.* The significant increase in trips and benefits between 2012 and 2013 is explained by the expansion of the ECOBICI programme during 2012 (with an addition of 170 stations). Increments in benefits per trip for 2010-14 are explained by the progressive increase in the average distance and speed of ECOBICI trips. 2. Travel time reduction is calculated based on the estimation of car, taxi and motorcycle trips that were substituted for ECOBICI, and taking into account the average speed of each type of vehicle. 3. Monetary savings are calculated by multiplying time reductions by the social value time factor used by the Mexican Ministry of Finance and Public Credit (SHCP). This factor reflects an individual's average willingness to pay for avoiding travel time. The number used for the study was MXN 21.60 per hour (USD 1.6) which corresponds to the social value time factor calculated by the Ministry of Finance for the 2010-12 period (CTS EMBARQ, 2013).

*Source*: SEDEMA (2015b), statistics and information prepared for OECD, unpublished.

Figure 3.2. **Location of ECOBICI stations and flows from top 500 frequent trips**

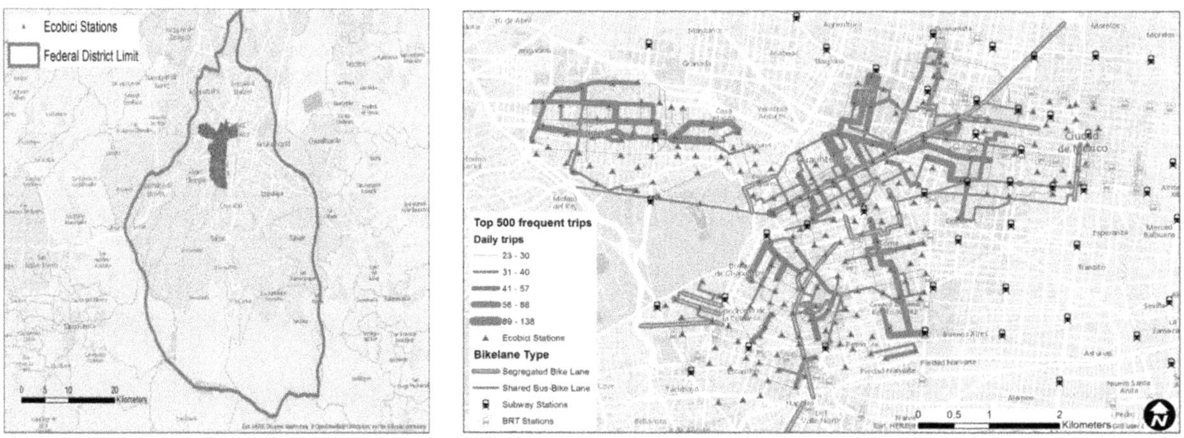


*Source*: Hernandez, U. and A. Ward (2015), "Shifting gears: Spatial analysis of Mexico City's ECOBICI bike-share system", unpublished research poster, University of California Berkeley, May.

Changes in road infrastructure allocation priorities in Mexico City have also been reflected in improving conditions for walking and in shifting away from free on-street parking policies. Pedestrianisation of major corridors and expansion of public walkable space have been conducted by the Public Space Authority (Autoridad del Espacio Público, AEP), under the Ministry for Urban Development and Housing (Secretaría de Desarrollo Urbano y Vivienda del Distrito Federal, SEDUVI). In addition, this entity has introduced a new programme for on-road parking charging called *ecoParq*. A distinctive feature of the programme is that 30% of the income generated is hypothecated for urban renewal in local neighbourhoods. Projects are selected by a public consultation process, which is carried out by neighbours in the framework of a Committee for Transparency and Accountability. The programme is currently operating in a small area in central Mexico City but is expected to be expanded in the near future (AEP, n.d.). In the State of Mexico, some parking meters have also been installed in some of the municipalities of the ZMVM.

### *Sustainability and inclusiveness are being incorporated in the legal and planning framework*

The Federal District has made significant progress in transforming the legal and planning framework for mobility policy, to encourage sustainability and inclusion. Changes in the institutional and legal structures began in 2013, when the Ministry of Transport and Roads of the Federal District (Secretaría de Transportes y Vialidad del Distrito Federal, SETRAVI) became the Ministry of Mobility (Secretaría de Movilidad del Distrito Federal, SEMOVI). More recent improvements have included the changes introduced by a new Mobility Law, and its mobility programme, as well as the reform of the fiscal code making public and non-motorised transport projects subject to funding through betterment charges (*contribuciones de mejoras*). Authorities of the State of Mexico have announced they are developing their corresponding new Mobility Law and programme, but details are not yet available. This section analyses the changes introduced by the Federal District.

#### *The new Mobility Law has made great progress in normalising sustainable and inclusive mobility principles*

Among the most important changes introduced by the new Mobility Law (Ley de Movilidad, LMDF) are: 1) the introduction of mobility as a right; 2) the explicit prioritisation of road space and financial resources according to a new user hierarchy and; 3) the enactment of explicit sustainability and inclusive principles to guide policy.

The new law declares that mobility is a right for citizens and the community, to have a mobility system that can guarantee effective travel, in order to satisfy their needs and ensure their personal development (Article 5 of the new Mobility Law). The new legislation reflects a shift from a transport policy focused on road management, evident in Article 3 of the former Law for Transport and Roads (Ley de Transporte y Vialidad, LTyV), to a mobility policy focused on "providing the necessary means to the population so that they can choose freely between different modes of transport in order to access goods, services and opportunities offered by the city" (Government of Mexico City, 2014a: Article 6).

The new legal framework has also standardised the new criteria for allocation of road space and financial resources (which many of the projects described above already reflected). According to Article 6, "priority for the use of road space and distribution of budget resources will correspond to the following hierarchy of mobility: I. Pedestrians, especially disabled people and people with limited mobility; II. Cyclists; III. Users of public transport services; IV. Service providers of passenger public transport; V. Service providers of cargo and distribution of goods; and VI. Private automobile users" (Government of Mexico City, 2014a: Article 6).

The Mobility Law also introduced explicit principles to guide the design and implementation of policies regarding mobility: safety, accessibility, efficiency, equity, quality, resilience, multimodality, sustainability and low-carbon objectives, social participation and joint responsibility, and technological innovation.

In addition to the changes to general principles guiding mobility policy, as described above, the new Mobility Law also specified modifications in a set of elements of mobility policy. Table 3.4 summarises some of the most important changes.[17] Overall, it should be acknowledged that many of the new institutions and instruments require secondary legislation before they can be implemented. Where this is the case, this has been noted in the table.

In accordance with the requirements of the new law, the Integral Mobility Programme (*Programa Integral de Movilidad*, PIM) 2013-2018 is an improved planning instrument with explicit objectives, strategic axes and indicators. Box 3.1 provides a description of the main elements that make up the PIM 2013-2018.

### Box 3.1. **Main elements of the Integral Mobility Programme for the Federal District 2013-2018**[1]

Through the Integral Mobility Programme (*Programa Integral de Movilidad*, PIM), the Federal District authorities seek to fulfil two core objectives: 1) improve the traveling experience of all users, regardless of the transport mode chosen; 2) maintain the current modal share, in which seven out of ten trips are performed in public and non-motorised transport modes, while lessening incentives for the use of private cars.

The PIM is divided into six strategic axes: 1) Integrated Transport System; 2) streets for all [users]; 3) more mobility with fewer cars; 4) a culture of mobility; 5) efficient distribution of goods; and 6) transport-oriented development.

The PIM proposes a diagnostic of the Metropolitan Zone of the Valle de México's current situation in each of these six strategic areas and establishes a list of short-term (2013-15) and mid-term (2015-18) goals. The PIM also provides for a set of indicators to monitor the achievements of the Ministry of Mobility and the other ministries and public agencies involved.

*Note:* 1. In October 2014, the Federal District adopted and published the Integral Mobility Plan 2013-2018 (PIM), drafted by the Ministry of Mobility.

*Source*: OECD, based on Government of Mexico City (2014b), "Acuerdo por el que se aprueba el Programa Integral de Movilidad 2013-2018", Secretaria de Movilidad, *Gaceta Oficial del Distrito Federal*, available at: www.ordenjuridico.gob.mx/Documentos/Estatal/Distrito%20Federal/wo99436.pdf.

### *Betterment charges to fund public and non-motorised transport infrastructure in the Federal District*

The inclusion of public transport, cycling and new multimodal station (CETRAM) projects into the betterment charge (*contribuciones de mejora*) framework is an important step in building wider financial capacity and advancing sustainable and inclusive mobility goals. This is an explicit recognition of the social benefits that such infrastructure offers. Among other reforms to the fiscal code implemented in 2014 was the inclusion of several transport-related infrastructure projects in the list of works subject to a betterment charge. Before this reform, construction, maintenance or expansion of roads were the only mobility-related projects that qualified to use this mechanism. Currently, new

## Table 3.4. Summary of some major changes introduced by the Federal District's new Mobility Law

| | |
|---|---|
| Planning | The former Law of Transport and Roads (LTyV) was not explicit about the criteria that should guide mobility planning or the minimum requirements for planning tools, such as the Integral Programme for Transport and Roads (PITV).<br>Chapter 1 of Title 2 of the new Mobility Law (LMDF) is dedicated to planning.<br>– Introduction of specific criteria for mobility and road safety planning (Article 37): Encourage modal, operational and payment integration of public transport; ensure safety and design infrastructure for universal access; incentivise the use of public transport and the rational use of cars; promote public consultation; encourage sustainable urban development and reduce the distance between housing and employment centres and other public services (education, health, etc.); prioritise planning of public transport and non-motorised mobility; encourage efficient distribution of goods; improve resilience of the mobility system; and make efficient use of public resources.<br>– Sets minimum requirements for the Integral Mobility Programme (PIM) and the Integral Programme for Road Safety (Articles 41 and 42): These planning tools should include diagnostics, objectives, goals, co-ordination mechanisms with other programmes and governmental agencies, and monitoring indicators (for the period of validity of the plan). A minimum list of issues to address is also included. |
| Co-ordination between agencies | The LTyV only acknowledged metropolitan commissions as co-ordination bodies to support mobility policy.<br>The LMDF establishes three new additional bodies:<br>– The Advisory Council for Mobility and Road Safety (Articles 20 and 21): consultative body.<br>• Competency: establish public policy proposals, issue opinions on priority projects, participate in the formulation of the PIM and integrated programmes for road safety, and issue opinions on relevant tools for follow-up and evaluation of policies.<br>• Composition: head of government (chairman); Minister of SEMOVI; ministries in charge of policies relevant to mobility outcomes; heads of public decentralised bodies in charge of public transport; members of academia and civil society; the chair and two deputies of the Mobility, Transport and Roads Commission at the legislative assembly.<br>– The Committee for the Integrated Public Transport System (Articles 24 and 25):<br>• Competency: establish programmes, guidelines and methodologies for the implementation of an integrated public transport system; develop financial schemes and technological proposals for centralised fee collection and clearing and distribution of income mechanisms; evaluate the performance of the integrated public transport system and present an annual report to the head of government.<br>• Composition: Minister of SEMOVI (chair); directors general of SEMOVI, and heads of the public decentralised bodies in charge of public transport.<br>– The Roads Classification Commission (Articles 27 and 28):<br>• Competency: classification and revision of road categories, development of a geo-referenced directory of roads, and responsibility to inform the Ministry of Urban Development about changes in road categories.<br>• Composition: Secretary of SEMOVI (chair), SEMOVI's Director General for Planning and Roads, and representatives from other ministries in charge of policies relevant to mobility outcomes. |
| Private bus concessions | Under the LTyV, concessions could be granted to individuals or companies.<br>– Introduction of new concessioning rules (Article 86): Where passenger transport is organised in corridors, only companies are allowed to operate transport services. Companies integrated by incumbent operators are granted preference to operate in corridors.<br>– Creation of the Regulatory Body for Transport (ORT) (Articles 148, 151 and 152): The LMDF creates the ORT as a body (*desconcentrado*) under the authority of SEMOVI. The ORT is in charge of planning, regulating and controlling the operation of public transport in corridors, except those regulated by Metrobús. It has authority over concessions, infrastructure projects and safety measures, although SEMOVI may override its decisions. Its structure has not yet been determined. |

Table 3.4. **Summary of some major changes introduced by the Federal District's new Mobility Law** (*continued*)

| | |
|---|---|
| Monitoring, evaluation and control | The LTyV did not provide for any instruments of this kind. |
| | – Databases (Articles 47 and 48): SEMOVI is to implement the Information and Monitoring System on Mobility and the Information and Monitoring System on Road Safety. These systems are to collect, process, monitor and update information related to mobility and road safety.<br>– Annual reporting and auditing (Articles 50 and 51): SEMOVI is required to provide a report every year on 30 November on mobility-related improvements. It is also entitled to perform mobility and road safety audits for infrastructure projects or works, to identify corrective measures and assess their coherence with the Integral Mobility and Road Safety Programmes.<br>– Public survey and consultation (Article 46, VI and VII): The LMDF also provides for SEMOVI to perform "citizen surveys" and public consultations.<br>Secondary legislation with further details on the functioning of these tools is still pending. |
| Urban development | Under the LTyV, the Ministry of Transport and Roads had no authority to intervene in urban development policy and decisions. |
| | Submission of a mobility assessment (Article 53): The LMDF requires developers to submit a mobility assessment to SEMOVI. The assessment will evaluate the impact of work conducted on passenger and freight travel and ensure that developments are in line with the Integral Programmes for Mobility and Road Safety, the General Programme for Urban Development, and the principles stated in the LMDF.<br>Secondary legislation establishing details of the contents of the mobility assessment as well as its role in final decisions on construction authorisations (which is the responsibility of the Ministry of Urban Development and Housing, SEDUVI) is still pending. |
| Funding | The LTyV did not provide for any similar instruments. |
| | Creation of the Public Fund for Mobility and Road Safety (Articles 32 and 33): This fund is designed to collect and administer financial resources to contribute to infrastructure and road safety improvements. Its activities will mainly cover the performance of studies and proposals for improving infrastructure, in line with the PIM. The fund will receive the fees charged to developers, on submission of mobility assessments and other governmental contributions. It is also expected that the fund will be allocated resources coming from compensation charged for negative impacts to mobility and life quality. Its structure has not yet been determined. |

*Sources*: OECD, with support from ITDP (2015a), Para entender la nueva Ley de Movilidad, Institute for Transportation and Development Policy, Mexico City, available at: http://mexico.itdp.org/wp-content/uploads/Para-entender-la-nueva-Ley-de-Movilidad-del-DF.pdf, based on Government of Mexico City (2010), "Acuerdo por el que se aprueba el Programa Integral de Transorte y Vialidad 2007-2012", *Gaceta Oficial del Distrito Federal*, Secretaria de Transporte y Vialidad, available at: www.transparencialinea3.df.gob.mx/normatividad/programa_integral_transportes.pdf; Government of Mexico City (2014a), Ley de Movilidad del Distrito Federal, Secretaria de Movilidad, *Gaceta Oficial del Distrito Federal*, available at: http://aldf.gob.mx/archivo-ba20960fb6570ec7d4ee34c30ee2d733.pdf.

infrastructure for mass transit (Metrobús, underground, trolley buses) is also subject to raising funds from the betterment charge. In the case of road infrastructure, bridges (for pedestrians and cars) and cycling lanes were also added to the list. Finally, another set of projects that is now authorised to be funded through this mechanism includes new construction for CETRAM, bus stations and transport terminals.[18]

The logic of the betterment charge is that individuals and enterprises whose properties benefit directly from public works also contribute directly to paying for them. The charge is paid by owners whose property is close enough to the infrastructure to receive more benefits than the general public. The charge can only be paid after construction has been completed and is paid over six two-month periods.[19] Three areas of direct impact are identified, and the properties closest to the construction pay a higher share, the contributions declining with distance. In each area, contributions are adjusted to topographical conditions and the properties' rateable value.[20] Betterment charges have already been used in the State of Mexico, although it was only in 2014 that they were used for the first time in the Federal District.[21] Effective collection of the betterment charge (which was to begin in 2015 for the first time in Mexico City) will be essential if the instrument is to have real potential for funding public and non-motorised transport projects.

One feature of this framework (compared with other land-value capture mechanisms) is that while increases in land values justify the charges, the amount of the charge does not correspond to calculated land-value increases. Rather, amounts covered by each of the influenced areas are calculated as a percentage of the cost of the project, with the restriction that total coverage by this mechanism may not exceed 50% of the total cost of the project.[22]

### *The national government has increasingly recognised the importance of urban mobility*

Local initiatives have coincided with the introduction of urban policy on the national agenda, through the consolidation of the Ministry of Agrarian, Territorial and Urban Development (Secretaría de Desarollo Agrario, Territorial y Urbano, SEDATU).[23] This ministry recently developed a National Sustainable Urban Mobility Strategy (*Estrategia de Movilidad Urbana Sustentable*, EMUS) that is coherent with the strategic axes stated by the Federal District's Integral Mobility Programme. The National Ministry of Finance and Public Credit (Secretaría de Hacienda y Crédito Público, SHCP) recently presented the list of categories to be included in the 2016 budget. The list includes a Programme to Promote Sustainable Urban Mobility (*Programa de Impulso a la Movilidad Urbana Sustainable*, or PIMUS). Effective allocation of funds to this programme will be key for promoting SEDATU's Sustainable Urban Mobility Strategy.[24] In addition to this potential source of funding, urban mobility projects are eligible for financial resources from other federal funds. In particular, the Federal Programme for Supporting Urban Mass Transport (*Programa Federal de Apoyo al Transporte Masivo*, PROTRAM) and the Metropolitan Fund have provided resources for urban mobility projects.

## Obstacles to further mobility improvements

The achievements described in the previous section are a promising start on aligning policies towards inclusive and sustainable mobility goals in the ZMVM. However, a coherent policy framework is needed to shift current transport policy away from car-oriented development. Two major issues have held this back: 1) limited metropolitan co-ordination for mobility and spatial planning; 2) a lack of solid planning, regulatory and financial capacity in the institutions in charge of mobility policy in state-level entities.

### *Metropolitan co-ordination of mobility policy planning is limited*

Attempts at metropolitan co-ordination have fallen short of generating the planning tools that can effectively support mobility strategies for the ZMVM. While CAM achieved exceptional success in encouraging metropolitan co-ordination for several transport policies focused on improving air quality, other relevant metropolitan commissions have been significantly less successful. The Metropolitan Transport and Road Commission (Comisión Metropolitana de Transporte y Vialidad, COMETRAVI) has made little headway towards meeting its objectives, which include: establishing mechanisms to study and solve problems related to transport and roads; improving transport services and road infrastructure in the metropolitan area, promoting the standardisation of legal frameworks for transport and roads; and providing the information needed to design the Master Plan for Transport and Roads in the Metropolitan Area (SEMOVI, n.d.b).[25] In fact, COMETRAVI activities are currently suspended. The Metropolitan Commission for Human Settlements (Comisión Metropolitana de Asentamientos Humanos, COMETAH), has developed the spatial planning programme for the ZMVM (POZMVM). But while the document includes a range of relevant subjects (including transport), it does not offer a long-term plan and is not used as a guiding tool for mobility policies or fund allocation.

The Metropolitan Fund's (Fondo Metropolitano, FM) impact has also been limited in encouraging co-operation and joint planning and implementation of transport projects.[26] In the ZMVM, resources from the FM were used for Line 12 of the underground and Line 1 of Mexibús. However, the framework has not been able to create incentives to develop a common portfolio of metropolitan projects. The two state-level entities make their own list of projects, which they submit jointly, but each subsequently administers its corresponding part of the funds. No clear framework exists for prioritising resources from the FM (or other funds) along sustainable and inclusive mobility goals. Apart from the two megaprojects mentioned, only a small share of funds has been allocated to infrastructure for non-motorised and public transport users (ITDP, 2014b).

### *Lack of metropolitan mobility and spatial planning encourages car-oriented development and hampers public transport*

An absence of integrated long-term mobility and spatial planning has contributed to increased trip distances and car-oriented development. The lack of a metropolitan project and the persistent division between spatial and transport planning has obscured the implications of the ZMVM's population and employment dynamics for mobility trends and accessibility needs. The fact that origin-destination surveys for the whole metropolitan area have not been conducted regularly is evidence of this.[27] Without an integral vision, urban development policy was reduced to finding a solution to the housing deficit and for many decades involved the construction of isolated and low-density housing in the periphery, without considering accessibility.[28] The rapidly growing population in the State of Mexico and Hidalgo is far from employment, which is concentrated in the central *delegaciones* of the Federal District. Thus, there are a significant number of long-distance daily trips between the entities of the ZMVM.[29] Meanwhile, the possibility of expanding mass transit, available almost exclusively in the Federal District, has been limited by the constraints of scattered housing developments, since mass transit requires a minimum density of demand for financial and operational sustainability.

In recent decades, *microbúses* and *combis*, as well as cars, have become the most important transport modes accompanying urban expansion. *Microbúses* and *combis* are characterised by low quality and poor safety conditions. In addition, users of these services, especially those travelling across administrative borders, face a growing number of transfers, which typically results in high commuting costs (PUEC-UNAM, 2013). This has made the option of owning a car increasingly appealing. Many peripheral areas have relatively high percentages of households with cars, even at relatively low income levels. For example, several areas on the north-eastern periphery have 50-75% of households that own at least one car (Figure 3.3).

Figure 3.3. **Percentage of households owning cars in the Metropolitan Zone of the Valle de México, 2010**

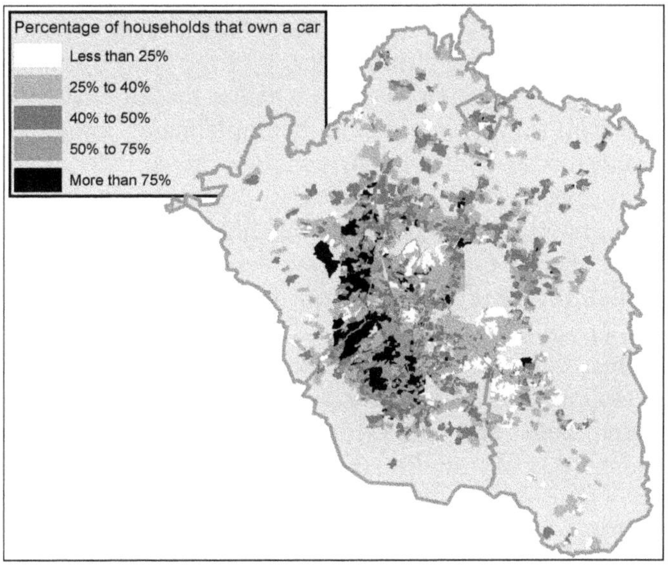


*Note:* This document and any map included herein are without prejudice to the status of or sovereignty over any territory, to the delimitation of international frontiers and boundaries and to the name of any territory, city or area.

*Source*: OECD based on data from INEGI.

The lack of a long-term plan for mobility and urban development for the ZMVM continues to put a drag on recent initiatives to boost public transport while discouraging car use. Since urban development and transport infrastructure are not planned in tandem, new transport projects do not fully correspond to accessibility needs. The suburban rail provides a good example. The project's location was chosen based on the existing rail tracks and rights of way, as a means to lower costs. However, this has meant sacrificing the possibility of constructing a direct, rapid connection between the Federal District and isolated housing developments on the periphery in the State of Mexico. As an alternative, State of Mexico authorities committed to reorganise bus routes to link remote areas such as Huehuetoca and Zumpango (both at a distance of about 20 kilometres from the suburban rail terminal) to the suburban rail infrastructure. This solution involved extra transfers and costs for users, and meanwhile, the reorganisation of routes, which proved more challenging than expected, has not yet been implemented. Taking into account the rail tracks and rights of way before constructing housing developments would have avoided such undesirable outcomes.

As this example shows, the lack of co-ordinated transport and spatial plans can be an issue for developers, population, private transport concessionaires and even transport authorities. The delays in implementing transport services between isolated housing developments and working areas has contributed to many homeowners abandoning houses on which they had already started paying monthly credit fees.[30] This has caused significant losses for construction companies. The suburban rail, despite its efficient service and high user ratings, is operating at half the projected demand. This has required the operator (CAF) to draw heavily on the contingency fund established with public funds at the beginning of the project. In addition, the federal government has had to provide extra financial support for operations.

The benefits of recent initiatives are also jeopardised by the lack of a metropolitan portfolio of projects based on an analysis of both short-term problems and longer term projections. The fact that some of the BRT corridors are already operating above capacity has raised questions about the long-term adequacy of the BRT system to meet residents' demand for transport. The issue is not so much whether the ZMVM should bet on BRT or the underground, but that projects continue to be implemented on a reactive basis, rather than following a multimodal strategy that can take advantage of different modes of transport. Isolated projects are thus quickly overtaken by unanticipated needs. Co-operation on a metropolitan portfolio would also ensure that projects are complementary, rather than competing with one another, as in the case of the Mexibús line that runs parallel to the suburban train instead of feeding passengers into it. Collaboration on a metropolitan portfolio could align investment across entities towards sustainable and inclusive mobility goals. The misalignment of fund allocation with transit-oriented development is evident, for example, in the fact that investment in road infrastructure between 2004 and 2013 for the business and commercial district of Santa Fe was double the cost of installing the five lines of Metrobús (Medina, 2014).

### *Uncoordinated actions among states have obstructed common goals*

Lack of metropolitan co-ordination has restricted the development of an integrated transport system since different institutions handle transport at the state level, and no common framework exists for project planning, implementation, operation and funding. As a result, projects are limited by the lack of physical and operational complementarity, and they cannot benefit from shared knowledge and good practices.

The varying frameworks have prevented BRT schemes from becoming part of a common strategy for bus reform. Both the regulatory framework for Metrobús and Mexibús and the financial schemes for implementing corridors are significantly different.[31] Segmented implementation limits knowledge sharing and harmonisation of quality. No common rules of operation, studies for corridor planning or evaluation procedures for BRT exist for the ZMVM as a whole. Knowledge sharing would have let the experience of Metrobús guide Mexibús (which was implemented after Metrobús had several corridors in operation). For Metrobús, conditions negotiated with incumbent operators were progressively modified to avoid barriers for tariff integration and fleet optimisation across Metrobús lines (Flores-Dewey and Zegras, 2012). Building on the Metrobús experience could have helped Mexibús avoid running into such difficulties. Instead, Mexibús users pay additional fees when transferring between lines, and even use different paying cards on each line in the Mexibús system.

Lack of co-ordination in the two BRT systems has also reduced the possibilities for building seamless public transport connections in the metropolitan zone. A common framework for implementing Metrobús and Mexibús could have made it possible to integrate Mexibús with the payment card used by both the underground and Metrobús, which is soon due to be extended to other modes of transport operated by the Federal District government. The different frameworks for funding and regulating BRT corridors prevent setting up metropolitan-wide BRT corridors, which would significantly improve mobility.

### *Lack of a metropolitan project jeopardises the future of infrastructure expansion and management*

The institutional configuration for the underground reflects the deficient co-operation between the Federal District and the State of Mexico for finding adequate arrangements for infrastructure expansion and management. When the agency in charge of the underground (STC) was created in 1967, the federal government funded its expansion and operational subsidy. After the 1997 reform, the government of the Federal District assumed responsibility for the underground system (Medina, 2013).[32] As a consequence, under the current framework, the Federal District has to provide the operational subsidy for the underground in the State of Mexico, and is also responsible for the maintenance and management of this infrastructure (Medina, 2013). This is far from ideal, since better connections for population in the State of Mexico necessarily mean higher financial pressure for the Federal District, which is already operating the underground at a deficit.

### *Administratively segmented services do not serve metropolitan mobility needs*

Providing a well-integrated public transport system at the metropolitan scale is also hindered by the persistent attempt to separate public transport service routes according to administrative boundaries. The new Mobility Law for the Federal District stipulates that: 1) transfer areas for transport services from surrounding entities should be established in the cross-border areas of the Federal District (Article 190); and 2) the concessionaires or permit holders of an adjacent entity can only access the Federal District through the nearest CETRAM (Article 91). This obliges millions of users to make at least one extra transfer per day that could be avoided if the transport system was planned on a metropolitan scale (ITDP, 2015a). Users also have to pay both the tariff for the State of Mexico transport services and, after transferring, another fee for transport services in the Federal District. Taxis' rate per kilometre doubles after crossing from Mexico City into the State of Mexico.

Segmenting services by administrative boundaries limits efficient allocation of resources and encourages informal agreements that often generate negative social outcomes. The need to create cross-border transport routes in this context has led to a series of informal agreements between operators. In some cases, bus services from the State of Mexico are allowed into the Federal District provided they do not carry passengers on their way back, a significant loss of efficiency. On their way in, buses from the State of Mexico duplicate services provided by Federal District transport services. This further reinforces the idea that the services of both entities are competing with each other. Transport providers from the Federal District have, as a result, increased pressure on their government to restrict entrance to State of Mexico buses. Meanwhile, the *de facto* CETRAM, which are not recognised as such, do not benefit from the necessary infrastructure investments. In addition, in many cases, informal arrangements are widely thought to result in corruption and extortion between operators.

### *Uncoordinated vehicle regulation undermines stringent standards and limits local financial capacity*

Conflicting policies and levels of surveillance in the different entities of the ZMVM have allowed the owners of private, public and freight vehicles to skirt more stringent environmental standards. For instance, inspection and maintenance programmes for light-duty private vehicles were homogenised in the 1990s between the Federal District and the State of Mexico. However, while emission standards were made uniform, anti-corruption procedures in monitoring centres and the fines imposed were not (Excelsior, 2014).[33] To benefit from lax policies, a large number of vehicle owners transferred the registration of their vehicles from the Federal District to the State of Mexico. As a result, the effectiveness of the programme was reduced by: 1) allowing many vehicle owners to use their cars on certain weekdays where they would normally not have been allowed to do so;[34] 2) imposing a different effective cost of owning a polluting vehicle in different parts of the metropolitan area; and 3) diluting the incentive to renew the fleet. An auto-regulation programme for freight transport is also significantly different across entities of the ZMVM, incentivising the registration of a significant part of the fleet in the State of Mexico.

The vehicle ownership tax (*tenencia*), a state-level tax since 2012, has a differentiated threshold for vehicles subject to payment across local entities in the Valle de México.[35] The three state-level entities in the ZMVM currently grant a 100% subsidy for vehicles with a market price below a certain value threshold. In the Federal District, this threshold is set at MXN 250 000 (USD 18 800), in the State of Mexico at MXN 350 000 (USD 26 300), and in Hidalgo at MXN 550 000 (USD 41 350).[36] This has led many car owners to transfer registration of their vehicles from the Federal District to the other entities. According to Federal District authorities, this represented a loss of MXN 500 million (USD 38 million) in 2012, and undercuts attempts to manage the private car fleet in the ZMVM efficiently.

## ***Institutional capacity for carrying out mobility policy needs to be strengthened***

As the Federal District notes in the new Integral Programme for Mobility, transforming the ZMVM's mobility system into one that can guarantee inclusiveness, efficiency and sustainability requires comprehensive mobility policies. The new legal framework adopted by the Federal District (and which is in the process of being developed by the State of Mexico) sets an important foundation for this by enlarging the scope of mobility policy and the responsibilities of mobility authorities. Success, however, will depend on strengthening the planning, regulatory and financial capacity of the authorities in charge of mobility policy. A crucial part of this process involves clarifying responsibilities where the outcomes depend on multisectoral strategies. Box 3.2 outlines the institutional framework of mobility policy in each state-level entity of the ZMVM. This section describes the main challenges for state-level institutions in charge of mobility in aligning policies with sustainable and inclusive mobility goals.

### *Mobility and urban development authorities need to co-operate on an effective framework for mobility and spatial planning*

In addition to the lack of metropolitan co-ordination, mobility and spatial planning in the ZMVM has been hampered by the absence of adequate mechanisms for evaluating the impact of urban development on mobility. The framework for linking urban development

### Box 3.2. Institutional framework for mobility policy in state-level entities in the Metropolitan Zone of the Valle de México

**The Federal District**

The Ministry of Mobility (SEMOVI) is in charge of regulating private vehicles, taxis, freight transport, roads, off-street parking and public transport concessions. Several regulatory bodies (*órganos descentralizados*) manage and operate public transport modes: the Collective System of Transport (STC), which regulates the underground; the Electric Transport System (STE), which includes the trolley bus and the light train; the Passenger Transport Network (Red de Transporte de Pasajeros, RTP), the system of publicly owned and operated buses; and Metrobús, which regulates the system of bus rapid transit (BRT) corridors and whose operation is mostly concessioned to the private sector (a small percentage is operated by RTP buses).

The Ministry of Mobility is in charge of off-street parking concessions. The Ministry of Housing and Urban Development (SEDUVI) runs the *ecoParq* programme for on-street parking fees. It also has the authority to grant construction development permits, including evaluation of the urban impact assessment (*estudio de impacto urbano*) required from developers, which includes a road and transport component. The Ministry of Environment (SEDEMA) is the entity in charge of expansion and management of the bike-sharing system ECOBICI. Finally, *delegaciones* have authority over local roads and particular local standards for infrastructure projects, including zoning for parking spaces.

**The State of Mexico**

In the State of Mexico, the Ministry of Transport and Communication was divided into two different ministries in 2002. Planning and regulation of concessioned public transport and freight are the responsibility of the Ministry of Mobility, while mass transit (including BRT) and highways are run by the Ministry of Communications. The Ministry of Communications issues opinions on the feasibility of incorporating into the existing road infrastructure vehicle and pedestrian flows generated by urban development (*dictamen de incorporación e impacto vial*). An approval on this issue, along with approvals from the Ministries of Urban Development, Interior, Environment, and Water and Works on the capacity to deal with other impacts is needed before the State Commission of Urban Development and Housing can issue a proof of viability (*constancia de viabilidad*).[1] This last document is required before the Ministry of Urban and Metropolitan Development grants construction authorisation. Parking policy is the responsibility of each municipality.

**Hidalgo**

The State of Hidalgo has no Ministry of Transport or Mobility. In 2013, a new Transport Law was passed, which established the Organisation for Conventional Transport and created a new Organisation for Mass Transport as a public body (*descentralizado*) under the Ministry of the Interior. Evaluation of the urban and roads assessment (*estudio de impacto urbano y vial*) for new developments is under the Ministry of Public Works and Land Management. Municipalities are in charge of local and secondary roads. Parking policy is run by each municipality.

*Note:* 1. The State Commission for Urban Development and Housing involves the Ministries of Urban Development, Government, Environment, Water and Works, and Communications.

decisions to transport considerations in the ZMVM is inadequate and is not aligned with transit-oriented development goals. In all three states, the legal framework for the development of urban areas and human settlements requires developers to provide state authorities with information on the impact that future construction will have on roads and vehicle flows. For Hidalgo and the Federal District, evaluating the impact of development on road access and vehicle traffic is a component of the urban impact assessment, which is required and appraised by the ministries in charge of urban development as part of the procedure for granting construction authorisations. These ministries can ask for opinions from other relevant authorities for evaluating different components of the urban impact assessment (e.g. mobility-related authorities for impacts on road access and vehicle traffic flows) but they are not obliged to do so, or to take this opinion into account in their final decision on granting the construction permit. In the State of Mexico, the Ministry of Communications (through the department in charge of roads) always issues an opinion on the feasibility of incorporating road and pedestrian flows generated by developments in the existing road infrastructure. A positive opinion is required for the State Commission of Urban Development and Housing (which includes representatives of various ministries including the Ministry of Communications) to issue a proof of viability. This document is needed in turn for the Ministry of Urban and Metropolitan Development to grant construction authorisations. The framework in the State of Mexico has the advantage of assigning evaluations of each of the potential impacts of a development to the pertinent authority, and formally linking construction authorisations to the assessment conducted by each of these authorities. However, just as in the Federal District and Hidalgo, transport-related impact assessment is limited to determining the availability (and eventual need for expansion) of road infrastructure. No provisions are in place for developers to turn in an intermodal assessment. This would help authorities evaluate the feasibility of providing developments with public transport (in particular mass transit infrastructure) and non-motorised transport connections.

In the Federal District, a lack of clarity in the division of responsibilities between mobility and urban development authorities is an obstacle to the current initiatives to align urban development decisions with transit-oriented development goals. The new Mobility Law for the Federal District has recently required developers to provide a mobility impact assessment to the Ministry of Mobility (SEMOVI) before beginning construction. Secondary legislation describing the elements to be included in this new assessment has yet to be issued. However, SEMOVI has stated that this assessment will aim to conduct a multimodal evaluation of the mobility impacts generated by developments, with a focus on public and non-motorised transport accessibility and eventual infrastructure development needs. SEMOVI is taking the lead in conducting an integral mobility assessment, after being charged under the Federal District's new Mobility Law to work with SEDUVI to discourage urban development in areas not covered by the public transport network (Article 37 of the new Mobility Law for the Federal District). Implementation and effectiveness of this new instrument to integrate mobility and spatial planning is likely to be held back if SEMOVI and SEDUVI cannot reach an agreement on the role of the mobility impact assessment in the process of granting construction permits.

The mobility impact assessment introduced by SEMOVI will cover road access, in addition to broader mobility issues like public and non-motorised transport connections. This new instrument should replace the current road and transport component of the urban impact assessment, which has the same purpose but is less comprehensive. However, the mobility impact assessment is acknowledged, so far, as a requirement independent of the urban impact assessment conducted by SEDUVI. Such overlap between ministries' authority will reduce the legal certainty for developers, who will potentially lose the benefit of a one-stop shop (*ventanilla única*) in applying for development permits, which was recently implemented by the Urban Development Ministry in Mexico City. In addition, if the new mobility impact assessment does not play a role in SEDUVI's decision to grant construction authorisations, it cannot serve the purpose of ensuring that new development can be served by good public transport and non-motorised infrastructure and services. Furthermore, under these conditions, the obligation of developers to turn in the new mobility impact assessment could easily be ignored overall.

### *Poor co-ordination between transport agencies in charge of public transport has stalled efforts to build a multimodal, seamless transport system*

Poor co-ordination between the many agencies in charge of public transport within each state-level entity has resulted in fragmentation between different modes of public transport. A transport system regulated by many separate public agencies does not make for seamless origin-destination travel. All the entities of the ZMVM suffer from non-synchronised routes, schedules and information, as well as a lack of tariff integration. Some efforts have been made in the Federal District, with the introduction of a single transport card for the underground and Metrobús. However, users continue to pay separate fares when they transfer between the underground and Metrobús, rather than paying a fare for a certain distance, regardless of the transfer between the two modes. Trolley buses, RTP buses, the suburban train, *microbúses* and *combis* do not use the common card. The State of Mexico has no common payment method for any of the services provided, with separate cards used even for each corridor of the Mexibús.

The new Mobility Law for the Federal District has introduced a new Committee for the Integrated Public Transport System.[37] It is intended to improve co-ordination between the different directorates of SEMOVI that are in charge of public transport planning and regulation, and the public bodies (*descentralizados*) in charge of different transport modes. Its goal is to strengthen the co-ordination of public transport by establishing programmes, guidelines and methodologies that can implement an integrated public transport system; developing financial schemes and technological proposals for centralised fee collection; and evaluating the performance of the system, including presenting an annual report. The success of the committee will depend on the allocation of human and financial resources to support its expanded role, given that it will be composed of high-level officials with many other responsibilities.

### *Transforming CETRAM has been hampered by the lack of adequate decision-making frameworks*

The transformation of modal transfer centres (CETRAM) is a key element in integrating the public transport modes and introducing transit-oriented development. CETRAM were first conceived by the Federal District government in the 1970s, to facilitate transfers between the underground and other modes of transport. The Federal District currently has 47, and over time, these nodes have come to be seen not only as a way of optimising transport services, but integrating transport into the urban landscape (ITDP, 2014c).

The governments of the Federal District and the State of Mexico have been modernising CETRAM, which are typically surrounded by deteriorated urban space, invaded by informal commerce and high vehicle congestion. Transfer areas are insecure, and users are forced to walk long distances, sometimes through traffic. To make things worse, they often face unpredictable waiting times. The government of the Federal District has recognised the many challenges posed by CETRAM and the need for a strategy to improve them. This includes granting concessions to the private sector to manage the building spaces where CETRAM are located, as well as the public space around the CETRAM owned by the government of the Federal District and that could benefit from modernisation of the CETRAM. In turn, private parties pay a financial compensation to the Federal District government. In the State of Mexico, the concept of CETRAM is less developed, and no institutional framework or overall strategy exists for co-ordination with private operators or between governmental agencies for modernisation of transfer centres. Nonetheless, the government has expanded and modernised some transfer centres, including the Ciudad Azteca transport node linking the underground, taxis, inter-city buses and Mexibús. This project was also carried out by granting concessions to the private sector.

The first projects for modernisation of CETRAM in the Federal District and in the State of Mexico have fallen short in improving access to public transport and encouraging transit-oriented development. A recurrent problem has been that improving accessibility between public transport modes has been subordinated to ensuring the financial profitability of private concessionaires. Users still face long transfers on foot between modes. In the Mexipuerto, for example, to transfer from the underground to Mexibús, users have to cross the whole commercial centre. This ensures flows of customers to businesses, but requires users to change floors six times. In the case of the CETRAM Zapata, most commercial development has been connected to car park facilities, with no connections to the CETRAM.[38] The overall result has little to do with encouraging transit-oriented development and the use of public rather than private transport. Another shortcoming of the modernisation projects is the limited access to the facilities for people with disabilities. The persistence of a divided public space within CETRAM and between the centres and their surrounding areas makes walking difficult (Medina, 2013).

Quite apart from specific design issues, modernisation efforts have been hampered by the lack of a coherent decision-making framework where legal, financial and design features are all guided towards clearly identified principles and objectives. To be successful, the modernisation of CETRAM requires co-ordinating actions from a multiplicity of private and governmental actors: the Ministries of Mobility (and the Ministry of Communications in the State of Mexico), the Ministries of Housing and Urban Development, the Ministries of Finance, the Ministries of Public Works, and in the case of the Federal District, the Administration Unit (Oficialía Mayor del Gobierno del Distrito Federal). The principles, objectives and guidelines for mobility, housing, urban development, economic and social development, need to be identified and addressed in a general framework. SEDUVI's new guidelines for the modernisation of CETRAM are a significant step forward in co-ordinating actions with the private sector.[39] However, the framework would also benefit from allocating clear responsibilities and co-ordination mechanisms among the relevant government agencies. The State of Mexico and Hidalgo have not yet issued similar guidelines.

### *Efforts to support public and non-motorised transport have not involved adequate transport demand management*

Weak transport demand management policies significantly decrease the impact of attempts to support public and non-motorised transport improvements. They also limit funding sources for further expansion of such programmes. The gradual phasing-out of the gasoline subsidy in Mexico by the national government has been an important step towards achieving more efficient pricing of private vehicle use, but complementary polices are needed. Effective parking policies are a basic element of transport demand management that need to be strengthened in the ZMVM.

On-street parking charges are not enforced throughout the ZMVM, and where they exist, their impact is limited by the imposition of a fixed rate. In the Federal District, only central neighbourhoods have them, although the Ministry of Urban Development and Housing, and the Authority for Public Space have plans to expand the *ecoParq* programme. Outside Mexico City, the decision to implement on-street parking charges depends on each municipality, rather than on state-level authorities. Only a few of the municipalities of the ZMVM in the State of Mexico (e.g. Ecatepec and Naucalpan) have instituted on-street parking charges. In many cases, the charges are continually reversed due to disagreements between different members of the city council. In Naucalpan, on-street parking charges had been implemented in 11 zones of the municipality but were suspended earlier this year (Reforma, 2015). Another constraint is that prices for on-street parking are set in the state's fiscal codes and can only be modified after an arduous and time-consuming legislative process.[40] These low and virtually fixed fares are effectively a subsidy for car use (especially in areas where space is scarce and land prices are high).

Parking policy needs better methodologies for increasing its effectiveness and generating revenues for public transport infrastructure. Both on-street and off-street parking policies would benefit from detailed analysis of how much parking space is needed to achieve modal shift objectives. The fee structure for off-street parking only accounts for the operational costs of the private sector, not the social costs of car use. This is a lost opportunity for generating revenues that could be used to cross-subsidise infrastructure and improvements for public and non-motorised modes. In the Federal District, on-street parking fees are allocated for renewal of public space, but in the State of Mexico these funds are not hypothecated.

The current legal framework regulating parking spaces in new developments should also be revised to align parking policy with sustainable and inclusive mobility goals. All municipal-level administrations in the ZMVM are subject to technical standards that establish a minimum number of parking spaces for each new development. In each municipality, minimum requirements are calculated based on several criteria, such as land use and square metres of construction. In the Federal District, as shown by an Institute for Transportation and Development Policy study, the minimum parking spaces regulation has accelerated the growth in construction space allocated for parking. The number of parking spaces increased at a 33% average annual growth rate between 2009 and 2013 in Mexico City, resulting in an oversupply (ITDP, 2014d). The current minimum policy regulation incentivises car use and reduces the competitiveness of public transport and non-motorised transport modes.

### *Planning tools developed by mobility agencies are constrained by a short-term vision, poor data collection and modelling, and limited instruments for monitoring progress*

Mobility programmes are the central tool for co-ordinating actions of all relevant agencies into a coherent strategy. While important improvements have been introduced to the Federal District's mobility planning framework, a persistent limitation for all entities in the ZMVM is the short-term vision of mobility programmes. In the Federal District, the PIM 2013-2018 has made progress in setting out clear objectives and quantifiable goals to measure success. It has also identified agencies responsible for each of the goals specified. These changes should be taken into account by the State of Mexico and Hidalgo for improving their own plans. However, the long-term impact on mobility will remain uncertain if short- and mid-term strategies in the current six-year programmes are not coherent with a long-term strategy (20-25 years ahead).

Improving collection and analysis of mobility data is a crucial issue that needs to be addressed in all entities of the ZMVM, to carry out adequate planning. Regular origin-destination surveys and annual monitoring of mobility trends are not currently conducted. To a great extent, this is due to a lack of human and financial resources dedicated to such activities. Regular data gathering is currently limited by the lack of an integrated fare collection system that could provide the possibility of generating data from smart cards. Among the agencies operating public transport in the ZMVM, only Metrobús, ECOBICI and the suburban railway are collecting and making use of the data provided by smart cards for planning and optimisation.

The absence of a centralised platform where information being collected by different entities can be organised, compared and analysed further limits the development of better planning tools. In many cases, data collection and several modelling exercises (e.g. origin-destination for certain areas of the city, estimation of modal shift and $CO_2$ emission mitigation, demand forecasting, environmental impact assessments) are carried out with the aim of implementing specific projects (underground line extensions, BRT corridors, bike lanes). However, information is currently neither used nor verified between agencies or gathered into an integrated model that could guide overall mobility planning. Poor long-term modelling and forecasting capacity will limit the ZMVM's long-term vision for mobility planning.

An important constraint for better planning is the absence of detailed documentation on project and policy implementation that can allow *ex post* assessment. In the light of the many changes planned, information on the impact of the different projects, policies and programmes will be crucial in shaping a strategy. In the Federal District, the set of indicators introduced in the PIM 2013-2018 provide a head start for monitoring the progress achieved by the agencies responsible for the programme's goals. SEMOVI is also working on expanding the list of indicators, to monitor progress on each of the actions stipulated in the document. Again, targets for these indicators only cover a six-year time span, and long-term targets need to be developed.

### *Mobility authorities' limited capacity to regulate the microbus sector is an obstacle to high-quality, safe bus services*

The public-private arrangements defining operation of the microbus sector have severely limited the regulatory capacity of mobility authorities in all of the states of the ZMVM. The microbus sector is defined by an arrangement through which mobility authorities grant right of way permits and concessions to the private operators. Certain operational standards are included in concessions, but few regulations for quality and safety standards have been set by transport authorities (USAID Mexico, 2014). Procedures to verify compliance with existing standards tend to be lax or non-existent. In return, the private sector has been expected to cover all costs, including maintenance, operation, investment and any subsidies to vulnerable population required by authorities, while allowing the fares to be set by the government (Molinero, 2014). Vehicle and service improvements in the system are subject to constant negotiations between authorities and private sector leaders, rather than by periodically revised standards and clear procedures. So are grants of new concessions, tariff adjustments and financial support from the government for acquiring vehicles that meet higher quality, security and sustainability standards.[41] A crucial consequence is that transport authorities (now mobility authorities) have not only ceded regulatory authority to the private sector, but lost important regulatory expertise, because many of the staff has much more developed skills for political negotiation than for technical transport planning (see Flores, Muñoz and Paget-Seekins, forthcoming).

The configuration described above has allowed transport authorities to withdraw substantial public financial support for buses, while creating rapidly expanding services that are relatively affordable and highly flexible in responding to rapid urban expansion.[42] However, service is highly inefficient, with poor performance in terms of quality, safety and environmental sustainability. The large number of uncoordinated individual concessionaires has made it hard for single operators to function as companies and for the different routes to be organised into a single system. Both of these trends prevent the creation of economies of scale in the sector and increase the obstacles to integrating bus services with other public transport modes. Furthermore, fare collection is not centralised, and fares are collected by drivers. As a consequence, service providers are constantly competing with each other, both on the same routes and between routes, while sacrificing service quality and security. Buses travel more slowly and spend longer at bus stops, to attract more passengers, and many stop providing services on routes with lower demand and/or during less popular periods (Medina, 2011). Without clear parameters for granting new concessions, negotiations have resulted in a general oversupply in the sector that has further compromised the financial sustainability of operators and increased competition on some routes, without necessarily addressing the needs of the population.

The lack of minimum quality, safety and technical standards set for operators has reduced incentives for fleet renewal and service improvement. As government initiatives to support fleet renewal show, the single-operator status of most service providers hampers access to finance and increases operators' difficulties in conducting regular fleet renewal (USAID Mexico, 2014).[43] Uncertainty about future tariff adjustments has also deterred concessionaires from investing in fleet renewal and service improvements. Without a clear mechanism for adjusting tariffs according to cost increases, and with lax regulation, operators maintain utility levels by sacrificing quality and maintenance (Molinero, 2014).

### *Bus rapid transit schemes face financial challenges and are hampered by discretional negotiations between authorities and operators*

The introduction of BRT is a first step in rebalancing the roles of the public and private sector for better quality bus services in the ZMVM. The difficulty lies in striking a balance between securing the participation of incumbent operators in a more regulated system and ensuring that conditions offered to operators do not compromise financial sustainability. Negotiations on bus reform are particularly challenging since incumbent operators have political clout and, as has happened in Rio de Janeiro, can potentially suspend all services to put pressure on the authorities. The negotiations with operators of Mexibús failed to incorporate enough microbus owners into the new system or to relocate them into feeder routes. As a result, microbus services run parallel to the Mexibús system, a source of unregulated competition that dampens demand for BRT services.[44] The gap between expected and actual demand has required financial support from the government, in addition to the funds provided to support low fares in all corridors.[45]

In the case of Metrobús, negotiations have been more successful in avoiding unfair and damaging competition. Nonetheless, ensuring inclusion of incumbent operators also came at a significant cost for the project. Many of the conditions agreed upon, especially with respect to the implementation of the first corridor, have also compromised the project's financial sustainability. For instance, the remuneration scheme, based on a payment per kilometre operated by CISA (the company formed by incumbent operators to run the first corridor) was negotiated to ensure pre-BRT revenues for incumbent operators, prioritising this over financial criteria.[46] Higher per-kilometre payments for the operator were made possible through cross-subsidising revenues from the public RTP services. Per-kilometre remunerations for RTP operations were set at much lower rates than those for CISA.

While negotiations with incumbent operators in the case of Metrobús have shown significant adjustments in the conditions offered by SEMOVI, remunerations being paid on Line 1 continue to be an important financial constraint for the system. Conditions negotiated by SEMOVI have been adjusted through time relative to those offered for implementation of the first corridor. Later negotiations have been able to attain a better balance between private commitments and governmental support.[47] Despite this significant success, costs for running the first corridor put financial strain on the Metrobús system (Flores-Dewey and Zegras, 2012). CISA's remuneration constitutes an important financial constraint for the overall system, as CISA's guaranteed profits plus payments for bus loans constituted 72% of the deficit registered by Metrobús in 2011.[48] Likewise, the necessary resources for the Metrobús regulatory agency (which were planned to be covered by BRT revenues) are also covered by general city funds (Flores-Dewey and Zegras, 2012).

An important pending issue of BRT implementation is moving away from highly discretionary negotiations between the public and the private sector. This is particularly important in the case of concession granting, as well as tariff setting and adjustment. Giving priority to enterprises formed by incumbent operators has limited the possibility of awarding contracts through a competitive tendering process with clear rules. Negotiations for each corridor have been conducted on a case-by-case basis. This has resulted in a lack of certainty for all parties and has continued to be extremely time and resource consuming for mobility authorities. Moreover, without a competition process, it is difficult for authorities to guarantee that the operations carried out by the concessionaires offer the highest value for money.

In the case of tariff setting, the procedure also continues to be highly dependent on political decisions rather than on an established formula based on a technical assessment of costs and affordability standards. In this respect, no formal procedure for collecting periodical financial data from operators has been instituted. The framework does not include periodical adjustments that respond to cost increases, and there is no clear procedure for determining what affordable tariffs are.

Having long periods of fixed fares followed by unexpected and significant increases, as opposed to small progressive tariff adjustment, continues to intensify political pressures and trap tariff setting into political debates. Just as in the case of the microbus framework, rigid and discretionary fares can impose major restrictions on guaranteeing high-quality services. Furthermore, without a transparent fare calculation and adjustment formula, the framework continues to fail to offer certainty for operators on their ability to recover investments or have future cost increases reflected in their revenues.

Lack of assessment on operational costs and affordable tariffs are also reflected in the unclear policy for governmental support for bus fares. BRT corridors are implemented on the principle that no public funds should be used to support tariffs.[49] However, certainty about costs and clear standards for affordability are needed in order to determine to what extent targeted levels of quality and safety can be achieved without governmental support. Until now, both Mexibús and Metrobús have been receiving governmental support, but neither of them has recorded this as an explicit subsidy.[50] This makes it difficult to have clarity on the elements that drive the need for additional resources and to determine the improvements that the scheme requires in order to reduce (and possibly suppress) this need.[51] An exception has been the funding of infrastructure by the Federal District in the case of Metrobús that has been a clearly established arrangement.

All of the challenges mentioned in this section apply not only to the future developments of the BRT schemes but to future initiatives continuing the process of bus reform in the ZMVM. This is the case of BRS corridors and the corresponding regulatory body that will soon be implemented. In the case of Metrobús, the fact that various concessions are close to termination opens the possibility of adjusting operation conditions and making progress on financial sustainability and more technical decision making.

### *Capacity to invest in publicly operated transport modes has been damaged by high and generalised subsidies*

Transport modes operated by Mexico City's government (underground, trolley bus, RTP buses) are heavily subsidised, without adequate analysis of cost structures and affordability of tariffs. In contrast to concessioned bus services, transport modes operated by the government are run on the assumption that a high subsidy needs to be granted in order to provide services at affordable prices. However, just as in the case of concessioned bus services, there is a lack of technical analysis about cost structures and affordability of tariffs. Without conducting this analysis, all publicly run transport modes are highly and equally subsidised for all individuals, regardless of their capacity to pay. Table 3.5 compares the user price per trip and the calculated cost per trip for different public transport services operated by the Federal District government. Tariffs are also fixed regardless of travel times and distances. Additionally, free entrance or further discounts to the already subsidised tariff are offered in particular cases (e.g. students and the elderly). Just as in the case of concessioned buses, no fare adjustments are conducted regularly, and when increases happen, these are quite significant and are not expected by the population. This has increased political pressure to keep tariffs low, as social protest arises each time a substantial increment is implemented.

Table 3.5. **Fare and calculated operation costs of a trip on public transport, 2015**

| | Price per trip (MXN) | Calculated cost per trip (MXN) |
|---|---|---|
| Metro | 5.00 | 11.50 |
| RTP ordinary service | 2.00 | 7.50 |
| RTP Ecobus service | 5.00 | 12.00 |

Despite the general discontent expressed in response to tariff increases, there is also evidence that significant segments of public transport users would accept fare increases as long as they were accompanied by significant improvements in service quality and safety. A December 2013 survey of underground users showed that 56% of respondents agreed with a fare increase from MXN 3 to MXN 5 if the government could guarantee a decrease in crowding, waiting times, delays in service, as well as improvement of trip conditions, such as air conditioning and improved safety (Mitofsky, 2013).[52] This fare increase was implemented in 2014. The STC has made considerable effort to engage in modernisation projects and to meet users' expectations after fare increases. However, public faith in its ability to realise the promised improvement has been dented by major events, such as the need to stop operations of the newly constructed Line 12 (due to the acquisition of unsuitable trains) and the collision of two trains in May 2015 (El Economista, 2015).

The high levels of generalised subsidies have hugely restricted financial capacity for infrastructure expansion, maintenance, improvements of both infrastructure and vehicles, and the possibility of carrying out regular vehicle fleet renewal. In the case of the underground, the gap between real and actual fares meant a loss of almost MXN 12 000 million in revenues in 2012. If the revenue that was not received due to users with free access is also taken into account, the amount rises to MXN 13 500 million (USD 1 million). Substantial funds from the Federal District government are provided as compensation every year (MXN 6 460 million, or USD 490 million in 2012).[53] This income accounted for between 50% and 60% of the yearly budget of the underground between 2008 and 2012. However, even with this support, the SCT is far from having a budget that could allow operation in optimal conditions. In 2013 for example, funds assigned by the Federal District Congress to the underground were 33.7% of what the institution had requested based on calculations of the total budget needed for optimal operation and required maintenance (MXN 6 676 million were authorised, although the institution requested MXN 16 738 million; STC, 2013).

As the STC acknowledges, the budget constraint has a negative impact on the performance of the underground. Among other things, it results in "lack of compliance with maintenance programmes for fixed infrastructure and rolling stock, which results in the unavailability of trains in service, saturation, and incidents that cause delays and discontinued service; absence of investment for projects dedicated to modernise and develop the system; decrease in ridership caused by bad service; and increase in the risk of accidents that impact users, workers, infrastructure, and equipment" (STC, 2013: 25). It is important to mention that while fare revenues constitute about 40% of the budget, they account for much less of the total funds than would be needed for adequate operation, maintenance and fleet renewal. The financial capacity of the STC is further compromised by the fact that it also has to cover financial support for underground operations in the State of Mexico.

In the case of RTP buses, budget restrictions have severely limited regular bus renewal. A large number of buses running the ordinary services have long exceeded their lifecycle and do not comply with current emission standards. The lack of funds has also complicated the introduction of cleaner vehicle technologies. While the entity would ideally have substituted a higher percentage of buses run on compressed natural gas (CNG), only 72 of the fleet of 1 360 buses have this kind of engine.

Budget restrictions have significantly reduced the capacity to expand the public transport network. Expansion towards the suburban areas in the State of Mexico has become increasingly necessary, and transport services need to provide a denser network, with alternative itineraries for corridors that are close to or above capacity. Supplementing segments of the system to create itineraries better suited to origin-destination demand may also help increase ridership in segments operating far below capacity.

#### *Vehicle ownership tax subsidies conflict with new mobility goals and drain local financial capacity*

In addition to subsidies for public transport, the Federal District and the State of Mexico and Hidalgo offer 100% subsidies for the payment of the vehicle ownership tax for cars of a market value below a certain threshold.[54] This has been a drain on public finances. Apart from the impact on the budget, this has particularly hit non-hypothecated funds and the overall capacity of increasing own revenues (Moody's, 2011).[55]

While exceptions based on social considerations could be considered, subsidising 100% of this tax for a majority of the population is in complete contradiction with the government's goal of promoting public and non-motorised transport modes and reducing dependence on cars. The vehicle ownership tax is one of the few mechanisms currently capturing the social costs of car use. Exempting a high percentage of car owners from this tax shelters them from the full costs of owning and using cars. Moreover, in the Federal District, income from the vehicle ownership tax has been used to support the underground system.[56] This decision intended to cross-subsidise efficient modes used by a majority of the population with revenues raised by taxing less efficient modes used by a small percentage of the population. The vehicle ownership tax subsidies are a step backward and conflict with air quality goals (see Chapter 4).

## Towards a high-quality mobility system

This section provides specific recommendations for the ZMVM to embrace fully co-ordinated sustainable and inclusive mobility policies, based on international good practices. Where relevant, the instruments and institutions introduced by the new Mobility Law in the Federal District are analysed.

### ***Achieving metropolitan co-ordination for building an efficient, well-integrated mobility system***

#### *Restore and strengthen the metropolitan commissions in charge of supporting joint mobility strategies*

These commissions should prioritise the harmonisation of legal frameworks and development of a long-term mobility master plan for the ZMVM. It is key that the metropolitan commissions evolve into solid institutions backed by legally binding mechanisms that ensure state and municipal co-operation, even in the absence of political will. International experience shows that metropolitan mobility projects can be facilitated by establishing a metropolitan-scale mobility authority (as in London, Paris, Singapore and Curitiba), with jurisdiction over the whole functional urban area. Box 3.3 describes examples of metropolitan transport authorities that have successfully improved the coherence of mobility policy throughout a functional urban area. Without the legal structure to allow this possibility (at least in the short and medium term), improving the current metropolitan co-ordination framework for mobility planning is a priority of the first order for the ZMVM.

Restoring the Metropolitan Commission for Transport (COMETRAVI) is of particular importance, since its objectives are central to the development of an integral metropolitan mobility strategy.[57] In the light of the wide scope of these objectives, permanent human and financial resources will be needed to build adequate expertise in this commission.

## Box 3.3. Metropolitan transport authorities

### Transport for London – United Kingdom

In the United Kingdom, Transport for London (TfL) is a statutory body created by the Greater London Authority (GLA) Act 1999. This act gives the Mayor of London a general responsibility to develop and apply policies to promote and encourage safe, integrated, efficient and economic transport facilities and services to, from and within London. The TfL is directed by a board of between 8 and 17 members, appointed by the Mayor. Decisions are made by majority vote. The TfL is in charge of the operation of public transport, highway construction and management, including congestion charges and vehicle licensing.

The financial capacity for continuous investments and improvements are ensured by six main sources: income from fares and the congestion charging scheme, central government funding, a proportion of London business rates, prudential borrowing, commercial development of their estate – including advertising and property rental, and development and third-party funding for specific projects.

### Land Transport Authority – Singapore

In Singapore, the Land Transport Authority (LTA) is a statutory board under the Ministry of Transport, established in 1995 as a result of a merger of four government agencies: the Registry of Vehicles, the Road Transport Division of Public Works Department, the Land Division of the Ministry of Communications and the Mass Rapid Transit Corporation.

The LTA is responsible for planning, operating and maintaining land transport infrastructure and systems, including road safety, vehicle licensing and electronic road pricing. The LTA continually improves and expands its public transport network, complementing it with parking policies and electronic road pricing. This has resulted in a shift from private to public transport in recent years. Investment mainly stems from government grants and operating income, such as management fees from taxes, fees and charges relating to land transport services.

### Syndicat des transports de l'Île-de-France – France

Transport authorities (known as GARTs in French) have been created in France since 1980 to promote urban transport alternatives to private cars. The Syndicat des transports de l'Île-de-France (STIF) is the transport authority for the Île-de-France and is jointly supervised by the region of Île-de-France, the departments that make up the region and the city of Paris.

The STIF assumes a broad range of public transport planning responsibilities that include defining general operational and service-level targets, setting fares and negotiating performance-based contracts with public service providers. The STIF also develops an Urban Mobility Plan (*plan de déplacements urbains*, PDU) that includes land-use and transport plans to guide all lower levels of government. The programme of actions included in the PDU is subject to approval from regional, general and municipal councils; transport users; experts and environmental associations. Revenue from a dedicated transport tax (*versement transport*) levied on employers and based on payrolls has enabled the STIF to extend and maintain the public transport network and non-motorised transport facilities.

### Urban Transport Planning Authority Curitiba – Brazil

Curitiba's bus rapid transit system (BRT) is widely known as an example of a pragmatic, integrated, cost-effective and efficient transport system. The city's success results from close co-operation between its Urban Transport Planning Authority (URBS), responsible for transport, and the urban development authority (IPUCC), which is in charge of land-use planning. From its start in 1974, the Curitiba BRT was notable for its careful alignment with the 1965 Curitiba Master Plan, which focused the city's growth along major corridors, through land-use and zoning regulations. Building on this core concept, the Curitiba BRT has continually improved efficiency and expanded access. The integration of feeder and inter-district buses, with transfer stations and a single fare, created the Integrated Transport Network (Rede Integrada de Transporte, RIT), considerably improving the system's coverage and utility.

### Box 3.3. **Metropolitan transport authorities** (*continued*)

The URBS is responsible for the planning, management, operation and control of the transportation system in Curitiba. It defines routes, capacity and schedules; regulates and controls the bus system; and collects all fares. Bus operations are contracted to private sector operators. Fare revenues are pooled and paid to the contracted operators on the basis of the services provided.

*Source*: Aguilar Jaber, A. and D. Glocker (2015), "Shifting towards low carbon mobility systems", Discussion Paper 2015-17, International Transport Forum, Paris, available at: www.internationaltransportforum.org/jtrc/DiscussionPapers/DP201517.pdf.

One objective of particular relevance will be to harmonise the legal framework for mobility planning in the ZMVM. This can help avoid a situation where municipalities in the State of Mexico and Hidalgo lag behind improvements realised in the Federal District. The COMETRAVI should also prioritise the development of a mobility master plan for the ZMVM.[58] Box 3.4 describes elements that, according to international experience analysed by the International Union of Public Transport (Union Internationale des Transports Publics, UITP), have proven to be essential in master plans for improving urban mobility. All elements of this structure should be included in the master plan developed for the ZMVM.[59]

### Box. 3.4. **A common structure for developing successful integrated mobility plans**

The International Union for Public Transport (Union Internationale des Transports Publics, UITP) develops action points, sets of recommendations in specific fields of public transport policy. As part of this work, the institution has analysed international experience in developing integrated mobility plans and identified the following elements as essential for such planning tools:

- Vision: The long-term political vision of the city/region, including the future role of sustainable mobility.
- Context: Setting the scene, detailing the transport geography of the area and studying the integration with land use and other policy areas, including plans for growth.
- Challenges and strategic policies: Outlines the challenges that need to be overcome, through clear objectives, supported by an analysis of future scenarios. Policies are also developed to support the achievement of these objectives through the delivery of the strategy.
- Transport proposals: Sustainable multimodal transport proposals to deliver the strategy's objectives and overcome future challenges.
- Expected outcomes: An analysis of the impact of the transport proposals on delivering the objectives.
- Implementation plan: Short-, medium- and long-term plans for delivery.
- Costs and resourcing: Identifying funding sources for the strategy.
- Monitoring and reporting: A framework of indicators and targets to measure the strategy's performance.

*Source*: UITP (2014a), "Action points for the public transport sector. Connecting people and places. Integrated mobility plans for sustainable cities", Union Internationale des Transports Publics, Brussels, available at: www.uitp.org/sites/default/files/cck-focus-papers-files/AP%20-%20Integrated%20mobility%20EN_0.pdf.

One of the main principles to consider is that any mobility plan will have to be integrated with spatial and economic development strategies (UITP, 2014a). In London, for example, the "Mayor's Transport Strategy (MTS) is a statutory document, developed alongside the London Plan and Economic Development Strategy (EDS), as part of a strategic policy framework to support and shape the economic and social development of London over the next 20 years" (GLA, 2010).[60] Close co-ordination between these strategies has made it possible to build a decision-making framework that ensures that transport is built to serve key development areas. The viability of creating transport links also influences decisions on urban development. For instance, construction at Battersea in Central London was supported by the recent approval of an extension of the Northern Line of the London Underground.

Long-term mobility and spatial plans will require close co-ordination between COMETRAVI and the Commission for Human Settlements (COMETAH), which is in charge of generating the ZMVM spatial development plan. Efficient mechanisms will be needed to ensure that transport and development projects effectively follow the plans developed. In Paris, only projects included in the PDU (see Box 3.3) are subject to financing. In London, all development projects that do not conform with the development plan are automatically required to produce a transport assessment (which is normally only required for large projects considered to have major transport implications).

Development of mobility and spatial plans will also require adequate data, including regular metropolitan-wide origin-destination surveys, and models capable of simulating land-use and transport interactions for the entire ZMVM. Box 3.5 describes the principal models used by Transport for London to carry out such simulations. A major role of the COMETRAVI and the COMETAH will be to co-ordinate metropolitan-wide data collection and modelling.

### Box 3.5. **Strategic models used by Transport for London for modelling land-use and transport interaction**

The following are the modelling tools Transport for London has developed to guide transport planning and investment:

- The London Transportation Studies Model (LTS): A model that uses population and employment forecasts and other inputs to forecast the number of trips to be made in London in the future, where people travel to and from, when they travel and which transport mode they use.
- The London Land-Use and Transport Interaction Model (LonLUTI): A model that predicts the use of land for different human activities, depending on government policies and transport investment.
- Rail plan Public Transport Assignment Model: A public transport model that predicts the public transport mode (e.g. rail, underground, bus) and route that passengers choose to get to their destination, as well as the associated crowding impacts.
- Highway assignment models (HAMs): Five models covering the whole of London, which predict the routes drivers choose and the impact of the associated congestion and delay on London's roads.
- The London Regional Demand Model (LoRDM; still under development): A demand-balancing model that is similar to LTS but uses the HAMs and Rail plan to model the choice of route.

*Source*: TfL (2014a), "TfL's strategic transport and land-use models", Transport for London, London, available at: https://tfl.gov.uk/cdn/static/cms/documents/tfls-strategic-transport-and-land-use-models.pdf.

Effective co-ordination will also be needed between the Environmental Commission for the Megalopolis (CAMe) and the restored COMETRAVI. This will allow the COMETRAVI to build on the CAMe's actions on the standardisation and improvement of mobility policies linked to air quality and the environment. It will be important to make sure that the studies and proposals developed by the CAMe (e.g. analysis for possible implementation of low-emission schemes) are harmonised with the transport master plan and other actions carried out by the COMETRAVI.

### *Readjust and strengthen federal financial incentives for metropolitan mobility projects*

Existing financial incentives from the federal government can be powerful tools to encourage metropolitan co-ordination, if adequately adjusted. Box 3.6 provides international examples, which show that linking national funds to urban planning can significantly improve urban transport and land-use planning. By this logic, the functioning of the Metropolitan Fund (FM) and the federal programme supporting mass transit (PROTRAM) could be significantly improved by requiring metropolitan zones to turn in spatial and transport master plans and to justify that the projects to be funded are a high priority. This would increase incentives for carrying out metropolitan-wide planning instruments and would avoid cases such as Mexibús Line 4, where funds from PROTRAM have been granted and invested but the project has been suspended because of disagreements between the Federal District and the State of Mexico over its implementation. Clear guidelines showing what master plans need to contain could be drawn up (referring to the elements in Box 3.4 for transport master plans).[61] Since this framework might take time to build, a schedule for gradually meeting all requirements could be introduced into both the requirements for the FM and PROTRAM.

#### Box 3.6. **National financial incentives for co-ordinating urban transport and land-use planning**

Linking national urban transport funds to integrated urban planning has proven useful to increase co-ordination of urban transport and land-use planning.

- In **India**, this has been facilitated by national funds made available for urban transport projects as part of a larger urban development project led and funded by the Ministry of Urban Development, the Jawaharlal Nehru National Urban Renewal Mission (JnNURM). In order to be eligible for funding under the JnNURM, projects have to be part of a comprehensive city development plan.
- In the **United States'** New Starts Program, project sponsor agencies are required by the Federal Transit Administration (FTA) to submit information of existing land use, transit-supportive plans and policies, performance and impacts of policies.
- In **Germany**, planning procedures involving interest groups and the public are part of the requirements to national funds for urban transport projects. Developing an environmental impact assessment and a cost-benefit analysis are part of these requirements.

*Source*: Aguilar Jaber, A. and D. Glocker (2015), "Shifting towards low carbon mobility systems", Discussion Paper 2015-17, International Transport Forum, Paris, available at: www.internationaltransportforum.org/jtrc/DiscussionPapers/DP201517.pdf.

A relevant challenge for adjusting the FM and PROTRAM frameworks in this direction will be to build the adequate expertise to evaluate the coherence between project proposals and priorities of master plans (as well as creating the guidelines for such evaluation).[62] This expertise could be created within the Ministry for Agricultural, Territorial and Urban Development (SEDATU), the leading agency for urban development, and sustainable urban transport, at the federal level. An evaluation of transport project proposals to be funded by the FM and PROTRAM carried out by SEDATU could offer a double benefit: making sure resources from these funds are used for metropolitan-wide sustainable and inclusive mobility objectives, and providing SEDATU with rich and standardised information about mobility in different metropolitan zones and cities across the country. This would constitute an important input for developing the National Sustainable Urban Mobility Strategy (EMUS).

Increasing the funds of both the FM and PROTRAM, as well as allocating significant resources to the Programme to Promote Sustainable Urban Mobility will help incentivise metropolitan planning. Finally, given the pressing need to build expertise in metropolitan commissions, resources from the FM would be particularly useful for supporting permanent technical teams within the metropolitan commissions, including COMETRAVI. Having technical expertise within the CAMe has been useful for providing leadership in co-ordinated project implementation, creating regional-wide evaluation tools and developing common strategies.

### *Build common frameworks for implementing mobility projects and share good practice guidelines*

The implementation of transport projects by the different entities in the ZMVM needs to be carried out under a common framework that facilitates physical, operational and financial integration, especially for projects in the same mode of transport (such as Metrobús and Mexibús). Having a common framework will make it easier to undertake metropolitan-wide projects (e.g. BRT corridors). This is unmanageable at present because of the different configurations of public-private participation, institutional structure of regulatory bodies, and legal conditions for granting concessions, among other things. Sharing knowledge between governments and building common good practice guidelines in areas such as rules of operation, feasibility studies, granting concessions and evaluation, will also help governments improve and homogenise quality and safety standards in the metropolitan transport system. Co-operation between entities in the ZMVM and with the federal government is key for expanding the network of longer distance trains (commuter as intercity rail), which could improve mobility not only in the ZMVM but in all of Mexico.[63]

Finding an adequate institutional configuration for the underground is a first-order priority for advancing the sustainable and inclusive mobility strategy. It is vital to restructure the framework so that the State of Mexico has planning and financial responsibility over infrastructure constructed in its territory. Any arrangement decided upon will need to allow for seamless connections (physical, operational and fare-wise) between underground services in the different entities.

### *Co-ordinate a reconfiguration of transport services at metropolitan scale*

Metropolitan transport planning should attempt to reduce unnecessary transfers for metropolitan trips. The requirements for compulsory transfer of passengers at Federal District borders should be revised. State-level entities should also aim to reconfigure transport routes to conform to origin-destination demand. This will allow for a more efficient allocation of routes in each administration, avoiding duplication of services in some areas while others are poorly served.

Institutionalising agreements for inter-state services will help reduce opportunities for corruption and extortion between concessionaires that negotiate informal agreements. A redistribution of transport routes, taking into account origin-destination dynamics in the ZMVM, will help governments identify new modal transport nodes that should be recognised as CETRAM and where infrastructure improvements and urban redevelopment projects can promote transit-oriented development.

#### *Harmonise vehicle fleet standards and enforcement*

These should be aligned with the most stringent regulations in the ZMVM, to secure significant benefits and prevent leakage from jurisdictions with stricter regulation. Regulation of the vehicle fleet needs to be consistent throughout the ZMVM, from the perspective of both standards and enforcement. This is essential if the incentives for modal shift, earlier fleet renewal, and improving safety and environmental standards are to be effective. Harmonising the regulation of the vehicle fleet will not only prevent owners from changing the registration of their vehicles to avoid meeting the most stringent standards, but will also preserve the revenues of administrations that are pursuing more active regulation.

The CAMe has played an important role in advancing harmonisation of vehicle regulation and enforcement between jurisdictions, not only within the ZMVM, but throughout the megalopolis. Progress in standardising the inspection and maintenance programme has been accompanied by an agreement from all the states in the megalopolis to allocate revenues to help fund activities for future progress. While political support has allowed the CAMe to set this framework up in a relatively short time, introducing legally binding mechanisms for continued co-operation will ensure continuity should the political climate change.

### ***Aligning public and private agents to develop coherent policies and projects***

#### *Ensure co-operation between mobility and urban development authorities to advance initiatives that encourage transit-oriented development*

The mobility impact assessment introduced by the new Mobility Law for the Federal District is an opportunity to improve evaluation of the mobility impacts of urban development and to link spatial planning to transit-oriented development goals. According to the Ministry of Mobility (SEMOVI), the new mobility impact assessment will analyse public transport, walking and cycling, as well as road connectivity. To avoid duplicating proceedings and charges for developers, the mobility impact assessment should replace the existing road and transport component of the urban impact assessment, which is required by the Ministry of Urban Development and Housing (SEDUVI). To realise the potential benefits of this improvement, SEDUVI and SEMOVI will need to make sure that the process for awarding construction authorisations is linked to the approval of the mobility impact assessment. It is also important that SEMOVI uses some of the funds, which according to the new law, are hypothecated for the Public Fund for Mobility and Road Safety, to build the expertise required for evaluating the mobility impact assessment.

The State of Mexico and Hidalgo, where sprawl is rapidly increasing, would also need to adjust their transport assessment tools. At present, these are focused on the evaluation of road connectivity and traffic flows, rather than on a multimodal appraisal of the feasibility of connecting developments through public and non-motorised transport. In the State of Mexico, expanding the Ministry of Communications' evaluations to cover analysis of public and non-motorised transport accessibility can automatically help align the construction permit-granting process with transit-oriented development goals. At present a favourable opinion from the Ministry of Communications is needed for granting construction authorisations. As in the Federal District, multimodal assessment tools for evaluating transport impacts of urban development in Hidalgo will need to be accompanied by a mechanism that binds decisions on construction permits to the result of such assessments. Improving the assessment tools needs to be carried out while ensuring co-ordination between state-level entities to achieve consistency across the ZMVM. Transparency in developing mobility assessments and in applying for construction permits in general is necessary. In the United Kingdom, a guiding document (*Guidance on Transport Assessment*) is publicly available to help developers understand the type of assessment they need to turn in, the elements it needs to include and the role of the different public agencies involved in the process. Such transparency in the role of municipal- and state-level agencies, and good co-ordination between them, is particularly important in the State of Mexico and Hidalgo, where municipal governments usually receive the documents from the public but pass them on for evaluation by state-level agencies.

Information required from developers through mobility impact assessments should take into account best international practices. Table 3.6 summarises the main studies required from developers included in the UK framework and notes the need for strong analytical capacity in authorities evaluating this instrument. In the United Kingdom, transport statements are required for developments considered to have relatively small implications, but transport assessments are obligatory for developments likely to have more impact.[64]

### *Strengthen expertise in appraisal and decision making on CETRAM modernisation projects*

The modernisation of transfer nodes is highly technical and involves cross-sectoral goals (e.g. development of neighbouring areas, seamless connectivity, positive environmental impact, etc.). This demands a strong framework for co-ordinating all stakeholders. The *Guidelines and Criteria for Proposals for the Reorganisation of Modal Transfer Centres* issued by SEDUVI in 2014 are a solid starting point to help authorities and private partners build expertise in designing projects in accordance with principles of accessibility and transport-oriented development (see Government of Mexico City, 2014c). These guidelines could be further developed to include case study references and examples that can increase expertise in evaluating private proposals. The *Mobility Hub Guidelines* issued by the transport agency of Ontario, Canada (Metrolinx) provides relevant starting material. It is also crucial that authorities in the State of Mexico and Hidalgo develop similar guidelines, to ensure coherence across the metropolis.[65]

CETRAM modernisation needs to be accompanied by complementary actions, such as restructuring transport routes or urban renewal in adjacent areas. Additional guidelines could help identify responsibilities and co-ordinate the actions of different government agencies. The SEDUVI guidelines identify the actions needed for certain objectives and principles. They also indicate whether each action is the responsibility of the private stakeholder making the proposal. These guidelines should be further developed to assign clear responsibilities to the multiple public stakeholders for carrying out the complementary actions necessary.

Table 3.6. **Minimum requirements in transport statements and assessments in the United Kingdom**

| Type of evaluation | |
|---|---|
| Transport statement | Transport assessment |
| **Existing site information** | |
| – A site location plan of the proposed development site in relation to the surrounding area and transport system<br>– The permitted and existing use of the site<br>– A detailed description of the existing land uses in the vicinity of the site<br>– Whether the location of the site is within or near a designated air quality management area (AQMA)<br>– Any abnormal load uses of the current site | |
| **Baseline transport data** | |
| – Qualitative description of travel characteristics, including pedestrian and cyclist movements and facilities<br>– Existing public transport provision<br>– Description and functional classification of the highway network<br>– Analysis of the injury accident records on the public highway of the site | – Quantification of trips and modal distribution<br>– Existing public transport facilities<br>– Parking facilities<br>– Pedestrian and cyclist traffic<br>– Description and functional classification of the road network<br>– Current traffic flows on links and at junctions<br>– Current personal injury accident records for the study area<br>– Summary of planned transport improvements (including type, implementation schedule and sponsoring agency)<br>– Current peak periods on adjacent road network<br>– Levels for air quality and noise for the highway network<br>– Baseline carbon emissions data, by mode |
| **Additional detailed evaluations** | |
| Not needed | Public transport assessment[1] |
| Not needed | Walking/cycling assessment[1] |
| Not needed | Road network assessment[1] |
| Not needed | Traffic data and forecast |
| Not needed | Safety considerations and accident analysis |
| **Proposed development** | |
| – Plans and drawings showing site location, layout and use<br>– Proposed land use<br>– Scale of development<br>– Main features (layout and access points)<br>– Trip generation and modal distribution<br>– Qualitative and quantitative analysis of travel characteristics proposed<br>– Proposed improvements to site accessibility via sustainable modes of travel<br>– Transport impacts of site construction works<br>– Proposed parking strategy | – Plans and drawings showing site location, layout and use<br>– Proposed land use<br>– Scale of development and site area in hectares<br>– Hours of operation<br>– Proposed access and servicing arrangements<br>– Traffic impacts of site construction works<br>– Proposed parking strategy<br>– Development phases |

*Notes:* 1. The three assessments serve as an input for determining modal split and travel plan objectives at a later stage of the transport assessment process. They also serve for determining public transport, non-motorised infrastructure and vehicular capacity enhancements needed as part of the mitigation package.

*Source*: OECD, based on UK Department for Transport (2007), *Guidance on Transport Assessment*, The Stationery Office, London, available at: www.gov.uk/government/uploads/system/uploads/attachment_data/file/263054/guidance-transport-assessment.pdf.

### *Improve institutional arrangements for co-ordination between agencies in charge of public transport*

These should synchronise routes, schedules and information, as well as achieve fare integration for multimodal and multi-segment trips. Improving co-ordination of the institutions responsible for different public transport modes in state-level administrations is essential for achieving an integrated public transport system. Significant progress has to be made in synchronising routes, schedules and information. Integrating all modes into the new smart cards is also essential. In the State of Mexico, the introduction of smart cards requires effective ticket integration, rather than a system with multiple cards (as in the case of Mexibús). Increasing regulation of the bus sector is essential for fully integrated public transport services, since most bus operations are still carried out by microbuses, with fares collected directly by drivers.

Integration of the public transport system in the ZMVM will involve more than a single card for different transport modes, and needs to allow users to pay a single fare for multi-segment and multimodal trips. In São Paulo, Brazil, for instance, introduction of the smart card was accompanied by the introduction of a time-based arrangement that allowed passengers to pay one fare and transfer as many times as needed between bus and underground services over a period of two to three hours. The origin-destination survey conducted some years later suggested that this was one of the main reasons the city was able to reverse a trend of rapidly increasing private transport shares in detriment of public transport use (UITP, 2013).

### *Make sure that new institutional configurations for integrating public transport have the financial and human resources to take well-informed decisions*

Achieving the proposed mandate of the Committee for the Integrated Public Transport System would be a significant step forward in integrating public transport in the Federal District. Given the complexity of issues involved (e.g. technological proposals for centralised fee collections, performance evaluation, development of guidelines, etc.), it is important to complete the proposed framework with designated, regular staff who can build expertise and conduct the research necessary for the committee to take well-informed decisions (especially since its members are high-level officials with many other responsibilities). As the example of Transport for London suggests, SEMOVI's planning department would be a good location for this staff, and providing the necessary resources is key.

### *Match efforts to improve public and non-motorised transport travel with efficient transport demand management*

Adequate pricing and regulation of parking is a priority. Efforts to improve conditions for public and non-motorised transport use will need complementary transport demand management policies to discourage private transport. While congestion charges or low-emission zones can be useful demand management tools, a more immediate priority is to align parking regulation and pricing with the new mobility policy. The *ecoParq* programme has shown positive results, and expansion of parking meters to the rest of the Federal District and across municipalities in the State of Mexico and Hidalgo would be an important step forward for the ZMVM. On-street parking charges are only one of a wide range of strategies that can be used to regulate parking. As international experience shows, significant results will only be obtained with an integrated parking plan using various complementary strategies for parking management and pricing. Box 3.7 describes the range of parking regulations used in Amsterdam, which include on-street parking charges with prices differentiated by city zone.

### Box 3.7. Integrated parking management strategy in Amsterdam

Amsterdam has implemented an integrated parking management strategy composed of a wide range of instruments. A list and explanation of each of the components follows:

- Zone-specific rates: There are three types of zones: blue zones, 10-cent zones and pay-and-display (P&D) zones. The blue zones are free and are used for short-term parking. The 10-cent zones are also used for short-term parking (to a maximum of one hour). The hourly rates for the metered zones (P&D) are between USD 1.10 and USD 6.40, and rates go up the closer the space is to the city centre.
- Residential permits: Parking cap management in central residential zones gives residents the option of buying a parking space. As an alternative, residents can wait for someone to give up, or sell, or exchange a residential parking permit for an annual public transport pass.
- Park-and-ride: Parking spaces on the outskirts of the city cost about USD 7.70 and include a 24-hour public transit pass for up to five people.
- Payment and monitoring technology: Pay-by-mobile-phone service was introduced in 2006. The system is managed by private companies, which are paid a fee of 4-5% of the revenue collected by the city. In addition, parking meters are gradually being replaced by license plate recognition technology.

*Source*: IDB (2013), *Practical Guidebook: Parking and Travel Demand Management Policies in Latin America*, Inter-American Development Bank, Washington, DC, available at: http://publications.iadb.org/bitstream/handle/11319/3577/PracticalGudebookParkingLaSinglePage20131207.pdf;jsessionid=6C19B9E8CD8B53AF95DCF6AC3544A0CB?sequence=5.

In developing a new integrated parking plan for the entities in the ZMVM, particular attention needs to be given to the following issues:

- Guidelines for the optimal amount of parking spaces in different areas of the ZMVM need to be generated by state-level authorities. This will allow the decisions of municipal authorities to be aligned with overall mobility policy. Methodologies for developing such guidelines should build on the experience of international cities that have aligned parking regulations with sustainable and inclusive mobility goals. This suggests that parking space regulations should reduce supply where density and land-use mix is higher, and public transport, walking and cycling facilities are available (Litman, 2013). Parking caps have been implemented in business districts of Zurich and Hamburg that have good access to public transport (Litman, 2011). Achieving results will require co-ordination of on- and off-street parking and coherence between guidelines set by the three states of the ZMVM.
- Prices set for parking should reflect not only the infrastructure needed and the cost of managing parking services, but the opportunity cost of allocating scarce public space to parking rather than other uses. Prices should also incentivise behaviour in line with policy objectives promoting the use of public and non-motorised transport. Efficient parking pricing is a highly effective tool. Evidence from cities around the world show that parking pricing can reduce the amount of parking required by 10-30%, and also reduce vehicle traffic (Litman, 2011). In San Francisco, smart parking meters with real-time fare adjustments have increased the effectiveness of variable-rate on-street parking pricing. These principles can already be used for off-street parking. For on-street parking, removing legal restrictions to allow flexibility in tariffs is essential.

- The current policy that establishes minimum requirements for parking spaces in development projects does not conform to sustainable and inclusive mobility objectives and should thus be eliminated. Abolishing such requirements is common practice in metropolitan areas seeking to shift from car-oriented to transit-oriented development. Examples include Denver, Colorado; Nashville, Tennessee; and São Paulo (ITDP, 2014d). In addition to abolishing minimum parking requirements, the ZMVM should explore alternative policies for regulating parking space in constructions to support current mobility policy. In some cities, like New York and Portland, Oregon, maximum parking spaces have been established in central areas of the city. In Paris, a maximum of one parking space for every 100 $m^2$ of construction has been established for housing developments. Policies regulating parking spaces in developments could also be linked to the availability of public transport, as in the case of Ottawa and Paris (ITDP, 2014d).

### *Building expertise for long-term mobility planning and evaluation of progress*

#### *Improve planning and monitoring tools, focusing on creating capacity to develop a long-term strategy*

Government agencies in charge of mobility need to develop long-term plans with a perspective of 20-25 years. Only in this way can governments create certainty about the effectiveness of strategies and avoid unanticipated effects. Strategies outlined in short-term programmes (the current six-year frameworks) should be the first steps for a long-term approach. All state-level programmes should conform with the mobility plan for the ZMVM (which should be developed through COMETRAVI). State-level mobility programmes should also include the elements described in Box 3.4.

Developing data collection and modelling expertise in mobility ministries and other relevant public bodies will be essential for developing long-term mobility plans. Centralising information collected by agencies in charge of different modes of transport in each state-level jurisdiction will be important. All the information can then be used on a metropolitan-wide platform. Data collection should take advantage of future fare integration initiatives to collect information on whole origin-destination travel, rather than trip segments only. Solid models based on long-term population and employment trends should be developed and used to decide on the projects that should be included in the mobility plans. This should also guide resource allocation. Modelling exercises conducted by public agencies in charge of mobility should be linked to metropolitan-wide models.

Detailed documentation for conducting *ex post* assessment of projects is needed to build expertise in policy and project implementation. This will improve insight into the impact of chosen strategies and indicate any adjustments needed. Clear indicators for measuring progress with also be needed, since only the Integral Mobility Programme (PIM) for the Federal District now establishes indicators to measure progress. The two states in the metropolitan zone could also benefit from such monitoring tools. In all cases, long-term targets should be set. Annual progress reports, like the one introduced for the Federal District by the new law, would also be useful for the other states in the ZMVM. The *Travel in London* yearly report is a good reference for a comprehensive tool of this kind (see TfL, 2014b).

Planning, monitoring and *ex post* assessment tools should help authorities identify how far mobility projects and policies are encouraging economic development and contributing to citizens' well-being. Indicators and assessment methodologies should therefore explicitly aim to measure the impact of mobility policies on economic development and the different dimensions of well-being, while explicit targets for improvement in these domains also need to be set. While convenience is a key element in the decisions of transport users, current transport evaluation methods worldwide tend to be more focused on measuring speed and price than comfort, convenience and reliability. This has systematically resulted in underinvestment in public transport service quality, which in turn makes public transport less attractive (ITF, 2015). The international evidence suggests that authorities in the ZMVM should evaluate the attractiveness of public transport and the value users assign to different dimensions of convenience.[66] The document "Valuing convenience in public transport" offers guidance on the key factors involved, as well as on methodologies for measuring convenience (see ITF, 2015).

## *Increasing regulatory capacity and expertise to continue bus reform*

### *Approach bus reform with an emphasis on building technical expertise in mobility authorities*

This is essential to justify greater governmental intervention in the public bus industry and to renegotiate operation rules without compromising the new bus schemes' financial sustainability. The ZMVM needs a sector-wide bus reform to achieve a well-integrated, high-quality and safe public transport system. This will not only mean renegotiation of rules of operation to expand the BRT projects, but renegotiating rules of operation in bus services beyond BRT corridors. The Federal District's new Mobility Law has explicitly opened the door with the creation of a new Regulatory Body for Transport (Órgano Regulador del Transporte, ORT), which will regulate bus services in corridors operating in exclusive lanes as well as in those with preferential right of way (BRS corridors). International cases of city-wide bus reform, as in Santiago de Chile, and previous experience with BRT implementation, suggest that success will depend on specialised staff who can progressively acquire the technical expertise to regulate and help justify government intervention.

One of the challenges of bus reform in the ZMVM will be for mobility authorities and new regulatory bodies to recover regulatory powers without compromising the new bus system's long-term financial sustainability. Institutions should build on the lessons learnt from previous BRT experience and the precedent set by Metrobús in offering tighter conditions in the latest corridor negotiations. Co-operation between existing and new regulatory bodies is essential. Financially sustainable conditions will be particularly important for negotiations in BRS corridors, since the RTP will not be running service in them (and RTP operations will not be able to cross-subsidise payments to private companies in the future). New regulatory bodies such as the ORT should build on public support for the BRT project already acquired.

### *Shift towards a bus regulatory framework with clear rules for granting concessions*

Priorities for the bus system include the creation of clear rules for granting concessions, as well as for setting and adjusting tariffs. This is essential both for renegotiation of existing BRT concessions (which are impending for several Metrobús corridors), and for new BRT and BRS corridor projects. The Metrobús and Mexibús frameworks remain subject to highly discretional negotiations between authorities and private parties in these two aspects. In addition to providing greater certainty for everybody involved, a framework with clear rules will allow authorities to allocate resources for purposes other than constant negotiations with bus operators.

Implementing a tendering process should remain a general objective. Effective competition will help authorities implement clear rules and secure certainty about achieving value for money. The authorities' decision not to implement competitive tendering processes for BRT and BRS corridors was intended to give incumbent operators the time to consolidate into professionally run, competitive companies. To increase certainty for operators and incentivise gradual preparation for competition, authorities need to define schedules for competitive tendering processes to be held (e.g. after the first period of concession expired, companies formed by incumbent operators would have to be subject to a competitive tendering process).

During the transition period, authorities can encourage incumbent operators to conform more closely to the operations they would need to abide by under competitive tendering:

- Companies formed by incumbent operators should be required to provide information allowing authorities to perform an assessment of their operational costs and ability to meet quality and safety standards.
- Authorities could introduce quality incentive contracts similar to those used by Transport for London (Box 3.8).
- Following the example set by Singapore's Public Transport Authority, the PTC, mobility authorities could introduce mechanisms to encourage efficiency in operations with a fare adjustment formula (Box 3.9). This would require periodical tariff adjustments in the bus system (addressed below).

### Box 3.8. **London's quality incentive contracts for bus services**[1]

Concession contracts stipulate a set of bonuses and deductions to bus service remuneration, depending on over- or under-compliance with the minimum performance standards established by the authority. Bonus and deductions payments are applied to performance on waiting time, driving quality, internal and external presentation of vehicles, and operated mileage. The contracts also establish an "extension threshold", rewarding compliance with specific minimum performance standards with an extension of two years in the concession.

Note: 1. A detailed description can be found on TfL (2008).

*Source*: OECD based on TfL (2008), "London's bus contracting and tendering process", Transport for London, London, available at: www.tfl.gov.uk/cdn/static/cms/documents/uploads/forms/lbsl-tendering-and-contracting.pdf.

In addition, the option of gradually introducing tendering for partial segments of the transport system should not be discarded, as it would: 1) provide authorities with benchmarking information on operation costs; and 2) enable authorities to cross-subsidise less-efficient segments assigned to incumbent operators until the efficiency gap was closed.

**Box 3.9. Formula for public transport tariff adjustment in Singapore[1]**

Singapore's Public Transport Authority (PTC) regularly adjusts public transport tariffs using a fare-cap regulation. A maximum fare adjustment cap is set according to an exogenous price index. The index is composed of a weighted average of the consumer price index, wages and a newly introduced energy price index. The three price indices are weighted according to the cost structure in the bus industry, and the weights are reviewed every three years.

An extraction productivity factor is then deduced from the cap. This deduction is calculated as a percentage of the profitability per employee (change in value-added per employee per unit of labour input) of the service provider. The PTC sets the productivity extraction for a fixed period (three years), based on a pre-set level of productivity improvement. Thus, to maintain or increase their levels of profitability, public transport operators need to meet at least this level of productivity improvement.

*Note:* 1. A full description of the tariff setting and adjusttment procedure in Singapore can be found at: www.mot.gov.sg/news/FRMC%20Report%201%20Nov.pdf.

*Source:* Fare Review Mechanism Committee (2013), "Affordable fares, sustainable public transport: The Fare Review Mechanism Committee Report", The Fare Review Mechanism Committee, Singapore, available at: www.mot.gov.sg/news/FRMC%20Report%201%20Nov.pdf.

### ***Boosting financial capacity by improving the methodology for granting subsidies and widening funding sources***

#### *Conduct regular, planned and modest public transport fare adjustments, and make clear to the public the corresponding service improvements*

Public transport services in the ZMVM need to replace the practice of maintaining fixed fares for long periods, followed by significant and unexpected increases. Regular, planned and small fare adjustments are preferable. Introducing this practice will be easier if fare adjustments are linked to clearly identifiable quality improvements. Shifting towards higher fares, reflected in higher quality, will be more effective in attracting users than low fares and poor services. Analysis of various underground networks globally shows that quality improvements have higher demand elasticities than lower fares (UITP, 2014b).

In the case of concessioned buses, regular tariff adjustments, linked to cost increases, will provide operators with greater certainty of recovering future costs. Introducing this mechanism will be an important asset for authorities to shift from negotiations based on ensuring fixed levels of profits and instead set remunerations based on cost structure.

#### *Replace generalised subsidies with targeted subsidy schemes and differentiated fares*

Use the new technologies in place, and existing poverty alleviation frameworks, to increase the effectiveness of targeted subsidy schemes. Public transport fare policies need to strike a balance between economic and social sustainability. Service provision should move away from granting generalised subsidies and instead set public transport prices at or near cost-recovery levels, while granting targeted subsidies to certain segments of the population. The World Bank has recently conducted research on targeted subsidies in cities in Latin America. Among the main conclusions is that developing better subsidy schemes for lower income populations in the region is now possible given the use of smart cards and better methodologies for defining and identifying beneficiaries. Mexican cities could benefit from the framework used by the *Prospera* programme to identify beneficiaries of public transport subsidies. In addition to subsidies targeted at lower income and other vulnerable groups, public transport services in the ZMVM should explore differentiated fares for peak and off-peak travel. Besides helping increase revenues, this should also help to reduce crowding at peak hours. Free public transport for the elderly could be limited to off-peak hours as practiced in the United Kingdom, outside London.

Elements for effective design and implementation of targeted subsidies in the ZMVM include: 1) clearly identifying who needs support; 2) understanding current travel and changes that would be caused by the scheme; 3) analysing the impacts of the new scheme in terms of both financial sustainability and accessibility; and 4) avoiding fraud and unintended consequences (World Bank, 2014). Box 3.10 describes a recently implemented targeted subsidy scheme in Bogotá that combines information from a poverty targeting system developed in Colombia with information from an electronic fare system.

### Box 3.10. **Targeted public transport subsidy in Bogotá**

In 2014, the District of Bogotá, in Colombia, implemented a transport subsidy programme that builds: 1) the introduction of a smart card technology for Bogotá's public transit system; and 2) the development of a national poverty targeting system and database (National System for Selection of Beneficiaries, or SISBEN). Individuals classified as "SISBEN 1 and 2 users" are eligible for a public transit subsidy equal to a 40% discounted fare, which is capped at 40 trips per month.

The smart card system allows the government to keep better track of the subsidies granted and is also efficient in targeting demand instead of supply. The process for users to become beneficiaries of the public transport subsidy is simple and fast. Users can register online or in a city service centre, and if their status as a SISBEN 1 or 2 user is confirmed, they can receive their smart card within three business days.

*Sources*: World Bank (2014), "Targeted subsidies in public transport: Combining affordability with financial sustainability", World Bank, Washington, DC, available at: http://siteresources.worldbank.org/INTURBANTRANSPORT/Resources/340136-1152550025185/Targeted-Subsidies-Public-Transport-Note-04-23-2014.pdf; SITP (n.d.), *Sistema Integrado de Transporte Público de Bogotá*, Bogotá, Colombia, www.sitp.gov.co/publicaciones/beneficios_de_transporte_para_personas_sisbenizadas_pub (accessed 6 July 2015).

### *Use progress on improving cost identification and affordability calculation methodologies to develop a transparent policy for subsidies of public transport*

Improving understanding of both operation costs and affordability should help develop clear policies on subsidies for public transport (both for concessioned and publicly operated modes). This will allow authorities to move away from: 1) continually allocating unexpected "temporary" funds to projects that had been expected to operate without subsidies (as in the case of BRT schemes); or 2) assuming levels of subsidies greater than the needs of large segments of the population, while straining budgets for necessary management and investment costs (as in the case of modes operated by the Federal District).

### *Enlarge the funding base for public and non-motorised transport projects by removing subsidies to private vehicles and extending the possibility of using betterment charges*

Authorities in the Federal District should make increasing use of betterment charges to fund projects for public and non-motorised transport. In the other two states, the introduction of betterment charges to fund this type of project would be a step forward. While exceptions based on social considerations could be considered, eliminating the subsidy for the vehicle ownership tax in all three entities is fundamental. Key to public acceptance will be conducting a communication strategy pointing out both the incoherence of this subsidy with inclusive and sustainable mobility goals, and the significant reductions it has meant for the underground budget in the case of the Federal District. These have amounted to about half of the gap between resources requested by the STC from the Federal District government and those granted by the latter in 2014. In the case of the State of Mexico and Hidalgo, making use of resources explicitly for public transport and/or non-motorised mobility projects, and communicating this to the population, would help gain public support. In the longer term, revising the current structure of the vehicle ownership tax for introducing environmental parameters would be desirable.

### *Explore funding sources used in cities worldwide*

New sources of funding for public and non-motorised transport projects that could be explored include funds from advertising space and/or private sponsorship to cover, for example, costs of the ECOBICI system. In Paris, these funds complement user charges in order to cover costs for the *Vélib* bike-sharing system (ITF, 2013). In London, a seven-year sponsorship from Santander has secured GBP 43.75 million for the shared bike system's expansion and maintenance. Another useful strategy would be to cross-subsidise public and non-motorised transport developments with charges introduced to road users. This could be done by imposing charges that account for externalities, such as congestion and air pollution from car use to current prices set for toll roads, or introducing charges corresponding to these social costs in certain roads that are currently toll-free. In the Seoul Metropolitan Area, for example, public transport improvements are funded by a congestion charge in a tunnel connecting the central and southern business districts (ITF, 2013). Finally, in addition to the proposed mobility impact assessment for developments, other mechanisms to improve co-ordination between urban expansion and transport planning can contribute to funding public transport projects. One example is the Community Infrastructure Levy used in London, which requires developers who want higher densities to help fund public transport.

## Federal transport projects and the Valle de México's sustainable and inclusive mobility goals

Future mobility in the ZMVM will be influenced by the construction of two major infrastructure projects planned and funded by the national government: a train from Mexico City to Toluca, and a new international airport.[67] Box 3.11 gives a brief description of the main features of each of the projects. The present section provides insights on key conditions, to ensure that both can contribute to inclusive and sustainable mobility goals in the Valle de México. Analysis and recommendations build on international experience of similar projects.

Box. 3.11. **Main features of the Mexico-Toluca train and the New Mexico City International Airport**

**The train from Mexico City to Toluca**

The Mexico City-Toluca train is one of the major transport projects included in the National Programme for Infrastructure 2014-2018. Operation is planned for 2017. The 57-kilometre rail corridor is expected to connect Mexico City and Toluca within 39 minutes from terminal to terminal, at a cost of MXN 53 (USD 4) per trip. The Mexico City terminal will be located in the underground Observatorio station, while the terminal in Toluca will be located in Zinacantepec. The itinerary will cover four intermediate stations. The first intermediate station will be situated in the business district of Santa Fe, in the Federal District. The other three intermediate stations will be located in municipalities of the State of Mexico outside the ZMVM, that are part of the Metropolitan Zone of Valle de Toluca (ZMVT). Travel between the Mexico City station, in Observatorio, and Santa Fe is expected to take five minutes, and tickets for this section will cost MXN 12 (USD 0.9) per trip. Projections prepared by the Ministry of Communications and Transport (SCT) estimate a total demand of 270 000 passengers a day, with the segment between Mexico City and Santa Fe accounting for 70 000 passengers per day. The SCT also estimates that the project will help cut about 13 000 trips per day on the Mexico-Toluca highway. An important characteristic of the project is that its construction is divided into three sections: two segments that correspond to infrastructure in each of the state entities and a tunnel linking the two through mountains along the border. Tendering for each of the segments is being conducted separately. While the project is an intercity train, its dimensions and expected flows between Mexico City and Santa Fe, as well as between the city of Toluca and its surrounding areas, define it as a commuter rail project as well.

**The New Mexico City International Airport**

The New Mexico City International Airport (NAICM) was planned to respond to the saturation of the current airport. The project will be located in Texcoco (in the eastern ZMVM) and will have an area of six times that of the present airport (4 431 hectares). The first phase of the project is planned to begin operations by 2020. In this first phase, the airport will be composed of one terminal and three runways. Demand for the new airport is projected to reach 50 million passengers per year (37 000 daily passengers). This is 50% higher than 2014 figures for the current airport (34 million passengers). A later phase of the project foresees expansion to two terminals and two satellites, operation of six runways, and a demand of 120 million passengers per year (329 000 daily passengers).

*Sources*: OECD, with information from SCT (n.d.), "Secretaría de Comunicaciones y Transporte", Mexico, www.sct.gob.mx/transporte-y-medicina-preventiva/transporte-ferroviario-y-multimodal/tren-interurbano-mexico-toluca (accessed 6 July 2015); GACM (n.d.), www.aeropuerto.gob.mx (accessed 25 June 2015).

### *The Mexico City-Toluca train will need complementary land-use strategies, high-quality public and non-motorised transport links, and coherent decisions about regional transport infrastructure*

To meet the expected demand and the goals for modal shift, and to make a contribution to transit-oriented development, the Mexico City-Toluca train will need: 1) a parallel land-use strategy; 2) a solid plan for ensuring seamless overall origin-destination trips, including easy access to stations; and 3) coherent regional infrastructure decisions to promote the train over car use. Experience worldwide shows that these three conditions have been key to the success of a wide range of rail projects, such as Washington, DC's Metrorail system (linking Washington, DC to suburban areas such as Arlington County), the Tokaido line of Japan's Shinkansen heavy-rail system (connecting Tokyo and Osaka), and metros in Copenhagen and Stockholm linking central cities to suburban areas (Cervero, 2009).

The land-use strategy should include adequate modifications to current density regulations and land zoning that would address the current low densities, underutilised land and limited commercial activity around several of the planned stations. A recent study commissioned by SEDATU and conducted by the Inter-American Development Bank concludes that densities around the train corridor in the segment located in the ZMVT are in general low when studied at a micro level. It also concludes that commercial activity and pedestrian flows in many areas along the ZMVT segment of the corridor are insignificant (BID, SEDATU, forthcoming). The case of Arlington County near Washington, DC shows that rail infrastructure can result in compact and mixed land-use areas (the Metrorail Orange line in that case). However, this example highlights the importance of carefully analysing current conditions for the Mexico City-Toluca rail project and developing land-use strategies to ensure sufficient ridership. In the Washington, DC project, zoning classifications were changed after developing both county-wide and station-area plans that reflected necessary land-use, density and circulation systems around the project. Successful planning for growth around the rail corridor is indicated by Arlington County as having one of the highest shares of mass transit use in the Washington, DC region. In addition, the creation of both housing and commercial use has allowed the project to cope better with demand, since it created more balanced two-way travel flows (Cervero, 2009).

A solid plan for upgrading public and non-motorised transport links to the México City-Toluca train will be essential to ensure that it is competitive with car use. While the station-to-station travel times that will be offered by the train project are attractive, the expected modal shift will only materialise if complete origin-destination trips can be accomplished much faster than travel by car. The many accessibility limitations in the region will have to be addressed. Firstly, the ZMVT has a lack of mass transit services and an absence of infrastructure for cycling. Public transport demand is met by privately concessioned microbuses and vans, which operate under a deregulated system. As indicated in the case of the suburban rail, negotiating route modifications to ensure that concessioned microbuses connect with stations on the Toluca rail line will be a major challenge for the Ministry of Mobility of the State of Mexico. This could severely limit ridership. In addition, Toluca's roads along the rail corridor are notorious for their poor levels of safety and elevated exposure to risk (BID, SEDATU, forthcoming). In the ZMVM, Santa Fe has been developed around the car, and its new station risks poor accessibility by non-motorised and public transport unless this is planned for. For example, the Federal District should assign new BRS corridors to serve this area, co-ordinating with train schedules.

Prioritising investment in high-quality public transport, walking and cycling connections to the train could present a once-in-a-lifetime opportunity to shift from car-oriented mobility in the ZMVT and the Santa Fe region. This could contribute to tackling congestion, which in the case of Santa Fe has become a major issue affecting economic activity. Such a transformation would also greatly improve access for low-income residents and workers commuting to these areas. Careful analysis of full origin-destination demand patterns will shed light on the extent to which planned upgrades, such as the extension of a second underground line to reach the train station in Mexico City, can solve accessibility problems, especially at times of high demand. Projected park-and-ride facilities in terminals and stations along the project should be planned as an integral part of the multimodal accessibility strategy, with a special focus on effective traffic management and road safety improvements.

The design of the train stations and improved security in surrounding areas will be particularly important. The stations should be designed to accommodate peak period entrances and exits safely without overcrowding. Similarly, they should minimise walking distances and ensure good facilities for walking and waiting. Empirical evidence shows that walking and waiting in crowded conditions, and excessive walking distances, are a deterrent to using public transport in Tokyo, Seoul and Paris (ITF, 2015). Box 3.12 also shows some useful principles identified by researchers from the California Polytechnic State University and the University of Berkeley for encouraging accessibility in rail stations.[68] One issue to address for the Mexico City-Toluca train is safety of neighbourhoods around some of the stations. An urban renewal strategy will be needed in the area surrounding the Observatorio terminal in Mexico City, where the crime rate is high and informal commerce has invaded the underground station. Without improving safety around the Observatorio terminal, it will be hard to meet ridership forecasts, in particular for services between Mexico City and Santa Fe.

### Box 3.12. **Conditions for promoting accessibility in station area planning**

The following conditions are important for promoting accessibility in rail stations:

- Ensure availability of multimodal access to the station, including non-motorised modes for trips with origins and destinations in close proximity to the station and both shared and private modes for trips of longer distances.
- Determine where to place stops for different modes of transport by giving priority to the highest occupancy modes. The stops for modes with the highest occupancy should be located closest to the station platform or centre, while stops for modes with lower occupancy should be placed farther away.
- Plan for land use that requires frequent use of the station to be closer to it and place others successively farther away from the station platform (commercial vs. residential).
- Plan for densities to be higher in areas closer to stations and progressively decline in locations that are farther away.
- Create mixed-use corridors along axes that radiate from the station centre.

*Source:* Nuworsoo, C. and E. Deakin (2009), "Transforming high-speed rail stations to major activity hubs: Lessons for California", paper prepared for the 88th Annual Meeting of the Transport Research Board, January, http://digitalcommons.calpoly.edu/cgi/viewcontent.cgi?article=1045&context=crp_fac (accessed 25 June 2015).

The development of stations for the rail project will need a common regulatory and financial framework. Given the importance of station design in the success of rail projects, governments across the world have issued guidelines for their development. Examples include the *Station Design Principles for Network Rail* in the United Kingdom and the *Mobility Hub Guidelines* used by Metrolinx in Toronto, Canada. Authorities in Mexico City and the State of Mexico can build on the guidelines for CETRAM already developed by SEDUVI to include principles and strategies appropriate for the train. These guidelines would need to be adopted by the State of Mexico authorities. In financing the construction of these stations, those built in the Federal District territory will be able to implement a betterment charge. Reforming the fiscal framework in the State of Mexico to allow for betterment charge revenues would be useful for funding development of stations in this territory.

Seamless connections between the train and other complementary transport modes can also be fostered with initiatives to pay for urban transport services along with the train ticket. In the United Kingdom, for example, PLUSBUS is a discount bus ticket users can buy with their train ticket, giving users the right of unlimited bus travel at both ends of the train journey. These tickets are available in daily, weekly, monthly, three-month and yearly configurations (PLUSBUS, n.d.).

Parallel investments planned for increasing capacity in the Mexico City-Toluca highway should be assessed, taking into account their impact on demand for the train project and the expected modal shift. International implementation of rail projects demonstrates that high congestion levels in the area of implementation are a pre-condition for making rail attractive relative to cars (Cervero, 2009). Initiatives to alleviate congestion for road users in the Mexico City-Toluca highway should not be evaluated as being independent of the rail project or bringing additional benefits to it. Rather, modelling exercises should carefully analyse the impact that congestion alleviation in the highway will have on expected ridership and the potential to meet targeted modal shifts. Investing such resources in complementary public and non-motorised transport infrastructure is more coherent with objectives set for the project. By the same logic, the Ministry of Communications and Transport (SCT) and the Federal District government should reconsider the decision to place an elevated highway running above the train, since this is likely to reduce demand for the train and interfere with modal shift goals.[69]

Decisions on connecting the train to airports in the region should be taken in the light of potential changes in the air travel market. The current decision to connect the train to Toluca Airport by shuttle services rather than stopping directly at the airport terminal was taken based on current demand at the airport. However, analysing how much of the demand of the Toluca Airport (currently operating way below its capacity) is due to the lack of direct connections to Mexico City could shed new light on the way in which a direct link could benefit both the project and the airport. The potential for extending the train to connect Santa Fe with the New Mexico City International Airport should also be examined.

Developing complementary land-use strategies, adequate transport links and aligning infrastructure decisions will require co-ordinated planning among federal, state and municipal agencies. One limitation is that neither the ZMVM nor the ZMVT have metropolitan spatial and transport plans. The recent study commissioned by SEDATU provides relevant information on current characteristics of the population, land use and employment, but only in municipalities of the ZMVT surrounding the project. The train will act both as an interurban and commuting service, and an integrated diagnostic of the whole region, rather than a partial analysis, will be needed. Long-term forecasts of population and employment, as well as clear plans for future urban development, will be necessary. In addition, municipal-level development plans will have to be adapted to allow for the required land-use policies. Urban development regulations in municipalities of the ZMVT now impose major limitations on building high densities around the rail corridor (BID and SEDATU, forthcoming). Finally, clear division of responsibilities and authority between SEDATU, the SCT and local ministries will be essential.

The Mexico City-Toluca train will probably be the first of a series of rail projects connecting the ZMVM with various states in the megalopolis and a future nationwide passenger rail network.[70] In this context, it will be essential to build a solid long-term planning framework to ensure financial sustainability and regional benefits for rail projects. In Hong Kong, China for example, all railway development proposals (urban, commuter rail and links to mainland China) are carefully studied in terms of transport, land use, economic return, environmental impact and engineering viability (Transport and Housing Bureau, 2014). Projects considered in line with wider development goals and the *Planning Vision and Strategy* (the long-term spatial plan) are included in the Railway Development Strategy. This document serves as a development blueprint for the long-term railway expansion (whose current span runs until 2031). Detailed individual assessment of each project is carried out at a later stage, before moving forward with implementation. Projects are developed within a 20-year timeframe, so each project can undergo a robust planning process including public consultation, development of land-use policies, and timely planning of complementary public transport expansion and improvements. The Hong Kong, China government considers eight to ten years the period necessary for adequate planning and implementation of rail projects (Transport and Housing Bureau, 2014).

### *The New Mexico City International Airport requires a multimodal surface transport access plan*

The absence of a solid multimodal surface transport access plan for the New Mexico City International Airport (NAICM) may compromise the ambitious goals set for the project for improving economic, social and environmental conditions in the Valle de México. Airport authorities have extensive objectives for the airport, including becoming an international reference for sustainability, developing a regional hub, helping the Valle de México reach urban equilibrium, improving connectivity and mobility, and transforming the ZMVM into a polycentric, articulated and functional urban area.[71]

Policy makers and airport managers around the world are recognising that regional benefits from expanded airport capacity require planning for the impacts of the increased travel generated (TCRP, 2002). For major airports around the world, as at Heathrow, Sydney and Zurich, requests for expansion or building of new airports are required to be accompanied by a thorough assessment of the surface transport implications. Authorisation in these cases has been conditional on the development of a sustainable transport plan and commitment to significant public transport upgrades. Public consultation has also been a key input in the development of the transport plans for these projects. In contrast to international good practice, the NAICM project has not only been granted authorisation without a solid and publicly available sustainable ground transport access plan, but has initiated construction bids without this planning instrument. This has raised justified public concerns about the impact of the project on congestion, air quality and accessibility.

Addressing the urgent need to develop a sustainable surface transport access plan calls for solving the current gaps in co-ordination between governmental agencies and levels of government, and clearly setting responsibilities for each of them. The Ministry of Agrarian, Territorial and Urban Development (SEDATU), the national agency in charge of urban transport policy, hired experts to address surface transport access. More recently, the SCT initiated work to support the Airport Group of Mexico City (Grupo Aeroportuario de la Ciudad de México, GACM) in addressing surface transport access. Particularly since the development of the plan is behind schedule, it is essential that these two efforts complement each other and tenders for new studies build on analysis already developed for SEDATU. It would also be advisable for the SCT to reconsider the decision to open new tenders for studies only to local consultants. In view of the large scale of the project, opening tendering to include proposals from international experts should bring significant additional value. Finally, local transport authorities need to be formally included in formulating the transport plan for the NAICM project. In Los Angeles, for example, a member of the aviation staff was appointed to work closely with specialists from different modes of transport within the Municipal Planning Organization (MPO). The aim was to develop a Regional Transport Plan that included strategies to cope with the increased travel demand caused by airport expansion. The ZMVM has no body like the MPO, but a comparable taskforce could be set up. Given the emphasis on regional sustainable mobility, the restored COMETRAVI or the CAMe could provide one framework for this.

Development of a comprehensive transport plan for the NAICM will also need input from a formal public consultation process. While no formal public consultation process has been established, a Citizen Observatory has been created by three non-governmental organisations.[72] The initiative has synthesised public concerns about the project and generated a forum for discussions between experts in relevant domains (including mobility) and other members of civil society. Formal mechanisms for including this and other input from stakeholders and the general population in the transport plan are essential.

The surface transport access plan should take into account the congestion and limited accessibility faced by the current airport. The existing airport already suffers from the lack of solid strategies to encourage greater use of public transport by passengers and staff. The underground line to the current airport, which may potentially be extended to the new airport, skirts the central areas of the city. This involves a transfer at the busiest CETRAM in the city and travel on the busiest line in the underground to reach many of the main areas of economic activity and entertainment (CEMDA/CTS Embarq Mexico/IMCO 2015). The airport station is at some distance from the terminal building, with little pedestrian access. Apart from the underground, only one recently constructed Metrobús corridor connects the airport with the historic centre, and many areas of the city are unreachable by public transport within acceptable time and transfer conditions. The lack of data on origin-destination movements and the behaviour of both passengers and staff are an important limitation in plans for integrating the airport within an efficient mobility network. The limited amount of information provided so far by the government on access to the NAICM refers mostly to adjustments to road infrastructure and construction of toll roads. Public transport works planned include only extensions of two Metrobús lines and connection to underground lines that currently operate over capacity. The airport's planning process should acknowledge clear objectives to generate high shares of travel on public transport. The expansion of Heathrow Airport, for example, has increased the modal share of public transport in airport related trips from 30% to 40%. The recently approved expansion is expected to increase public transport use to over 50% by 2030 (Airports Commission, 2015). Better analysis of mobility trends generated by the existing airport and detailed modelling of future accessibility needs will be required to formulate a coherent, sustainable surface transport access strategy for the NAICM.

Authorities should carefully analyse the need to redesign the airport to achieve coherence with the developed surface transport access plan. The example of the Zurich airport shows that introducing ambitious objectives for sustainable travel is likely to require redesigning the airport facilities. In that case, the commitment to increase public modal share from 34% to 42% (a condition required for expansion approval) became "a driving force in the redesign of the airport, including the decision to place all of the new check-in facilities – 60 counters – within the rail stations and the addition of a shorter more direct walking path from baggage pick-up to the rail station" (TCRP, 2002). Going through the process of developing a sustainable land access strategy and conducting the required redesign will impose short-term costs on the NAICM project. However, these will pale by comparison with the costs that construction without this process will impose in the medium and long term. Added to the high social costs of increased congestion and air quality problems, the lack of easy access for passengers, staff and freight will severely limit the airport's potential for developing into a regional hub (and reaching the anticipated demand). As shown by many airports that are suffering from not having developed a sustainable land-access strategy, retrofitting existing infrastructure to promote public transport use is particularly costly.

## Conclusion

Car-oriented policies have brought high social, economic and environmental costs to the ZMVM, and thus authorities want to move towards a more sustainable and inclusive mobility system. Their efforts are reflected in a series of projects that promote walking and cycling, and prioritise allocation of road space and investment in favour of public and non-motorised transport. Planning and legal instruments linked to mobility policy have also been modified in the Federal District, to introduce principles of sustainability and inclusiveness. Locally driven initiatives have also coincided with a growing role of urban mobility in the national agenda. These efforts have laid important foundations and made considerable progress. However, the limited metropolitan co-ordination for developing mobility and spatial policy, and the lack of solid planning, regulatory and financial capacity of institutions in charge of mobility policy, impede further progress.

Metropolitan commissions responsible for supporting joint mobility strategies in the ZMVM need to be restored and strengthened (in particular COMETRAVI). They need adequate financial and human resources, and to be backed by legally binding mechanisms. In addition, federal financial incentives for metropolitan co-ordination need to be adjusted to ensure that projects are aligned with spatial and mobility metropolitan strategies. State-level authorities in the ZMVM will also need to co-operate to build common frameworks and good practice guidelines for projects, harmonising vehicle regulation and enforcement procedures, and reconfiguring transport services at a metropolitan scale. Improved co-ordination among public and private agents inside state-level entities is also crucial.

Efforts should focus particularly on: 1) ensuring that mobility and urban development agencies set efficient mechanisms to guide mobility and spatial planning towards transit-oriented development; 2) building a solid decision-making framework to guide modernisation of transfer nodes (CETRAM) towards improved access to public transport and significant urban renewal; 3) making sure that the multiple agencies in charge of different public transport modes co-ordinate and build expertise to synchronise routes, schedules and information, and integrate fares for multimodal and multi-segment trips; and 4) aligning improvements in public and non-motorised travel, with effective transport demand management tools (in particular setting efficient pricing and regulation of parking).

Agencies in charge of mobility policy need to move from short- to long-term planning, and the current six-year mobility programmes should constitute the first steps of a 20-25-year strategy. Adequate human and financial resources to improve expertise in data collection, modelling and *ex post* analysis is fundamental. Mobility agencies also need to continue bus reform, with an emphasis on building technical expertise, renegotiating operation rules without compromising financial sustainability, and setting a bus regulatory framework with clear rules for concession granting and tariff setting. Agencies in charge of mobility need to strengthen their financial capacity by conducting regular, planned and small public transport fare adjustments and substituting generalised subsidies with targeted subsidy schemes for lower income and vulnerable groups, and differentiating fares depending on distances or peak hours. Mexico City can also take advantage of its capacity to use betterment charges to fund public and non-motorised projects. Removing the generalised subsidy for the vehicle ownership tax can generate important resources for non-motorised and public transport projects. The ZMVM can also explore funding sources used in cities worldwide. Finally, national transport projects (e.g. the Mexico City-Toluca train and the New Mexico City International Airport) will require adequate urban infrastructure and land-use strategies to support attainment of sustainable and inclusive mobility goals in the ZMVM.

## Notes

1. Automobile-oriented refers to transport policies that favour automobile access and provide relatively inferior alternatives (VTPI, 2014).

2. In 2010, 74% of trips in all modes of transport, except for walking, realised in the ZMVM used public transport or bicycle (the latter accounting for 1%). While transport services like bus rapid transit and the commuting rail have been introduced in the past decade, most public transport trips are still on microbuses and *combis* operating under low safety and environmental standards. Such vehicles accounted for over 60% of total trips on public transport in 2010 (Government of Mexico City, 2012).

3. Population growth has been calculated based on data from the National Council for Population (CONAPO), while GDP per capita growth is based on data from the OECD *Metropolitan Database*. For further information, see Chapter 1.

4. This information has been provided by the Ministry of Environment of the Federal District and corresponds to the data collected through the inspection and maintenance programme conducted in the Federal District and the State of México. The number of vehicles differs significantly from the data reported by the National Institute of Statistics and Geography (INEGI), according to which there are 6.8 million vehicles in the ZMVM. The gap is presumably due, to a great extent, to the lack of accurate deregistration of vehicles that are scrapped or no longer in use, which is reflected in the fact that these vehicles are not enrolled in the inspection and maintenance programme.

5. The Institute for Transportation and Development Policy based its estimations for congestion costs using European time cost factors, due to the lack of specific estimates for Mexico (ITDP, 2012).

6. The costs estimated for traffic accidents include material costs as well as the estimated cost of deaths and injuries (ITDP, 2012).

7. Two features that strengthened the role of this commission were: 1) having a presidential decree for its creation; and 2) the agreement of state-level entities to impose an additional charge for gasoline, which was transferred to a trust to fund its activities. Nonetheless, the role of the CAMe (like that of other metropolitan commissions) has been limited by the lack of a legal framework with binding mechanisms for ensuring co-operation from state- and municipal-level governments. The metropolitan commission framework is explained in detail in Chapter 5.

8. The group of actions listed have been part of the PICCA and ProAire programmes. In the case of the vehicle restriction scheme, *Hoy No Circula*, considerable controversy about its effects on air quality improvements has arisen. Among other things, evidence has emerged that the scheme has resulted in both a large part of the population buying additional cars (which are used not only to substitute for the car that is not permitted to be used on a certain day), but also a significant acceleration of the fleet's renewal. Concerns about equity issues have also emerged, especially since the criterion for vehicle use has recently become more restrictive. The PICCA and ProAire programmes, as well as the *Hoy No Circula* scheme, are further addressed in Chapter 4.

9. Activities carried out by the CAMe will be supported by federal yearly funds (MXN 42 million in 2015), and a fund integrated with resources allocated by state-level governments from the inspection and maintenance programmes. This mechanism substituted for the funds allocated to the CAM from the gasoline charge.

10. Area integrated by the Federal District; the State of Mexico; and the states of Hidalgo, Morelos, Tlaxcala and Puebla.

11. The period from 1988 to 2000 witnessed significant slow-downs in expansion of the underground, and the system did not expand at all between 2002 and 2011 (Medina, 2013). The public enterprise Ruta 100 was dissolved in 1995, mostly because of financial problems, and the industry turned back to private operators. Only a small percentage of services was maintained under public domain through the public body (*descentralizado*) RTP (Flores-Dewey and Zegras, 2012).

12. A sixth corridor is currently under construction.

13. The next section of the report highlights key challenges that BRT schemes still have to address.

14. In this report, the word *secretaría* is translated as ministry (both for the agencies at the state-level and at the national level of government).

15. This ranking is the result of analysis conducted by the Ministry of Environment of the Federal District (SEDEMA) and last updated in February 2015. The criteria taken into account are the number of stations and bicycles. SEDEMA only took into account bicycle-share systems that had official data available. In the case of the People's Republic of China, this was only the case for Hangzhou.

16. By the end of 2014, Mexico City had 48 kilometres of dedicated bike lanes and 9.4 kilometres of lanes shared between buses and bicycles.

17. Table 3.4 is not meant to provide a literal translation of the articles of the new Mobility Law for the Federal District but to offer a summary and analysis of the most important changes that the introduction of this new law entails.

18. Article 166 of the Fiscal Code of the Federal District.

19. Through equal and consecutive payments.

20. The reduction from five to three areas considered as having direct impacts (and therefore the reduction of the total area of direct impact from 1 260 metres to 500 metres around the new infrastructure) was also part of the 2014 reform.

21. A betterment charge was levied in order to fund road and public space improvements in the neighbourhood of Polanco.

22. Another modification due to the reform is that financing expenses are now included in the calculation of total cost (Article 168 of the Fiscal Code of the Federal District).

23. Before 2013, this was the Ministry of Agrarian Reform.

24. The funding categories included in the 2015 budget also included the PIMUS, but no funding was allocated to it (ITDP, 2015b). As part of the process for receiving funds for the PIMUS, SEDATU needs to provide the Ministry of Finance with technical details on expected results from funds invested in the PIMUS (Cletofilia, 2015).

25. COMETRAVI was created in 1994 under an agreement between the federal Ministry of Communications and Transport and the governments of the Federal District and the State of Mexico.

26. The Metropolitan Fund is described in Chapter 5.

27. The last available origin-destination survey for the whole metropolitan zone is from 2007, and before that from 1994.

28. Since 2013, the National Housing Policy and the National Housing and Urban Development Programmes 2014-2018 have established new goals that aim to enhance co-ordination of urban planning and housing institutions; a sound and sustainable urban development model; the reduction of the housing deficit; and the procurement of appropriate housing solutions. A more detailed analysis on housing policy in Mexico can be found in OECD (2015). Further analysis on housing policies in the ZMVM can be found in Chapter 2 of this report.

29. The last origin-destination survey conducted showed that 4.4 million daily trips cross the State of Mexico-Federal District border (almost 20% of total trips). See PUEC-UNAM (2013).

30. Under current connectivity conditions, residents from Paseos de San Juan (located in Zumpango, in the State of Mexico) pay around MXN 12, the equivalent of three to four metro tickets or two Metrobús tickets, to get to the centre of Zumpango or Tecamac (both within a radius of less than 15 kilometres) and MXN 57 for a round-trip ticket to Mexico City. This means that, on average, residents in this neighbourhood have transport expenses of MXN 1 500 per month, which represents 80% of the average monthly payments for houses acquired in the neighbourhood. Based on various sources (inhabitants, commercial agents, transport service providers and field visits), it is estimated that 30-40% of houses in Paseos de San Juan are vacant (Negrete, and Paquette Vassalli, 2011).

31. In the Federal District, implementation of the BRT system entailed the creation of a public body in charge of managing, planning and controlling the BRT corridors (*órgano descentralizado*). In the State of Mexico, no similar body was created. In the Federal District, infrastructure construction costs are funded by the Federal District government, which has also remained in charge of the system's maintenance and management. Meanwhile, operation of the corridors is concessioned to private

companies. In the case of the State of Mexico infrastructure construction, maintenance and management is concessioned to the private sector.

32. Further details on the 1997 reform of the Federal District are provided in Chapter 5.

33. Harmonisation of the programme has been co-ordinated by the Environmental Commission for the Megalopolis (not only for the ZMVM but at the megalopolis level). By 2014, the CAMe achieved harmonisation of measuring methodologies and instruments across member states of the megalopolis. In July 2015, all the states in the megalopolis agreed to remove the age of vehicles from the criteria used in the inspection and maintenance scheme. Only emission standards now remain a parameter of the evaluation conducted through the programme.

34. The vehicle restriction programme classifies vehicles according to their compliance with emission standards, evaluated through the inspection and maintenance programme. Less stringent anti-corruption and monitoring programmes imposed in some states allow vehicles to be classified as less polluting than they really are. They are thus granted the right to be used for more days than if they were correctly classified.

35. The vehicle ownership tax is described in detail in Chapter 5.

36. These thresholds are those in force in 2015 (AMDA, 2015).

37. The Committee for the Integrated Transport system is described in Table 3.4.

38. In the case of this project, concessions were granted for the surrounding areas, but the administration of the CETRAM is still carried out by the Federal District government.

39. SEDUVI's guidelines for modernisation of CETRAM were published on 1 April 2014 and are available at: www.consejeria.df.gob.mx/index.php/gaceta.

40. In the Federal District, the rate is currently set at MXN 2.08 every 15 minutes (USD 0.15). In the State of Mexico it is set at 2.6% of the applicable minimum wage every ten minutes. This is equivalent to about MXN 1.8 or USD 0.08.

41. While regulations governing transport in the three states explicitly mention various technical criteria to take into account for setting tariffs, in practice, this process has involved intensive, time- and resource-consuming negotiations between the government and private operators.

42. Ruta 100, the public entity in charge of bus operations before privatisation required major public financial support.

43. The scrapping programme implemented by SEDEMA, for example, faced this limitation.

44. In the case of Line 3, for example, unfair competition from microbuses has made a significant difference in the effective demand. While the corridor was designed to serve between 130 000 and 140 000 passengers per day, it is now serving only 75 000 daily passengers.

45. The Mexibús fare is MXN 6 per ride, while the operational cost is calculated at MXN 8.5 (USD 0.45 and USD 0.63 respectively).

46. "Many operators overestimated their net income, ignoring unpaid taxes, non-existent insurance policies, high maintenance expenses, frequent bribes and their own salaries as drivers and mechanics" (Flores-Dewey and Zegras, 2012).

47. For example, loan reimbursement costs were not included in remunerations per kilometre in corridors implemented later. Authorities also adjusted remunerations by negotiating that costs that do not increase directly with travel would not be paid if operators travelled extra.

48. Since the RTP does not receive full payment from revenues of the Metrobúses it runs, its operations are subsidised by funds from Mexico City.

49. Meeting this condition is also a requisite for funding from PROTRAM.

50. In the case of Metrobús, public funds have been used to cover the RTP buses' operations as well as activities of the regulatory body.

51. While unfair competition in corridors and high arbitrary remuneration have contributed to the need for additional funding, there is no certainty that operations are cost-efficient.

52. All the elements mentioned were already included in the question.

53. Funds from the federal government are marginal (1.3% of total income in 2013).

54. As previously noted, this subsidy has been granted ever since this charge became a state-level tax in 2012. The value threshold over which vehicles are no longer eligible for the 100% subsidy is MXN 250 000 (USD 18 800) in the Federal District, MXN 350 000 (USD 26 300) in the State of Mexico and MXN 550 000 (USD 41 400) in Hidalgo.

55. Revenue from this tax is not hypothecated, while a high percentage of transfers from the federal government to the states are hypothecated funds.

56. Funds from the vehicle ownership tax are not formally hypothecated for supporting the underground, but the Ministry of Finance of the Federal District explained in interviews with the OECD delegation that income generated from this charge has been spent on supporting the underground system for several years.

57. Or an equivalent body, in case it is considered that reforms are needed to align the commission with the transformation of transport authorities into mobility authorities.

58. While the new Mobility Law for the Federal District considers implementation of a metropolitan programme for mobility, in co-ordination with bordering states (Article 12), there are no formal or legally binding mechanisms in place to ensure the development and implementation of such a programme.

59. The term master plan is here used as a general nomenclature. This planning instrument takes different names depending on the country. In many contexts the word "plan" is substituted by "programme".

60. The London Plan is the Spatial Development Strategy.

61. In the case of PROTRAM, the Intermodal Sustainable Urban Mobility Plan, which is currently required, could be the basis for developing the transport master plan. Its contents will therefore have to be adjusted to include all the elements, in line with best practice in developing transport master plans (see Box 3.4).

62. An important limitation of the current Intermodal Sustainable Urban Mobility Plan required in the PROTRAM framework is that these are not evaluated by a specialised team. The criteria for evaluating this requirement have been reduced to the turning in of the document, rather than to the evaluation of specific information and analysis in it.

63. Analysis of the Mexico City-Toluca rail project is provided in the next section of this chapter.

64. More information on the kind of projects that qualify for each type of study, as well as further details on each requirement and further processes in the framework can be found in the *Guidance on Transport Assessment*, developed by the UK Department for Transport, available at: www.gov.uk/government/uploads/system/uploads/attachment_data/file/263054/guidance-transport-assessment.pdf.

65. The Metrolinx Mobility Hub Guidelines are available at: www.metrolinx.com/en/projectsandprograms/mobilityhubs/mobility_hub_guidelines.aspx (accessed 18 August 2015).

66. Convenience is related to "absence of effort" in utilising transport services (ITF, 2015).

67. The city of Toluca is the capital of the State of Mexico. The Toluca metropolitan zone is composed of 23 municipalities in the State of Mexico.

68. While these principles were developed for high-speed rail stations, they are also useful for commuter and traditional inter-urban rail.

69. Co-operation between the Ministry of Communications and Transport and the Federal District government for both the Mexico City-Toluca train and the elevated highway projects was announced in 2014. See Government of Mexico City (2014d).

70. The Mexico-Querétaro train was already part of the National Infrastructure Programme 2013-2018, although it has been suspended indefinitely at present.

71. All these objectives are announced on the website of the NAICM project: www.aeropuerto.gob.mx.

72. Mexican Institute for Competitiveness (IMCO), CTS-EMBARQ Mexico and Mexican Centre for Environmental Law (CEMDA).

## *Bibliography*

AEP (n.d.), www.aep.df.gob.mx (accessed 2 July 2015).

Aguilar Jaber, A. and D. Glocker (2015), "Shifting towards low carbon mobility systems", Discussion Paper 2015-17, International Transport Forum, Paris, available at: www.internationaltransportforum.org/jtrc/DiscussionPapers/DP201517.pdf.

Airports Commission (2015), *Airports Commission Final Report*, Airports Commission, London, July, available at: www.gov.uk/government/uploads/system/uploads/attachment_data/file/440316/airports-commission-final-report.pdf (accesed 10 September 2015).

AMDA (2015), "¿Cómo quedaron las tenencias en 2015?", Asociación Mexicana de Distribuidores de Automotores, Mexico, D.F., www.amda.mx/index.php?option=com_content&view=article&id=598:como-quedaron-las-tenencias-en-2015&catid=73&Itemid=485 (accessed 11 August 2015).

BID and SEDATU (forthcoming), "Plan de Acción para la Integración Urbana y Funcional del Tren Toluca – México, D.F. en su travesía por la Zona Metropolitana del Valle de Toluca (ZMVT)", unpublished paper.

CEMDA/CTS Embarq Mexico/IMCO (2015), *Observatorio Ciudadano del Nuevo Aeropuerto de la Ciudad de México*, Instituto Mexicano para la Competitividad, A.C., Mexico City.

Cervero, R. (2009), "Urban development on railway-served land: Lessons and opportunities for the developing world", Working Paper, UCB-ITS-VWP-2009-13, UC Berkeley Center for Future Urban Transport, University of California, Berkeley, California, available at: www.its.berkeley.edu/publications/UCB/2009/VWP/UCB-ITS-VWP-2009-13.pdf.

Cletofilia (2015), "En manos de Murillo Karam presupuesto para proyectos de Movilidad Urbana Sustentable", 1 July, http://cletofilia.com/?p=324 (accessed 10 August 2015).

CTS EMBARQ México (2013), "Estudio de la reducción de emisiones y los co-beneficios generados por la implementación del Programa ECOBICI (2010, 2011, 2012)", May, Centro de Transporte Sustentable EMBARQ México, Mexico, D.F., available at: www.ecobici.df.gob.mx/sites/default/files/pdf/reduccion_gei_y_co-beneficios_generados_por_la_implementacion_del_programa_ecobici_201020112012.pdf.

Department for Transport of the United Kingdom (2007), *Guidance on Transport Assessment*, The Stationery Office, London, available at: www.gov.uk/government/uploads/system/uploads/attachment_data/file/263054/guidance-transport-assessment.pdf.

El Economista (2015), "Hasta agosto primer tramo de la Línea 12 del metro", *El Economista*, 12 May, Mexico City, http://eleconomista.com.mx/distrito-federal/2015/05/12/hasta-agosto-primer-tramo-l12-metro (accessed 15 June 2015).

Excelsior (2014) "Homologan verificación vehicular en la Megalópolis", Excelsior, Mexico City, www.excelsior.com.mx/comunidad/2014/06/19/965961 (accessed 29 September 2015).

Fare Review Mechanism Committee (2013), "Affordable fares, sustainable public transport: The Fare Review Mechanism Committee Report", The Fare Review Mechanism Committee, Singapore, available at: www.mot.gov.sg/news/FRMC%20Report%201%20Nov.pdf.

Flores-Dewey, O. and C. Zegras (2012), "The costs of inclusion: Incorporating existing bus operators into Mexico City's emerging bus rapid transit system", Department for Urban Studies and Planning, Massachusetts Institute of Technology, Cambridge, Massachusetts, available at: http://web.mit.edu/czegras/www/Flores_Dewey_and_Zegras_Metrobus_FinalDraft.pdf.

Flores, O., J.C. Muñoz and L. Paget-Seekins (eds.) (forthcoming), "BRT as tool for negotiated re-regulation", in: *Restructuring Public Transport through Bus Rapid Transit*, Policy Press, Bristol, United Kingdom.

GACM (n.d.), Airport Group of Mexico City, www.aeropuerto.gob.mx (accessed 25 June 2015).

GLA (2010), *Mayor's Transport Strategy: Executive Summary*, Greater London Authority, May, London, p. 6, available at: www.london.gov.uk/sites/default/files/MTS_Executive_Summary.pdf.

Government of Mexico (2014), *Programa Nacional de Infraestructura 2014-2018*, Presidencia de la República, http://presidencia.gob.mx/pni/consulta.php?c=1 (accessed 7 August 2015).

Government of Mexico (1999), "Acuerdo de la Comisión Metropolitana de Asentamientos Humanos, por el que se aprueba el Programa de Ordenación de la Zona Metropolitana del Valle de México", Secretaria de Desarrollo Social, *Diario Oficial de la Federación*, www.dof.gob.mx/nota_detalle_popup.php?codigo=4945401 (accessed 15 June 2015).

Government of Mexico City (2015), *ECOBICI 5 Años Cambiando la Movilidad en la CDMX*, Mexico City.

Government of Mexico City (2014a), *Ley de Movilidad del Distrito Federal*, Secretaria de Movilidad, Gaceta Oficial del Distrito Federal, available at: http://aldf.gob.mx/archivo-ba20960fb6570ec7d4ee34c30ee2d733.pdf.

Government of Mexico City (2014b), "Acuerdo por el que se aprueba el Programa Integral de Movilidad 2013-2018", Secretaria de Movilidad, *Gaceta Oficial del Distrito Federal*, 15 October, available at: www.ordenjuridico.gob.mx/Documentos/Estatal/Distrito%20Federal/wo99436.pdf.

Government of Mexico City (2014c), *Lineamientos y Criterios para la Presentación de Propuestas para el Reordenamiento de los Centros de Transferencia Modal*, Secretaría de Desarrollo Urbano y Vivienda, available at: www.alcani.com.mx/soporte/protocolus/DF/Arancel/JORNADAS_2014.pdf.

Government of Mexico City (2014d), *Convenio de coordinación de acciones que celebran por una parte el Ejecutivo Federal a través de la Secretaría de Comunicaciones y Transportes y el Gobierno del Distrito Federal, que tiene por objeto establecer las bases de coordinación de acciones y apoyo entre el Ejecutivo Federal por conducto de "LA SCT" y "EL GDF" para que en el ámbito de sus competencias y jurisdicción participen en forma coordinada para la implementación de "El Proyecto Ferroviario" y el "Viaducto Vehicular"*, available at: www.consejeria.df.gob.mx/portal_old/uploads/gacetas/73ba5f5175a8dd180f899e5f148fa5b5.pdf.

Government of Mexico City (2012), "Programa de ordenación de la Zona Metropolitana del Valle de México. Actualización 2012: Síntesis ejecutiva", Government of Mexico City, Mexico, D.F., available at: https://workshopcdmx.files.wordpress.com/2014/06/8-programa-de-ordenamiento_zmvmpdf.pdf.

Government of Mexico City (2010), "Acuerdo por el que se aprueba el Programa Integral de Transorte y Vialidad 2007-2012", Secretaria de Transporte y Vialidad, *Gaceta Oficial del Distrito Federal*, available at: www.transparencialinea3.df.gob.mx/normatividad/programa_integral_transportes.pdf.

Government of Mexico City (2005), "Decreto por el que se crea el organismo público desconcentrado Metrobús", *Gaceta Oficial del Distrito Federal*, http://cgservicios.df.gob.mx/prontuario/vigente/919.htm (accessed 15 June 2015).

Government of the State of Mexico (2015), "Sistema de Transporte Masivo y Teleférico, Gobierno del Estado de México", presentation given to the OECD delegation, April.

Heathrow Airport (2014), "Sustainable Transport Plan 2014-2019", Heathrow Airport Limited, Hounslow, Middlesex, United Kingdom, available at: www.heathrowairport.com/static/HeathrowAboutUs/Downloads/PDF/Sustainability/Heathrow_STP_inter.pdf.

Hernandez, U. and A. Ward (2015), "Shifting gears: Spatial analysis of Mexico City's ECOBICI bikeshare system", unpublished research poster, University of California, Berkeley, California.

IDB (2013), "Practical guidebook: Parking and travel demand management policies in Latin America", Inter-American Development Bank, Washington, DC, available at: http://publications.iadb.org/bitstream/handle/11319/3577/PracticalGudebookParkingLaSinglePage20131207.pdf;jsessionid=6C19B9E8CD8B53AF95DCF6AC3544A0CB?sequence=5.

ITDP (2015a), "Para entender la nueva Ley de Movilidad", Institute for Transportation and Development Policy, Mexico City, July, available at: http://mexico.itdp.org/wp-content/uploads/Para-entender-la-nueva-Ley-de-Movilidad-del-DF.pdf.

ITDP (2015b), "Con la reciente publicación de la estructura programática del PEF 2016, sabemos que la movilidad está incluida en sus programas", *ITDP México Noticias*, Institute for Transportation and Development Policy, 2 July, http://mexico.itdp.org/noticias/con-la-reciente-publicacion-del-pef-2016-sabemos-que-la-movilidad-esta-incluida-en-sus-programas (accessed 10 August 2015).

ITDP (2014a), *Caminar la Ciudad, Políticas de Seguridad Peatonal en la Ciudad de México*, Institute for Transportation and Development Policy, Mexico City, available at: http://mexico.itdp.org/wp-content/uploads/CaminarLaCiudad1.pdf.

ITDP (2014b), *Invertir Para Movernos, Diagnóstico de Inversiones en Movilidad en las Zonas Metropolitanas de México 2011-2013*, Institute for Transportation and Development Policy, Mexico City, October, available at: http://mexico.itdp.org/wp-content/uploads/Invertir-para-movernos2.pdf.

ITDP (2014c), *Megacentralidades. Propuesta de Integración de los CETRAM al Desarrollo Urbano de la Ciudad de México*, Institute for Transportation and Development Policy, Mexico City, available at: http://mexico.itdp.org/wp-content/uploads/Megacentralidades_final.pdf.

ITDP (2014d), *Menos Cajones, Más Ciudad – El Estacionamiento en la Ciudad de México*, Institute for Transportation and Development Policy, Mexico City, available at: http://mexico.itdp.org/wp-content/uploads/140922_FINAL_Menos-cajones-m%C3%A1s-ciudad.pdf.

ITDP (2012), *La Importancia de la Reducción del Uso del Automóvil en México: Tendencias de Motorización, del Uso del Automóvil, y de Sus Impactos*, Institute for Transportation and Development Policy, Mexico City, October, available at: http://mexico.itdp.org/wp-content/uploads/Importancia-de-reduccion-de-uso-del-auto.pdf.

ITF (2015), "Valuing convenience in public transport: Roundtable summary and conclusions", Discussion Paper 2014-02, International Transport Forum, Paris, April, available at: www.internationaltransportforum.org/jtrc/DiscussionPapers/DP201402.pdf.

ITF (2013), "Funding urban public transport: Case study compendium", International Transport Forum, Paris, available at: www.internationaltransportforum.org/pub/pdf/13Compendium.pdf.

Litman, T. (2013), "Parking management: Strategies, evaluation and planning", Victoria Transport Policy Institute, Victoria, British Columbia, Canada, 5 November, available at: www.vtpi.org/park_man.pdf.

Litman, T. (2011), "Parking pricing implementation guidelines: How more efficient parking pricing can help solve parking and traffic problems, increase revenue, and achieve other planning objectives", Victoria Transport Policy Institute, Victoria, British Columbia, Canada, 24 August, available at: www.vtpi.org/parkpricing.pdf.

Medina, S. (2014), *Santa Fe y Obras Viales: Cuando el D.F. Se Sometió al Desarrollo Inmobiliario*, Nexos, 30 September, http://labrujula.nexos.com.mx/?p=81#_ftn10 (accessed 21 August 2015).

Medina, S. (2013), "Reciclaje y aprovechamiento de nodos de transporte: El caso de los centros de transferencia modal ligados al metro", Universidad Nacional Autónoma de México, Mexico City, available at: http://132.248.9.195/ptd2013/junio/097529895/097529895.pdf.

Medina, S. (2011), "El transporte público en la Ciudad de México: Incentivos a la ineficiencia", *Distintas Latitudes*, 12 January, www.distintaslatitudes.net/el-transporte-publico-en-la-ciudad-de-mexico-incentivos-a-la-ineficiencia (accessed 5 July 2015).

Metrobús (2015), "Metrobús, movilidad sustentable", presentation given to the OECD delegation, 22 April 2015, Mexico City.

Metrolinx (2011), *Mobility Hub Guidelines for the Greater Toronto and Hamilton Area*, Metrolinx, Toronto, Canada, September, available at: www.metrolinx.com/en/projectsandprograms/mobilityhubs/MobilityHubGuidelines.pdf.

Mitofsky (2013), "Estudio de opinión, Sistema de Transporte Colectivo Metro, principales resultados", Consulta Mitofsky, Mexico, D.F., available at: www.metro.df.gob.mx/imagenes/organismo/boleto/mitofsky.pdf.

Molinero, A. (2014), "Situación actual del transporte urbano en México", Asociación Mexicana de Transporte y Movilidad, Mexico City.

Moody's (2011), "Comentario especial: La eliminación de la tenencia: Un factor crediticio negativo", Moody's Investor Services, Mexico City, 24 May, http://bmv.com.mx/eventoca/eventoca_moodys_1330_2796.pdf.

Negrete, M.E. and C. Paquette Vassalli (2011), "Interaction between public transportation and urbanization in the Mexico City metropolitan area: An expansive model reaching its limits", in: *Territorios*, Vol. 25, Universidad del Rosario, Bogotá, Colombia, pp. 9-14.

Nuworsoo, C. and E. Deakin (2009), "Transforming high-speed rail stations to major activity hubs: Lessons for California", paper prepared for the 88th Annual Meeting of the Transport Research Board, January, http://digitalcommons.calpoly.edu/cgi/viewcontent.cgi?article=1045&context=crp_fac (accessed 25 June 2015).

OECD (2012), "Mobilising private investment for bus rapid transit systems: The case of Metrobús, Mexico City", Towards a Green Investment Policy Framework – Case Study Series, Prepared by CTS EMBARQ Mexico, OECD, Paris, available at: www.oecd.org/env/cc/Case%20study%20Mexico.pdf.

PLUSBUS (n.d.), www.plusbus.info (accessed 2 July 2015).

PUEC-UNAM (2013), *Diagnóstico y Proyecciones de la Movilidad del Distrito Federal 2013-2018*, Universidad Autónoma de México, Mexico City.

Reforma (2015), "Analiza Naucalpan reactivar medidores", 19 July, www.reforma.com/aplicaciones/articulo/default.aspx?Id=594755 (accessed 11 August 2015).

RTP (n.d.), www.rtp.gob.mx (accessed 5 July 2015).

Rutzen, B., N. Hutson and L. Loftus-Otway (2010), "Mexico City, Mexico, commuter rail: Planning and implementation of a multi-jurisdictional, PPP project", in: *Transportation Research Record: Journal of the Transportation Research Board*, Vol. 2 146, pp. 119-126, The National Academies of Sciences, Engineering and Medecine, Washington, DC, http://dx.doi.org/10.3141/2146-15.

SCT (n.d.), Secretaría de Comunicaciones y Transporte, Mexico, www.sct.gob.mx/transporte-y-medicina-preventiva/transporte-ferroviario-y-multimodal/tren-interurbano-mexico-toluca (accessed 6 July 2015).

SEDEMA (2015a), "Proaire 2011-2020", presentation given to the OECD delegation, Secretaría de Medio Ambiente del Distrito Federal.

SEDEMA (2015b), statistics prepared for OECD, unpublished.

SEDEMA/CEMCA (2015), *Encuesta ECOBICI 2014 Principales Resultados*, Secretaría de Medio Ambiente del Distrito Federal, Mexico City.

SEMOVI (n.d.a), "Información Nochebús", Secretaría de Movilidad del Distrito Federal, Mexico City, www.semovi.df.gob.mx/wb/stv/nochebus.html (accessed 6 August 2015).

SEMOVI (n.d.b), "Comisión Metropolitana de Transporte y Vialidad", Secretaría de Movilidad del Distrito Federal, Mexico City, www.semovi.df.gob.mx/wb/stv/comision_metropolitana_de_transporte_y_vialidad.html (accessed 6 August 2015).

SITP (n.d.), "Sistema Integrado de Transporte Público de Bogotá", Bogotá, Colombia, www.sitp.gov.co/publicaciones/beneficios_de_transporte_para_personas_sisbenizadas_pub (accessed 6 July 2015).

STC (2013), *Informe a la Comisión de Movilidad, Transporte y Vialidad – VI Legislatura de la ALDF*, *Sistema de Transporte Colectivo Metro*, Mexico City, www.metro.df.gob.mx/organismo/informes.html (accessed 5 July 2015).

STE (n.d.), Servicio de Transportes Eléctricos del Distrito Federal, Mexico City, www.ste.df.gob.mx (accessed 2 July 2015).

Tarriba, G. and G. Alarcón (2012), "Movilidad competitiva en la Zona Metropolitana de la Ciudad de México: Diagnóstico y soluciones factibles", Instituto Mexicano para la Competitividad, Mexico, D.F., January, available at: http://imco.org.mx/wp-content/uploads/2012/1/costos_congestion_en_zmvm2_final_abril.pdf.

TCRP (2002), *TCRP Report 83 – Strategies for Improving Public Transportation Access to Large Airports*, Transportation Research Board of the National Academies, Washington, DC, available at: http://onlinepubs.trb.org/onlinepubs/tcrp/tcrp_rpt_83a.pdf.

TfL (2014a), "TfL's strategic transport and land-use models", Transport for London, London, October, available at: https://tfl.gov.uk/cdn/static/cms/documents/tfls-strategic-transport-and-land-use-models.pdf.

TfL (2014b), "Travel in London, Report 7", Transport for London, London, available at: www.tfl.gov.uk/cdn/static/cms/documents/travel-in-london-report-7.pdf.

TfL (2008), "London's bus contracting and tendering process", Transport for London, London, available at: www.tfl.gov.uk/cdn/static/cms/documents/uploads/forms/lbsl-tendering-and-contracting.pdf.

Transport and Housing Bureau (2014), "Railway development strategy", Transport and Housing Bureau, Hong Kong, China, September, available at: www.thb.gov.hk/eng/psp/publications/transport/publications/rds2014.pdf.

UITP (2014a), "Action points for the public transport sector. Connecting people and places. Integrated mobility plans for sustainable cities," Union Internationale des Transports Publics, Brussels, available at: www.uitp.org/sites/default/files/cck-focus-papers-files/AP%20-%20Integrated%20mobility%20EN_0.pdf.

UITP (2014b), "Better public transport fare policy for more resilient funding", Union Internationale des Transports Publics, Brussels, January, available at: www.uitp.org/sites/default/files/cck-focus-papers-files/UITP_Policy_Brief_Fare_Policy_20140131.pdf.

UITP (2013), "Electronic ticketing system in Latin America", Union Internationale des Transports Publics, Brussels, May, http://growpublictransport.org/wp-content/plugins/download-monitor/download.php?id=127 (accessed 5 July 2015).

USAID Mexico (2014), "Apoyo a la preparación de proyectos para movilidad interurbana y transporte de carga para la Comisión Ambiental de la Megalópolis (CAMe) con co-beneficios locales, regionales y globales", unpublished technical report, Mexico City.

VTPI (2014), "Automobile dependency, transportation and land use patterns that cause high levels of automobile use and reduced transport options", TDM Encyclopedia, Victoria Transport Policy Institute, Victoria, British Columbia, Canada, www.vtpi.org/tdm/tdm100.htm (accessed 15 June 2015).

World Bank (2014), "Targeted subsidies in public transport: Combining affordability with financial sustainability", World Bank, Washington, DC, available at: http://siteresources.worldbank.org/INTURBANTRANSPORT/Resources/340136-1152550025185/Targeted-Subsidies-Public-Transport-Note-04-23-2014.pdf.

# *Chapter 4.*

# Enhancing environmental sustainability in the Valle de México

*This chapter looks at the key environmental challenges of the Valle de México. It begins with an overview of the water, air, solid waste and land conservation problems that threaten the sustainability of the metropolitan zone. This is followed by an exploration of the governance obstacles that authorities face in addressing environmental challenges. It next considers the lack of a metropolitan vision, weak institutional arrangements, multiplicity of actors, sub-national governments' limited capacity and citizens' lack of awareness as the main barriers to environmental policy success. The main section considers some alternatives for tackling environmental concerns, as well as the need to use urban planning and a metropolitan resilience strategy to ensure policy coherence. It ends by making some recommendations for overcoming the governance obstacles to facilitate policy implementation and promote green growth.*

Urban growth in the Valle de México, as in the other Mexican metropolitan zones, has largely been left to improvisation based on a reactive approach to urban policy challenges dictated by political priorities. A growing population, urban sprawl, lack of regional planning, corruption and mismanagement, as well as poor law enforcement and compliance, are just some of the causes of the environmental challenges that the Valle de México faces. Ensuring the competitiveness and attractiveness of the Valle de México while at the same time protecting the environment and natural resources is a difficult balance to achieve. The environment needs to be seen as an economic asset; the cleaner and greener the Metropolitan Zone of the Valle de México (Zona Metropolitana del Valle de México, ZMVM) is, the more opportunities it will have to attract investment and human capital to encourage economic growth and build resilience to global environmental change. Protecting the environment also has a direct impact on people's health and is a way of contributing to citizens' well-being.

This chapter looks at the environmental challenges and opportunities of the Valle de México. It begins with an overview of the main environmental problems of the metropolitan zone: water, air quality, waste management and conservation land. The discussion then turns to the main governance obstacles that prevent or limit an effective response to environmental concerns. Then the chapter makes some particular recommendations to address those environmental problems, in particular linking environment and urban policy. Finally, it discusses some governance alternatives to better tackle environmental problems and even boost the economic potential of the metropolitan zone. This chapter's overriding message is that to face the Valle de México's environmental problems, it is necessary to integrate environmental issues into urban planning. However, to achieve this aim, governance arrangements must be reinforced, as they provide a basis for that integration.

## Key environmental problems: Water, air, solid waste and conservation land

The ZMVM faces critical environmental challenges that threaten its sustainability. The growing demand and low supply of drinking water, the poor air quality, the inefficient management of solid waste and the high risk to conservation land are the four main environmental threats that will be discussed in this section.

### *The Valle de México faces a dual water challenge*

Water constitutes a dual challenge for the Valle de México. Authorities face a situation in which there is simultaneously too little and too much water. There is too little water for current and future demand for potable water to be met from local sources. At the same time, torrential rainfall during the rainy season results in frequent flooding that affects residents, houses and infrastructure. Moreover, growing water demand, overexploited local and neighbouring aquifers and basins, ageing infrastructure, lack of investment, artificial low tariffs and high operation costs, and the deterioration of water quality have taken the water system to the limits of its physical and financial operability.

#### *The metropolitan zone is liable to floods*

Mexico City was founded on an island, surrounded by the Lake Texcoco, the largest among an interconnected chain of lakes within the Valle de México basin.[1] Starting in the early 17th century, efforts to drain the vast system of lakes continued until the 1970s and left only small remnants of the once vast expanse of surface water. Lake Texcoco covered almost 700 km² in 1521, but today only 70 km² of the area remain, of which only 15 km² are covered by permanent bodies of water. The largest body of water is the artificially created lake "Nabor Carrillo", with a surface area of about 10 km², the sixth-largest lake in Mexico (CONAGUA, 2014a). Even with the tremendous effort of draining the basin, seasonal floods remain a concern. Between 1980 and 2011, rain-related flooding incidents occurred every year and caused severe traffic disruptions, damages to business, homes and residents.[2] During the rainy season, the metropolitan area experiences high-intensity rainfall in a short amount of time. A single storm can produce as much as 10% of the total average annual precipitation (see ANIS, 1995).

Flood risk in the Valle de México is high compared to most parts of the country. The southern parts of the metropolitan zone, along the area with the highest elevation, exhibit high risk levels. But the area at risk extends north beyond high-risk municipalities and *delegaciones* along the border between the Federal District and the State of Mexico. From 2010 to 2013, the *delegaciones* and municipalities along the northeastern border between the Federal District and the State of Mexico experienced several severe spells of rain that led to declarations of states of emergency (Figure 4.1, left panel). Beyond these very severe events, annual flooding regularly leads to disruptions in traffic flows and displacement of residents in these areas.

Figure 4.1. **Flood-related risks and flood-related states of emergency, 2010-13**

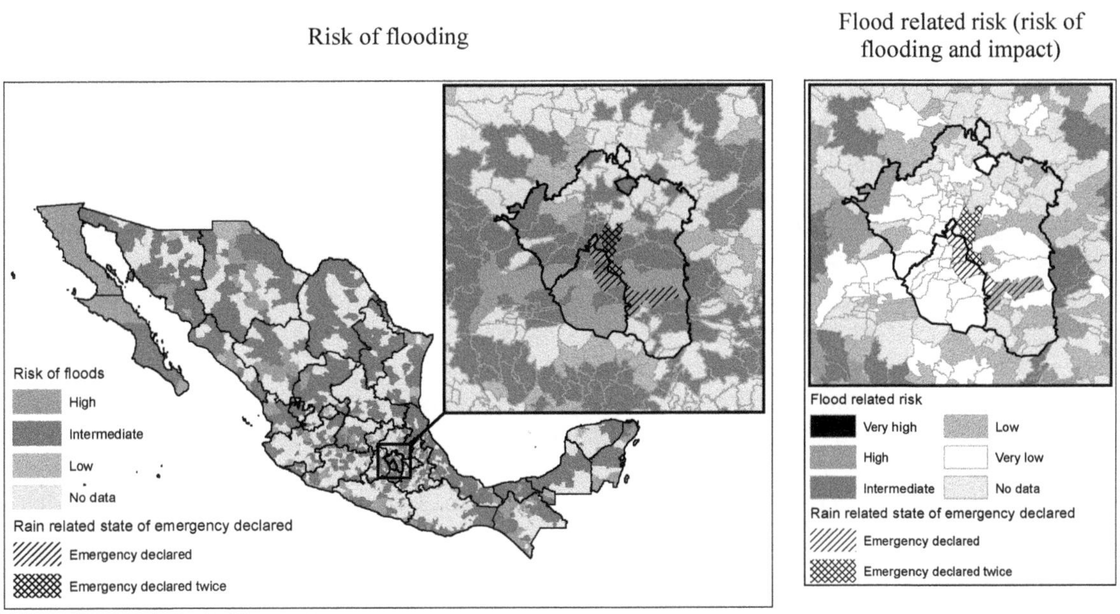


*Note:* This document and any map included herein are without prejudice to the status of or sovereignty over any territory, to the delimitation of international frontiers and boundaries and to the name of any territory, city or area.

*Source*: OECD calculations based on SEGOB (2015), *Atlas Nacional de Riesgos*, CENAPRED, Mexico, DF.

While the risk of floods is significant, the anticipated impact of damage is relatively low. Nearly all municipalities are considered in the lowest two categories when it comes to the expected impact of flooding (Figure 4.1, right panel). However, since drainage typically mixes rainwater with sewage, floods are associated with high health risk and severe impact on the liveability of local neighbourhoods. This is particularly relevant for neighbourhoods that are not connected to subterranean drainage but rather use open sewer canals. One such area is the municipality Valle de Chalco, located within the State of

Mexico and just east of the Federal District, where dwellings of poor residents have been flooded twice within two years by sewage from the local open-air canal (see Chelleri, Schuetze and Salvati, 2015). In 2010, heavy rain flooded the municipality, followed by flooding from a rupture in the canal in 2011. The direct cost can be sizeable. An estimate for the damages from the 2010 flood for six neighbourhoods[3] in the municipality was MXN 43.5 million (USD 3.4 million; see Díaz-Delgado et al., 2012).

To address the recurring floods, Mexico's National Water Commission (Comisión Nacional del Agua, CONAGUA) invests heavily in expansion of the drainage network. Currently, two major tunnels are being constructed to support the existing network. The Eastern Drainage Tunnel, a new tunnel that runs through several municipalities in the State of Mexico along the border with the Federal District and into the state of Hidalgo, is the single largest expected investment in CONAGUA's current strategic projects (CONAGUA, 2015). The total estimated costs for the six-year project were MXN 37.5 billion (USD 2.8 billion) as of early 2015.[4] Once completed, the tunnel will drain both waste and rainwater. While such a dual use could be considered efficient, it also increases the cost of treating rainwater. Additionally, draining excess water means that opportunities for storing, treating and reusing rainwater inside the Valle de México are foregone. While current plans do not include an expansion of local storage, like the lake Nabor Carillo, the planned construction of the New Mexico City International Airport (Nuevo Aeropuerto Internacional de la Ciudad de México, NAICM) is likely to change this.

The NAICM is to be built in the State of Mexico in the former lakebed of Lake Texcoco. Located just north of the artificial lake Nabor Carillo and east of the urban centre of the Federal District, the airport will require substantial precautionary measures to guard against hydrological risks. In plans presented by the Ministry of Agrarian, Territorial and Urban Development (Secretaría de Desarollo Agrario, Territorial y Urbano, SEDATU), investments include the development of five lagoons in and around the area of the airport, which are planned to become a system of six lagoons until 2018, covering most of the former lakebed to the south of the new airport and substantially expanding the surface water storage capacity. The efforts to prepare the area around the new airport also include dredging works along the existing open-air sewage canals and the construction of a 3.6-kilometre drainage tunnel to alleviate pressure on the main sewage canals. This main canal is currently open-air, but is planned to be covered until 2018 along a 10.6-kilometre stretch passing the newly developed lagoons and the airport (SEDATU, 2014).

### *A growing scarcity of potable water*

In the Valle de México, with most of the local surface water depleted, the main source of potable water is from wells that tap into the aquifers underneath the metropolitan area. But the rapid growth of the city, combined with a high per capita use of water and infrastructure-related water losses, has severely drained resources and overstrained the local aquifers (see Chapter 1). To cope with the demand, water supply has been supplemented by piped surface water from outside the Valle de México basin since the 1940s. Even with this effort, access to piped water remains uneven across the city. While on average, more than 95% of residents in the metropolitan zone had access to piped water, outside the metropolitan zone's densely populated urban centre, access to piped water remains far from universal (Figure 4.2). Thus water has become a national and sub-national priority established in the national and state development plans and a key element of the inclusive green growth goals of the national government.[5]

Figure 4.2. **Percentage of residents with access to piped water, 2010**

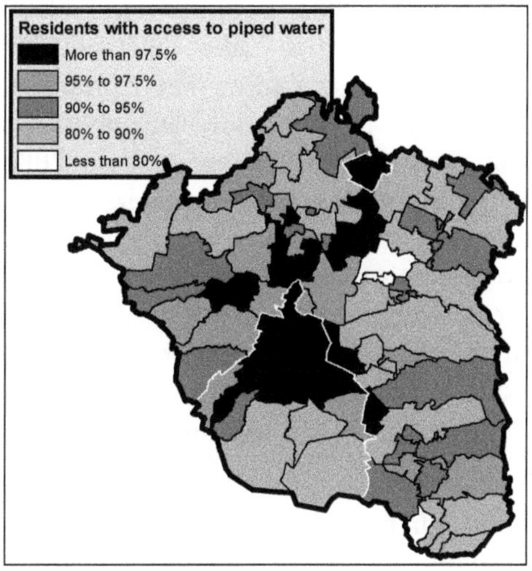


*Note:* This document and any map included herein are without prejudice to the status of or sovereignty over any territory, to the delimitation of international frontiers and boundaries and to the name of any territory, city or area.

*Source*: INEGI (2010a), *Censo de Población y Vivienda 2010*, Instituto Nacional de Estadística y Geografía, Aguascalientes, Mexico.

While the rainy season brings excessive amounts of rainwater, potable water is scarce and becoming scarcer. The local subterranean aquifers are under severe stress. Among the water concessions for the metropolitan area's main aquifers, 98% come from overexploited aquifers, i.e. aquifers in which abstractions exceed refill. The main aquifer underneath the Federal District, which accounts for nearly two-thirds of the concessions, is being drained rapidly (Table 4.1). Overexploitation has required wells to become deeper. They range up to a depth of 400 metres, where a depth of 70 metres was sufficient for older wells.[6] Due to the soil composition, extraction from deeper wells tends to be less efficient.

Table 4.1. **Overexploitation of the Valle de México's main aquifers**

| Aquifer | Abstractions (concessions in m³/s) | Recharge deficit (m³/s) |
|---|---|---|
| ZM Ciudad de México | 38.9 | -22.6 |
| Cuautitlán-Pachuca | 10.5 | -4.1 |
| Texcoco | 6.3 | -1.6 |
| Chalco-Amecameca | 2.9 | -0.5 |
| Soltepec | 0.6 | 1.1 |
| Apan | 0.3 | 1.9 |
| Tecocomulco | 0.0 | 0.8 |
| Total | 59.5 | -25.0 |

*Source*: World Bank (2013), "Agua urbana en el Valle de México: ¿Un camino verde para mañana?", World Bank, Washington, DC, available at: www.agua.unam.mx/sacmex/assets/docs/AguaUrbana_ValleMexico.pdf.

The excessive abstraction from local aquifers has visible and significant effects on the urban landscape. Reduction in water in the clay soil that supports a large part of the city leads to densification of the soil and subsidence. The annual subsidence – the downward shift – of the soil can reach up to 30 centimetres per year. The effect is particularly pronounced around the northeastern border between the Federal District and the State of Mexico, around the lakebed of the former Lake Texcoco.[3] The unsettled earth creates significant challenges for urban infrastructure. The "Grand Canal", a major drainage outlet for the Valle de México, used to rely solely on gravity for sewage disposal. Due to subsidence, the outflow was no longer sufficient, and in 2008, a pumping station was built to raise wastewater by 30 metres (see Jiménez, 2014). Differential subsidence creates strain on pipes and results in cracks and breaks in the infrastructure. The resulting leakage not only results in losses of potable water, but creates severe health hazards. Breaks in drainage pipes can cause contamination of surface and underground water sources, and combined with cracks in the potable water network, can also create cross-contamination. Cracks also reduce the potential pressure in pipes for potable water, further increasing the potential for contamination of drinking water (see Soto Montes de Oca, 2007).

To meet the high demand for potable water, an intricate water delivery system has been developed. The first part of today's system was built in the early 1940s and transported water from the Lerma basin, outside the Valle de México basin, to the metropolitan zone. In the 1970s, the Lerma system was complemented by a new system of long-distance water delivery, the "Cutzamala system". This system today is the main source of water delivered from outside the basin. The Cutzamala system pumps surface water across 127 kilometres from a set of 3 reservoirs and 4 dams. The water from the Cutzamala system is not only pumped across a long distance, but has to be elevated from a height of 1 600 metres above sea level to 2 700 metres.[8] The associated costs are significant. In 2013, 0.5% of the country's total electricity consumption was used by the Cutzamala system.

The transfers from external basins cover 22% of the total supply, while 68% are abstracted from local aquifers. Slightly more than half these abstractions are sustainable, i.e. balanced by refill. The vast majority of refill is natural infiltration. Surface water and treated wastewater account for the remaining 10% of total supply (Table 4.2). Nearly three-quarters of potable water is consumed in domestic use, with the industrial, commercial and service sector consuming the remaining fourth.[9]

Table 4.2. **Potable water by source in the Metropolitan Zone of the Valle de México**

| | Local aquifer (sustainable) | Local aquifer (overexploitation) | Surface water | Transfer Lerma | Transfer Cutzamala | Treated wastewater | Total |
|---|---|---|---|---|---|---|---|
| Volume ($m^3/s$) | 31.6 | 27.9 | 2.9 | 4.8 | 14.7 | 6.1 | 88 |
| Percentage | 36% | 32% | 3% | 5% | 17% | 7% | 100% |

*Source*: World Bank (2013), "Agua urbana en el Valle de México: ¿Un camino verde para mañana?", World Bank, Washington, DC, available at: www.agua.unam.mx/sacmex/assets/docs/AguaUrbana_ValleMexico.pdf.

Despite the intense efforts in water delivery, supply does not reach all residents of the Valle de México. While nearly all households are connected to the water network, in some neighbourhoods, tapped water is only available at certain times or days (*tandeo*) and shortfalls have to be compensated by supplying residents via mobile water tanks. In the Federal District, 268 neighbourhoods (*colonias*) in 11 of the 16 *delegaciones* officially receive only limited piped service.[4] Survey evidence suggests that coverage outside the Federal District is even lower. Among residents who have access to piped water in their home, less than 50% in the northern parts of the Valle de México and only 50-75% in the south receive water daily (Figure 4.3).

Water quality in the Valle de México is difficult to assess. Data on some indicators is available on a regular basis. For example, CONAGUA publishes information on the quality of water in the Cutzamala system. But this data is limited to colour and turbidity, acidity and hardness (pH scale, residual chlorine and $CaCo_3$ level), and taste and odour.[5] Information on contaminants is not provided, and neither is information on the quality of the water once it leaves the Cutzamala system and enters the local delivery networks. Aggregate measures for the presence of total organic matter and total biodegradable organic matter, as well as total suspended solids, are available annually for surface water in CONAGUA's statistical yearbook,[6] and show a low level of quality across most surface water in the Valle de México.[7] For groundwater, less information is available. Tests carried out in December 2007 and July 2008 found that only 35% and 47% of wells provided potable water that was norm compliant.[8] The remainder showed elevated bacteriological or chemical contamination. In 2008, only 4 out of 16 bodies of surface water had "acceptable" water quality or better, and the majority exhibited high levels of organic matter pollution.[9] Information on the quality of supplied water is limited. A recent study finds that pollution is most concentrated in the southern part of Valle de México, where local wells are contaminated by industrial production and past industrial activities, as well as intrusion from local sewage (see Soto Montes de Oca, 2007; and Jiménez, 2014).

Figure 4.3. **Percentage of residents with access to piped water who are supplied daily, 2010**

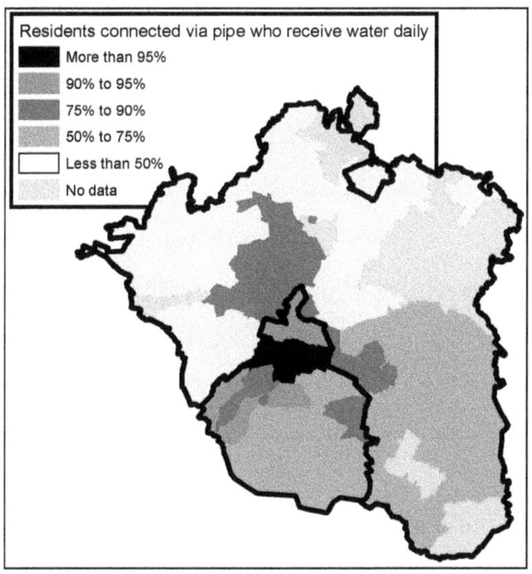


*Note:* 1. Adjacent municipalities/delegations have been aggregated to ensure that each spatial aggregate is based on a sample of at least 100 households.

This document and any map included herein are without prejudice to the status of or sovereignty over any territory, to the delimitation of international frontiers and boundaries and to the name of any territory, city or area.

*Source*: OECD calculations based on INEGI (2010b), *Encuesta Nacional de Ingresos y Gastos de los Hogares (ENIGH) 2010* [National Survey of Mexican Household Income and Expenditures], Instituto Nacional de Estadística y Geografía, Aguascalientes, Mexico.

Water tariffs are set locally and exhibit substantial variation. Tariffs have to be politically approved. For the Federal District, the legislative assembly approves changes in tariffs. In the State of Mexico, tariffs are set out for all municipalities (split into four groups) by the state, but the municipal councils have the option to grant general subsidies, surcharges or cancel fines.[16] In practice, this leads to a wide range of tariffs within the metropolitan area, which makes comparisons difficult. CONAGUA has established a national tariff register, which currently contains information up to 2012.[10] More recent tariffs tend to be available on the website of the providers the Water Utilities of Mexico City (Sistema de Aguas de la Ciudad de México, SACMEX) and the Water Commission of the State of México (Comisión del Agua del Estado de México, CAEM).

Tariffs typically distinguish between domestic and commercial use, with some allowing for mixed use, e.g. in the Federal District. They further apply different schedules, according to some measure of need within the neighbourhood. In the Federal District, for example, need is assessed based on a block-level development index that combines data on social marginalisation, income and property values. Comparability across tariffs is further limited by the inclusion or exclusion of fixed fees and drainage. Despite the challenge in creating comparable indices, studies tend to find that the price for water in the Federal District is very low by comparison with the municipalities across the metropolitan area. For example, compared to the municipality of Naucalpan, tariffs for households with about average levels of consumption are lower in all categories, with significant gaps for households that fall into the lowest two tariff categories (Figure 4.4).

Figure 4.4. **Average price per m$^3$ for 35 m$^3$ consumption in two months, 2015**

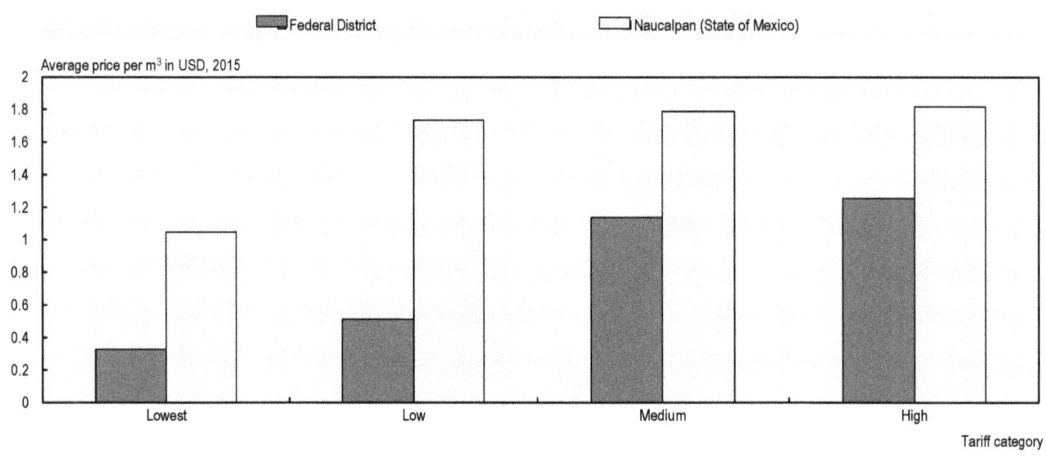


*Note:* Tariff categories for the Federal District/Naucalpan are *popular/popular con tandeo* (lowest); *baja/popular* (low); *media/medio* (medium); *alta/alto* (high). Tariffs are for 2015 and converted from MXN to USD using the average exchange rate for 2014. Tariffs in Naucalpan are reported in multiples of the daily minimum wage, which is converted using the minimum wage valid from April 2015 (MXN 70.10).

*Source*: Tariffs: Government of the Federal District (2014), "Decreto por el que se reforman, adicionan y derogan diversas disposiciones del Código Fiscal del Distrito Federal", *Gaceta Oficial Distrito Federal*, No. 2012(I), 22 December, available at: www.sacmex.df.gob.mx/sacmex/doc/3_atencion_a_usuarios/tarifas/6_tarifas172.pdf; Government of Naucalpan (2014), *Gaceta del Gobierno*, 18 December, p. 106, available at: http://caem.edomex.gob.mx/sites/caem.edomex.gob.mx/files/files/TramitesServicios/Tarifas2015/Naucalpan2015.pdf. Exchange rate: OECD (2015a), "PPPs and exchange rates", *OECD National Accounts Statistics* (database), http://dx.doi.org/10.1787/data-00004-en (accessed 30 June 2015); Minimum wage: CONASAMI (2015), "Tabla de salarios mínimos generales y profesionales por áreas geográficas", Comisión Nacional de los Salarios Mínimos, www.conasami.gob.mx/t_sal_mini_prof.html (accessed 7 April 2015).

The low rates do not set strong incentives to conserve water, especially in the Federal District, where 75% of consumers fall into the two lowest tariff categories.[11] As a result, water is heavily subsidised, both at the local and the national level. CONAGUA's budget includes about one-third of duties paid for water, SACMEX's budget to about two-thirds.[12] The remainder of CONAGUA's operating budget is covered nearly completely by fiscal contribution from the central government, SACMEX is subsidised by both the federal government and the government of the Federal District.[13]

## *The quality of air is not yet satisfactory*

The Valle de México is the most polluted area in the country in terms of ozone, and the fourth for particulate matter $PM_{10}$ (Centro Mario Molina, 2014). This represents a high cost to public health, and has a negative effect on the productivity, competitiveness and attractiveness of the metropolitan zone. The OECD's work on cities and climate change has observed that if their current pollution trends continue, even cities such as Chicago, Los Angeles, New York, Osaka, Paris, Seoul and Tokyo are at risk of losing economic attractiveness (OECD, 2010). In the international scene, Mexico is committed to reducing 30% carbon emissions by 2020 and by 40% by 2030 (a combined effect of reducing $CO_2$ emissions by 70% and greenhouse gas emissions by 36%) compared to the emission level in 2012.

### *Encouraging results on $SO_2$ and CO are being obtained ...*

Federal and local authorities in the Valle de México have been relatively successful in improving the air quality in the metropolitan area. Over the last two decades, thanks to the implementation of four consecutive comprehensive programmes called ProAire (Box 4.1) there has been a dramatic reduction in local air pollution (Figure 4.5). Since 2003, the levels of $SO_2$ and CO have not been above the limit established by the Mexican Official Norm (NOM) of 0.130 ppm average per 24 hours and 11 ppm average per 8 hours respectively. The levels of lead (Pb) have been below the accepted limits since the component was removed from fuels in 1997. In spite of these achievements, local authorities acknowledge that additional efforts are needed to reduce the level of pollutants that are still beyond the national standards such as ozone and particulate matter. The measures adopted to improve air quality have been diverse, from closing the most polluting factories to banning cars in the metropolitan area one day per week through the *Hoy No Circula* programme ("No driving today"). Mexico City's government has introduced the Atmospheric Monitoring Network (*Red de Monitoreo Atmosférico*, SIMAT), which provides data for informed policy making and has led to the adoption of the Metropolitan Index of Air Quality, and the establishment of contingency and pre-contingency protocols.

Despite encouraging results and continuation in air quality improvement programmes, air quality is one of the main concerns of authorities and residents in the Valle de México. The effects of air pollution are being manifested in health effects that can range from a little irritation to acute sickness (decreased respiratory capacity, asthma, heart diseases or lung cancer) or even to premature death.[14] For example, the Mexican standard of ozone ($O_3$) – 0.11 ppm – is frequently exceeded, and its effects on human health are detected in the form of irritated eyes, persistent headaches and increased hyper-reactivity. Particulate matter and aerosols are other important pollutants caused by tobacco smoke, metal dust, metallic and fibrous particles, and exhaust fumes, which have long-term health effects such as cardiovascular disease, emphysema, cataracts, bronchitis, asthma and coughs. According to OECD calculations, the total number of deaths from ambient PM and ozone pollution in Mexico increased from 17 954 in 2005 to 21 594 in 2010. Similarly, the years of life lost (YLL) from ambient air pollution increased from 377 739 to 448 436 in the same period. The same trend was reported in Australia, Canada, Chile, Japan, Korea and New Zealand for the same period, but 20 other OECD countries achieved a reduction in air pollution-related deaths (OECD, 2014).

Figure 4.5. **Emissions of sulphur dioxide ($SO_2$) and carbon monoxide (CO) in the Valle de México**

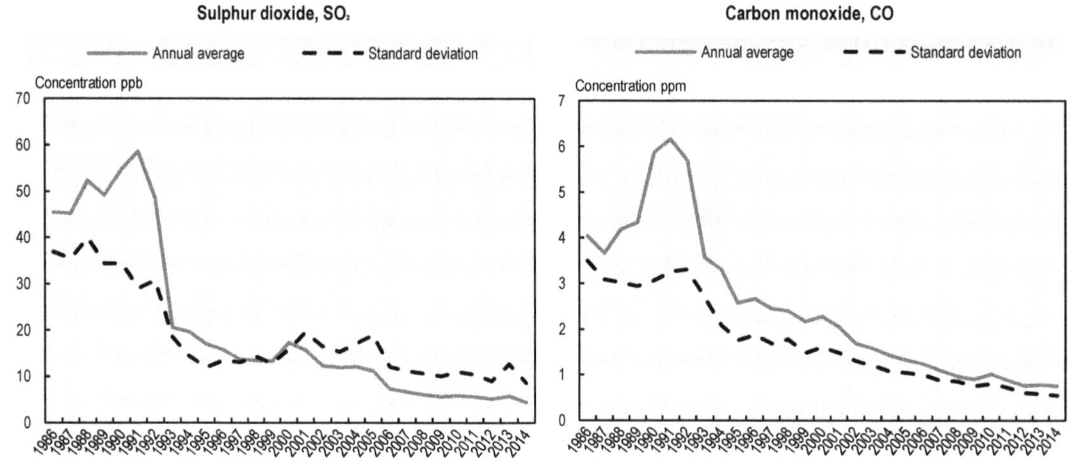


*Source*: Information provided by the Ministry of Environment of the Federal District (SEDEMA).

Box 4.1. **Improving air quality in the Valle de México: ProAire**

In 1990, the Mexican federal government, the Federal District and the State of Mexico presented the first Comprehensive Programme Against Air Pollution (PICCA) as a systematic plan to combat air pollution. It included restricting the circulation of private cars on certain days, depending on registration plate. During the period the second programme, ProAire II 1995-2000, was in force, the Metropolitan Environmental Commission was created to co-ordinate the actions of the federal and the two local governments in the Valle de México. During ProAire III 2002-2010, the Metrobús and the shared bike programme ECOBICI were introduced. Emission reductions over this period were estimated at 5 078 tonnes/year of $PM_{10}$, 506 tonnes/year of $SO_2$ and 817 132 tonnes/year of CO. In the Valle de México, the implementation of ProAire has made significant progress in reducing air pollution. It is estimated that between 1997 and 2005, 1 928 deaths were averted due to the reductions of $PM_{10}$ concentrations and 794 due to reduction in ozone concentrations. ProAire has also been reinforced by the implementation and constant updating of Mexico City's Atmospheric Monitoring System (SIMAT), which has made it possible to monitor air quality from 40 different points in the metropolitan area. It includes a laboratory for the physico-chemical analysis of samples and a centre for the processing and diffusion of air quality data.

ProAire IV 2011-2020 is the main guideline for establishing an eco-systemic approach in the management of the air quality in the Valle de México. It has 81 measures and 116 actions across 8 strategic themes to further improve air quality and reduce greenhouse gas emissions by 2020. The eight strategic themes are: reduction of energy consumption; cleaner and more efficient energy across all sectors; promoting public transport and regulating fuel consumption; technology shift and controlling emissions; environmental education; creating a sustainability culture and citizen participation; green areas and reforestation; and institutional capacity building and scientific research. The expected results include 490 000 tonnes of fewer emissions of "criteria" pollutants: hydrocarbons, carbon monoxide, sulphur oxides, nitrogen oxides, $PM_{10}$ and $PM_{2.5}$ and ozone; 5 000 tonnes of toxic pollutants; and 5.5 million tonnes of greenhouse gases. Mexico City's ProAire programme has been awarded the C40 & Siemens Climate Leadership Award in the Air Quality category for its results in reducing local air pollution, as well as $CO_2$ emissions.

Box 4.1. **Improving air quality in the Valle de México: ProAire** (*continued*)

One of the main problems of dealing with air pollution is that the Mexican standards are not fully in line with international standards established by the World Health Organization (WHO). In some cases, the discrepancy is due to the fact that the Mexican standards were formulated before the international standards were set.

Table 4.3. **Mexican and WHO standards for measuring air quality**

| Pollutant | Mexican standard | WHO standards |
|---|---|---|
| Particulate matter $PM_{2.5}$ | **NOM-025-SSA1-1993**<br>15 µg/m³ annual mean<br>65 µg/m³ 24-hour mean | 10µg/m³ annual mean<br>25 µg/m³ 24-hour mean |
| Particulate matter $PM_{10}$ | **NOM-025-SSA1-1993**<br>50 µg/m³ annual mean<br>120 µg/m³ 24-hour mean | 20 µg/m³ annual mean<br>50 µg/m³ 24-hour mean |
| Ozone ($O_3$) | **NOM-020-SSA1-1993**<br>0.110 ppm 1-hour average not to be exceeded more than once a year<br>0.080 ppm 8-hour average – Fifth maximum taken over a period of one year | 100 µg/m³ 8-hour mean |
| Nitrogen dioxide ($NO_2$) | **NOM-023-SSA1-1993**<br>021 ppm 1-hour mean – not to be exceeded once per year | 40 µg/m³ annual mean<br>200 µg/m³ 1-hour mean |
| Sulfur dioxide ($SO_2$) | **NOM-022-SSA-1993**<br>0.130 ppm 24-hour mean – not to be exceeded once per year<br>0.030 ppm annual mean | 20 µg/m³ 24-hour mean<br>500 µg/m³ 10-minute mean |

*Sources*: Government of the State of Mexico (2011), *Programa para Mejorar la Calidad del Aire de la Zona Metropolitana del Valle de México 2011-2020*, Government of the State of Mexico, SEMARNAT, Secretaría de Salud, SEDEMA, www.sedema.df.gob.mx/flippingbook/proaire2011-2020 (accessed 15 August 2015); OECD (2013a), *OECD Environmental Performance Reviews: Mexico 2013*, OECD Publishing, Paris, http://dx.doi.org/10.1787/9789264180109-en; C40 Siemens (2014), "City Climate Leadership Awards: Mexico City climate close-up", available at: www.siemens.com/press/pool/de/events/2014/infrastructure-cities/2014-06-CCLA/mexico-climate-close-up.pdf; Background Questionnaire for the OECD review answered by Mexico City's Ministry of Environment; WHO (2005), "WHO air quality guidelines for particulate matter, ozone, nitrogen dioxide and sulphur dioxide, Global update 2005, Summary of risk assessment", World Health Orgnization, Geneva, available at: http://apps.who.int/iris/bitstream/10665/69477/1/WHO_SDE_PHE_OEH_06.02_eng.pdf; Secretaría de Salud (2002), *Modificación a la Norma Oficial Mexicana* NOM-020-SSA1-1993, www.salud.gob.mx/unidades/cdi/nom/m020ssa13.html (accessed 15 August 2015).

Reducing the levels of emissions in the ZMVM is considered a shared responsibility among the Federal District, the State of Mexico and the federal government. Table 4.4 shows that most of the pollutants originate in the municipalities in the State of Mexico where the majority of the sources of emissions are located, including industries (manufacture) and private vehicles. The responsibility of the federal government is to regulate chemical industry, metals production, the generation of electric energy, freight transport vehicles and inter-state bus services, etc.

### *... but the lack of an efficient transport strategy undermines progress on air quality improvement*

The Valle de México currently has no efficient transport solution between most of the municipalities in the State of Mexico and Mexico City. Urban sprawl, long commuting distances and the increase in the number and use of private vehicles are just part of the environmental challenge. The underground system in the State of Mexico is still limited, and most commuting is done in low-capacity and polluting buses (*microbúses*). Private vehicles represent 78% of the vehicle fleet in the ZMVM, but only cover one-third of the

Table 4.4. **Inventory of emissions in the Valle de México by jurisdiction, 2012**

| Jurisdiction | Emission (t/year) | | | | | | | | | | |
|---|---|---|---|---|---|---|---|---|---|---|---|
| | $PM_{10}$ | $PM_{2.5}$ | $SO_2$ | CO | $NO_X$ | COT | VOCs | $NH_3$ | Toxics | CN | $CO_2$eq. |
| Federal District | 6 552 | 2 185 | 217 | 594 116 | 79 287 | 232 949 | 199 483 | 16 210 | 75 001 | 293 | 13 401 215 |
| State of Mexico | 23 335 | 4 749 | 1 052 | 944 674 | 117 734 | 536 841 | 314 436 | 27 799 | 97 489 | 597 | 24 576 236 |
| Federal | 4 790 | 2 517 | 3 598 | 67 258 | 42 111 | 125 579 | 118 829 | 183 | 23 325 | 1 226 | 11 525 559 |
| Total | 34 677 | 9 451 | 4 867 | 1 606 048 | 239 132 | 895 369 | 632 748 | 44 192 | 195 815 | 2 116 | 49 503 010 |
| | Emissions (%) | | | | | | | | | | |
| Federal District | 19 | 23 | 4 | 37 | 33 | 26 | 31 | 37 | 38 | 14 | 27 |
| State of Mexico | 67 | 50 | 22 | 59 | 49 | 60 | 50 | 63 | 50 | 28 | 50 |
| Federal | 14 | 27 | 74 | 4 | 18 | 14 | 19 | N/S | 12 | 58 | 23 |
| Total | 100 | 100 | 100 | 100 | 100 | 100 | 100 | 100 | 100 | 100 | 100 |

*Note:* N/S = Not significant.$PM_{10}$ and $PM_{2.5}$ (particulate matter); $SO_2$ (sulphur dioxide); CO (carbob monoxide); $NO_X$ (mono-nitrogen oxides); COT (total organic compounds); VOCs (volatile organic compounds); $NH_3$ (ammonia); CN (black carbon); $CO_2$ eq (carbon dioxide equivalente)

*Source*: Government of the Federal District (2012), *Inventario de Emisiones Contaminantes y de Efecto Invernadero, Zona Metropolitana del Valle de México*, Secretaría del Medio Ambiente.

mobility needs. The public transport fleet represents 8% of the vehicles in the ZMVM and covers two-thirds of the transport needs. Figure 4.6 shows that the number of privatevehicles is increasing, mostly in the State of Mexico, whereas the levels of ozone, although decreasing, are not entirely satisfactory. According to Mexico City authorities, the number of cars rose from 2 million in 1990 to 5 million in 2012, but reports from the National Institute of Statistics and Geography (Instituto Nacional de Estadística y Geografía, INEGI) suggest that the number is even higher, at approximately 6.8 million.[22] However, the implementation of the ProAire programme, improvements in gasoline fuels and the adoption of greener technologies for the vehicle fleet may have contributed to a decrease in levels of ozone.

Figure 4.6. **Evolution of car ownership levels and ozone emissions in the Metropolitan Zone of the Valle de México**

Main environmental initiatives

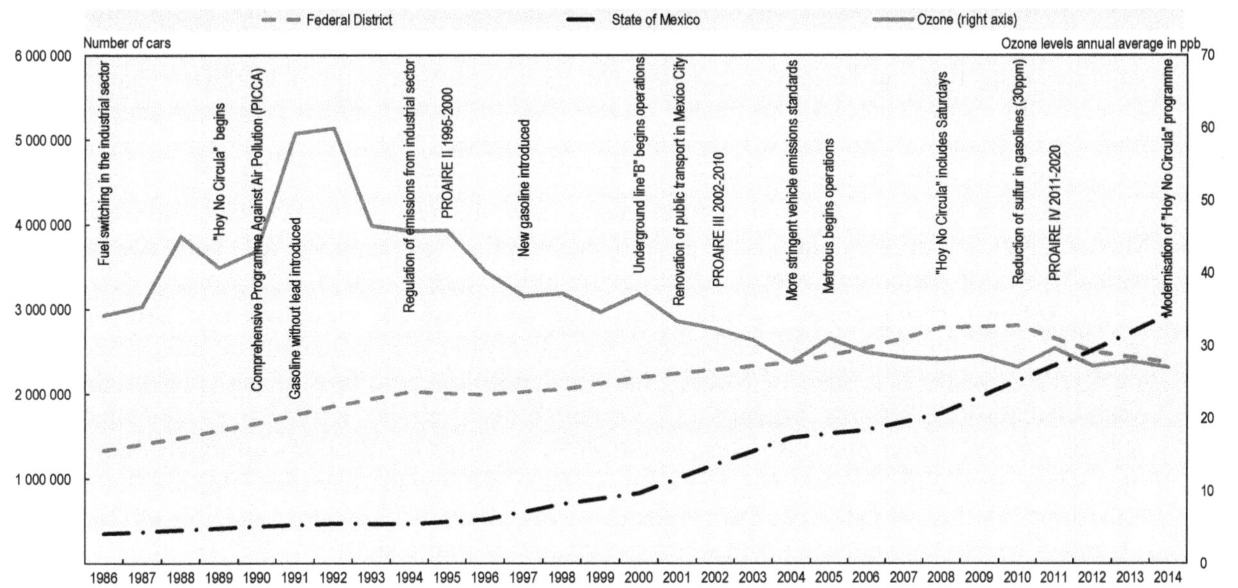


*Source*: Information provided by the Ministry of Environment of the Federal District (SEDEMA).

The increasing number of cars, the inefficient traffic signal system and the road layout have reduced the average vehicle travel speed of cars, which is currently 17 km/h. Mexico City authorities consider that there is a risk this may drop in the coming years, which could led to higher levels of pollutants such as volatile organic compounds (VOCs), CO and NOx. A large majority of car trips transport only one or two passengers (SEDEMA, 2012). The vehicular fleet that uses fossil fuels represents 95% of the total fleet and consumes 21 million litres of fuel every day. In addition, the inadequate zoning of some businesses, which lack parking spaces for customers and providers, and the use of part of the road lanes by informal businesses (*comerciantes ambulantes*) obstruct the traffic, causing congestion, low speeds and higher emission levels. All these facts underline the urgent need for better managing private vehicles in order to improve air quality in the ZMVM.

Another critical problem is freight transport, which relies on highly polluting diesel fuels, which requires stricter regulation. No local government has competency in this area, as it is regulated by the federal government. The only area over which local governments have discretion is on regulating when trucks are allowed to circulate. Freight transport represents 14% of the transport fleet (700 000 freight vehicles are registered in the ZMVM), most of them highly polluting. Monitoring this sector is highly complicated and expensive (SEDEMA, 2012).

### *An inadequate management of solid waste is threatening land, water and air quality*

The Valle de México lacks a comprehensive solid waste management system. One of the main problems is that even the existence of landfills does not guarantee an adequate treatment of waste. A number of studies conducted by Mexican institutions report an insufficient and inadequate infrastructure for managing solid waste (Barreda Marín, 2009). Mexico City produces 12 800 tonnes of solid waste every day (an average of 1.5 kg per capita). Only between 3.9% and 6.7% of the waste that enters into the selection plants is recuperated, and the rest is deposited in landfills. Managing solid waste costs MXN 3 billion yearly (USD 185 million approximately). Mexico City has 13 transfer stations to select, store and concentrate solid waste. It also has two selection plants to separate waste that can be recycled. There are six composting plants that reuse organic waste. Solid waste that cannot be treated by any biological or chemical process is sent to final disposal sites in the State of Mexico and in Morelos (7 613 tonnes per day). From waste that is received at the transfer plants, 56% is sent to final disposal sites, 25% goes to composting plants, 19% to selection plants and the rest to the cement industry. Mexico City's government has issued an integral plan for the management of solid waste, with the aim of generating energy based on organic waste by 2018. The *Basura Cero* ("Zero Rubbish") programme is a valuable effort to minimise waste generation, maximise recycling and improve waste collection, but it should be extended to the entire metropolitan zone. The State of Mexico has ten landfills where half of the solid urban waste is deposited. The rest is sent to 37 controlled disposal sites and 52 non-controlled sites or garbage dump opencast sites. In the ZMVM, there are 22 non-controlled dump sites where any kind of waste is disposed of without restrictions (Barreda Marín, 2010). According to the Ministry of Environment of the State of Mexico, one-fifth of the generated waste is not collected and is left in clandestine dump sites.

The problem of waste in the ZMVM is not just the amount produced but also the lack of a preventive plan and of available spaces for its concentration and final disposal. This has led to the proliferation of non-controlled dump sites or clandestine sites in many areas of the Valle de México.[23] This situation is affecting the recharge of aquifers, leading to loss of habitat and biodiversity, increasing the emissions of greenhouse gases (GHG), generation of vermin, loss in the quality and productivity of land, and the obstruction of waterways. Since 50% of the dump sites are opencast, an uncontrolled production of biogas and leachate is damaging the environment and causing health problems. The production of leachate is polluting groundwater, as many landfills, principally the uncontrolled ones, are not properly prepared to store solid waste, and many are located in conservation land or in areas close to the aquifers in the State of Mexico. In some cases, mine shafts are used as dump sites, and many are located close to watersheds. Opencast dump sites close to sewage canals are potential generators of GHG and the proliferation of vermin, increasing the potential for disease.

One of the problems in analysing waste management is the lack of good data on the generation, disposal and composition of waste at national, state and municipal level (Barreda Marín, 2009). Data are mostly dated and incomplete. Several clandestine dump sites of urban solid waste have neither been inventoried nor monitored by any authority.

There are no records of recycled materials in the State of Mexico and most of the work in the metropolitan zone is conducted by informal workers (*pepenadores*). The sewage canals of the ZMVM, located mainly in the State of Mexico, also contain liquids produced by the decomposition of the urban solid waste deposited in them and are a source of GHG, but they are not included in the garbage-related registry. National urban solid waste data are presented by state or regions (Centre, North, South, Northern Border and Federal District) and on occasion based on the size of population centres. However, none of these criteria is sufficient to quantify the generation of waste in the ZMVM. Only about half of the municipalities of the State of Mexico are part of the ZMVM, others are part of the Metropolitan Zone of the Valle de Toluca, and the rest are semi-urban or rural communities with very different characteristics. The data thus have a very low level of certitude. Grouping the State of Mexico with a large number of other entities makes it impossible to analyse waste management at the metropolitan level.

### *Lack of planning is putting conservation land at risk*

Conservation land is of great importance to the sustainability of the metropolitan zone, affecting all three major environmental problems (water, air and solid waste). According to the 2013-2018 Development Programme of the Federal District, 59% of the city's territory is conservation land, located mainly in the south and southwest (see Chapter 1). The conservation land is critical for recharging the aquifers, improving air quality, protecting biodiversity, regulating weather and providing recreational opportunities, which in turn promotes eco-tourism. Nonetheless, the lack of urban planning, urban sprawl, deforestation, fragmentation of the forest, irregular human settlements and the pollution of the soil through residual waters and uncontrolled, inadequate landfills are putting conservation land at risk.

To address the problem, Mexico City's government has implemented ecological management and urban development programmes to regulate the use of land and productive activities, both to prevent irregular settlements and protect the biodiversity and ecosystems (e.g. in the lake area of Xochimilco). Authorities have been identifying areas in conservation land with a particularly high potential for the generation of environmental services and are negotiating with the private owners on a compensation scheme to protect the land and develop sustainable environmental services. Communication strategies on the environmental and urban regulation aimed at raising awareness of the importance of the conservation land for the sustainability of the city are being adopted. Some efforts are also being made to train environmental inspectors and officials to improve the implementation of regulations. The State of Mexico has an initiative to protect forest lands, under which the government gives a type of subsidy to land owners as an incentive not to build on the land. However, this scheme applies mainly to municipalities that are not part of the ZMVM. The preservation of the conservation land will not only require legal reinforcement, but adopting the technical instruments, such as land-use planning.

## Governance obstacles for addressing environmental problems

The Mexican authorities are working to address the environmental challenges in the Valle de México, but much remains to be done. Interviews conducted for this review suggested that the origin of the environmental problems is largely governance-related. How effective organisational arrangements and how efficient policy instruments are to address environmental challenges seem to be the primary concern of national and local policy makers and academics. Current governance arrangements are creating bottlenecks that slow down progress and prevent a comprehensive response to environmental challenges.

### *A "megalopolitan" dimension to improve governance for a better environment*

In 2013, to confront the socio-economic and environmental challenges in Mexico's Central Region and based on the positive experience of the former Metropolitan Environmental Commission (Comisión Ambiental Metropolitana, CAM), Mexican federal and local authorities created the Environmental Commission for the Megalopolis (Comisión Ambiental para la Megalópolis, CAMe). It includes the six central entities: Mexico, Hidalgo, Morelos, Puebla, Tlaxcala and the Federal District.[24] The CAMe is designed to be the environmental governance platform to support policies, programmes and actions that encourage sustainability and green growth in the Central Region of the country. It allows policy makers to meet and discuss environmental issues on a regular basis. The commission has neither implementation nor enforcement responsibilities. It does not intend to replace local or municipal governments in their environmental responsibilities, but to support them by facilitating understanding, co-operation and co-ordination in areas of common interest, and to provide evidence for informed policy- and decision making. One recent example of environmental protection at megalopolitan level is the harmonisation of standards for vehicle environmental assessment and the extension of the *Hoy No Circula* programme to the six entities of the megalopolis. According to Mexican authorities, these measures are expected to contribute to a reduction of environmental pollution of 11% every year.[25] Moreover, policy makers have realised that reaching agreement on the macro level is not a problem but the challenge is to work on details for implementing the decisions agreed upon. Governments will need to be willing to pay the political costs of implementing the decisions taken by the CAMe.

#### Box 4.2. **The Environmental Commission for the Megalopolis (CAMe)**

Created in 2013, the Environmental Commission for the Megalopolis (CAMe), which replaces the Metropolitan Environment Commission, aims to: establish a regional environmental policy framework; design and implement environmental projects with an integrated regional vision; encourage informed decision making and build consensus; provide technical support and training to the different entities of the megalopolis; and conduct research. The territorial demarcation for the CAMe includes the 16 *delegaciones* of the Federal District, and some municipalities from the states of Hidalgo (29), Mexico (79), Morelos (34), Puebla (22) and Tlaxcala (61). They constitute the Central Region of the country. The CAMe intends to provide an integral approach to the megalopolitan region for diagnostics, analysis and actions on environmental protection. It also aims to create synergies to tackle common problems and facilitate transversal decision making. Moreover, the CAMe intends to create a critical mass by facilitating citizens' participation in the discussion of environmental problems.

The commission has an Organ of Government (*Órgano de Gobierno*), as the highest decision-making body, composed of the governors of the states of Mexico, Hidalgo, Puebla, Tlaxcala and Morelos; the Mayor of Mexico City; and the federal Minister of Environment and Natural Resources. It meets every two months. The Advisory Scientific Committee (Comité Científico Asesor) is a body for technical consultation composed of 12 members of academia, think-tanks and non-governmental organisations. Its membership is renewed every two years and works on an honorary basis. The Executive Co-ordination (*Coordinación Ejecutiva*) body acts as the secretariat of the commission.

*Sources*: CAMe (2014), *La CAMe a 6 meses de su creación*, Coordinación Ejecutiva de la Comisión Ambiental de la Megalópolis, 4 April; Secretaría del Medio Ambiente y Recursos Naturales (2013), "Convenio de coordinación por el que se crea la Comisión Ambiental de la Megalópolis", *Diario Oficial de la Federación*, 3 October.

### *A lack of a shared vision and the particularities of the political system constitute a bottleneck*

The lack of a widely shared environmental vision and strategy to tackle urban challenges seems to be an obstacle to a co-ordinated metropolitan response to environmental challenges. Interviews conducted for this review did not show strong evidence that every organisation has the same vision or that municipal-level governments have the same level of commitment to protecting the environment. The federal and state governments acknowledge the importance of working on climate change and environmental sustainability, but responses have been largely fragmented and, on some occasions, divergent. Moreover, although the Federal District and the State of Mexico have environmental and climate change policies, plans and programmes, there is little evidence that the two entities work as a team in the Valle de México. For example, whereas Mexico City has a mobility strategy that covers all its territory, the State of Mexico has only a mobility strategy for the Metropolitan Zone of the Valle de Toluca, where the state's capital is located. Furthermore, while Mexico City's Climate Action Programme emphasises mass transport initiatives, the State of Mexico is basing its strategy on building more motorways and roads to reduce traffic congestion, which is totally at odds with its Climate Action Programme.[26]

The different entities in the Valle de México appear to be moving at different speeds, and sometimes in different directions, due to policy fragmentation and uncoordinated actions. It is particularly revealing that Mexico City has made more progress on environmental sustainability and climate change mitigation and is now working on a resilience strategy, whereas the State of Mexico and Hidalgo are lagging behind. The State of Mexico has just begun work on a risk atlas for climate change, a first step towards resilience, but no systematic efforts have been made towards building a resilience strategy or moving in that direction. ProAire seems to be one of the few examples where co-ordinated action has taken place and where positive results have been achieved. Similarly, there is no concrete evidence that environmental policies are aligned with the interests or the needs of private sector stakeholders. Not all local governments seem to be willing to pay the political costs policies may entail. For instance, the CAMe is considering a proposal to harmonise the car-ownership tax. It is up to every state-level government whether it will collect the tax, and some states in the megalopolitan area have refrained from collecting it for political reasons. Adding an extra day per week without a car has reduced the popularity of the state governments that took this decision.

It is unclear to what extent municipal-level governments are active in environmental protection and climate change mitigation and adaptation. Some municipalities are taking steps to protect the environment and encourage the use of non-motorised transport, such as bicycles, but this does not seem to be the case across all municipalities and *delegaciones* in the ZMVM. Where such initiatives exist, they do not appear to be part of strategic urban planning, but one-off projects.

The political system is not conducive to co-ordination and co-operation. At the municipal level, neighbouring municipalities of different states do not co-ordinate their actions, as they need the approval and support of their state governments. The problem is exacerbated when those municipal-level governments belong to different political parties, which leads to no communication and co-ordination at all. Co-ordination for environmental protection in the metropolitan zone and the megalopolitan region seems to be easier at state level. The creation of the CAMe, under the leadership of the federal government, has brought together state governments from different political parties.

Nonetheless, this level of co-operation does not seem to be replicated at municipal level. A lack of political continuity also complicates co-operation, as there is no guarantee that the next administration will have the same disposition to co-operate. An environmental strategy at metropolitan level underpinned not only by political will but, more importantly, a political and social mandate, would be preferable. The reported lack of continuity in state programmes started by previous administrations, in particular in the State of Mexico, is a major difficulty for implementation, evaluation and adaptation of the programmes.

### *The CAMe's weak institutional arrangements …*

The creation of the CAMe to replace the CAM and cover a larger territory has somehow weakened effective governance structures. The reason for this may be the limited institutional capacity of the CAMe, its lack of adequate funding and the fact that it has no enforcement capacity. The other factor is that the CAMe will have to generate agreements and understanding among six local governments and the federal government, something that will require strong efforts and resources beyond its capacity. Although the commission is still in its infancy, it needs to show it has the political and technical muscle to lead and implement the strategic orientations agreed by governors and the federal government.

In addition, the CAMe presents two further weaknesses that may compromise its effectiveness. First, the capacity at the Executive Co-ordination is insufficient. At least until 2015, there were only 11 full-time officials appointed to the Executive Co-ordination, although the staffing level is not expected to exceed 30 officials. So far, most of the technical work has been done by external consultants financed by donations from international co-operation agencies. Second, the financing of the commission is progressing slowly. The Megalopolitan Environmental Trust needs to be approved to act as the financial instrument of the CAMe. In February 2014, the members of the commission agreed to give MXN 5.00 to the trust for every environmental vehicle inspection carried out in their territory. The funds will be used to meet the objectives of the CAMe and support the operation and administration of the Executive Co-ordination. Federal funds are also used for the financing of the commission.

### *… and the multiplicity of actors complicate co-ordination*

At the federal level, the Ministry of Environment and Natural Resources (Secretaría del Medio Ambiente y Recursos Naturales, SEMARNAT) combines policy making, regulation and implementation functions, while some bodies, called *desconcentrados*, also have policy-making functions.[27] The environment sector at federal level, led by SEMARNAT, includes decentralised bodies but also *desconcentrados*. These are autonomous in decision making but controlled by SEMARNAT in administrative issues such as human resources and finances. They include the National Water Commission (CONAGUA), the National Protected Areas Commission (Comisión Nacional de Areas Naturales Protegidas, CONANP), the National Ecology and Climate Change Institute (Instituto Nacional de Ecología y Cambio Climático, INECC) and the Federal Attorney for Environmental Protection (Procuraduría Federal de Protección al Ambiente, PROFEPA). Decentralised bodies exist as legal entities with their own budgets, such as the Mexican Institute of Water Technology (Instituto Mexicano de Tecnología del Agua, IMTA) and the National Forestry Commission (Comisión Nacional Forestal, CONAFOR). Most of the financial resources for the environment sector go to water and forests. CONAGUA accounts for nearly three-quarters of SEMARNAT's budget, and CONAFOR a further 13%.

In the water sector, in the Federal District, the provision among the 16 *delegaciones* is pooled in a single provider, the Water Utilities of Mexico City (SACMEX). Municipalities in the State of Mexico provide services mostly themselves, with the Water Commission of the State of Mexico (CAEM) having responsibilities transferred by some smaller municipalities. The CAEM co-ordinates action between municipalities and the federal government to improve water management, water and sanitation services and it provides technical assistance and develops infrastructure. In practice, all bodies of water are administered centrally by CONAGUA, which provides major infrastructure and water-related permits. Exploitation of water sources is permitted through concessions for the private sector and allocations to states and municipalities. All abstraction rights are recorded in a Public Registry of Water Rights and typically last for several decades, with the option of renewal. Concessions are tradable, and sales need to be registered. The recorded number of trades is likely to be an underestimate, as informal, i.e. unrecorded, lease agreements for concessions occur. For Mexico, estimates suggest that more than 15% of the population uses water without a permit or concession (see OECD, 2013d).

Moreover, the 1992 National Water Law established basin councils as co-ordinating and consultative authorities that bring representatives from CONAGUA, the federal states, municipal commissions and civil society together. In an effort to improve water governance, in 2004, an amendment to the law established 13 watershed organisations as autonomous structures with technical, administrative and legal prerogatives, acting as CONAGUA implementing agencies. In parallel, basin councils were to remain the main institutions under federal authority for water management at the basin level (see OECD, 2013d). Commissions and committees that focus on specific local areas or topics support the work of the basin councils and organisations. The ZMVM falls into the Valle de México basin. The basin and its organisation and council cover a significantly wider area in the states of Hidalgo and Mexico and include parts of Tlaxcala (Figure 4.7, left panel). The basin combines two hydrological zones, the Valle de México area, consisting mainly of the metropolitan zone, and the Tula Valley in the north (Figure 4.7, right panel). The basin council combines representatives from the Federal District (SACMEX), the three states, the CAEM and CONAGUA via the Valle de México Basin Organisation (Organismo de la Cuenca de Aguas del Valle de México).[28] At least for the provision of potable water, the main decisions are taken at the local level, with little co-ordination across municipal boundaries. Collaboration in flood prevention appears to be stronger and well-established.

The environmental responsibilities of local governments are specified in the General Law on Environmental Protection (Ley General de Equilibrio Ecológico y la Protección al Ambiente, LGEEPA). In the Federal District, the Ministry of Environment (Secretaría de Medio Ambiente del Distrito Federal, SEDEMA) is responsible for the design and implementation of an environment protection strategy, and the promotion of a sustainable urban environment. It focuses on six main areas: air quality and climate change, sustainable mobility, conservation land and biodiversity, green urban infrastructure, provision and water quality, and environmental education and communication. The State of Mexico's Ministry of Environment (Secretaría del Medio Ambiente del Estado de México, SMA) is also in charge of the formulation, implementation and evaluation of the environment strategy, and in particular the State Programme for Environment Protection and the State Climate Action Programme. It is responsible for co-ordinating the state environment strategy with the municipalities, including its 59 municipalities that are part of the ZMVM. The state government has also created the Institute for Climate Change to co-ordinate and support work in this area.

Figure 4.7. **Valle de México basin and administration**

Valle de México: Basin and metropolitan zone

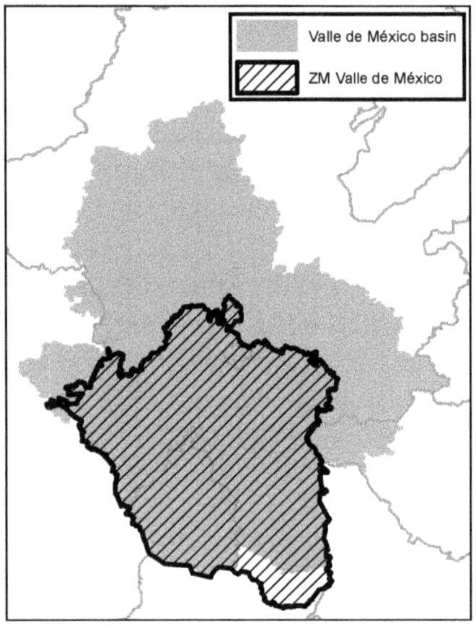


Hydrological zones in the Valle de México river basin

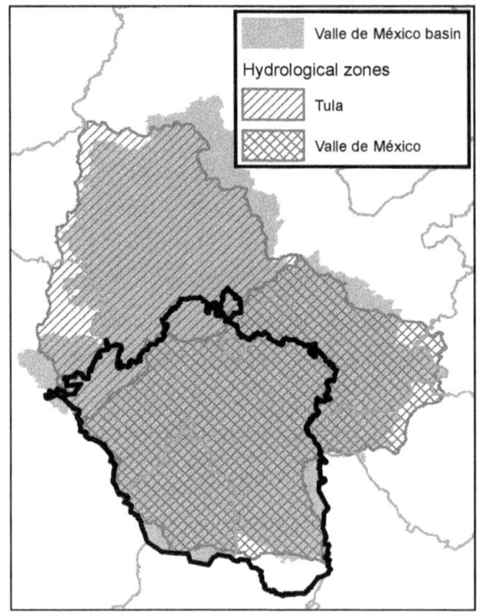


*Note:* This document and any map included herein are without prejudice to the status of or sovereignty over any territory, to the delimitation of international frontiers and boundaries and to the name of any territory, city or area.

*Sources*: CONAGUA (2007a), "Regiones hidrológicas administrativa (organismos de cuenca)", Comisión Nacional del Agua, www.conabio.gob.mx/informacion/metadata/gis/rha250kgw.xml?_xsl=/db/metadata/xsl/fgdc_html.xsl&_indent=no (accessed 28 May 2015); CONAGUA (2007b), "Subregiones hidrológicas, escala 1:250 000. República Mexicana", Subdirección General Técnica, Comisión Nacional del Agua, www.conabio.gob.mx/informacion/metadata/gis/sbrh250kgw.xml?_xsl=/db/metadata/xsl/fgdc_html.xsl&_indent=no (accessed 28 May 2015).

## *The implementation of environmental policies is beyond sub-national governments' capacity*

Across the Valle de México there seems to be insufficient technical expertise, infrastructure and money to design, implement and follow up sustainable development policies, particularly at municipal level. Financing environmental strategies such as those included in the climate action programmes constitutes a major barrier to implementation. The federal budget continues to be the main source of funding for environmental expenditure (see Chapter 5).

Municipal-level governments lack the technical and institutional capacity to implement sustainability strategies, in particular those regarding climate change. Interviews with officials from several municipalities and authorities in the State of Mexico suggested that there is weak regulation of activities such as energy, transport and solid waste management, whereas the use of solar energies is not encouraged. The problem is aggravated by weak enforcement of environmental law on the part of the state and municipal authorities, which results in low levels of compliance. Moreover, municipal-level governments do not appear to have the necessary personnel with the competencies, skills and experience to design and implement urban planning, zoning and environmental protection strategies.

The drawbacks of the waste management system epitomise the lack of capacity at municipal level. There is a large difference in the regulation, operation and inspection capacity for waste management between the Federal District and the State of Mexico. In the Federal District, the responsibility for ensuring collection and management of waste corresponds to the central government through the Ministry of Public Works (Secretaría de Obras y Servicios del Distrito Federal, SOBSE), whereas in the State of Mexico every municipality is responsible for the management of waste, and the state government sets guidelines for the integral management of waste. The problem is that the majority of municipalities do not have the infrastructure to collect and dispose of waste. The vehicles that collect waste, for example, are obsolete and do not allow the separation of waste (Gutiérrez, 2014). Insufficient personnel to conduct inspections, supervise the operation of landfills and ensure compliance with the norms is also an issue. Surveillance of the landfills is limited, to make sure that no other type of toxic, biological or infectious waste is deposited with urban solid waste, which can change its composition. Moreover, the operation of final disposal sites (landfills and controlled sites) is in many cases the responsibility of private enterprises that have obtained a concession. This situation often leads to discretional management of the registry of the quantity, composition and treatment of waste (Barreda Marín, 2009). Similarly, in the water sector, municipalities are responsible for the provision of drinking water, drainage, sewage and water treatment (under Article 115 of the Constitution). Some municipalities, however, struggle to provide these services for lack of funding and technical capacity.

The lack of systematic follow-up and measurement of outcomes of the different environmental protection strategies is an obstacle to assessment of progress and impact. The OECD (2013a) *Environmental Performance Review of Mexico* concluded that monitoring, reporting and evaluation of environment programmes was increasing but was not yet focused enough on outcomes. This also applies for the Valle de México. Reporting takes place through activity reports, implementation reports and annual working programmes' implementation reports in both the Federal District and the State of Mexico. Some evaluations are already providing useful feedback. The evaluation of the ProAire programme suggests that air-quality standards could be more stringent, to reap additional health benefits, and notes the need to strengthen compliance with particular standards. Some municipalities do not even have the technical capacity to follow up and assess results, given the lack of skilled staff and financial means.

### *Environmental and development goals are often in conflict*

The municipal authorities within the Valle de México, as in many other municipalities across the country, rarely take into account the recommendations of land-use planning in formulating municipal development plans. This has led, for example, to the use of land for housing when it is officially considered as conservation land. A lack of information and understanding persists of how environmental protection can contribute to economic development. State and above all municipal governments in the metropolitan zone still need to find a balance between development and environmental goals, particularly during the planning and enforcement stages. This issue also shows that achieving complementarities between economic growth and environmental priorities in the metropolitan area remain a challenge.

Although housing production, in the framework of sustainable development, widely uses eco-technologies, the authorities at all levels of government do not seem to take into account other aspects critical to sustainability, such as the urban and social impact of housing on citizens and on the habitat. Urban sprawl, the use of rural or conservation land, water demand, long commuting times and the difficulty for families of living in "dormitory cities" in small homes that cannot be adapted to their future needs are just some of the effects of housing policies on the environment (OECD, 2015b; Paquette, 2014). For example, 60% of the fuel used in the metropolitan area is to move commuters to and from their workplaces. This not only creates environmental damage through emissions but negatively affects the quality of life. State and municipal authorities in the State of Mexico and recently Hidalgo have largely focused on satisfying housing demand rather than on job creation in the municipalities, leading to the transformation of municipalities into dormitory towns.

### *Environmental awareness among citizens could be promoted*

Residents' awareness and understanding of environmental issues remains weak despite governments' efforts. Progress in environmental protection and climate change action depends on citizens' engagement. Residents in the Valle de México appear to lack environmental information and education and are resistant to changing their habits. For example, small businesses are not willing to change their traditional equipment and production systems for cleaner technology because of the cost. Resistance among people living in risk zones to moving to secure places is another example. Citizens are aware of environmental problems, but not of their role both in creating the problem and resolving it. The strategies for development and climate change in both Mexico City and the State of Mexico promote the need for public consultation in forums and seminars, but there is little evidence of a strategy to actively engage the public in policy decisions, and the voluntary sector's involvement in climate change actions is limited. Local governments in the Valle de México recognise the need for cultural change to reduce pollution levels. If owning a car continues to be a necessity, change will be harder to achieve.

## Urban planning as a tool for addressing environmental problems

In the Valle de México, the environmental problems related to water, air quality and solid waste and the threats to conservation land are the product of poor urban strategic planning and its dissociation from the environment. Integrating the environment into urban planning could be a significant contribution to pursuing climate change and resilience. For example, effective mass transit systems that prioritise non-motorised transport can reduce emissions and congestion and help improve public health. However, the urban form and density shape how efficient these systems can be. Moreover, efficient management of solid waste reduces the generation of methane, a powerful greenhouse gas. Effective landfill management can reduce emissions, and if located strategically, need not represent a threat to aquifers and soil. Architectural and urban design that reduces energy consumption and cost can reduce costs for residents and contribute to lower GHG emissions. Investing in water and sewerage treatment plants and on innovative urban design that integrates natural and built form to conserve ecosystem functioning could not only improve well-being but reduce the costs of conserving the environment.

### *Addressing the water challenge may increase environmental sustainability*

Urban planning and water services should be closely linked to increase environmental sustainability. The focus on four pillars should continue: reducing demand, eliminating leaks, raising awareness and availability of water from other areas, and refilling aquifers. International experience suggests that urban areas can be very successful in reducing demand (Box 4.3).

The first pillar consists in reducing water demand in the Valle de México. Attempts have been made to reduce demand through awareness campaigns, often targeting schools. Uptake among children seems to be satisfactory, but the impact of the measures is not clear. Consumption has been fairly stable, despite campaigns in the Federal District to raise awareness and reduce consumption. Reducing demand is not made easier by the relatively low cost of water. As with any other good, consumers respond to an increase in price with a reduction in demand. Estimates of the "price elasticity", a measure of the responsiveness of demand to changes in price, tend to range between -0.4 and -0.6, implying that a doubling in prices reduces demand by about 40-60% (Grafton et al., 2011; Fuentes, 2011).[29]

Box 4.3. **Declining urban water consumption**

Per capita water consumption is declining in cities in OECD countries, thanks to a combination of increased system efficiency, deindustrialisation and lower levels of domestic use. The only exceptions in an OECD survey on water governance in cities are Hong Kong, China; Lisbon, Portugal; and the Federal District of Mexico.

- Industrial uses are declining, driven by efficiency gains and the shift from industry to services. Similarly, hospitals and schools tend to reduce their water consumption.
- Households have also reduced their consumption. While per capita water consumption initially dropped due to reduced outdoor use, indoor water use (chiefly through low-flow toilets and efficient washing machines) has also decreased.
- A growing number of utilities operators are seeing an additional decrease in consumption because households are finding alternative water supply solutions – e.g. rainwater harvesting – driven by environmental motives (reducing the energy footprint) or financial concerns (reducing the water bill). These households usually remain connected to the main infrastructure, and in some cases discharge water they have not purchased into the sewer, free-riding on the sewer service.
- Authorities contribute to this trend when they encourage users to conserve water. In California, the 2009 Water Conservation Act requires the state to achieve a 20% reduction in urban per capita water use by the end of 2020.

*Source*: OECD (2015c), *Water and Cities: Ensuring Sustainable Futures*, OECD Studies on Water, OECD Publishing, Paris, http://dx.doi.org/10.1787/9789264230149-en.

Keeping prices artificially low not only encourages overconsumption, but also holds back investment in water-saving technologies and counteracts efforts to build an environmentally sustainable water culture. This applies to both private households and the public sector. Prices are heavily subsidised in the Valle de México, especially in the Federal District. In 2008, more than 55% of SACMEX's budget came from subsidies. By 2012, the percentage of subsidies was reduced to one-third, but the total budget decreased by 15%, from MXN 12.2 billion to MXN 10.4 billion (USD 800 million) in 2013 prices (SACMEX, 2013). This makes investment in major infrastructure difficult and creates obstacles in co-ordination across levels of government.[30]

Any adjustment to prices needs to be accompanied by measures to improve collection of tariffs. Only 74% of charges in the Federal District were recovered in 2013 (up from 61% in 2011). In the State of Mexico, payment rates vary significantly across municipalities. On average, 46% of bills were paid in 2013 (down from 67% in 2011). In response to the low rate of collection by municipalities, the CAEM, the Water Commission for the State of Mexico, introduced a chargeback system, in which transfers to municipalities are reduced if they do not collect their fees.

In addition to collecting fees, a necessary step in aligning incentives with reducing demand is to ensure that households are paying for their actual consumption. A lack of coverage with individual water meters results in a significant percentage of households paying fixed fees for their water. In the Valle de México metropolitan area, only 52% of households are metered. The percentage exceeds 90% in cities in other Latin American countries (see World Bank, 2013). Programmes for the expansion of meters have been implemented. Between 2007 and 2012, SACMEX increased the number of working meters from less than 600 000 to 1 253 626, but a significant shortfall remains, of about 25% of users, who mostly pay a fixed consumption fee.[31] A further advantage of having a meter installed is that awareness of actual consumption is raised. This can create a measurable impact on water demand by itself (Grafton et al., 2011) and amplify the reduction in demand that follows price increases.[32] Working meters are also essential to assess the efficiency of the water delivery system and to detect leakage.

Adjusting tariffs is difficult, both politically, because changes require legislative approval, and socially, as water and its tariffs quickly become hotly discussed topics in local media. Short political cycles increase the pressure on policy makers to keep public opinion in their favour. Nonetheless, a successful strategy in reducing demand needs to consider adjusting prices. The social impact can be alleviated by allowing for higher increases for wealthy customers and those with relatively high consumption levels. Gains from increased tariffs could then help subsidise improvements in infrastructure and the expansion of meter coverage. It would also allow for subsidising less-affluent households, while moving towards water and fiscal sustainability.

The current progressivity of tariffs is fairly steep (starting at a very low rate; see Figure 4.8) for the lowest two tariff categories. The subsidy for these consumers is reduced with increasing consumption. For the 25% of households that pay the middle and high tariffs, prices per cubic metre are flat until they reach 70 $m^3$ in two months, corresponding to 288 litres per person (assuming a four-person household). This exceeds both the required level for sustainable water supply and average consumption levels typically found across Latin America.[33] The incremental increase in the relevant consumption range, below 70 $m^3$, is unlikely to have a significant impact on the behaviour of affluent consumers.

The second pillar in achieving sustainability is reducing leakage. Leakage arises both in the public infrastructure, i.e. in the main pipes that deliver potable water and on the "last metre", i.e. between the public system and the households and even in the household's own appliances. For the latter, water meters can help raise awareness of losses generated by faulty appliances and incentivise replacement. Public infrastructure, however, requires significant investment. The existing network of pipelines is under severe stress, especially pipes that are more than 40 years old. Estimates for the total loss from leaks (and illegal abstractions) vary, but even estimates at the upper end, around

38-40% losses, are considered realistic (see IADB, 2012). To assess the extent of the loss, further monitoring along the pipe network is required. Full mitigation of leaks is not economically viable, and the investment in infrastructure needs to be balanced with the cost savings in water provision. In water-rich areas, higher leakage rates are typically found to be acceptable, e.g. in Grenoble in France. But given the severe strain on the water resources in the Valle de México, investment in leakage reduction is likely to create significant returns.

Figure 4.8. **Progressivity of bimonthly water tariffs in the Federal District, 2015**

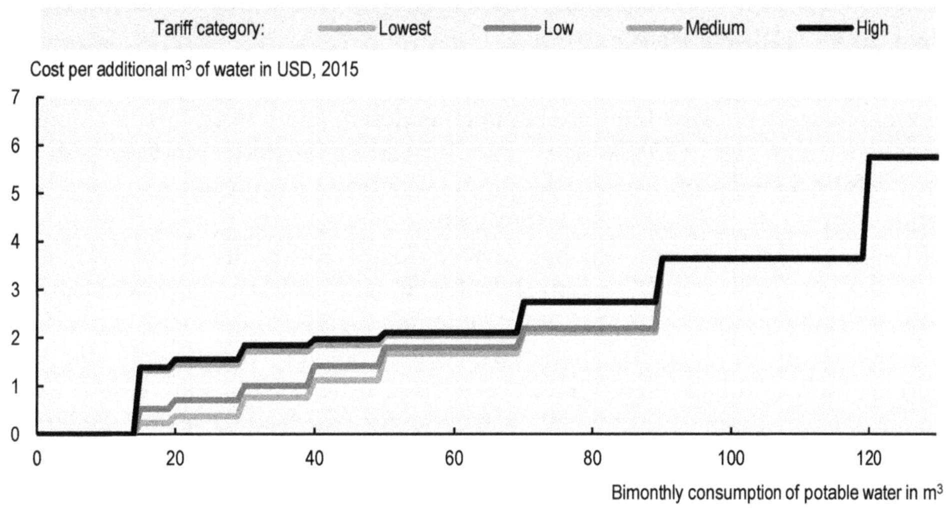


*Note:* Tariff categories for the Federal District are *popular* (lowest); *baja* (low); *media* (medium); *alta* (high). Tariffs are for 2015 and converted from MXN to USD using the average exchange rate for 2014.

*Source*: Government of the Federal District (2014), "Decreto por el que se reforman, adicionan y derogan diversas disposiciones del Código Fiscal del Distrito Federal", *Gaceta Oficial Distrito Federal*, No. 2012(I), 22 December, available at: www.sacmex.df.gob.mx/sacmex/doc/3_atencion_a_usuarios/tarifas/6_tarifas172.pdf.

Cracked and leaking pipes not only result in direct waste of potable water, but limit service delivery. The pressure at which water can be supplied is constrained, to avoid bursting pipes. This means that water will not be available to all households in the affected part of the network. Required replacements and an expansion of the existing network require significant investment, which is not covered in the operating budget of the utilities providers. This is seldom the case across the OECD. Among the three revenue sources for utilities providers, taxes, tariffs and transfers, governments decide on the most efficient mix of resources to manage trade-offs between economic efficiency, financial sustainability, environmental protection and social cohesion.

The third pillar to achieve a sustainable supply of water is to increase the available water. This pillar combines two strategies. The first is the utilisation of non-freshwater sources. For private households, collecting rainwater to use for watering green areas is encouraged. In the public sector, coverage of water treatment facilities is being expanded. The largest water treatment plant in Mexico is currently being constructed in the Tula Valley, north of the Valle de México. It has a planned capacity of 35 cubic metres per second ($m^3/s$), of which two-thirds will result in "safe to handle" water and one-third in water that can be drained into rivers and dams (see CONAGUA, 2015). Given the plant's location, the benefit of the plant will be outside the Valle de México. In the Tula Valley, the majority of the city's untreated wastewater is used to irrigate

100 000 hectares of agricultural land. The raw sewage is appreciated by the farmers, as it significantly increases yield for crops. But the higher yields come at a price. The sewage is detrimental to residents' health and given the high permeability of the agricultural soil, its use has the unintended side effect of artificially recharging the aquifer underlying the irrigated area with 25 $m^3/s$ of raw wastewater (see WHO, 2003: Chapter 3). While it might seem counterintuitive to construct water treatment facilities outside the metropolitan zone, the benefits of treating water to become "safe to handle" are likely to be higher in the Tula Valley than in the metropolitan zone. The possible use of "safe to handle" water in the urban parts of the Valle de México is probably limited. Its main use is for agriculture and gardening, and the majority of water used in these areas in the Federal District is treated water.

The second strategy to increase supply is the expansion of the water delivery systems from external aquifers. New lines are being considered, and a third line is planned for the Cutzamala system (see CONAGUA, 2015). Adding a third pipeline will facilitate required refurbishments of the existing pipes, which were built 40 years ago. However, importing water from neighbouring basins cannot be the main strategy to supply water to the ZMVM, because this practice has created social and political conflicts and led to regional deficits of water (Escolero Fuentes et al., 2010). The water tariff in the Valle de México does not reflect the environmental damage to the Lerman and Cutzamala basins. Moreover, the costs associated with water delivery across long distances (and heights) are high, and increased reliance on surface water systems increases vulnerability to climate change. Extended dry spells and droughts can lead to severe depletion of the reservoirs and make the water system susceptible to risk from climate change. In 2014-15, São Paulo experienced a severe drought and had to implement a range of immediate measures that helped alleviate the pressure on the water infrastructure, but short-term adjustments are unlikely to result in sustainable solutions (Box 4.4). Without addressing the dual water challenge, the Valle de México can neither achieve sustainability nor resilience to climate change. Both aspects require a concrete long-term strategy, developed jointly by all stakeholders in the metropolitan zone, the basin and at the national level. But both aspects also require immediate action to stop further depletion of resources and enhance the quality of life of the metropolitan zone's residents.

### Box 4.4. **Drought response by São Paulo's sanitation services**

In 2014, the Basic Sanitation Company of the State of São Paulo (Companhia de Saneamento Básico do Estado de São Paulo, SABESP) had to respond to the worst drought in 84 years. Water inflow was significantly reduced and remained even below values recorded in 1953, formerly the driest year on record. In addition, high temperatures well above summer averages led to greater consumption of water and greater evaporation, thereby causing a continuous decrease in the volume stored in the main surface water system. In response, the SABESP has implemented a series of measures:

- substitution of water supply from the most affected parts of the system to other sources
- introduction of discounts (bonus) to consumers using below-average amounts of water
- reduction in the pressure in the water distribution lines, to decrease leakage
- reduction of the volume of treated water sold wholesale to municipalities that own their distribution network

Box 4.4. **Drought response by São Paulo's sanitation services** (*continued*)

- installation of new pumps and delivery routes to extract water located below the intakes of the existing water storage system, from the so-called "technical reserve", which had never been used to serve the population.

The SABESP estimates that as of March 2015, the implementation of the bonus programme accounted for 19.8% of water savings in the most affected part of the system. The reduction of pressure in water distribution lines and initiatives mitigating water losses accounted for 41.2%, the transfer of water between production systems for 35.6% and the reduction of the volume of wholesale water transfers for 3.4%.

With the continuation of the drought into 2015 and a low level of inflow into the reservoirs, the SABESP implemented further measures:

- The period to which discounts (bonuses) apply was extended until the end of 2015, or until reservoir levels normalise, depending on which occurs first.
- The SABESP was authorised in January 2015 to introduce a contingency tariff that increases the water bill for above-average consumption. Customers who consume up to 20% more than the average pay 40% higher tariffs and consumption above 20% of the average results in a tariff increase of 100%.
- The intensification of the reduction in water pressure was extended, increasing the periods of reduced pressure.

Due to the crisis, a series of short- and medium-term emergency investments have been and will be required to continue providing water to the population. These investments resulted in an increase in costs and change in capital expenditure. If the drought does not end and further investments are not possible, the SABESP expects that more drastic measures might be required, including rotating rationing, to ensure continued service provision.

*Source*: SABESP (2015), "Form 20-F (filing date 29 April 2015)", Companhia de Saneamento Básico do Estado de São Paulo, available at: www.sabesp.com.br/sabesp/filesmng.nsf/04F592CBAA86C3EB83257E3600833CB6/$File/sbsform20f_2014.pdf.

The fourth pillar is to recharge local aquifers. Mexico City's main aquifer is recharged through natural infiltration in the Sierra de las Cruces and Sierra del Chichinautzin that form the western and southern boundary of the metropolitan area respectively. But sustainability can only be achieved if abstractions are significantly reduced or artificial refill is used and urbanisation in this area is controlled and there is a wide campaign of reforestation through the *Pago por Servicios Ambientales* (Payment for Ecosystem Services) programme.[34] Refilling aquifers via pumps risks contaminating the groundwater, and even refill via pumped groundwater from external aquifers can lead to contamination.[35] Moreover, using the New Mexico City International Aurport as a testbed, the long-term flood protection measures for the Valle de México should shift from costly drainage tunnels (to drain both waste and rainwater) towards the closing of open sewage canals (to separate waste and rainwater) and expansion of the local rainwater storage capacity at the local level. Smaller scale solutions, such as retention ponds and eco-roofs in industrial and residential neighbourhoods, could make a difference in reducing the pressure on the piped wastewater system and promoting reuse of rainwater. A good example can be found in Portland, Oregon, where a city-wide watershed management plan aims to increase natural drainage of rainwater to reduce the high cost of piped infrastructure investment (Box 4.5).

As part of the effort to build a resilience strategy for Mexico City, drought scenarios will be simulated, with different resilient investment portfolios. This could be the basis for a solid response in the event of serious drought. It is nevertheless important to protect the highest parts of the basins, the refilling zones and the local climate. Declaring refilling zones natural protected areas would be one useful strategy if it is accompanied by adequate enforcement. Including water issues in urban planning would help locate areas that could store rainwater (Escolero Fuentes et al., 2010).

### Box 4.5. **Portland's green infrastructure**

The City of Portland, Oregon, promotes green infrastructure, which is defined as interconnected natural systems and/or engineered systems that use plants and soil to slow, filter and infiltrate runoff close to its source in a way that strengthens and mimics natural functions/processes. The 2005 Portland Watershed Management Plan provides the scientific framework for watershed improvements, with an emphasis on hydrology. A big part of this is understanding that restoring the hydrologic cycle has a significant role in watershed health and protects both Portland's piped infrastructure investment (capacity) and its rivers and streams at less cost. Green streets and eco-roofs are among the most typical green infrastructures:

- **Green streets** consist of swales, linear facilities that collect and often convey storm water. Storm water flows into the swale and soaks into the ground as the vegetation and soil filter pollutants. This keeps storm water from flowing to sewers or into rivers and streams. It also replenishes the groundwater, which feeds cool, clean water to rivers and streams. The first curb extension was built in 2002. There are already more than 900 green street facilities in Portland. It was successful partly because the initiative was started as a pilot project that would have been discontinued if it had been unsuccessful. Different designs were then developed for different situations. Green streets have also enhanced pedestrian safety by shortening crossing distances, and are sometimes considered to slow traffic. Neighbours consider them a real asset to the neighbourhood because they provide water quality and habitat benefits and increase property values.
- More and more **eco-roofs** are being built in Portland. As of 1 July 2010, Portland had a total of 250 projects for over 12 acres. Since 2008, nearly 100 incentive projects have been accepted for an additional 5.6 acres, despite the recession and economic downturn. The approach seems to be working. Incentive funds have been awarded and interest is growing.

*Source:* OECD (2012d), *Compact City Policies: A Comparative Assessment*, OECD Green Growth Studies, OECD Publishing, Paris, http://dx.doi.org/10.1787/9789264167865-en.

## *Urban air quality management could be boosted by synergies with other sectors*

Improving air quality requires synergies from different sector activities. For instance, reducing air pollution produced by cars would require reforming vehicle inspection (*verificación vehicular*), imposing uniform inspection and maintenance standards in the entire megalopolis. This programme should accelerate the disposal of old and inefficient cars. Buses, trucks and motorcycles should be included in the compulsory vehicle inspection. Improving fuel quality should also be part of this strategy. Using less diesel would address the problem of black smoke from heavy diesel-powered buses and trucks that operate in the metropolitan zone. The introduction of alternative fuels such as compressed natural gas (as India has done), biofuels from crops, or used cooking oils or biogas from sewerage and waste should be analysed as long-term alternatives. The city of Kyoto, Japan, collects used cooking oil from the residents to make fuel, under the biodiesel fuel project launched in 1996. The city's 92 buses and 136 garbage collection trucks are now operated on biodiesel fuel (City of Kyoto, 2015). Promoting the use of three-way catalysts that can reduce emissions or particle filters for diesel vehicles, and the adoption of hybrid technology could have a positive impact in air quality. Moreover, as discussed in Chapter 3, authorities must re-examine urban transport demand from a metropolitan perspective and devise new strategies that provide maximum accessibility. The challenge is to expand and improve public transport supply so that the automobile becomes part of the transport system rather than its central focus. But discouraging the use of cars will only be possible if efficient and economic transport alternatives are offered (bus, light rail, underground, ferries, walking or cycling). Improving the transport system will require a combination of policies that reinforce each other and help avoid adverse side effects. The OECD has found that in cities where more people commute by public transport, $CO_2$ emissions per capita from transport tend to be lower, whereas in cities where people commute by car, $CO_2$ emissions per capita tend to be higher (OECD, 2013b).

The *Hoy No Circula* programme could be updated. Adopting more stringent restrictions for poorly performing vehicles, including motorcycles and freight transport in the programme, and gradually scrapping cars more than 20 years old are some options (Centro Mario Molina, 2014). Other alternatives could include taking out of service public transport vehicles that do not have environmental technology, promoting the yearly renewal of catalytic converters in buses, taxis and trucks, or even implementing the *Hoy No Circula* only during contingencies – based on odd and even numbers on license plates – as in Paris. The *Hoy No Circula* programme alone will not help to improve air quality; it will need to be complemented with strategic urban planning, transport-oriented policies and zoning. Better transport would allow government to enforce stricter regulations, reducing the number of old cars in circulation. Imposing a uniform car-ownership tax (*tenencia vehicular*) across the six entities of the megalopolitan region would improve air quality and increase the financial resources of state-level governments.

Mass public and non-motorised transport should continue to be part of the environmental strategy, but with a metropolitan approach. Individually, the Federal District and the State of Mexico have introduced a number of mobility initiatives (see Chapter 3) in a quest to improve the air quality in the metropolitan area and reduce energy consumption. For example, the Federal District's BRT Metrobús system is expected to help reduce pollution (120 000 tonnes of $CO_2$ emissions per year) and to help with the urban regeneration of green areas. The ECOBICI bike-sharing programme has helped reduce 1 395 tonnes of $CO_2e$, equivalent to planting 4 100 trees between 2010 and 2014.[36] Authorities in Mexico City are also renewing the Passenger Transport Network (Red de Transporte de Pasajeros, RTP) bus fleet with new, less-polluting buses. In 2014, the RTP bus introduced 2 lines of the EcoBus, with 2 hybrid buses and 72 natural gas buses (in a fleet of 1 360 buses).[37] The RTP faces two main challenges: the fact there are only three natural gas stations in Mexico City and the lack of financial resources to replace old buses. Such initiatives need to complement each other as part of a metropolitan transport strategy if they are to be effective.

One desirable step would be to consider aligning Mexican air quality standards with the international standards set by the World Health Organization (WHO). This would provide policy makers with appropriate targets for air quality management and ensure buy-in from national environmental groups. The new standards would be based on an extensive international body of scientific research relating to air pollution and its health consequences. Although WHO acknowledges that every country should consider its own circumstances, technological feasibility and economic needs before adopting international guidelines as legally based standards, authorities in the Valle de México have shown they have the experience, political commitment, economic means and technology to upgrade their standards.

Efforts to reduce air pollution from industrial sources in the Valle de México should also be reinforced. Better information is needed on polluting industries, the type of pollutants emitted, the trends of the pollutants and what is currently being done to reduce the trend. Some strategies to reduce industrial pollution could include physical planning or zoning by: 1) restricting the location of new industries close to residential zones; 2) relocating existing industries, if economically viable; 3) creating special control areas or smoke-free zones; 4) area planning based on emission assessments and air quality objectives, to determine the type of control needed; and 5) compulsory environmental impact assessments for new major industries, to assess potential air pollution and develop recommendations for improvement in choice of location and pollution equipment.[38] Promoting cleaner production is another option available. This would mean increasing the efficiency of industrial processes and the use of products to prevent the pollution of air, water and land, reducing waste at its source and minimising health risks. Poor solid waste management also contributes to air pollution, and a comprehensive system of waste collection is essential (see below).

Authorities in the Valle de México should ensure the compatibility of new and existing environmental strategies at city, regional and national level. Integration of land-use planning with transport planning and air quality management, all of which directly influence the metropolitan zone's air quality, requires greater co-ordination. The aim should be to avoid sending contradictory messages to the wider public. The experience of the US Clean Air Act, which seeks to ensure that transit and highway projects are consistent with ("conform to") air quality goals, could be a valuable example for the Valle de México. The mobility impact assessment proposed by the Ministry of Mobility of the Federal District (Secretaría de Movilidad del Distrito Federal, SEMOVI) is a step in this direction.

Greening of the building sector and other key urban infrastructure requires greater integration of environmental concerns and investment decisions. Valuable initiatives are already in place at federal and local level, but they need to be co-ordinated and integrated into regional/metropolitan planning. In the area of housing construction, to reduce energy consumption and reach its target of reducing $CO_2$ emissions by 50% by 2050, Mexico's federal government is adopting the "whole house approach" that includes technological development and housing design. In 2012, Mexico's National Housing Commission (Comisión Nacional de Vivienda, CONAVI) adopted the National Appropriate Mitigation Action (NAMA) for sustainable housing. Since 2013, all new social housing in the country has been built with eco-technologies. More recently, the Mexican government has been piloting a NAMA for existing social housing, which aims to improve the existing housing stock using eco-technology, in collaboration with local and municipal governments, and raise the standards used for new houses.

One of the most important projects of the NAMA is ECOCASA, which finances the construction of energy-efficient homes for low- to middle-income families. The Federal Mortgage Society (Sociedad Hipotecaria Federal, SHF) provides bridge loans with a preferential rate for developers to construct houses using eco-technology. This project is expected to help cut over 1 million tonnes of GHG emissions over 40 years, the estimated lifecycle of these houses. It also intends to support the construction sector and to promote

### Box 4.6. Conformity between transport and air quality management planning in the United States

The US government has introduced a policy of transport conformity, integrating air quality and transport planning. The air quality plan seeks to minimise emissions, while transport planning seeks to increase mobility. Transport activities are not funded or approved unless they conform to the purpose of the air quality plan. No transport activity should result in new violations of air quality standards or exacerbate existing violations, or in any delay in the planned improvement of air quality. The transport plan funds transport control measures in the air quality plan, calculates motor vehicle pollution inventory and matches the air quality budget. Conformity is required in areas that do not meet, or previously have not met, air quality standards for ozone, carbon monoxide, particulate matter or nitrogen dioxide. A conformity determination estimates emissions that will result from an area's transportation system, and demonstrates that those emissions are within the limits outlined in the state's air quality implementation plan. The conformity process is administered jointly by the US Environmental Protection Agency (EPA) and the US Department of Transportation. This requires shared data and identical assumptions between transport and air quality plans to generate realistic measures.

Several US cities have added new projects and measures to meet their air quality and transportation goals for the one-hour ozone air quality standard. For example, Beaumont-Port Arthur, Texas, provided truck stop electrification to reduce vehicle idling; Houston, Texas, implemented a heavy-duty diesel retrofit and replacement programme; Atlanta, Georgia, used the conformity process to assist agencies in addressing a significant increase in vehicle miles travelled, re-evaluated transportation planning goals, and added new transit and land-use initiatives; and Charlotte, North Carolina, addressed increased vehicle miles and the resulting emissions increases by creating a long-term transit and land-use plan.

*Sources*: US Environmental Protection Agency (2006), "The bridge to cleaner air: Transportation conformity", Office of Transportation and Air Quality, United States Environmental Protection Agency, Washington, DC, January, available at: http://epa.gov/otaq/stateresources/transconf/420f06001.pdf; UNEP (2005), "Urban air quality management toolbox", United Nations Environment Programme, United Nations Human Settlements Programme, Nairobi, available at: www.unep.org/urban_environment/PDFs/handbook.pdf.

the use of eco-technology; and increase the comfort of residents and lower their electricity bills. This is a complex project, as it requires the co-ordination of several actors in the housing sector, including CONAVI, the National Workers' Housing Fund Institute (Instituto del Fondo Nacional de la Vivienda para los Trabajadores, INFONAVIT) and housing developers. It has been necessary to build the technical knowledge of developers on eco-technology, to prepare suitable proposals, adopt adequate incentives to attract private developers and create a robust and feasible monitoring, reporting and validation framework.[39] As an example of sustainable housing construction, the ECOCASA programme won an award for climate protection from the United Nations during the COP19 in Warsaw in 2013. In 2007, INFONAVIT created a "Green Mortgage" (*Hipoteca Verde*). Almost all mortgages awarded by the institute to buy, build, remodel or improve a house are required to use eco-technologies to save water, electricity and gas. Initially, the green mortgage was allocated as an additional amount of credit to those who asked for it, but since 2011, all credits granted by INFONAVIT have been dedicated to houses using eco-technology.[40] Between January and July 2015, 96.2% of the credits for new housing and 94.4% of the credits for used houses were part of the green mortgage scheme. It would be helpful to align these projects with transport and air improvement plans, to avoid negative side effects due to, for instance, poor urban planning. In the same vein, in 2008, Mexico City's government introduced the Certification Programme for Sustainable Buildings, under which local authorities transform and adapt existing and future buildings using sustainability criteria and environmental efficiency. When a building receives the certification, the owners are entitled to fiscal incentives, of either a 40% reduction in payroll tax or a 20% reduction in property tax (SEDEMA, 2008).

### *The metropolitan zone needs a sustainable approach to waste management*

In the Valle de México, the main motivations for better solid waste management are to avoid groundwater contamination, soil pollution, the bad smell, generation of GHG emissions and health hazards. The ZMVM lacks an effective collection and disposal system. A first priority would be to develop an adequate waste management system and then focus on waste reduction measures. For the Valle de México, as for any large metropolitan area, managing waste properly requires addressing all three key drivers of a sustainable waste management system: public health, with a focus on waste collection and street sweeping; the environment, focusing on improving disposal to protect ground and surface water and avoiding air, water and soil pollution; and resource recovery, to close the loop of both materials and organics management (Wilson and Scheinberg, 2010). The overarching idea is that the metropolitan zone as a whole should aim at landfilling less waste and recycling more. The *Basura Cero* programme could be the basis for a comprehensive metropolitan initiative. However, its results need to be evaluated, so that it can be improved and eventually expanded to the entire metropolitan zone, in co-ordination with the authorities in the State of Mexico.

There are several areas where the Valle de México needs to act on waste management. First, authorities need to build new disposal sites and renovate existing sites, with adequate protection for the environment and public health, and also to gradually introduce recycling. Second, the authorities should phase out open dumps – as has already been achieved with the Bordo Poniente landfill – and inadequate collection systems. Lastly, measures could be taken to increase separation at the source and ensure that less waste goes to disposal sites. Since the Valle de México is somewhat heterogeneous in terms of capacity and resources, the modernisation of its solid waste management system should start with the identification of simple, appropriate and affordable solutions that can be implemented progressively. Early steps could include extending collection to the whole metropolitan zone and measures to raise awareness of the importance of waste separation. The experience of the Netherlands in managing solid waste could be helpful to authorities in the Valle de México, as an example of how growing environmental awareness among the Dutch people led the government to reduce the space for landfills (Box 4.7). The Valle de México should learn from the Dutch experience that without a system of laws and regulations for waste materials, and control measures established from the outset, all waste could end up in a landfill. If the authorities want to promote the participation of private waste-processing companies, it needs to give them the possibility of developing profitable activities. With mandatory and prohibitory provisions and taxes, a better grade of waste processing can be enforced.

The experience of OECD and EU countries provide authorities in the Valle de México with some policy instruments to incentivise a shift up the waste hierarchy. Table 4.5 presents a non-exhaustive overview of those policy instruments, which can be designed and implemented in different ways to influence their effectiveness. Those presented in Table 4.5 are options authorities in the Valle de México might explore. Important lessons for the Valle de México that can be drawn from OECD-EU countries' experience are that: 1) using a wide variety of instruments increases the chances of a higher level of waste recycling; 2) a regional waste management plan generally achieves good waste recycling results; 3) the management waste plan needs to be complemented with additional initiatives to establish better infrastructure or divert waste from landfills; 4) increasing the landfill tax by more than 50% in the medium term and introducing a landfill ban on organic waste or non-pre-treated waste can help achieve good results; 5) countries that have introduced mandatory separation of certain elements of waste, e.g. waste paper, in addition to packaging waste, or mandatory separation of biowaste, have high recycling levels; and 6) economic incentives for households to recycle their waste (e.g. pay-as-you-throw schemes, requiring payment fees based on the weight of the residual, and not separately collected waste, the size of the residual waste bin or the frequency of collection) have mostly performed better than waste collection fees based on the property value, size of the property, household size or similar criteria (European Environmental Agency, 2013). Experience suggests that users should be asked to pay for collection and street sweeping, since they can see the results and need the services. In the Valle de México, fees for collection and street sweeping should be collected by government and not by informal workers. State-of-the-art landfills are best financed by a combination of central government financing supplemented by cross-subsidies between rich and poor.

### Box 4.7. The Netherlands' "Lansink's Ladder" waste management system

The Netherlands has a highly efficient waste management system that allows it to recycle more than half of its waste. Most of the remainder is incinerated to generate electricity. As a result, only a small percentage ends up in landfills. The Dutch system avoids as much as possible creating waste, recovering the valuable raw materials from it, generating energy by incinerating residual waste, and only then dumping what is left over in an environmentally sound fashion. The Netherlands has little space for disposal sites and Dutch people are environmentally aware (more than 90% of Dutch citizens separate their household waste, and 75% seek to reduce water and energy consumption). As a result, the Dutch government took measures to reduce landfilling. This gave private companies the confidence to invest in environmentally sounder solutions to manage waste. The deciding factor was regulations known as "Lansink's Ladder", after the member of the Dutch parliament who proposed them in 1994. Over the years, recycling targets were set for the various waste streams, such as organic waste, hazardous waste and construction and demolition waste. Introducing a tax on every tonne of material landfilled was critical, because it gave waste-processing companies the incentive to look for other methods – such as incinerating and recycling – because they were more financially attractive. Landfilling waste in the Netherlands costs EUR 35 per tonne, plus an additional EUR 87 in tax if the waste is combustible, which overall is more expensive than incineration.

*Source*: Feller, G. (2015), "Dutch successes: Public and private sector aren't wasting their time", *Waste Management World*, www.waste-management-world.com/articles/print/volume-11/issue-1/features/dutch-successes.html (accessed 15 August 2015).

The Valle de México needs to make better use of economic instruments for waste management. Municipal-level governments in the Valle de México could follow the example of other Mexican cities, such as Aguaprieta, Mérida, Puebla and Tehuacán, in imposing charges for household waste collection. These cities levy flat-rate charges differentiated by city area, with lower rates for poorer areas. Authorities in the Valle de México could further make these charges quantity-based, to encourage waste reduction. One area of attention is the limited municipal institutional capacity and the role of informal workers (*pepenadores*) in the waste sector. In Mexico City, household waste charges are prohibited by law. While there is wide social resistance to paying for formal waste collection, much of the population pays tips to informal waste pickers, sometimes more than municipal waste charges would be. To introduce waste charges, local governments will have to work with informal workers to ensure effective implementation of a waste management system (OECD, 2013b).

Table 4.5. **Municipal solid waste management and selected policy instruments in European countries, 2001-10**

| Policy instrument | Austria | Germany | Belgium | Netherlands | Switzerland | Luxembourg | Norway | France | Finland | Poland | Czech Republic |
|---|---|---|---|---|---|---|---|---|---|---|---|
| Percentage of MSW recycled per MSW generated, 2010 | 63% | 62% | 58% | 51% | 51% | 47% | 42% | 35% | 33% | 21% | 16% |
| Two or more national waste management plans developed between 2001 and 2010 | X | X | | X | | X | | | X | X | |
| Only regional waste management plans | | | X | | X | | | | | | |
| Landfill tax increased more than 50% from 2001 to 2010 | X | | X | X (abandoned in 2012) | | | | X | X | X | X |
| Landfill tax at least 30 EUR/tonne MSW, 2010 | X | | X | X | | | X | | X | | |
| Incineration tax | X | | X | X (but zero) | X | | Until 2010 | X | | | |
| Landfill ban on organic waste or non-pre-treated MSW | X | X | X | X | X | X | X | X | X | X | |
| Mandatory separate collection of non-packaging waste | X | | X | | X | | X | | X | | |
| Mandatory separate collection of bio-waste fractions | X | | | X | | X | | | | X | |
| Economic incentives for recycling of MSW (pay-as-you-throw, etc.) | X | X | X | X | X | X | X | X | X | X | X |
| Selected innovative policies | (1) | (2) | (3) | | | (4) | | (5) | (1) | (6) | (7) |

*Notes:* MSW: municipal solid waste.

1. Separate collection of waste paper. 2. Introduction of a recycling bin for plastics and metals. 3. High household fines for non-compliance in source separation, maximum generation of residual MSW per capita, recycling quality standards. 4. Design standards for separate collection in new households, one container per 10 000 inhabitants, 100% of population covered by separate collection. 5. National extended producer responsibility introduced, e.g. on non-packaging paper, textiles and furniture. 6. Government fund co-financing recycling activities. 7. Quality standards on composted biowaste.

*Source*: European Environmental Agency (2013), “Managing municipal solid waste: A review of achievements in 32 European countries”, EEA Report No. 2/2013, European Environmental Agency, Copenhagen.

## *Climate change measures need to be linked to urban planning*

The Valle de México is exposed to a range of climate-related hazards, and many of its residents are highly vulnerable to climate change, mainly low-income people. Energy shortages, damaged infrastructure, increasing losses to industry, changes in rainfall patterns which could reduce freshwater availability and food production, heat-related mortality and illnesses are some of the likely economic and social effects of climate change. The vulnerability of the Valle de México and its residents to climate change is shaped not only by their exposure to particular hazards, but also by the sensitivity of social, economic and environmental systems, and by the capacity of these systems, including urban households and communities, to adapt. Some groups may be particularly affected: for example, children and the elderly are more susceptible to extreme heat and air pollution. The urban poor located in informal settlements are highly exposed to hazards such as floods. Adapting the Valle de México to climate change can be best achieved through addressing underlying development and infrastructure deficits. Integrating climate change mitigation and adaptation in urban planning and management has significant potential to address these issues, in association with other economic and social challenges. The experience of cities in Germany, the Netherlands, the United Kingdom and the United States suggests that a climate change action plan is not enough on its own. The most effective strategy is to incorporate the environment into existing planning tools, rather than developing stand-alone approaches.

In the Valle de México, the challenge for state-level authorities, as in many other OECD countries, will be to enlist the commitment of the different departments and units in the municipalities. Climate change needs to be seen as an issue for the whole municipal government and not just for an under-funded environmental unit. State-level governments will need to produce a clear high-profile public statement or declaration on climate change and environmental protection, setting out policies, targets and key actions. This should be linked to the more detailed urban planning and municipal development programmes, making clear what the plans and programmes seek to achieve. However, experience also suggests that the inclusion of environmental concerns in strategic development documents does not necessarily mean that these are taken seriously or result in meaningful changes. Much depends on changing budgets, laws, attitudes and politics. Given the governance challenges the Valle de México is facing, it may be more effective to concentrate support on a single issue that is a national priority, and is the responsibility of the state-level authorities, such as water service delivery.

Mexico City and the State of Mexico have issued climate change action laws and programmes to reduce the environmental, social and economic risks of climate change and promote the welfare of the population. Mexico City's Climate Action Programme (*Programa de Acción Climática de la Ciudad de México 2014-20*, PACCM) aims to increase the city's resilience as well as the population's adaptation capacities, particularly for the 5.6 million people most vulnerable to the consequences of extreme weather events, such as flooding. The State of Mexico's Climate Change Action Programme considers water, agriculture, forestry and human settlements key priority sectors, and includes issues such as gender equality and preservation of the cultural heritage as part of the programme. Its goal is to plan the metropolitan growth zones of the Valle de Toluca and the Valle de México with climate change adaptation criteria. However, a metropolitan climate change action programme developed and implemented by all relevant authorities in the Valle de México would provide a more coherent and co-ordinated approach. The ZMVM would be treated as a whole and would not be divided by two programmes with different priorities and levels of development.

The ZMVM is uneven in its socio-economic development: different areas face different environmental and urban challenges that require appropriate responses. Mexican authorities may wish to request the Environment Commission for the Megalopolis (CAMe) to provide guidelines for state- and municipal-level governments to link environmental concerns and urban planning that are broadly applicable, and which can be adapted to the needs of urban sub-centres in a range of situations. Flexibility in policy implementation can introduce urban-level policy responses that can be scaled up. Management practices should also be flexible and adaptable, and lessons learnt and local context-related knowledge should be taken into account when assessing climate change strategies (Frohlich and Knieling, 2013).

### Box 4.8. Mexico City's Climate Action Programme

The primary objective of Mexico City's Climate Action Programme 2014-20 (PACCM) is to improve the quality of life and low-carbon sustainable development in Mexico City. The PACCM is expected to achieve the direct mitigation of approximately 8 million tonnes of $CO_2e$ up to 2020. The criteria that govern the programme are: build consensus among agencies of the government of the Federal District; strive for social equity and gender equality; improve the quality of life of citizens in the framework of sustainable development; communicate between federal and local public programmes; include society and decision makers, and maintain flexibility to adapt the programme to technological advances. The PACCM was extended for two years beyond the current administration's term to allow the next administration to assess the current programme and design a new one. The PACCM has seven strategic priorities, aligned with the local climate action strategy: 1) urban and rural energy transition; 2) containment of urban sprawl; 3) environmental improvement; 4) sustainable improvement of natural resources and biodiversity; 5) building resilience; 6) education and communication; and 7) research and development.

All of the actions of the PACCM have been assigned a scope, objective, implementation strategy, and follow-up and impact indicators. Of the 69 measures, 20 were considered as priorities and fundamental to achieve the plan's goals, taking into account the availability of resources, which is a limitation for the programme.

*Source*: SEDEMA (2014), *Programa de Acción Climática de la Ciudad de México 2014-2020*, www.sedema.df.gob.mx/sedema/index.php/temas-ambientales/cambio-climatico (accessed 15 August 2015).

## *The call for a metropolitan resilience framework to inform urban planning and investment*

The authorities in the Valle de México may wish consider developing a resilience framework for the entire metropolitan area. The CAMe will lead the working group formulating a resilience agenda at the level of the megalopolis, which is a promising step, given that a comprehensive approach to resilience and overcoming the administrative fragmentation of the ZMVM is called for. This resilience framework should inform urban planning and investment patterns based on measurable evidence. It should also relate resilience to areas over which authorities have some control, such as infrastructure, public services, education, risk management, etc. A resilience framework for the Valle de México should include a metropolitan vision, an integral development strategy and plans that are regularly reviewed and updated. It is essential that the resilience framework consider the metropolitan zone as a whole, avoiding administrative, territorial divisions. The threat of climate change does not respect administrative borders, and addressing environmental shocks or stresses in isolation cannot serve resilience. A metropolitan resilience framework should be led by the federal and the three state-level governments, which should ensure adequate financial resources for the project. Municipal-level governments, private sector agents and NGOs should also be part of the discussions.

Mexico City's experience in building a resilience strategy could serve as a reference for a metropolitan-wide effort. Its underlying idea is to develop more capacity at the community and government level to confront disaster risks. It will also involve taking advantage of any natural or man-made disasters to improve urban development and the quality of life in the city. This strategy must be ready in early 2016. To this end, Mexico City's government has created a Resilience Steering Committee, involving 17 organisations from the Federal District government, the CAMe at the megalopolis level, civil society, members of the private sector and academic organisations. Five working groups, which represent the pillars of the strategy, have been established: 1) creation of a resilience agenda at the level of the megalopolis; 2) resilient urban and land-use planning; 3) building a resilient watershed in the Valle de Mexico; 4) resilient infrastructure and economy; and 5) sustainable and resilient mobility. So far, 290 initiatives for resilience have been identified, of which 90-95% are existing initiatives to be analysed for their impact. The different work streams of the resilience strategy still need to be ratified by the Climate Change Inter-ministerial Commission, but the political support of Mexico City's Mayor is expected to encourage the participation of all relevant actors. Mexico City's resilience strategy (and an eventual metropolitan equivalent) should assess how sensitive the region can be to ever-increasing uncertainty; how well-conceived, constructed and managed its physical assets are; whether it has spare capacity to accept disruption; how flexible and resourceful it can be in changing circumstances; whether there has been a broad consultation and engagement of communities, including the most vulnerable; and more crucially for the Valle de México, how consistent the system is, to ensure that all investments mutually support a common outcome.[41]

## Governance alternatives to environmental threats

Tackling the environmental challenges in the Valle de México will require paying attention to governance arrangements. Meaningful long-term changes in the environmental sphere cannot happen without sound governance and decision-making structures that are horizontally and vertically integrated (Dodman, Dalal-Clayton and McGranahan, 2013). Environmental challenges and solutions typically do not fall neatly into one specific area of expertise. A comprehensive strategy across sectors is necessary to balance and integrate different claims and to avoid or minimise conflicts between different aims. Governance arrangements provide a basis for the use of specific tools for including the environment in urban planning and management. At the same time, flexible environmental strategies are needed, because the scope of decisions is subject to considerable political and budgetary uncertainty (Frohlich and Knieling, 2013).

### *Building a long-term vision, and facilitating inter-municipal co-operation*

Moving the Valle de México towards a commonly agreed direction in sustainable development is of critical importance. A long-term vision is needed, considering all possible risk scenarios, for how the metropolitan zone should promote economic development and limit the impact on the environment and natural resources. The long-term impact of climate change, over the next 50-100 years, requires not only a long-term vision, but intergenerational thinking that far exceeds the timeframes of the existing responsibilities in policy making and planning (Frohlich and Knieling, 2013). For example, Portland's Climate Change Preparation Strategy builds on existing work to understand how climate is affecting the community, how those effects are expected to change in the coming century and what can be done to prepare for them.

A metropolitan view of environmental policy and programmes should underpin that vision. Clear progress has been made on environmental policy actions in air quality, but other issues, such as waste management and water provision are addressed in a more parochial manner.

The participation of a range of stakeholders in decision making is a key element of building a more resilient and environmentally aware metropolitan zone. Portland's experience suggests that the only way forward for implementing a climate action plan effectively is through collaboration and co-ordination with other public and private sector partners. This will require identifying lead bureaus, agencies and departments, and clarifying responsibilities to ensure accountability in the process.[42] Climate change strategies in London and Toronto and the green growth strategy of Kitakyushu in Japan have shown the importance of valuing and working with civil society. If climate action programmes are to be successful, they require high levels of public engagement. Local voluntary groups can help build that engagement, as they are often more trusted than local or central government by those they work with. However, it is equally important that voluntary groups focus on climate change and build their leadership skills.[43]

Pursuing a climate-sensitive form of governing could be a part of the vision and a way to achieve it. This would require, for instance, the integration of climate change adaptation and mitigation issues in different sectors such as energy, transport, housing and construction, urban planning, water management, conservation land, health and even agriculture. Authorities in the Valle de México may need to analyse the most appropriate instruments or regulatory tools needed, sector by sector, to direct the behaviour of the different actors towards climate-friendly development. Table 4.6 shows some of the formal, informal and economic instruments that could be used to enhance a climate-friendly governance model.

Table 4.6. **Instruments of climate change governance**

| Formal instruments | Economic instruments | Informal instruments |
|---|---|---|
| Regional development plans | Land-use taxes | Development concepts (local, regional) |
| Land-use plans | Soil-sealing charges | Development scenarios |
| Zoning plans | Water charges | Mission statements |
| Urban planning agreements | Tradable land-use rights | Area management (local, regional) |
| Plan approval procedures | Certificates | Networks |
| Environmental impact assessments | Climate standards | Aggregate liability indices |
| Strategic environmental audits | Incentive systems | Climate proofing |
| | Climate labels | Climate agencies |
| | | Flood protection associations |

*Source*: Frohlich, J. and J. Kieling (2013), "Conceptualising climate change governance", in: Knieling, J. and W. Leal Filho (eds.), "Climate change governance", *Climate Change Management*, pp. 9-26, Springer-Verlag, Berlin and Heidelberg, Germany, http://dx.doi.org/10.1007/978-3-642-29831-8_2.

The task of co-ordinating the Federal District, the State of Mexico and the municipal-level authorities is particularly challenging given the absence of a regulatory framework to guide inter-municipal climate change and environmental protection. The experience of Portland's Climate Change Strategy[44] and the London Climate Change Partnership[45] suggests that a seamless co-ordination from the outset, across and among governments, is critical for an effective implementation of climate adaptation strategies. Given the fragmented nature of the governance arrangements in the Valle de México (see Chapter 5), the CAMe constitutes an asset for better co-ordination and collaboration among the 6 central governments, the 225 municipalities and the 16 *delegaciones*. Meanwhile, it is essential to upgrade the institutional capacities of the commission. As a first step, the issue of funding needs to be accelerated so that the Executive Co-ordination has the necessary human capital and budgetary resources to finance research and co-ordination projects and assist local governments in capacity building. The commission has a large portfolio of topics to deal with, from air quality control to waste management, water treatment and forest protection. It needs the financial resources and qualified personnel. Secondly, the commission will require the support of all state Ministries (*secretarías*) of Environment and that of SEMARNAT and SEDATU at national level, to ensure that they all share the same vision. Although the commission has no implementation responsibilities, it should be given the role of supervising and assessing the agreed environmental strategies. These assessments should be used to benchmark progress and to give advisory assistance to governments that lag behind. Members of the Organ of Government should meet periodically to show not only political support for the commission but to follow up on decisions taken and agreements reached, and look for alternatives to improve their work and that of the commission.

## *Reconciling environmental objectives with economic growth*

Mexico has made green growth, and in particular sustainable water management and the reduction of carbon emissions, key national priorities (see Government of Mexico, 2013). The aim is to promote growth that preserves natural resources while encouraging competitiveness and employment.[46] For Mexico in general, and for authorities in the Valle de México in particular, focusing on green growth is a way to tackle poverty, provide sustainable livelihoods and job creation; mobilise resources and reduce the burden on public finances while improving the environment; reduce vulnerability to environmental disasters; and encourage new growth and job opportunities. Mobility, construction, water management and air quality are beginning to be managed with a green growth perspective, but these efforts are still somewhat isolated.

### *An explicit green growth agenda underpinned by pro-growth factors is needed*

The Valle de México requires a concrete metropolitan green growth strategy that stimulates growth through urban activities that reduce either: 1) negative environmental externalities, such as air pollution and $CO_2$ emissions; or 2) the consumption of natural resources and environmental services, including water, energy and underdeveloped land (OECD, 2013b). Policies to reduce environmental impact can only be sustained over the long term if they generate wealth.[47] Although green growth does not explicitly focus on social equity, improving the environmental performance of the Valle de México need not be at the expense of social progress. Green growth policies have the potential to benefit the poorest and most vulnerable indirectly, but authorities must design green growth policies that maximise benefits and minimise costs for the poorer groups. Some cities, for instance, Toronto, with its green jobs programme, and Chicago, with its Green Jobs for All initiative, have explicitly pursued equity objectives alongside environmental and economic goals, by focusing on jobs.

The Valle de México needs to be prepared for the new jobs that will be demanded in a green-oriented economy. The availability of skilled and trained people will facilitate the development of a more dynamic economy. Training and education need to be at the top of the national and local authorities' agenda, ensuring that vulnerable groups are not left behind. Local authorities need to capitalise on the recently approved national education reforms to ensure that there is a strong cluster of linked competencies in firms, universities and the workforce, to promote job creation and innovation with a green orientation. Skill creation for new jobs, as well as training to upgrade old jobs, can be more efficiently organised by pooling the learning resources of educational institutions and industries in the metropolitan area. All major national universities and technology institutes are based in the Valle de México, and this asset could be exploited to upgrade the skills of the labour force through partnerships between universities, enterprises and the public sector. At the same time, the universities in the metropolitan zone need to pay greater attention to the educational needs of the metropolitan workforce. For example, in the Chicago Tri-State Region, a number of regional or applied universities are actively promoting economic development and research. Universities like the University of Illinois at Chicago, Northern Illinois University and local private universities have explicit regional engagement missions and more applied academic programmes to help match curricula and research with regional needs (OECD, 2012b).

Partnering with the private sector is a critical step in transitioning to the green economy. National and local authorities will have to work closely with the private sector to identify their needs and enhance local efforts to develop skills. Linking local training initiatives with the overall economic development strategy and to an explicit metropolitan green growth strategy can help assess local needs. Particular focus should be placed on small- and medium-sized firms, which, compared to large companies, have greater difficulty in providing in-house training to employees.

### *Investments in infrastructure should have a green orientation*

High-quality infrastructure and services are accepted as being vital to a strong economy. Upgrading transport infrastructure, for instance, can shorten travel times, which in turn can affect property prices and economic rents and influence decision making of households (in residential location and patterns of consumption) and firms (production location, access to markets and investment decisions) (Hammer et al., 2011).

Some large-scale urban infrastructure programmes offer great potential for greening dirty economic sectors, and sometimes, re-employing displaced workers or creating new jobs, as well as generating new growth. The construction of the New Mexico City International Airport (NAICM) and its operation offer several possibilities for green growth (Box 4.9). If the Master Plan for the construction of the new airport is followed, the new terminal and its surrounding environment will be environmentally sustainable.[48] The construction of the new airport could also include measures to ensure using green technology and environmentally friendly procedures through green procurement. A condition for granting construction contracts should be the use of clean and green materials. The new airport offers the possibility of generating new growth through the renewable energy sector ($CO_2$ capture and storage; and solar panels on airport buildings, etc.), an area that needs to be further developed in Mexico.

### Box 4.9. Greening the construction and operation of the New Mexico City International Airport

The construction of the New Mexico City International Airport (NAICM) requires an eco-friendly airport planning approach. The Master Plan provides for the NAICM to have a positive impact on the quality of life and the environment in the Valle de México. It includes several green initiatives that cover the construction and operation of the airport, aimed at obtaining Leadership in Energy and Environmental Design (LEED) international certification. The use of renewable energy, water treatment and reuse, rainwater collection, use of recycled materials with low emissions, and the use of biogas for electricity production are some examples. An integrated management hydrology is expected to rehabilitate the area of the former Lake Texcoco. However, to ensure that a green NAICM does not only refer to the airport infrastructure but also to its operation in relation to the environment, Mexican authorities may consider the following points:

- Regularly conduct an environmental impact assessment associated with aviation activity that detects environmental consequences and control measures. The idea is to assess and manage all possible potential environmental impacts the NAICM may encounter and consider alternatives to address them.
- Integrate the NAICM into the resilience strategy for the Valle de México. This will require analysis of climate change impact scenarios in which the existence of the airport may alter environmental outcomes, such as flooding. The participation of the state-level governments in this exercise will be essential.
- Define guidelines on infrastructure for airport environmental management. All airport staff and stakeholders should be trained in the environmental management requirements. Authorities may also consider adopting a collaborative environmental management programme to ensure that all stakeholders have the same information and the vision of a more efficient, pollution-free and environmentally sound airport environment.
- Align land-use planning and administration with the construction and operation of the airport. Urban planning should cover the airport's construction and operation and its related activities. In Singapore, the construction of Changi Airport was in line with urban planning, land-use planning and environmental regulations, and required that the whole airport area be planted with lush vegetation.
- Include climate change resilience and adaptation strategies in the construction and operation plans of the airport. The underlying issue is to show how the airport can achieve national and sub-national objectives on climate change, such as reducing GHG emissions while encouraging economic development.
- Define and implement a mass public transport strategy, so as not to rely on road transport (see Chapter 3). This would reduce the motor vehicle traffic and emissions from the airport. In the United Kingdom, airport construction or expansion permits are granted only after plans for mass public transport have been defined.
- Define how the airport will contribute to the air quality improvement objectives of ProAire. A clear strategy for reducing the emissions of the airport activity should be agreed on. Following the example of Hong Kong International Airport and Warwick Airport in the United Kingdom, a Clean Air Charter could be signed by all stakeholders involved in airport operations.
- Implement a waste management system for collection, segregation, storage and safe disposal of waste. For example, both Charles de Gaulle Airport and Orly Airport in Paris recycle at least 30% of waste.

Box 4.9. **Greening the construction and operation of the New Mexico City International Airport** *(continued)*

- Undertake extensive flora and fauna studies to determine the biodiversity values within the airport boundaries. Flora and fauna could be rehabilitated with the help of federal and state environmental authorities and NGOs. Appropriate landscaping may also be considered by, for example, planting trees around the bodies of water. The construction of a dedicated pipeline network around the airport could irrigate the area with treated water, a strategy implemented at the Indira Gandhi International Airport in Delhi, India, and Charles de Gaulle Airport in Paris.
- Noise reduction should be central to the airport management, and introducing noise mitigation measures should be considered. These might include restricting the operation of old aircraft, the continuous descent approach, avoiding aircraft overflights in densely populated areas, etc.

### *Overcoming barriers to innovation is essential to shift towards green growth*

Innovation serves as an important bridge to the green economy. National and local authorities in the Valle de México will need to ensure that barriers to innovation, such as lack of funding, barriers to early-stage commercial development and demand-side policies, are dealt with. In Mexico, the National Development Plan 2013-2018 acknowledges the need for more funding for research. However, it is still unclear whether sub-national levels of government also consider it a priority and how they intend to promote it. Research on generic or general-purpose technologies, such as green chemistry, biotechnologies, etc., have not kept pace with growing environmental challenges. Transformative innovation in the green technology sector often results from spillover effects from other sectors. For example, enabling technologies (ICT and nanotechnologies) can significantly decrease the cost and increase the environmental efficiency of new infrastructure and network investments. In France, for example, the Paris suburb of Issy-les-Moulineaux, by providing superior broadband infrastructure, a business-friendly climate and innovative e-services, has managed in less than a decade to radically change its industrial structure, reducing local unemployment to virtually zero (Hammer et al., 2011). Mexican authorities in the Valle de México could fund research in the form of R&D tax credits or subsidy support.

State-level governments in the Valle de México could also support green innovation by targeting barriers to its early-stage commercial development, including access to finance. Mexico has a relatively immature market for green innovation. The challenge for Mexican authorities, as it is for many OECD countries, is that the dominance of existing design in energy and transport markets can create entry barriers for new technologies, due to the high fixed costs of developing new infrastructure. Authorities in the Valle de México could strengthen green innovation from the demand side through policies that incorporate environmental conditions, such as government standards and labelling. Building partnerships with academia could help set up eco-innovation clusters. Universities can facilitate local knowledge exchange and become effective pipelines of information exchange with national and global markets.

The Federal District and the State of Mexico could consider the creation of a metropolitan innovation system for the Valle de México through inter-state and inter-municipal dialogue. This would reduce zero-sum game competition and increase trust, develop a common approach to optimising the innovation-driven growth potential of the metropolitan area in the long term and enhance co-operation. The CAMe is in a key position to facilitate this dialogue. Producing relevant data on innovation at the metropolitan scale would be critical to help raise awareness of regional imperatives. The CAMe could be given the mandate to collect data and indicators from existing research centres, with the goal of providing strong evidence for future metropolitan green growth initiatives. It could link up with state, municipal and federal authorities responsible for the policies and programmes that affect economic development, workforce development, innovation, green growth capacity, and transport and logistics in the metropolitan zone. Authorities in the ZMVM would also need to critically review the economic development programmes for cost-neutral innovation-driven growth. This would help prioritise among different investments to make strategic choices with a common approach and, if needed, reorient public expenditure towards more durable sources of economic development for the metropolitan zone. Public procurement and regulation, cost-neutral to public budgets, are other potential tools to spur innovation.

Encouraging innovation could also be promoted by a joint strategic environmental assessment. Authorities in the ZMVM may wish to review the Scottish Environmental Assessment Act, which establishes the modalities for conducting an environmental assessment. It defines an environmental assessment as the preparation of an environmental report through public consultations whose results must be taken into account in decision making.[49] The Canadian Environmental Assessment Agency is also an interesting example, which not only ensures the timely completion of environmental assessments, but promotes co-ordination and co-operation between federal and provincial governments, communication with aboriginal people and ensures opportunities for a meaningful public participation during an environmental assessment.[50] A joint strategic environmental assessment would provide authorities in the Valle de México with valuable information on whether apparently green policies and programmes, such as subsidies, might have unintended consequences. It would also be useful in promoting good governance for green growth. Local environmental policies and programmes need to be assessed in terms of effectiveness (compliance and enforcement) and impact.

### *The use of market incentives for environmental policy could be strengthened*

OECD (2013c) has found that Mexico has made progress in using market-based instruments other than taxes to create incentives for using natural resources more efficiently and reducing pollution and environmental damage. These instruments generally take the form of subsidies. Fees have been implemented only in the area of water and, to a lesser extent, biodiversity management.

The federal and state-level governments in the Valle de México could reward environmentally sound goods and activities. Mexico has primarily used subsidy-based instruments to reward the purchase of supposedly more environmentally friendly goods. These have included soft loans and tax deductions for businesses' environment-related investment, tax credits for scrapping old buses, and subsidies to replace old home electric appliances and loans to low-income households to purchase energy- and water-efficient houses or for home retrofitting (ECOCASA, *hipoteca verde*). All these mechanisms can encourage businesses and consumers to make more environmentally friendly purchases. However, they come at a cost to the budget and discriminate against households and businesses that cannot afford such purchases and investments. From an environmental perspective, these measures are generally less efficient than instruments such as taxes that directly incorporate the cost of environmental damage into market prices. By targeting a limited range of cleaner products or activities, subsidy-based measures encourage firms and consumers to adopt the subsidies even when other options are more effective (OECD, 2013b).

Authorities in the Valle de México could also improve air quality, reduce traffic, increase revenue and green the economy by limiting the incentives to vehicle ownership and use, particularly company cars. Mexico is one of the few countries where company cars are fully exempt from employee income tax, which encourages employers to offer their employees income in this way. About one-third of all newly registered cars in 2009-11 were company cars, a higher share than in many OECD countries, including the United States (OECD, 2013c). Fuel expenses are deductible from corporate income up to MXN 250 (USD 16.5). Thus, employers have almost no incentive to limit the use of company cars by employees, and they in turn, having virtually no additional costs linked to car use, have no incentive to drive less or more efficiently. Some form of local taxation could be imposed on the ownership and use of company cars. Free parking provided by employers is also a non-taxed benefit in kind. In contrast, commuting expenses paid by employers are part of employees' taxable income, though with some tax advantage when public transport is used. In general, this mix of incentives encourages driving to work (mainly at rush hour and to/from particularly congested locations), exacerbating congestion, the risk of accidents and environmental problems. Including parking spaces in taxable benefits would remove this incentive, and meanwhile, efficient and reliable alternatives on public transport should be provided.

### *Local governments' institutional capacity for green growth needs to be upgraded ...*

The institutional capacity of state but above all municipal governments in the ZMVM needs to be substantially reinforced. This would involve sources of funding and building a professionalised public workforce with the right skills and competences (see Chapter 5). In Japan, the city of Kitakyushu is building green growth capacity by requiring staff to regularly transfer between administrative offices focused on economic development and those centred on environmental affairs. This policy is an explicit effort to build "green growth personnel" who understand inter-sectoral linkages and trade-offs between short-term economic imperatives and long-term sustainability goals (OECD, 2013b).

State- and municipal-level authorities in the Valle de México need to further explore mechanisms to mobilise public and private funds for promoting inclusive green growth. Many urban revenue sources can be designed to either stimulate or discourage green growth in the metropolitan zone. For example, well-designed property taxes and development fees can tackle urban sprawl and raise money for funding green infrastructure. In addition, private financing can be attracted to fill the funding gap for many urban green infrastructure projects. Some of the measures that can be adopted are: 1) real estate developer charges and fees to pay for the infrastructure needed to connect new development to existing infrastructure, and discourage urban sprawl; 2) land-value capture taxes aimed at seizing part of the value increases of real estate due to new nearby infrastructure development (this is the case in the redevelopment of Presidente Mazaryk Avenue in Mexico City); 3) public-private partnerships (PPPs) which transfer the long-term risk to the private sector (capacity to manage PPPs, however, needs to be developed); and 4) the use of loans, bonds and carbon finance to attract private investment.

Authorities in the Valle de México may also wish to promote local good practices in building resilience and mitigating and adapting to climate change, as a way to enhance capacity. This is a task that may be undertaken by the CAMe. Experience shows that when initiatives started in a locality are promoted to other areas in the same region, their chances of being adopted and emulated are higher. The experience of the City of London suggests that emerging good practices need to be monitored, assessed and promoted, along with the necessary toolkit for successful implementation (London21, 2008). In addition, the Valle de México could institutionalise climate change preparation planning by, for instance, establishing a multi-bureau or -department adaptive management co-ordination team, to review emergent trends and regulation and share information. It will also be critical to strengthen emergency management capacity to respond to natural emergencies such as heavy rain, floods or heat waves (OECD, 2013c). Valle de México authorities could also consider means to improve monitoring, evaluate the effectiveness of climate change preparation actions and advance new research to support climate change preparation efforts, as practiced in Portland and Toronto. Building databases and filling data gaps, supporting research and monitoring trends in natural developments are some options for building capacity.

To further enhance capacity, state-level authorities in the Valle de México could also fund research. Mexico City's climate action programme already includes research and development as a strategy for climate change action, but giving it a metropolitan approach would have a more relevant effect. For example, authorities in the Valle de Mexico can emulate the model of the Brainport Eindhoven Region in the Netherlands, where the municipality of Eindhoven and the Eindhoven Metropolitan Region have been supporting research and technology development to contribute to a safe, green, sustainable economic development and ensure the region's international economic competitiveness.[51] Similarly, the San Francisco Metropolitan Transport Commission finances innovative projects aimed at reducing GHG emissions, such as fleet-oriented vehicle programmes, to encourage housing construction in areas well-served by public transport.[52] The CAMe and RTP could develop similar investment projects.

### *… and the federal government should support them in pursuing green growth objectives*

One way the federal government can support green growth, not only in the Valle de México but nation-wide, is by incorporating green growth and sustainable development policies into structural reform agendas. It can define the overall vision and strategy for inclusive green growth, so as to frame national and sub-national policy reforms as positive long-term goals. Another option is to provide financial or technical support for setting targets and designing monitoring mechanisms for green growth policies. Price signals and standards could be set up through carbon taxes or other pricing mechanisms. The federal government could also help in greening typical local taxes, such as the property tax, and assisting in making better use of service charges to strengthen the budgets of local governments, which are responsible for providing basic environmental services (OECD, 2013c). The federal government could also review national policies' impact on local incentives to encourage green growth to identify and eliminate perverse incentives, for example in the housing sector. It can also encourage infrastructure investment in line with sustainable development and green goals.

It is critical that federal policies ensure policy coherence across levels of government. The greener the national framework, the easier it will be to address specific challenges in the ZMVM, and to ensure coherence and consistency between national and local policies. The national government should also ensure the adoption of a holistic approach for a green growth agenda, based on the objectives set in the National Development Programme 2013-2018. The experience of OECD countries suggests that efforts to encourage urban green growth may not always be equitable. These concerns should be addressed through national policies, particularly the tax and benefit system, rather than trying to ensure that individual policy measures fulfil both environmental and equity objectives. Furthermore, the federal government should ensure that sophisticated policy instruments such as those related to green growth be grouped within a simple policy package. The experience of OECD countries shows that an overly complex system of regulations, incentives and taxes makes impact assessment harder and raises the risk of unintended effects or perverse incentives.

The federal government may also be of assistance to local governments in the Valle de México by helping them to conduct a public environmental expenditure review. The aim is to examine, together with the federal Ministry of Finance and Public Credit (Secretaría de Hacienda y Crédito Público, SHCP), local governments' resource allocations within and among sectors. The efficiency and effectiveness of those allocations can then be assessed in the context of environmental priorities, while maintaining fiscal prudence. The final goal is to assist governments to redistribute spending to institutions responsible for environmental priorities, and on long-term goals, thereby increasing environmental budgets. This review would be useful for identifying, quantifying and maximising the public revenue potential of under-priced natural resources, such as water. The data and insights obtained from the review could help in designing policy reforms, government budgets and investment projects. In Mexico's political context, however, the national government can only intervene at the request of local governments if there is not enough technical capacity. A memorandum of understanding between federal and local authorities for carrying out the review could be signed and a review panel established.

## Conclusion

The Valle de México faces growing demand and low supply of drinking water, poor air quality, and lacks an efficient waste management system. To a large extent, the environmental problems are the product of poor urban strategic planning and its dissociation from environmental protection, and the administrative fragmentation and particularities of the political system. To address the specific urban environmental challenges, environmental issues could be integrated in all urban planning and development projects, and a metropolitan resilience strategy formulated. The water sector should focus on ensuring a sustainable provision of water; improving air quality by enhancing co-operation with the transport and construction sectors. A metropolitan waste management strategy is needed to boost air quality improvement efforts, and avoid polluting water reservoirs and soil. Better urban governance arrangements can facilitate the integration of environmental and urban planning. Thinking in metropolitan terms and facilitating inter-municipal co-operation on key environmental objectives are key issues for consideration. Environmental protection should also be regarded as an economic asset, and adopting a green growth approach to urban-environmental planning is critical in promoting economic development. The recommendations made in this review build on existing experience in Mexico and OECD countries. The authorities in the

Valle de México have been working on several of these issues for a long time, and now need to work as a team, building on each other's experience, to work towards a common goal.

## Notes

1. Only a small part of the system of lakes, the southern Lake Xochimilco, was freshwater. Most of the system was formed by saline lakes. During the rainy season, the lakes frequently expanded into a single body of water. Floods – sometimes lasting for several years – led to efforts to limit the extent of the lakes. In Aztec times, dykes separated freshwater and saltwater parts of the system of lakes and protected areas of the city from fluctuations in water levels. At the beginning of the 17th century, under Spanish rule, it was decided to drain the lakes (see Alcocer and Williams, 1996, for details).

2. Data from desinventar.net (accessed 17 April 2015).

3. Neighbourhood in this case refers to AGEB (*áreas geográfico estadísticas básicas*).

4. MXN to USD conversion is based on average 2014 exchange rate.

5. For further information see: Government of Mexico (2013); Government of the Federal District (2013); Government of the State of Mexico (2011).

6. See Soto Montes de Oca (2007) for details, though wells as deep as 105 metres were already dug in 1847 (Jimenez, 2014).

3. See the recently released images by the European Space Agency (2014).

8. See: http://cuidarelagua.df.gob.mx/costo.html for details.

9. For further details, see Government of the Federal District (2013).

4. See: www.sacmex.df.gob.mx/sacmex/doc/3_atencion_a_usuarios/tarifas/tandeo_2015.pdf for details. According to the government of the Federal District, more than 1.5 million residents receive water through the *tandeo* system; and 180 000 people do not have networks that connect the houses to the main supply system, because they are located in a non-authorised area (Ciudad de México, 2013).

5. See: www.conagua.gob.mx/CONAGUA07/Temas/CALIDADAGUA.pdf for current values.

6. See e.g. CONAGUA (2014a).

7. Surface water is treated more thoroughly than groundwater. Groundwater is treated with chlorine before being injected into the network, while surface water is treated by alum coagulation and sedimentation in addition to chlorination (Jiménez, 2014).

8. Norm NOM-127-SSA1-1994. See CONAGUA (2009) for details.

9. Ibid.

16. Article 129 of the Código Financiero del Estado de México y Municipios sets out the municipalities' rights in adjusting the state's tariffs specified in Article 130ff.

10. For further information, see: www.conagua.gob.mx/tarifas.

11. There were 1 358 134 registered users in 2012 (SACMEX, 2013).

12. 2013 data from CONAGUA (2014a) and 2012 data from SACMEX (2013).

13. See CONAGUA (2010) for CONAGUA's budget and 2012 data from SACMEX (2013) for SACMEX's budget.

14. For further information, see: www2.inecc.gob.mx/publicaciones/libros/394/cap4.pdf; and http://biophysics.sbg.ac.at/mexico/air.htm.

22. See: www.inegi.org.mx/est/contenidos/proyectos/registros/economicas/vehiculos/default.aspx.

23. See: http://midiariourbano.blogspot.fr/2012/02/diagnostico-de-la-basura-en-el-distrito.html.

24. The Environmental Commission for the Megalopolis (CAMe) is part of the wide array of efforts Mexican authorities have used to co-ordinate work on air quality management since the 1990s.

25. For further information, see www.df.gob.mx. However, there is a growing body of literature that suggests that *Hoy No Circula* has not had the desired effects and that this has contributed to more emissions and congestion. See, for example: Gallego, Montero and Salas (2013); Riveros Rotgé (2009); and Eskeland and Feyzioglu (1995).

26. Mexico City is reportedly also planning to build more second decks in urban highways. This decision is surprising, since there is wide empirical evidence that shows that building more roads increases congestion. See, for example: www.wired.com/2014/06/wuwt-traffic-induced-demand; www.vtpi.org/gentraf.pdf; and www.redalyc.org/articulo.oa?id=31200104.

27. In Mexico's administration, the bodies called *desconcentrados* refer to bodies subordinated to an organ of the central public administration. Their competences are regional and thematic, and determined by law. They do not have legal personality or their own assets. In contrast, a decentralised (*descentralizado*) body has legal personality, autonomy in decision making and its own assets.

28. The council's website shows significant activity in 2010 and 2011 but has not been updated since then. See: http://cuencavalledemexico.com.

29. The estimated responses are showing the average response. How much consumers will ultimately reduce demand is likely to differ based on their affluence and initial level of consumption.

30. The main obstacle for vertical co-ordination in water policy making cited in an OECD survey on water governance (2010-11) for Mexico was unstable or insufficient revenues. See OECD (2012c) for details.

31. See: www.agua.unam.mx/sacmex/assets/docs/granreto_sacmex.pdf and SACMEX (2013) for details.

32. See Fuentes (2011) and the cited literature.

33. Average consumption is 166.89 litres per day across 30 Latin American water service providers (ADERASA, 2012).

34. For further information see: www.conanp.gob.mx/acciones/programa.php.

35. See WHO (2003) for a detailed discussion.

36. Information provided by the Ministry of Environment of Mexico City (SEDEMA).

37. In 2015, the RTP expects to acquire 220 natural gas buses with environmentally friendly technology.

38. For an in-depth discussion on the toolbox for urban air quality management, see UNEP (2005).

39. For further information, see: www.iadb.org/en/topics/climate-change/mexico-ecocasa-ctf,9899.html.

40. For further information, see: http://portal.infonavit.org.mx/wps/wcm/connect/infonavit/trabajadores/saber+para+decidir/cuido_mi_casa/ahorro+y+cuido+el+medio+ambiente.

41. For further information, see The Rockefeller Foundation/Arup (2014).

42. For further information see: www.portlandoregon.gov/bps/climate.

43. For further information see: www.london21.org/uploads/files/london21/Newsletter.

44. For further information see: www.portlandoregon.gov/bps/climate.

45. For further information see: http://climatelondon.org.uk/lccp.

46. Mexico has also been a champion of inclusive green growth. In 2012, the Mexican presidency of the G20 introduced inclusive green growth as a cross-cutting priority on the G20 development agenda.

47. For an in-depth discussion, see Hammer et al. (2011).

48. The current Master Plan for the new airport for Mexico City includes several measures that would make it environmentally sustainable, such as installing better waste capture facilities, recycling water, generating energy through biogas, the establishment of parks and water reservoirs, etc.

49. For further information, see: www.gov.scot/Home.

50. For further information, see: Parliament of Canada www.parl.gc.ca/HousePublications/Publication and Canadian Environmental Assessment Agency www.ceaa-acee.gc.ca.

51. For further information, see: www.brainport.nl/en/work/brainport-eindhoven-region-makes-a-name-for-itself-in-the-world.

52. For further information, see: www.mtc.ca.gov.

# *Bibliography*

ADERASA (2012), *Grupo Regional de Trabajo de Benchmarking (GRTB): Informe Anual – 2012*, Asociación de Entes Reguladores de Agua Potable y Saneamiento de las Américas.

AfDB, OECD, UN, WB (2013), "A toolkit of policy options to support inclusive green growth", submission to the G20 Development Working Group by the AfDB, the OECD, the UN and the World Bank, www.oecd.org/g20/topics/development/atoolkitofpolicyoptionstosupportinclusivegreengrowth.htm (accessed 15 August 2015).

Alcocer, J. and W.D. Williams (1996), "Historical and recent changes in Lake Texcoco, a saline lake in Mexico", *International Journal of Salt Lake Research*, Vol. 5, No. 1, pp. 45-61.

ANIS (1995), *Mexico City's Water Supply: Improving the Outlook for Sustainability*, The Joint Academies Committee on the Mexico City Water Supply, Commission on Geosciences, Environment, and Resources, National Research Council, Academia Nacional de la Investigación Cientifica, National Academies Press.

Barreda Marín (2009), *Evaluación de los impactos de los residuos sólidos bajo cambio climático en la Ciudad de México*, Instituto de Ciencia y Tecnología del Distrito Federal, Centro de Ciencias de la Atmósfera de la Universidad Nacional Autónoma de México, Agosto, available at: www.cvcccm-atmosfera.unam.mx/sis_admin/archivos/rsu_barreda_informe_tecnico.pdf

C40 Siemens (2014), "City Climate Leadership Awards: Mexico City climate close-up", available at: www.siemens.com/press/pool/de/events/2014/infrastructure-cities/2014-06-CCLA/mexico-climate-close-up.pdf.

CAMe (2014), *La CAMe a 6 meses de su creación*, Coordinación Ejecutiva de la Comisión Ambiental de la Megalópolis, 4 April.

Centro Mario Molina (2014), "Evaluación del programa Hoy No Circula", Centro Mario Molina, available at: http://centromariomolina.org/wp-content/uploads/2014/06/RE_HNC_20141.pdf.

Chelleri, L., T. Schuetze and L. Salvati (2015), "Integrating resilience with urban sustainability in neglected neighborhoods: Challenges and opportunities of transitioning to decentralized water management in Mexico City", *Habitat International*, Vol. 48, pp. 122-130, http://dx.doi.org/10.1016/j.habitatint.2015.03.016.

City of Kyoto (2015), "Projects to create low-carbon City of Kyoto", presentation at the 6th High Level Seminar on Environmentally Sustainable Cities, 9-10 February, Johor Bahru, Malaysia.

CONAGUA (2015), "Strategic projects: Drinking water, sewage, sanitation", presentation on 5 March, available at: www.conagua.gob.mx/english07/publications/StrategicProjects.pdf.

CONAGUA (2014a), "Estadícas del agua en México: Edición 2014", Comisión Nacional del Agua, Mexico, D.F., available at: www.conagua.gob.mx/CONAGUA07/Publicaciones/Publicaciones/EAM2014.pdf.

CONAGUA (2014b), "Situación del subsector agua potable, drenaje y saneamiento: Edición 2014", Secretaría de Medio Ambiente y Recursos Naturales, November, available at: www.conagua.gob.mx/CONAGUA07/Publicaciones/Publicaciones/SGAPDS-6-14.pdf.

CONAGUA (2012), "Situación del subsector agua potable, drenaje y saneamiento: Edición 2012", Secretaría de Medio Ambiente y Recursos Naturales, September, Mexico, D.F., available at: www.conagua.gob.mx/CONAGUA07/Publicaciones/Publicaciones/SGAPDS-40-12.pdf.

CONAGUA (2010), "Statistics on water in Mexico: 2010 Edition", Ministry of Environment and Natural Resources, June, available at: www.conagua.gob.mx/english07/publications/EAM2010Ingles_Baja.pdf.

CONAGUA (2009), "Estadiísticas del agua de la Región Hidrológico-Administrativa XIII, Aguas del Valle de México: Edición 2009", Secretaría de Medio Ambiente y Recursos Naturales, September, Mexico, D.F., available at: www.conagua.gob.mx/CONAGUA07/Noticias/OCAVM-1-EAOCAVM2009.pdf.

CONAGUA (2007a), "Regiones hidrológicas administrativa (organismos de cuenca)", Comisión Nacional del Agua, www.conabio.gob.mx/informacion/metadata/gis/rha250kgw.xml?_xsl=/db/metadata/xsl/fgdc_html.xsl&_indent=no (accessed 28 May 2015).

CONAGUA (2007b), "Subregiones hidrológicas, escala 1:250 000: República Mexicana", Subdirección General Técnica, Comisión Nacional del Agua, www.conabio.gob.mx/informacion/metadata/gis/sbrh250kgw.xml?_xsl=/db/metadata/xsl/fgdc_html.xsl&_indent=no (accessed 28 May 2015).

CONASAMI (2015), "Tabla de salarios mínimos generales y profesionales por áreas geográficas", Comisión Nacional de los Salarios Mínimos, www.conasami.gob.mx/t_sal_mini_prof.html (accessed 7 April 2015).

CTS EMBARQ México (2013), "Estudio de la reducción de emisiones y los co-beneficios generados por la implementación del Programa ECOBICI (2010, 2011, 2012)", May, Centro de Transporte Sustentable EMBARQ México, Mexico, D.F., available at: www.ecobici.df.gob.mx/sites/default/files/pdf/reduccion_gei_y_co-beneficios_generados_por_la_implementacion_del_programa_ecobici_201020112012.pdf.

Davoudi, S., A. Mehmood and L. Brooks (2010), "The London climate change adaptation strategy: Gap analysis", *Electronic Working Paper No. 44*, Global Urban Research Unit, Newcastle University, United Kingdom, available at: www.ncl.ac.uk/guru/documents/EWP44.pdf.

Díaz-Delgado, C. et al. (2012), "Valoración económica de daños directos por inundación en Valle de Chalco Solidaridad, Estado de México", in: González-Sosa, E. et al. (eds.),

*La Importancia de las Inundaciones en la Gestión Integrada de los Recursos Hídricos en México*, Universidad Autónoma de Querétaro, Mexico, pp. 157-176.

Dodman, D., B. Dalal-Clayton and G. McGranahan (2013), *Integrating the Environment in Urban Planning and Management: Key Principles and Approaches for Cities in the 21st Century*, International Institute for Environment and Development (IIED), United Nations Environment Programme, available at: www.citiesalliance.org/sites/citiesalliance.org/files/publications/integrating_the_environment.pdf.

Escolero Fuentes, O. et al. (2010), "Vulnerabilidad de las fuentes de abastecimiento de agua potable de la Ciudad de México en el contexto de cambio climático", in: UNAM (2010), *La Ciudad de México Ante el Cambio Climático*, pp. 7-19, Instituto de Geología, UNAM.

Eskeland, G. and T. Feyzioglu (1995), "Rationing can backfire: The "Day Without a Car" in Mexico City", *Policy Research Working Paper 1554*, Policy Research Department, The World Bank, Washington, DC, http://dx.doi.org/10.1596/1813-9450-1554.

European Environmental Agency (2013), "Managing municipal solid waste: A review of achievements in 32 European countries", *EEA Report*, No. 2/2013, Copenhagen, www.eea.europa.eu/publications/managing-municipal-solid-waste (accessed 15 August 2015).

European Space Agency (2014), "ESA/DLR Microwave and Radar Institute – SEOM InSARap study", Copernicus data, European Space Agency, www.esa.int/spaceinimages/Images/2014/12/Mexico_City_subsidence (accessed 2 April 2015).

Feller, G. (2015), "Dutch successes: Public and private sector aren't wasting their time", *Waste Management World*, www.waste-management-world.com/articles/print/volume-.11/issue-1/features/dutch-successes.html (accessed 15 August 2015).

Fuentes, A. (2011), "Policies towards a sustainable use of water in Spain", *OECD Economics Department Working Papers*, No. 840, OECD Publishing, Paris, http://dx.doi.org/10.1787/5kgj3l0ggczt-en.

Frohlich, J. and J. Kieling (2013), in: Knieling, J. and W. Leal Filho (eds.), "Climate change governance", *Climate Change Management*, pp. 9-26, Springer-Verlag, Berlin and Heidelberg, Germany, http://dx.doi.org/10.1007/978-3-642-29831-8_2.

Gallego, F., J.P. Montero and G. Salas (2013), "The effect of transport policies on car use: Evidence from Latin American cities", *Journal of Public Economics*, Vol. 107, pp. 47-62, Elsevier BV, http://dx.doi.org/10.1016/j.jpubeco.2013.08.007.

Government of the Federal District (2014), "Decreto por el que se reforman, adicionan y derogan diversas disposiciones del Código Fiscal del Distrito Federal", *Gaceta Oficial Distrito Federal*, No. 2012(I), 22 December, available at: www.sacmex.df.gob.mx/sacmex/doc/3_atencion_a_usuarios/tarifas/6_tarifas172.pdf (accessed 20 April 2015).

Government of the Federal District (2013), "Programa de Desarrollo del Distrito Federal", *Gaceta Oficial del Distrito Federal*, No. 1689(II), 11 September, available at: www.prosoft.economia.gob.mx/organismos/docop/ESTRATEGIA_DF.pdf.

Government of the Federal District (2012), *Inventario de Emisiones Contaminantes y de Efecto Invernadero, Zona Metropolitana del Valle de México*, Secretaría del Medio Ambiente.

Government of Mexico (2014), "Programa Especial de Cambio Climático 2014-2018 (PECC)", *Diario Oficial de la Federación*, SEMARNAT, 28 April, available at: www.semarnat.gob.mx/sites/default/files/documentos/transparencia/programa_especial_de_cambio_climatico_2014-2018.pdf

Government of Mexico (2013) *Plan Nacional de Desarrollo 2013-2018*, Presidencia de la República, available at: http://pnd.gob.mx/wp-content/uploads/2013/05/PND.pdf.

Government of Mexico (2011), *Programa para Mejorar la Calidad del Aire de la Zona Metropolitana del Valle de México 2011-2020*, Government of the State of Mexico, SEMARNAT, Secretaría de Salud, SEDEMA, www.sedema.df.gob.mx/flippingbook/proaire2011-2020 (accessed 15 August 2015).

Government of Naucalpan (2014), *Gaceta del Gobierno*, 18 December, p. 106, available at: http://caem.edomex.gob.mx/sites/caem.edomex.gob.mx/files/files/TramitesServicios/Tarifas2015/Naucalpan2015.pdf.

Government of the City of Toronto (2007), "Change is in the air: Climate change, clean air and sustainable energy action plan: Moving from framework to action Phase 1 – Highlights", Toronto Environment Office, June, available at: www.toronto.ca/legdocs/mmis/2008/ex/bgrd/backgroundfile-13957.pdf.

Government of the State of México (2013), *Programa Estatal de Acción Ante el Cambio Climático del Estado de México 2013*, Gobierno del Estado de México, available at: www.uaemex.mx/cambioclimatico/PEACC.pdf.

Government of the State of Mexico (2011), *Programa de Desarrollo del Estado de México 2011-2017*, available at: www.edomex.gob.mx/legistelfon/doc/pdf/gct/2012/mar133.PDF.

Government of the State of México (1984), *Ley de Planeación del Estado de México*, Decreto Número 212, available at: www.edomex.gob.mx/legislatelfon/doc/pdf/ley/abr/leyabr045.pdf.

Grafton, R.Q. et al. (2011), "Determinants of residential water consumption: Evidence and analysis from a 10-country household survey", *Water Resources Research*, Vol. 47, No. 8, http://dx.doi.org/10.1029/2010WR009685.

Gutiérrez, C. (2012), "Problemas y Soluciones en el Manejo de los Residuos Sólidos en México, presentation at UNAM "Semana Verde", 10 September, available at: www.iingen.unam.mx/es-mx/BancoDeInformacion/MemoriasdeEventos/SemanaVerde2012/03_Miercoles/ConstantinoGutierrezPalacios.pdf.

Hammer, S. et al. (2011), "Cities and green growth: A conceptual framework", *OECD Regional Development Working Papers*, No. 2011/08, OECD Publishing, Paris, http://dx.doi.org/10.1787/5kg0tflmzx34-en.

IDB (2012), "Modelo de marco institucional para la gestión de los recursos hídricos en el Valle de México", Inter-American Development Bank, November, available at: www.agua.unam.mx/sacmex/assets/docs/IDBDOCS_GRH_ValleMexico.pdf.

INEGI (2010a), *Censo de Población y Vivienda 2010*, Instituto Nacional de Estadística y Geografía, Aguascalientes, Mexico.

INEGI (2010b), *Encuesta Nacional de Ingresos y Gastos de los Hogares (ENIGH) 2010* [National Survey of Mexican Household Income and Expenditures], Instituto Nacional de Estadística y Geografía, Aguascalientes, Mexico.

Jiménez, B.J. (2014), "The unintentional and intentional recharge of aquifers in the Tula and the Mexico Valleys: The megalopolis needs mega solutions?", Chapter 8, in: Garrido, A. and M. Shechter (eds.), *Water for the Americas: Challenges and Opportunities*, Rosenberg International Forum on Water Policy, Buenos Aires, Argentina.

London21 (2008), "Thirty-three ways forward? Climate change in London: Action by local government", A survey of local councils by the London 21 network.

OECD (2015a), "PPPs and exchange rates", *OECD National Accounts Statistics* (database), http://dx.doi.org/10.1787/data-00004-en (accessed 30 June 2015).

OECD (2015b), *OECD Urban Policy Reviews: Mexico 2015: Transforming Urban Policy and Housing Finance,* OECD Publishing, Paris, http://dx.doi.org/10.1787/9789264227293-en.

OECD (2015c), *Water and Cities: Ensuring Sustainable Futures*, OECD Studies on Water, OECD Publishing, Paris, http://dx.doi.org/10.1787/9789264230149-en.

OECD (2014), *The Cost of Air Pollution: Health Impacts of Road Transport*, OECD Publishing, Paris, http://dx.doi.org/10.1787/9789264210448-en.

OECD (2013a), *OECD Environmental Performance Reviews: Mexico 2013*, OECD Publishing, Paris, http://dx.doi.org/10.1787/9789264180109-en.

OECD (2013b), *Green Growth in Cities*, OECD Green Growth Studies, OECD Publishing, Paris, http://dx.doi.org/10.1787/9789264195325-en.

OECD (2013c), *OECD Reviews of Risk Management Policies: Mexico 2013: Review of the Mexican National Civil Protection System*, OECD Publishing, Paris, http://dx.doi.org/10.1787/9789264192294-en.

OECD (2013d), *Making Water Reform Happen in Mexico*, OECD Studies on Water, OECD Publishing, Paris, http://dx.doi.org/10.1787/9789264187894-en.

OECD (2012a), *OECD Territorial Reviews: The Chicago Tri-State Metropolitan Area, United States 2012*, OECD Publishing, Paris, http://dx.doi.org/10.1787/9789264170315-en.

OECD (2012b), *Redefining "Urban": A New Way to Measure Metropolitan Areas*, OECD Publishing, Paris, http://dx.doi.org/10.1787/9789264174108-en.

OECD (2012c), *Water Governance in Latin America and the Caribbean: A Multi-level Approach*, OECD Studies on Water, OECD Publishing, Paris, http://dx.doi.org/10.1787/9789264174542-en.

OECD (2012d), *Compact City Policies: A Comparative Assessment*, OECD Green Growth Studies, OECD Publishing, Paris, http://dx.doi.org/10.1787/9789264167865-en.

OECD (2010), *Cities and Climate Change*, OECD Publishing, Paris, http://dx.doi.org/10.1787/9789264091375-en.

Paquette, C. (2014), "Retos del desarrollo urbano", in: Jourcin, E. (co-ord.) (2014), *Los Desafíos del Desarrollo Urbano en América Latina: Dinámicas Socioecnómicas y*

*Políticas Públicas*, Institut des Amériques, Agence Française de Développement, pp. 185-211.

Riveros Rotgé, H. (2009), "Análisis del programa Hoy No Circula", *Ciencia*, January-March, pp. 76-83, UNAM, available at: www.fisica.unam.mx/personales/hgriveros/docu/10-HoyNoCircula.299122533.pdf.

SABESP (2015), "Form 20-F (filing date 29 April 2015)", Companhia de Saneamento Básico do Estado de São Paulo, available at: www.sabesp.com.br/sabesp/filesmng.nsf/04F592CBAA86C3EB83257E3600833CB6/$File/sbsform20f_2014.pdf.

SACMEX (2013), "Foro: La crisis del agua en la Ciudad de México – Retos y soluciones – Documento base", Sistema de Aguas de la Ciudad de México, available at: www.agua.unam.mx/sacmex/assets/docs/doc_base.pdf.

SACMEX (2012), "El Gran Reto del Agua en la Ciudad de México", Sistema de Aguas de la Ciudad de México, Mexico, D.F., available at: www.agua.unam.mx/sacmex/assets/docs/granreto_sacmex.pdf.

Secretaría del Medio Ambiente y Recursos Naturales (2013), "Convenio de coordinación por el que se crea la Comisión Ambiental de la Megalópolis", *Diario Oficial de la Federación*, 3 October.

Secretaría de Salud (2002) Modificación a la Norma Oficial Mexicana NOM-020-SSA1-1993, www.salud.gob.mx/unidades/cdi/nom/m020ssa13.html (accessed 15 August 2015).

SEDATU (2014), "Propuesta territorial: Para una implantación optima del NAICM", presentation, August.

SEDEMA (2014), *Programa de Acción Climática de la Ciudad de México 2014-2020*, www.sedema.df.gob.mx/sedema/index.php/temas-ambientales/cambio-climatico (accessed 15 August 2015).

SEDEMA (2012), "Inventario de emisiones contaminantes y de efecto invernadero – Zona Metropolitana del Valle de México 2012", Secretaría del Medio Ambiente, www.sedema.df.gob.mx/flippingbook/inventario-emisioneszmvm2012 (accessed 15 August 2015).

SEDEMA (2008), "Programa de Certificación de Edificaciones Sustentables", *Gaceta Oficial del Distrito Federal*, 25 November, available at: www.sedema.df.gob.mx/sedema/images/archivos/tramites/auditoria-regulacion-ambiental/edificaciones-sustentables/programa-certificacion-edificaciones-sustentables.pdf.

SEDUVI (2013), "Agenda: hacia una ciudad compacta, dinámica, policéntrica y equitativa 2013-2018", Gobierno del Distrito Federal.

SEGOB (2015), *Atlas Nacional de Riesgos*, CENAPRED, Mexico, DF.

SEMARNAT (2013), "Convenio de Coordinación por el que se crea la Comisión Ambiental de la Megalópolis", *Diario Oficial de la Federación*, Secretaría de Medio Ambiente y Recursos Naturales, 3 October.

Soto Montes de Oca, G. (2007), *Agua: Tarifas, Escasez y Sustentabilidad en las Megaciudades: ¿Cuánto Están Dispuestos a Pagar los Habitantes de la Ciudad de*

*México?*, Sistema de Aguas de la Ciudad de México, Universidad Iberoamericana, Centro de Estudios Jurídicos y Ambientales, Procuraduría Ambiental y del Ordenamiento Territorial del Distrito Federal, Mexico, DF.

The Rockefeller Foundation/Arup (2014), *City Resilience Framework*, City Resilience Index, April, Ove Arup & Partners International Limited, London, available at: https://assets.rockefellerfoundation.org/app/uploads/20150530121930/City-Resilience-Framework1.pdf.

UNEP (2008), "UNEP background paper on green jobs", United Nations Environment Programme, Nairobi, available at: www.mi.gov/documents/nwlb/UNEP_Background_on_Green_Jobs_236033_7.pdf.

UNEP (2005), "Urban air quality management: Toolbox", United Nations Environment Programme, United Nations Human Settlements Programme, Nairobi, available at: www.unep.org/urban_environment/PDFs/handbook.pdf.

US Environmental Protection Agency (2006), "The bridge to cleaner air: Transportation conformity", Office of Transportation and Air Quality, United States Environmental Protection Agency, Washington, DC, January, available at: http://epa.gov/otaq/stateresources/transconf/420f06001.pdf.

WHO (2005), "WHO air quality guidelines for particulate matter, ozone, nitrogen dioxide and sulphur dioxide, Global update 2005, Summary of risk assessment", World Health Orgnization, Geneva, available at: http://apps.who.int/iris/bitstream/10665/69477/1/WHO_SDE_PHE_OEH_06.02_eng.pdf.

WHO (2003), "Health risks in aquifer recharge using reclaimed water", Chapter 3 in: Aertgeerts, R. and A. Angelakis (eds.), *Water, Sanitation and Health*, World Health Organization, Geneva, www.who.int/water_sanitation_health/wastewater/wsh0308/en (accessed 17 May 2015).

Wilson, D. and A. Scheinberg (2010), "What is good practice in solid waste management?", *Waste Management & Research*, Vol. 28, No. 12, pp. 1 055-1 056, SAGE Publications, http://dx.doi.org/10.1177/0734242X10392106.

World Bank (2013), "Agua urbana en el Valle de México: ¿Un camino verde para mañana?", World Bank, Washington, DC, available at: www.agua.unam.mx/sacmex/assets/docs/AguaUrbana_ValleMexico.pdf.

# *Chapter 5.*

## Revitalising metropolitan governance in the Valle de México

*This chapter looks at the major features of metropolitan governance in the Valle de México. It begins with an exploration of the institutional framework and co-ordination mechanisms, looking at the politico-administrative system as it affects the metropolitan governance dynamics. It then looks at the fiscal system operating in the metropolitan zone, proposing some changes to the Metropolitan Fund as an instrument for metropolitan co-operation. A major section focuses on options to bridge co-ordination gaps for urban development where the political reform of the Federal District, inter-municipal arrangements and the construction of the New Mexico City International Airport could help improve governance. It ends with some recommendations to encourage institutional capacity at the sub-national level of government. Overall, the chapter emphasises that the governance problem is not the lack of institutions, but how they work. A shift to metropolitan governance is a precondition for comprehensive policy responses.*

The Metropolitan Zone of the Valle de México (Zona Metropolitana del Valle de México, ZMVM) is the economic, financial, political and cultural heart of Mexico. Nonetheless, the Valle de México lacks an adequate governance structure to take on the challenges of urban development, environmental sustainability and building a competitive and liveable metropolis. The ZMVM needs to find a formula to capture a share of its economic resources that is adequate to current and future public expenditure needs. It also requires organising governance arrangements so that public services are delivered in a high-quality, timely and cost-efficient manner. Part of the solution would be to rethink the existing formal structures of metropolitan governance, and the instruments of finance and expenditure assignment, as well as to give citizens a voice in defining priorities and course of action.

The overriding message of this chapter is that the problem with the current governance arrangements of the Valle de México is not the lack of institutions, but how they operate. The challenge is to plan in a territory that covers several jurisdictions that must be united under a common vision. Ensuring operational capacity of the municipal-level governments is critical to improving governance arrangements. The Mexican authorities have two major opportunities to bolster metropolitan co-ordination: the political reform of the Federal District and the building of the New Mexico City International Airport (Nuevo Aeropuerto Internacional de la Ciudad de México, NAICM).

This chapter thus looks at the major metropolitan governance challenges in the Valle de México and explores some options for overcoming them. It begins with an overview of the institutional framework and co-ordination mechanisms, focusing on the fragmented nature of governance and a sectoral approach to policy making. It then looks at the fiscal system that operates in the metropolitan zone, highlighting the disparate revenue capacity of the local government, and in particular at the attempt to incentivise inter-governmental co-ordination through the Metropolitan Fund. The discussion then turns to exploring some alternatives to reinforce the institutional governance architecture and bridge the co-ordination gaps. It finally makes some suggestions for strengthening institutional capacity.

## Institutional framework and co-ordination mechanisms

The ZMVM is a highly complex zone, given the features of its politico-administrative organisation. It is easy to distinguish two administrative systems that are not complementary, and their co-existence complicates the organisation of a dynamic, functional metropolitan zone.

### *The politico-administrative system is highly complex and does not encourage co-ordination*

The Valle de México may be characterised as a socially divided, politically and administratively fragmented metropolis, with large and increasing differences in the coverage and quality of public services, as discussed in the previous chapters of this review. It has incomplete structures of governance, and presents mismatches between the politico-administrative realities and socio-political and economic needs. As Chapter 1 showed, the Valle de México is a complex administrative zone consisting of the 16 *delegaciones* (boroughs) of the Federal District, the 59 municipalities of the State of Mexico and 1 from the State of Hidalgo, plus the 3 state-level government (Federal District, Mexico and Hidalgo) and the federal government (INEGI-CONAPO-SEDESOL, 2010).

The ZMVM is a metropolis with two politico-administrative systems: the Federal District and its *delegaciones*, and the states and their municipalities. The Federal District is a distinct entity with a unique legal status. Unlike the states, the Federal District does not have a constitution, it is not integrated by municipalities, it is not autonomous, and its legislative assembly is not a congress and does not have a voice in constitutional reforms at national level. Its debt has to be approved by the federal government, and the Senate can remove the head of government (Mexico City's Mayor). The states of Mexico and Hidalgo have the opposite characteristics. Although the Federal District is much like a geographically small state in its spending responsibilities, it is not legally a state, but neither is it a municipality. Despite having a legal status that ties it more closely to the federal government than the states, it has far greater revenue-raising power than the states. Nonetheless, within the Federal District, some key functions that are usually the responsibility of the states – such as education – are administered directly by the federal government. As the capital of the country, the Federal District has certain additional responsibilities that do not apply, or that are less important for other states. At the municipal level, whereas municipalities are more autonomous and have more financial power because they can collect taxes (i.e. property tax), the *delegaciones* are, to all intents and purposes, administrative units of the Federal District. Moreover, the variety and number of politico-administrative units found in the metropolitan zone make co-ordinated management a rather complicated issue. Politico-administrative units have a very different legal status and have several sources and capacities of funding.

### *The constitutional position is ambiguous*

Mexico has developed some avenues for inter-governmental co-operation (both horizontal and vertical) in recent decades, though metropolitan governance arrangements remain relatively weak, given their ambiguous treatment within the legislative framework. The Federal Constitution of Mexico has no provisions for a metropolitan level of government, contemplating only the federal, state and municipal tiers. Article 115 states that there is no intermediate authority between the *ayuntamiento* (City Council) and the state government. Both the Federal Constitution and the General Law for Human Settlements (Ley General de Asentamientos Humanos, LGAH) define the term "metropolitan" somewhat ambiguously.[1] Article 115 also states that municipalities can co-ordinate their activities when there is a demographic continuity between two or more municipalities (i.e. the municipalities are adjacent); if such an urban centre covers the territory of municipalities located in two or more states, then, following Article 115, the federal, state and municipal governments should co-ordinate the development of such a centre. This article offers the possibility – but not the mandate – of creating metropolitan agencies for co-operation and co-ordination.

The Constitution and the LGAH acknowledge the concept of "conurbation", as the geographic continuity between two or more urban centres, but not the concept of "metropolitan zone", as the territorial space of influence of a dominant urban centre. This lack of a constitutional definition of a metropolitan zone and the absence of an official rule for delimiting which localities to include in defining metropolitan zones have created several co-ordination problems, such as the lack of common investment for public service delivery. Inter-governmental co-operation and collaboration may occur through loosely defined and structured urban metropolitan commissions (see below), national councils for mayors (Conferencia Nacional de Municipios de Mexico, CONAMM) and governors (Conferencia Nacional de Gobernadores, CONAGO), or other forms of voluntary inter-governmental agreements, councils and commissions. The legal framework also includes the local laws on metropolitan development but, in the case of the Federal District, for instance, they are rather ambiguous on what the government can do for better co-ordination of several domains of metropolitan impact. A direct consequence of this is that the national and local governments lack the resources and structures for joint metropolitan projects, which is why the federal government distributes resources and plans for its actions through purely local and/or sectoral schemes.

### *Inter-governmental co-ordination and co-operation is widely needed but poorly facilitated*

Direct co-ordination and co-operation between the Federal District and the State of Mexico and Hidalgo is not as straightforward as it might be between states where the legal and fiscal frameworks are similar. One first obstacle is that the federal government has not provided clear rules for metropolitan co-ordination that operationalise the constitutional precepts (Articles 115, Fr VI and 122, Fr VI .p G)[2] on inter-governmental relations and co-ordination. Moreover, the fragmentation of the ZMVM prevents an efficient co-ordination of public service delivery at the metropolitan level. An example of the lack of co-ordination is the existence of two disjointed bus rapid transit (BRT) networks (Metrobús and Mexibús), one per state-level entity, managed by different financing and regulatory frameworks. This limits the possibility of setting up a metropolitan bus service with a uniform fare scheme. Moreover, the absence of co-operation at the metropolitan level is preventing the expansion of the underground system into the municipalities of the State of Mexico, as the government of the Federal District has to subsidise any expansion of the network into this state. Uncoordinated vehicle regulation also allows vehicle owners to avoid stringent environmental standards by registering the vehicles in the State of Mexico and not in the Federal District. This situation reveals a persistent mismatch between administratively segmented services and metropolitan-wide mobility needs. Co-operation among neighbouring municipalities from the states and the *delegaciones* is not just hindered by legal and financial constraints, but also by political identification: when their governments come from different political parties, co-operation is almost non-existent. This can also apply to municipalities within the same state.

Within public administrations, there are units in charge of encouraging co-ordination. The federal Ministry of Agrarian, Territorial and Urban Development (Secretaría de Desarollo Agrario, Territorial y Urbano, SEDATU) has a general directorate in charge of metropolitan co-ordination; in particular, it operates in inter-state metropolitan areas, when municipalities of two or more states constitute a metropolitan area. The federal government takes part in the co-ordination meetings, and its role is twofold: it has a normative role (i.e. sets rules and guidelines) in metropolitan development programmes, and oversees the management of the Metropolitan Fund. The State of Mexico has a Ministry of Metropolitan Co-ordination, and the Federal District has a General Directorate for Metropolitan Co-ordination.

The number of authorities from the three levels of government represented in the Valle de México creates the problem of having to co-ordinate with a large number of decision makers (76 municipal-level governments, 3 state-level governments and the federal government). This may be holding back socio-economic development. The OECD (2015a, 2015b) has found that an increasing fragmentation of a metropolitan area into different municipalities is correlated with lower levels of labour productivity (see Chapter 1). Moreover, the political and ideological diversity in the Valle de México, together with the intense national electoral agenda, make dialogue, co-ordination, planning and the effective participation of citizens more challenging (Iracheta Cenecorta and Iracheta Carroll, 2014).

### *Metropolitan co-ordination is based on commissions, committees and covenants but has limited impact*

Ensuring effective metropolitan governance in the Valle de México creates some challenges of its own, including the need for coherent cross-government collaboration, multi-stakeholder engagement, interagency co-ordination, private sector engagement, and definition of relevant long-term goals and indicators. The importance co-ordination has for the ZMVM is reflected in the plethora of co-ordinating and planning bodies, commissions, committees and councils between the states of Mexico and Hidalgo, the Federal District and the federal government, intended to strengthen collaboration in areas of common interest. Unfortunately, the existing co-ordinating mechanisms and programmes do not seem to have created much co-ordination. Poor follow-up to decisions and agreements reached and the lack of rigorous assessments of results and outcomes as well as accountability channels have called into question the legitimacy and relevance of those co-ordination mechanisms.

Other obstacles to metropolitan co-ordination are related to the fiscal regime and the absence of a culture of institutional co-operation. The lack of a co-operative culture can be partially linked to the effects of the three-year term limits for municipal governments without the possibility of re-election, which makes long-term commitment to accountable policy making and public spending difficult. In the State of México, mayors will be able to be re-elected once, as of 2018, and although a three-year term remains short by OECD country standards, this is a positive step forward. There are no incentives for municipal leaders to increase co-operation or to have a long-term or inter-municipal policy focus. The Mexican Congress and SEDATU, acknowledging the need for a long-term vision, are currently working on changes to the LGAH to make co-ordination for metropolitan projects compulsory, enhance public participation in decision making on urban development and establish the basis for long-term planning of metropolitan development. Changes to this law could be seminal in addressing the lack of culture of co-operation and creating the incentives for collaboration.

The Executive Commission for Metropolitan Co-ordination (Comisión Ejecutiva de Coordinación Metropolitana, CECM), created in 1998, is considered the first instance of tripartite co-ordination in the Valle de México.[3] The CECM defines the topics of the metropolitan agenda; sets priorities; and establishes the basis for the collaboration among the municipalities of the State of Mexico, Hidalgo and the *delegaciones* of the Federal District.[4] The aim of the CECM is to co-ordinate, assess and follow up on the plans, programmes and projects of the different sectoral metropolitan commissions, providing them, in theory, with precisely the general view that they lack when they operate unconnected as single-sector bodies. The CECM needs to reposition itself as a centre for metropolitan co-ordination, as its members have not met for a long time, due to the lack of political support from state-level and federal governments. The commissions that the CECM is, at least in theory, in charge of co-ordinating are:

- the Metropolitan Commission for Water and Sewage (Comisión de Agua y Drenaje del Área Metropolitana, CADAM), created on 27 June 1994
- the Metropolitan Commission for Transport and Roads (Comisión Metropolitana de Transporte y Vialidad, COMETRAVI), created on 27 June 1994

- the Metropolitan Commission for Public Security and Justice (Comisión Nacional de Seguridad Pública y Procuración de Justicia, COMSPJ), created on 27 June 1994
- the Metropolitan Commission for Human Settlements (Comisión Metropolitana de Asentamientos Humanos, COMETAH), created on 23 June 1995
- the Metropolitan Environment Commission (Comisión Ambiental Metropolitana, CAM), created on 13 September 1996, and transformed into the Environmental Commission for the Megalopolis (Comisión Ambiental para la Megalópolis, CAMe) in 2013
- the Metropolitan Commission for Civil Protection (Comisión Metropolitana de Protección Civil, COMEPROC), created on 6 March 2000.

The principal drawback of the sectoral commissions is that they are single-sector bodies and tend to be reactive to specific problems, without being able to address the range of possible causes or contributing factors. It is difficult to make the Valle de México a functional metropolis and encourage its urban development via sectoral approaches, and this remains a key underlying problem that influences outcomes in many different sectors. In addition, it is not clear how effective the work of these commissions has been in ensuring metropolitan co-ordination and in overcoming obstacles to implementation of metropolitan projects. Another problem is that the actions recommended by these commissions have to be carried out by sectoral organisms that do not necessarily follow the recommendations. These sectoral organisms also often lack the structure to create integrated projects with a metropolitan approach or the necessary resources to that end (Iracheta Cenecorta, 2003).

Co-ordination covenants (*acuerdos de coordinación*) are another mechanism for inter-governmental co-ordination in the ZMVM. But reaching these covenants depends on political agreements, not on a legal mandate. The Federal Constitution (Article 122 Ap. G) states that the Federal District "may" celebrate covenants for the creation of metropolitan commissions created by joint agreement – of wills – of the participants. Their main drawbacks are the lack of incentives for compliance, as they were created in good will; they do not constitute a legal framework for co-ordination in the solution of common problems. They also only include the main agreements reached, and there are no elements to follow up their implementation or to assess their results (Meza Urías, 2004).

The instruments used to encourage co-ordination seem to be evolving over time, for example, in the case of the creation of the CAMe. However, despite the comprehensive nature of institutions currently in place, there is still a sense that this has not translated into a metropolitan approach overall. This does not seem to be a problem of lack of institutions, but rather how these institutions operate. Three reasons could be distinguished. Firstly, these institutions do not act under a common metropolitan vision that guides how actions should be implemented, co-ordinated and monitored. Secondly, the regulatory framework for metropolitan co-ordination for development is not facilitating the work, as it is rather dated. For example, there is no region-wide framework for sharing responsibilities or pooling resources. Thirdly, there is a financial disequilibrium between the different actors in the metropolitan zone. The fragmentation of metropolitan governance also raises concerns over accountability. As in the rest of the country, institutional fragmentation leads to responsibility overlaps, and confusion over who is responsible for what and accountable to whom (OECD, 2015c).

### *A fragmented, sectoral approach to planning, policy making and financing prevails*

In the Valle de México, there is growing awareness of the need for a more integrated approach to policy making, but policies are still largely defined based on sectoral needs and priorities. The prevalence of unidimensional planning is holding back several urban policy domains that are too large or complex for any unit or level of government to address alone, and require synergies with other sectors to be successful. Issues such as urban renewal, housing, public transport, environment, groundwater management and the quality of life are not managed under a regional/metropolitan approach. Moreover, Mexican legislation regulates sectoral and territorial planning through different bodies without articulation. The General Law for Human Settlements (LGAH) is administered by SEDATU and the Planning Law (Ley de Planeación, LP) is implemented by the Ministry of Finance and Public Credit (Secretaría de Hacienda y Crédito Público, SHCP), but no synergies between the two could be found. Since the Planning Law depends on the SHCP, it has more influence on practical decisions such as fund allocations. Article 12 of the LGAH establishes the metropolitan planning programmes (*programas de ordenación de las zonas conurbadas)* as a mechanism for territorial planning and resource allocation, but it is underused.

There are limited synergies across policy domains within each local entity. Every sector – housing, transport, urban renewal, etc. – still conducts its planning in a strictly vertical way, setting its objectives, goals, programmes, projects and actions exclusively based on the national and the states' development plans. This leads to inconsistencies in urban development projects. For instance, the gaps between transport and urban (housing) development have led to the construction of isolated and low-density housing in the peripheries of the metropolitan zone. Since urban development and transport infrastructure are not jointly planned, new transport projects do not fully correspond to accessibility needs. The problem is exacerbated if it is considered that certain sectors are also fragmented, such as police, transport and water delivery. This is leading to fragmented sectoral policies with a fragmented vision. For example, a metropolitan transport system for the Valle de México is still pending because of the fragmentation that exists in the governance system and within the sector itself (see Chapter 3). Indeed, in the State of Mexico two different bodies are in charge of transport/mobility issues, whereas the Federal District has only one.[5] This problem is also found at national level. For instance, the planning for the New Mexico City International Airport has been predominantly sectoral, led by the federal Ministry of Communications and Transport (Secretaría de Comunicaciones y Transporte, SCT). Territorial planning that ensures an integrative decision-making process linked to a shared vision and an overall development strategy for the region has been minimal.

The Valle de México has had several metropolitan or urban planning initiatives. Every state-level government has a large number of plans of different kinds, at different geographical scales, following different timelines and sponsored by different bodies. Most of these plans seem to be poorly linked to the political/decision-making channels through which public investment choices and budget allocations are made. Even when the plans themselves are articulated in a horizontal, integrated manner, their implementation is still carried out by generally uncoordinated sectoral departments. Spatial planning lacks a strategic co-ordination between land-use, transport, housing and economic development issues.

Planning is not just largely sectoral but localised, or rather covers only the territory of the state/municipality where it is conceived, and not the region. This is a reflection of the jurisdiction problems, as no state is entitled to plan developments in another state. This situation is not surprising, considering that states are sovereign and municipalities are autonomous. The challenge is to find the way to plan regionally without undermining the legal, political status of every territory.

The National Development Plan (Plan Nacional de Desarrollo, PND) is the basic instrument for allocating resources and assigning responsibilities. The SHCP is responsible for co-ordinating the implementation of the PND and following through on a local scale with the states and municipalities by means of a range of co-ordination agreements between the federal and state governments. For these co-ordination efforts to be reflected at a municipal scale, the corresponding agreement may contain the specific procedures in that regard. Every state, including the Federal District, has to prepare a development plan articulating the principles of the PND at state level. This plan is typically prepared by a state planning committee (Comité de Planeación del Desarrollo Estatal, COPLADE), and generally includes a proposal for investments at state and municipal levels and supervises co-ordination of actions across levels of government. At the municipal level, the planning committee for municipal development (Comité de Planeación para el Desarrollo Municipal, COPLADEM) is responsible for formulating a municipal development plan that includes more specific expenditure proposals. Both the COPLADEs and COPLADEMs find their legal grounds in the local planning laws. On the basis of these municipal plans, the state government conducts municipal development agreements with each municipality, setting out the transfer of resources and defining shared responsibilities for project implementation and financing in the case of joint activities. This is the principal framework for policy planning across levels of government, and given the heavily centralised nature of the Mexican fiscal regime, this system of planning also governs fiscal relations to a large extent. Some municipalities have a municipal planning institute, but information and studies provided by them is generally not used. An additional problem is that these plans are not fully implemented, and even if they are, they tend to be limited in their coverage and the functions considered. State and municipal governments are elected entities and are defined by political boundaries that fragment the metropolitan area.

### *The capacity of municipal-level governments is weak*

Mexican municipalities, and the *delegaciones* of the Federal District, need to be able to provide basic public services such as water, waste collection, street lighting, public security, markets, cemeteries, parks, gardens and other public facilities. Municipalities are entitled to adopt urban municipal development plans, take part in the creation and management of territorial reserves and ecological reserves, authorise and control land use, grant construction permits, and intervene in the formulation and implementation of public transport programmes.[6] However, not all municipal governments conduct urban planning, and even the richest municipalities lack enough resources and incentives to update urban development plans and programmes (OECD, 2015c). Thus, municipalities lack an important instrument for guiding spending, accountability and measuring success. Their decision making is often improvised and based on good will, but with little planning and vision.

The reasons for this poor planning are threefold. First, as already mentioned, the short municipal terms and the features of the political system do not favour political commitment to long-term planning. Lack of continuity prevents progress, since with each new administration, all plans change. Second, qualified staff to conduct and implement urban planning are lacking; some municipalities have to outsource the creation of a plan to universities or consultancy firms, rather than build internal know-how. High levels of turnover every three years and the complete absence of a career system often preclude the formation of a professional, competent workforce in charge of municipal administration. In addition, timely and adequate training of the workforce is usually lacking. Finally, a lack of adequate funding also holds back urban development. State-level governments, on the other hand, appear to have more qualified staff to conduct urban planning.

## Fiscal relations across levels of government

Improving inter-governmental relations by clearly defining who does what, and who charges which taxes and fees, has been an ongoing challenge for Mexico. Finding a close correlation between the income and expenses of the local governments and developing a system that assumes both fiscal and political responsibilities are just part of this problem. Fiscal intergovernmental relations do not allow for the healthy development of metropolitan areas, making the most of scarce resources. Across the country, sub-national governments have limited own-revenue sources (mostly taxes, fees and contributions) with high levels of spending responsibility and low fiscal autonomy. As Figure 5.1 shows, there is a fiscal imbalance at the sub-national level of government regarding expenditure and revenue. Mexican local governments have basically four sources of income: own income, federal transferred resources, decentralisation covenants and public debt. As most of their spending is funded by federal transfers, sub-national governments have little incentive to spend wisely or to be fiscally prudent. This is reflected in growing levels of sub-national government debt (OECD, 2013a; 2015a), which is also evident in the fiscal landscape of the Valle de México.

Figure 5.1. **Fiscal imbalances among OECD countries at the sub-national level**

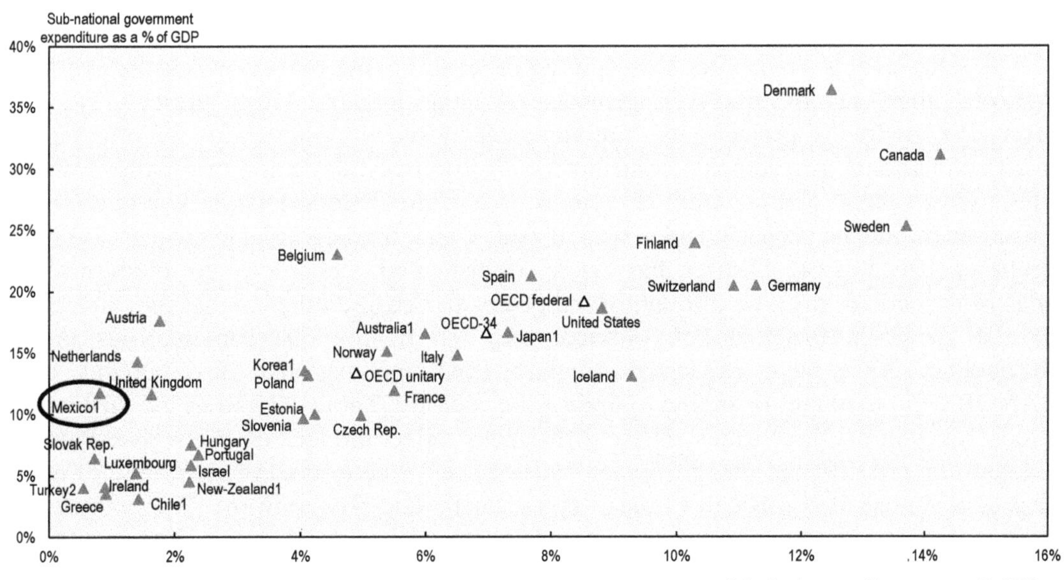


*Notes:* 1. 2012 figures 2. 2011 figures. Tax revenues include both own-source taxes and shared taxes.

*Source*: OECD calculations based on OECD (2015d), "Sub-national governments in OECD countries: Key data" (brochure), OECD, Paris.

### *The fiscal system operating in the Valle de México is complex and heterogeneous*

The Federal District and the State of Mexico receive a large percentage of their income from federal transfers, which fluctuate every year, limiting long-term planning (see Chapter 1). The heterogeneity of the politico-administrative system carries over to the fiscal regime. The Federal District's fiscal regime differs from that of the states, and that of the *delegaciones* differs from the municipalities'. This complicates inter-governmental co-ordination and the funding of metropolitan projects. The Fiscal Co-ordination Law, rather than being an instrument for facilitating the financing of metropolitan projects, is an instrument by which the federal government distributes part of its income among the different sub-national governments. Inter-governmental transfers from the federal and subsequently state governments fail to provide incentives to increase municipal government revenue mobilisation. There is also considerable disparity between the fiscal capacity of the Federal District, and that of the states and municipalities (Table 5.1). The Federal District's debt is classified as federal debt, and considered low risk.[7] The income the Federal District receives from decentralised organisms[8] include, for example, revenues from underground fares.

Table 5.1. **Structure of total revenue by percentage, Federal District and State of Mexico, 2014**

| Type of revenue | Federal District % | State of Mexico % |
|---|---|---|
| Own-revenue | 43 | 18 |
| Federal transfers | 45 | 75.7 |
| Debt | 3 | 4.5 |
| Income from decentralised organisms | 9 | 1.5 |
| Other revenue | 0 | 0.2 |

*Source*: Based on information provided by the Ministry of Finance of the Federal District and the Ministry of Finance of the State of Mexico to the OECD.

The state-level governments have limited revenue-raising powers. With the available resources, they cannot invest in projects of large impact. Mega projects such as motorways, hydraulic projects, etc. are financed by the three levels of government, to which sub-national governments contribute with resources that come originally from the federal government. The main tax revenue source of the Federal District is a payroll tax. It also levies a tax on property and real estate sales, and taxes on vehicle property, use and purchase. The Federal District has used sophisticated technology to modernise its cadastre to increase revenue through property tax and ensure citizens that they are being charged fairly. In the State of Mexico, only 15 of the 59 municipalities in the metropolitan zone have requested support from the national development bank (BANOBRAS) to obtain financing to update the cadastre. Table 5.2 shows the differences in local taxes in the three states. These differences reflect the lack of fiscal co-ordination in determining tariffs and fees for goods and services. Due to the tax autonomy of every local government, it is difficult to make taxes, tariffs and fees uniform. The poor design of local tax instruments do not permit levying user charges and property taxes at rates high enough to cover the expenditures of the metropolitan area or to change behaviour.

Municipal governments do not have the necessary infrastructure and sophisticated tools to collect taxes. The problem is that the federal Constitution states that municipal governments will receive the contributions and other income related to real estate and municipal public services as defined by the local state congress. As a result, municipalities raise relatively little income. Table 5.3 shows that even the most developed municipalities in the State of Mexico that are within the metropolitan zone have limited fiscal capacity, since almost three-quarters of their income comes from transfers.

Table 5.2. **Differences in local taxes in the states of the Valle de México**

| Concept | Federal District | State of Mexico | State of Hidalgo |
|---|---|---|---|
| Real estate purchases | Fee (between MXN 200 and MXN 900 000) | x | x |
| Property tax | Fee (between MXN 156.9 and MXN 47 095) | x | x |
| Public events | 8% | x | x |
| Vehicle property use and purchase | Subsidy up to MXN 250 000 | Subsidy up to MXN 350 000 | Subsidy up to MXN 550 000 |
| Lotteries, raffles and contests | 6% | 6% | 4.5% |
| Accommodation services | 3% | 4% | 2% |
| Payroll tax | 3% | 3% | 2% |
| Purchase of used vehicles | x | 1% | 4 minimum salaries |
| Fees on professional services | x | x | 1.6% |

*Note:* x: not applicable.

*Source*: Information provided by the Ministry of Finance of the State of Mexico.

Table 5.3. **Structure of municipal revenues in the Metropolitan Zone of the Valle de México, 2013**

| Type of revenue | Atizapán | Coacalco | Ecatepec | Naucalpan | Tlalnepantla | Tultitlán |
|---|---|---|---|---|---|---|
| Own revenue | 37% | 28% | 26% | 25% | 38% | 36% |
| No own income (i.e. transfers) | 63% | 72% | 74% | 75% | 62% | 64% |
| Total | 100% | 100% | 100% | 100% | 100% | 100% |

*Source*: Ministry of Finance of the State of Mexico answers to background questionnaire (unpublished).

## *Encouraging inter-governmental co-operation through financing*

### *The Metropolitan Fund needs fine-tuning to pursue metropolitan objectives*

To support the sustainable development of metropolitan zones in Mexico, the federal government uses part of the national budget to subsidise state and municipal action on urban development through the so-called Metropolitan Fund (Box 5.1). The operation rules for the Metropolitan Fund require the creation of a Metropolitan Development Council (Consejo para el Desarrollo Metropolitano, CDM) to receive funds. In the Valle de México, the CDM is jointly chaired by the governors of the states of Mexico and Hidalgo and the Mayor of Mexico City. In principle, the CDM must define the mechanisms for sharing the resources with the municipalities; and determine the criteria to align investment and development plans and programmes with the National Development Plan, the National Urban Development Plan, as well as local urban development programmes. It should also establish the criteria for defining priorities and determine the metropolitan impact of those plans and programmes to receive financing from the Metropolitan Fund.[9] The CDM handles the areas of environment, sustainable mobility and public works. The aim is to co-ordinate actions to improve zoning, urban mobility, mitigate pollution and encourage economic growth. Nonetheless, the CDM has become a space for political negotiation on resource allocation rather than a forum for co-ordination. Most of the projects financed with the help of the fund's resources are related to road infrastructure, and only a small part of the revenues is spent on public transport infrastructure. Water projects are also financed by the fund, but so far have been limited to infrastructure for the provision of water and sewage. The federal Ministry of Agrarian, Territorial and Urban Development (SEDATU) does not participate in the fund allocation decisions or dictate priorities.

### Box 5.1. The Metropolitan Fund

Established in 2008 by the Ministry of Finance and Public Credit (SHCP), the Metropolitan Fund is a federal subsidy designed for the officially recognised metropolitan areas in the country, charged with financing studies, plans, evaluations, programmes, projects and infrastructure works that prove to be viable and sustainable. It seeks to promote adequate planning for urban and territorial development, and to enhance the economic competitiveness and capacity of metropolitan areas. These projects can be new or ongoing, implying that the funds can be used to complete the financing of projects that have run out of resources. The Metropolitan Fund aims to finance projects and plans that contribute to:

- sustainability, economic competitiveness and the strengthening of productive capacities
- diminishing the vulnerability or risks posed by natural phenomena or demographic and economic dynamics
- urban consolidation
- the optimal use of the competitive advantages or regional and urban functions in the metropolitan areas.

Hence, the Metropolitan Fund can be used to finance the elaboration or updating of regional and urban development programmes; infrastructure such as metropolitan transport, water provision and water treatment; acquisition of territorial reserves; the elaboration of cost-benefit analysis, environmental impact analysis and metropolitan risk-management projects. The Operation Rules suggest using part of the resources for the elaboration of the Metropolitan Development Plan and an urban non-motorised mobility plan. The financial resources of the Metropolitan Fund are managed by a trust whose fiduciary is a development bank. All actions funded with resources from the Metropolitan Fund must be aligned with the national state and municipal development plans.

Following the Operation Rules, all institutions co-ordinating the management of the Metropolitan Fund (Metropolitan Development Council, Technical Committee and the Technical Sub-Committee) need to include not only the federal, state and municipal authorities but also citizens, either as individuals or as members of non-governmental organisations.

*Source*: Government of Mexico (2015a), "Reglas de Operación del Fondo Metropolitano", *Diario Oficial de la Federación*, 31 March, available at: www.shcp.gob.mx/lashcp/MarcoJuridico/documentosDOF/2015/marzo/reglas_31032015.pdf.

The Metropolitan Fund has very limited resources given the size of metropolitan projects (OECD, 2013b). Its size varies from year to year, depending on the federal government's income, and represents between 4% and 10% of municipalities' public investment. One of the main drawbacks of the fund is that its resources are distributed among the three entities by political negotiation. The state of Hidalgo gets 25%, and the rest is divided between the other two entities in equal parts, leading to an imbalance in per capita terms.[10] To compensate for this differential, the federal government included the Federal District in the *fondo de capitalidad*, but there is no formula to calculate this, as it depends on political negotiations.[11]

The projects funded by the Metropolitan Fund are typically local, not metropolitan.[12] To decide which projects will be financed with resources from the fund, every local government proposes its priority projects to the Metropolitan Development Council. However, the Metropolitan Fund lacks clear objectives. The Operation Rules make reference to "enhancing economic competitiveness and productive capacity" of the metropolitan zones, but these are broad concepts that do not determine whether a project has a real metropolitan impact, or if the resources are to supplement insufficient resources for infrastructure (Iracheta Cenecorta and Iracheta Carroll, 2014). In addition, the Operation Rules do not take into account the particular characteristics of every metropolitan zone. It does not consider, for example, the particular politico-administrative system that operates in the Valle de México, as explained above, and the role of Mexico City as the country's capital.

The Metropolitan Fund aims to enhance metropolitan co-ordination through integrated, long-term planning, but the absence of metropolitan plans with a long-term vision to guide investment projects makes achieving this objective virtually impossible. The fact that the SHCP and state governments use different delimitations also limits the potential of the fund. Moreover, the fund is based on annual budgeting, as is typical of the budget procedure in Mexico; but metropolitan projects with real urban impact usually require several years to be carried out. In addition, local governments have no certainty when the resources of the Metropolitan Fund will be transferred, complicating the management of investment projects (Iracheta Cenecorta and Iracheta Carroll, 2014). Interviews for this review also underlined the fact that the procedures for complying with the Operation Rules and those of the legal framework for public works are not aligned, doubling the amount of administrative work.

### *The Operation Rules of the Metropolitan Fund require a metropolitan, integrated vision*

To enhance the potential of the Metropolitan Fund in the Valle de México, Mexican authorities may consider the following actions: 1) allow experts, civil society organisations and citizens to take part in the CDM to reflect their priorities in the decision making; 2) ensure more flexibility in the Operation Rules, to make it possible to use existing local planning and co-ordination structures and avoid creating additional structures for the Metropolitan Fund; 3) support the work of the CDM through a technical body – a Metropolitan Planning Institute for example – that conducts metropolitan planning and assesses and evaluates all projects technically and financially, together with their different sources of funding; 4) use information and communication technologies (ICT) to build databases to manage, control and assess investment projects financed by different funds, not just the Metropolitan Fund; and 5) ensure that all projects financed by the Metropolitan Fund are fully linked to a metropolitan development plan.

Iracheta Cenecorta and Iracheta Carroll (2014) propose new operational rules and a methodology for the distribution of resources of the Metropolitan Fund. They suggest the use of different criteria such as: size of the population, poverty and social inequality levels, vulnerability to natural phenomena, the capacity of the local administration, productive capacity, etc. The SHCP may well wish to consider using this proposal to modernise the operational rules of the Metropolitan Fund, as it would make the distribution of resources fairer, based on the particularities of each metropolitan zone. This proposal suggests that only those projects that promote inter-governmental co-operation and collaboration, operate in multi-annual cycles and build synergies with other projects should be supported by the Metropolitan Fund. This would help limit the possibility for state governments to divide the Metropolitan Fund along political lines.

The Metropolitan Fund should not be used only to finance road construction. It should give priority to projects with a metropolitan logic, such as mass transport systems and non-motorised transport programmes, integrated treatment of water, solid waste management, inter-governmental co-operation in the metropolitan areas, environment improvement and productive infrastructure (see Chapters 3 and 4). What is important is that metropolitan projects have a long-term, holistic vision.

## Bridging co-ordination gaps for urban development

The key challenge in the Valle de México is to find the approaches and technical methods for efficient and effective co-ordination that is also politically feasible. This would help reduce duplication of functions, clarify responsibilities and build links between strategy and its implementation. The caveat is that no single model of metropolitan governance can be emulated completely; it depends on the particular political, economic, social and historic background of each metropolitan setting in Mexico. Mexican authorities should also ensure that co-ordination be conducted in a practical fashion. It is not always necessary to wait until institutional frameworks such as mandates and legislation or co-ordination frameworks are in place. In the case of Mexico's busy electoral agenda (with municipal elections every three years), making a single government approach operational involves buy-in across party lines and by public servants at all levels. Political will and leadership is needed to separate a clear policy agenda from the means to achieve it. Gathering support for a whole-of-government approach involves a combination of short-term wins to build and maintain momentum, while preserving a long-term vision across election cycles.

### *Towards "Mexico City": The political reform of the Federal District*

The political reform of the Federal District is an opportunity to revamp the metropolitan governance structure of the Valle de México. The ongoing discussions on the transformation of the Federal District into a federal state called Ciudad de México raise important questions, which may have a long-term impact on the metropolitan and megalopolitan region as a whole. For example, what fiscal powers would the new state have? Would *delegaciones* become municipalities, and would they have fiscal responsibilities and be in charge of the police, like the other municipalities in the country? Would the reform consider a framework for metropolitan co-operation and collaboration with the State of Mexico and its municipalities? What mechanisms will be adopted to facilitate a dynamic management of the city that cultivates competitiveness and equality and reduces social, political and administrative fragmentation? How will service delivery be co-ordinated among the three levels of government within the metropolitan area? How will the national government support the new state, since it is also the capital city of the nation? For example, Mexico City is generally the focus of demonstrations expressing social and political discontent. People from different parts of the country travel to the capital to manifest their demands, often affecting the life of local residents, urban infrastructure and the city's economy. These demonstrations are not about local issues or local government, but it is often the local government that must provide security and the urban space.

Interviews conducted for this review revealed no clear consensus on the features of the future new state. There is no decision on whether Mexico City will be treated the same as other local governments or be given differential fiscal treatment. In the People's

Republic of China, for example, the four largest cities are treated as provinces and have the powers of both provincial and local government (OECD, 2015e). The Valle de México is already spread across jurisdictional boundaries, so the city-province status would only be assigned to the core city, which may not be adequate for metropolitan purposes. The future of the *delegaciones* is also unclear. There is some talk of transforming them into a hybrid type of government with characteristics of both municipalities and *delegaciones*. This risks complicating governance even more. Federal and state governments should regard municipalities as clients in charge of the front office, since they are in direct contact with citizens, unlike deconcentrated administrative units or service providers, as is currently the case with the *delegaciones* and to a large extent with the municipalities.

Political reform of the Federal District should aim to give municipal-level governments more support from higher levels of government, to meet its development objectives. Only services that require a wider vision, highly specific competencies and skills, and have an impact on the entire metropolitan area, such as transport, would need to be managed by the state-level governments in the form of a joint administration. The reform of the Federal District should help to formalise a generic long-term vision for the metropolitan zone. Municipal-level governments should be given more incentives to engage more actively in and become accountable for urban planning and development. They should be the main providers of public services and guide economic development in their territories. To use the political reform of the Federal District to revamp metropolitan governance, Mexican lawmakers may consider the following points:

- The reform process of the Federal District must take a metropolitan view of reform choices that institute co-ordination mechanisms, making co-ordination and consultation with other levels of government and peer governments mandatory rather than voluntary. The reform should consider updating the Law for Metropolitan Development of the Federal District, which should specify the attributions of the new entity (Mexico City) in terms of metropolitan co-ordination; or at the very least, allow the Federal District to issue the secondary legislation of the law (*reglamento*). It is important to define what the new state can do in terms of metropolitan co-ordination in the areas of environment, mobility, security, water management, etc. Ensuring coherence with the legal framework of the states of Mexico and Hidalgo is critical.
- Some talk persists about dividing some of the current *delegaciones* of the Federal District into different municipal entities, since they are considered to be too big territorially and with low density. OECD research has found that there is a risk in increasing the number of municipal-level governments. Statistically, increasing fragmentation of a metropolitan area is correlated with lower levels of labour productivity, although this could be mitigated by the right metropolitan governance structure (OECD, 2015b). Denmark, for instance, reduced the number of its municipalities from 271 to 98 in 2007, to deal with fragmentation of investment. In Italy, the creation of Roma Capitale reduced the number of municipalities from 19 to 15, to improve the management of the capital.[13] Creating new municipal governments could also increase the administrative cost of paying for additional elected and appointed personnel.
- There should be a clear and consistent definition of responsibilities and resources for each level of government to contribute to a dynamic system of inter-governmental relations in the Valle de México. Critical questions are: Who

does what? Who charges which taxes and fees? How should the imbalance between the income and expenses of municipal-level governments be dealt with? Would municipal-level governments be able to acquire debt and if so, how would it be supervised (Rojas, 2008)? The local and municipal-level governments could be given more discretion in taking decisions about service delivery and managing their budgets.

- A key element of improved urban management would be to ensure accountability of the service providers to their ultimate clients: citizens and business in the city. The reform could consider those accountability mechanisms, for example: political oversight, local councils, community and business advisory councils, citizens' report cards, contractual obligations, etc. Experience shows that without such accountability, public and private providers will have few incentives to improve the management and delivery of metropolitan public services.
- Effective policies and mechanisms for the election, appointment and removal of key officials will be needed. These mechanisms should promote proficient and trustworthy behaviour on the part of public officials at all levels of the administration. A clear distinction between local and national elections could help citizens focus on local issues. Moreover, when the elected officials' terms are short, with no possibility of re-election, their attitudes tend to be opportunistic. Longer incumbencies with the possibility of re-election may encourage elected officials to create long-term strategies fully committed to the community's interests. The experience of OECD countries suggests that a four-year municipal term with the possibility of one re-election would facilitate medium-term planning.
- There could be provisions for the installation of a Council of *delegados* chaired by Mexico City's Mayor to discuss and harmonise territorial and administrative policies (Rosique Cañas, 2006). Whether the *delegaciones* become municipalities or not, it would be important to give them an active role in metropolitan affairs, so that territorial and administrative issues could be discussed in the Council of delegados giving a voice and vote to each *delegación*. Brazil's metropolitan councils (i.e. São Paulo) could be of inspiration to Mexico in bringing all stakeholders together to find solutions. The reform should consider mechanisms to request municipal-level governments to work together irrespective of the entity where they are located, and submit projects to be financed by, for instance, the Metropolitan Fund, as in London's boroughs.
- Lawmakers may wish to explore the introduction of a metropolitan council, with members elected by citizens, and with responsibilities focused on metropolitan affairs and financing clearly established in the local constitutions of at least the State of Mexico and Mexico City. Mechanisms that facilitate citizens' participation in public affairs will be needed. Defining the power of the local councils will be essential for effectively representing the interests of the community and acting as a mechanism of supervision of elected officials.
- The reform should also help to redefine the duties of the mayor (municipal president), who should focus less on administrative issues and assume a more strategic role guiding municipal urban development plans, and bringing other mayors together with financial experts to explore new ways of financing essential urban infrastructure. The municipal president's new role should involve thinking

outside the box and beyond municipal borders. Introduction of a city manager could be considered, to ensure professional management of the city (OECD, 2015c).

- The capacity of local employees to deliver services will need to be improved. The Constitution of the new state could include elements that promote the professionalisation and the effective management of public employees in the local and municipal-level administrations. A career service system that eliminates favouritism and promotes specialisation and professional development would revitalise institutional development. Accountability of local officials, elected and appointed, for the quality of service delivery and management of resources, would need to be cultivated.
- A well-organised method of collecting taxes and tariffs, dynamic planning and budgeting mechanisms, and methods to evaluate results would contribute to the operational capacity of the local and municipal-level governments. Provisions for multi-year planning and financial execution will need to be considered.

To complement the reform of the Federal District, the federal government may consider granting the Metropolitan Zone of the Valle de México special status, because it includes the capital of the country. This could ensure a more functionally driven governance structure. Special status would mean more financial autonomy, the possibility of creating supra-municipal bodies for service delivery, and facilitating the creation of inter-municipal arrangements for service delivery among municipal-level governments of different states. Whether the Legislative Assembly of the Federal District is transformed into a local congress or not, it should be possible for the local legislature to take part in reforms to the federal Constitution, so it can have the same possibility as the other states to participate in the design of metropolitan forms of government. Given the importance of the Federal District in the national economy, ensuring its participation in the National System of Fiscal Co-ordination would grant it access to all federal transfers, which could also be an important contribution to the political reform of the Federal District.

### *Moving to a networked model of metropolitan governance may promote joint action*

In order to encourage greater co-ordination (shared information) and ultimately co-operation (joint intent) and collaboration (joint intent and peer-to-peer communication) among local authorities, OECD countries are moving away from hierarchical one-to-one structures toward a more strongly networked governance model (i.e. Estonia, Finland, Ireland and Sweden). The reason is that it allows greater connectivity between different sectors, agencies and levels of government, as well as with stakeholders outside the public sector. A networked model is significantly different from a hierarchical structure, where management is more streamlined and accountability is clearer, but information and knowledge flows are vertical, social capital can be limited and communication among peers is lacking. This co-ordination and integration model requires a whole-of-government approach,[14] which is the growing aspiration as OECD countries react to the silos and fragmentation in policy making and organisation (OECD, 2011a). In the Stockholm metro-region, networked governance rather than formal metropolitan institutions is seen as the best way to achieve stronger, more enduring policy implementation that can outlast political cycles and achieve multisectoral objectives. Networked governance brings together a multiplicity of public sector agencies, private sector firms, non-governmental organisations and other actors to deal with the complex problem of sustainability. Stockholm authorities point to such successes as the construction of the Citybanan (a railway tunnel through Stockholm) and the Stockholm Agreement on future transport infrastructure in the region. Because of the complexity of the Valle de México, with the powers to implement planning strategies spread out among a large number of private and public bodies, a genuine consensus on regional goals, strategies and commitments would make concerted regional action easier to achieve. It would also facilitate moving to a more cross-cutting, integrated policy-making approach.

A metropolitan governance system for the Valle de México should balance the competencies between municipalities and state governments, under the stewardship of the federal government. The challenge for Mexican authorities is to avoid duplicating functions across levels of government, and the creation of a fourth level of government. The political reform of the Federal District could be of assistance in this respect. Moving towards an effective form of metropolitan governance should take into account possible resistance from institutional actors and must remain within the specific legal and institutional context. In this sense, it might be easier to elaborate and incrementally implement alternatives that start with inter-municipal co-operation.

### *Effective metropolitan governance arrangements require a long-term vision ...*

The metropolitan idea seems to be gaining momentum in the Valle de México, so this could be the time to start the promotion of a metropolitan agenda with a common vision within the framework of the political reform of the Federal District. Without strong and unified political backing, the benefits from co-ordination are lost, because in the end, implementation depends on elected political authorities. The ultimate objective for the ZMVM should be to develop a strategy or a vision as to how the Valle de México should develop over time. If the Valle de México does not know where it wants to go, it is hard to correct its course in the face of complexity, adversity or shocks, whether expected or otherwise. This process requires horizontal and vertical networks between public and private actors at national and sub-national levels of government. It would allow for a more open-ended and multi-stakeholder learning process, with advances and setbacks, in which products (reduction of sprawl, collective goods, scale economy, public service delivery) and processes (voice, transparency and accountability) become increasingly interdependent (Klink, 2008).

A long-term vision could be a powerful tool for providing a clear direction to governments and public administration at all levels, and is also fundamental for measuring performance. Developing a vision means thinking beyond immediate government cycles and political concerns. This vision should be a statement of common interest and a commitment to co-operate towards shared objectives. To develop a vision, Mexican authorities need to be strategic, and this requires drawing on capacities and capabilities that are not often fully developed or easily implemented in government. This includes having well-established and regularly updated evidence bases, ensuring that the proper frameworks are in place to support evidence-based analysis, and that the public administration has the capability to provide evidence-based advice. Consultation with internal and external stakeholders, including civil society organisations and citizens, is paramount.

This new deal for the ZMVM should include reflection on two main perspectives:

- Internal vision or how residents see the Valle de México in the national context: a competitive and socially balanced metropolitan region. This should be based on an explicit assertion that all parts of the region are potentially valuable to the economic success of the country. The promotion of social development and the reduction of social problems and imbalances is not social policy per se but an integral element of a long-term strategy to ensure productivity and prosperity by developing the Valle de México's employment base. The ZMVM needs to be thought of as a metropolis within the regional framework of a megalopolis (composed of the six central states of the country); this requires a regional vision.

- External vision or how residents see the Valle de México in the international scene: a world metropolis for Latin America. This refers to the position of the Valle de México in the world economy. The prominence of the ZMVM on the world stage is due to its historical development and role. However, as the world economy changes, the competitive advantages that the Valle de México can offer, relative to those in other similar cities, need to be continually reassessed. This reassessment should include the assets found in the wider region. The New Mexico City International Airport could be used as leverage for this vision. Establishing Mexico City as an international transport hub could contribute to making the Valle de México the political, cultural and economic centre of Latin America.

### *... and a new working culture in the public service*

Given the wide variety of urban development issues, and the number of actors involved in policy making and implementation, the Valle de México needs a different approach to getting traction on some long-standing and often complex problem areas. The network approach offers that possibility. While informality may be highly desirable for its dynamic and often innovative qualities, a networked public administration requires a balance between institutionalised and informal relations. Informal networks could be complemented with institutional networks. This entails embedding networks more formally in the administrative culture of national and sub-national governments. Institutionalised networks are a means to build an organisation's social capital, where ties are formed between the institution and government bodies, civil society groups, thought leaders, individuals, etc. Links within and among institutionalised networks are maintained even when individuals leave the organisation. The experience of New Zealand could be an inspiration for authorities in the Valle de México. Since 2004, New Zealand has instituted a number of networks and teams to improve whole-of-government co-ordination across sectoral areas. The creation of "circuit-breaker teams" and "soft" and "hard" wired networks have been regarded as an innovative response to fragmentation and silo-based working. The core idea is to find solution collaboratively and locally, through the circuit-breaker teams and proposed regional networks. Another example is Finland's Finwin Programme. Although this was initiated at the central government level, the Finwin model may have some lessons for authorities in the Valle de México, as it builds a more co-operative administrative culture through information sharing and network building (Box 5.2).

Training of senior officials could be used not only as a capacity development exercise but as a way to build a vision, sharing information and networking at a professional level. The Australian New Zealand School of Government provides an excellent example of how this can be achieved (Box 5.3). Its collaborative partnership between government and universities ensures both academic rigour and direct application to public sector requirements, but also collaboration across jurisdictions, helping develop a focus on common problems.

### Box 5.2. Finland: The Finwin Programme

In December 2006, the Ministerial Committee for Economic Policy of Finland established the change management programme called Finwin – Towards a New Leadership. The aim of the programme was to cultivate a shared understanding and vision about future challenges and how to manage them. Finwin facilitated horizontal dialogue among senior managers from different ministries and agencies through discussion seminars. It intended to facilitate change through the dissemination of information and the exchange of positive and negative lessons on reform programmes in different areas and levels of government. The programme was organised around seminars on topics like well-being at work, social innovations, functions of the state sector and regional administration reform. Managers had the opportunity to discuss a common vision of where they were going, what they wanted from the future, where they would be in ten years and the level of operational quality they wanted to achieve. The seminars gave them the opportunity to share experiences and fears regarding the future and the challenges ahead. One of the concrete results of Finwin was the elaboration of a five-point programme for better management.

*Source:* Huerta Melchor, O. (2008), "Managing change in OECD governments: An introductory framework", *OECD Working Papers on Public Governance*, No. 12, OECD Publishing, Paris, http://dx.doi.org/10.1787/227141782188.

### Box 5.3. The Australia and New Zealand School of Government (ANZSOG)

The Australia and New Zealand School of Government (ANZSOG) is unique for its inter-governmental approach to public sector learning. The ANZSOG was established in 2002 through the collaboration of major Australian and New Zealand universities and the governments of the Australian Commonwealth, states and territories and of New Zealand. Its focus is on educating public sector leaders, building new public policy research and managing capability, and encouraging public sector innovation. To promote learning across jurisdictions, all students come from the public sector of the participating governments. An interactive learning model creates the opportunity for public sector managers to compare various approaches being tried by other jurisdictions. As participants come from various departments and agencies, they bring comparative knowledge and experience to the ANZSOG's classrooms. Participants work collaboratively on team projects. This encourages knowledge sharing, relationship building and the creation of lasting networks across governments. The school also has an alumni association, which facilitates networking and information sharing between participants after they have completed their studies.

*Source:* ANZSOG website: www.anzsog.edu.au/about-us/about-anzsog (accessed 15 June 2015).

Building a forum for policy dialogue and structured exchange of ideas and views on urban development issues would enhance networking and a new working culture of co-operation. Urban Toronto in Canada, the University of Chicago Urban Network in the United States, and the Viet Nam Urban Forum (VUF) are examples of platforms for networking and discussion on key urban issues among agents from different backgrounds. The VUF, for instance, chaired by the Ministry of Construction, has a membership that includes public, private and non-profit organisations (universities, think-tanks, etc.) and even international organisations. The VUF, as a platform for discussion on urban issues, regularly reviews and reports to stakeholders on the state of ongoing urban development programmes. It also contributes to a deeper understanding of urban upgrading projects. Donors use the forum to present their views and findings of the projects they finance.[15] The Valle de México could draw inspiration from these experiences to build a similar platform (Urban Forum of the Valle de México) where national, state and municipal actors and national and international expert groups get together to discuss urban issues and search for co-operation strategies. This would add transparency in building a vision for the metropolitan zone.

Resource capacity is often cited as a reason for lack of co-ordination, but whole-of-government approaches are undertaken precisely to build efficiency by capitalising on synergies, reducing overlap and pooling resources (whether knowledge, funding, staff or infrastructure). The United Kingdom has recognised that it can save more by working across government than by having individual units working alone. ICT-enabled networking and inter-connectivity provide new opportunities to identify and eliminate duplication and redundancies, and to remedy incompatible systems and processes across governments.

Developing shared services can help the Valle de México to promote a whole-of-government way of working in the metropolitan zone. Streamlining and aligning processes and utilising ICT to gather data for various corporate functions can provide efficiencies and increase the effectiveness of service to staff and government. Shared services are therefore increasingly being used to bring the over-reliance on decentralisation and devolution back into balance across OECD countries. Shared services are an area where the authorities of the Valle de México could explore joint action among the different governments in the metropolitan area. Denmark, for instance, has been using ICT to make interaction with government seamless. A citizen portal has been set up that will enable a broad array of public sector organisations – central and local – to use a common interface with citizens. Horizontal integration is also pursued across government through enhanced ICT standard setting by the Ministry of Finance, which will allow easy communication between all central and local government units (OECD, 2012).

### *Strategic regional planning should be the basis for metropolitan co-ordination*

One of the biggest challenges for authorities in the Valle de México is to shift from a physical and spatial to a regional and strategic dimension of planning. Economic, land-use and transport patterns have evolved, making the political boundaries into which the metropolitan zone is divided largely irrelevant to citizens and economic and social activities. To meaningfully influence land use, transport and service delivery, it is necessary to act at a level at which the city core and suburban area can be considered as a whole. For the Valle de México, regional strategic planning could be a tool and the basis for the establishment of co-operative networks where information can flow under a joint action framework. To be effective, regional strategic planning must be transformational, involve a large number of stakeholders and be backed by long-term finance. It should bring together a spectrum of social, economic and environmental sustainability goals. The challenge is to plan in a territory that covers several jurisdictions that must be united under a common vision. Regional planning does not necessarily imply a uniform approach, as the challenges and contexts of different parts of the metropolitan zone are distinct and diverse.

#### *The Valle de México needs a metropolitan planning authority*

Regional planning normally requires an administrative regional authority that implements the regional development plans in collaboration with both national and sub-national government authorities. To plan and guide metropolitan development with a long-term vision, authorities in the Valle de México may wish to establish a metropolitan planning and development body. This role is now partially played by SEDATU, but this is not ideal. The 2004 *OECD Territorial Review of Mexico City* recommended the creation of a Metropolitan Development Agency to act as the principal implementing body for a competitiveness strategy for the ZMVM. This is still a recommendation that authorities in the Valle de México may wish to consider. The purpose of this agency should be to improve the effectiveness of economic development measures through co-ordinating planning and implementation; it could be a quasi-public body reporting directly to a board composed of representatives of the federal government, as well as those of the Federal District and the states of Mexico and Hidalgo. The institution could be managed by a board composed of representatives of the three state-level governments. They should be professionals nominated by the state executives (governors) and ratified by the local legislative powers. Alternatively, the board could include some members (a minority) appointed by the federal and state-level governments and other members elected directly or by electoral college. Municipal-level election of members could be organised through metropolitan sub-regions. Voting powers should aspire to be proportional to the contributions of the different members, but avoid the dominance of the central city. This governance model would ensure independence, accountability and representation, without imposing another electoral layer on the Valle de México's multi-level governance system.

Two critical features of the proposed institution are that it must have a stable professional staff hired on the basis of capacity and proficiency, and not linked to political cycles. They could be transferred from their current state departments of planning and other relevant urban agencies. Secondments from municipal, state or federal government could be contemplated. In addition, the institution could be funded by its own rate-raising mechanism or from contributions from the three entities, established as recurrent expenditures in their annual budgets. It should work in direct communication and co-ordination with the different metropolitan commissions. The experience of the Melbourne and Metropolitan Board of Works in Australia suggests that it is essential that such an agency or planning body be seen to have an independent, if subsidiary, mandate to that of the state-level governments. This body should have clear responsibility for places and issues of metropolitan significance, including: all principal activity centres in the ZMVM, all public transport corridors that have major potential for growth, and the current and new airport zones. Outside these areas and issues, state- and municipal-level governments should have greater discretion to pursue localised planning solutions. Tasks it might undertake include:

- *Prepare long-term plans* to supply the territory with the infrastructure and services required by the development process, and propose development proposals above a threshold size or value. The decisions taken by the agency should be binding for all member governments.
- *Provide technical assistance* to the authorities responsible for urban services, such as public transport, water, sanitation and waste management, and *prepare plans and programmes* to improve urban services in the metropolis.
- *Advise the Executive Commission for Metropolitan Co-ordination (CECM), the CDM and other metropolitan commissions and councils*, through project preparation and evaluation services, on investments with high metropolitan priority that could be financed with federal transfers from the Metropolitan Fund or other federal programmes.

- *Prepare integrated metropolitan development projects*, co-ordinating the input from relevant sub-national governments and sectoral institutions.
- *Support municipal-level governments* in improving territorial management, providing technical assistance for activities such as the preparation of urban development programmes or land-use master plans, as well as for exercising their development control authority or updating and improving the management of land cadastres and land tax rolls.
- *Develop mechanisms for municipal evaluation* to distinguish which municipalities are working well and which ones are being left behind. It would be critical to give this body some power to impose sanctions for poor results.

Many examples exist of metropolitan-scale planning institutes financed by the public sector that could be relevant for a similar institute in the Valle de México, such as the Institut d'Aménagement et d'Urbanisme d'Île de France (IAU) in France, and Barcelona Regional in Spain (Box 5.4). A common feature is the multidisciplinary teams and the key role of these institutions in large-scale urban projects. In Mexico, the Metropolitan Planning Institute of the Metropolitan Area of Guadalajara (Instituto Metropolitano de Planeación del Área Metropolitana de Guadalajara, IMEPLAN) is another valuable example of how an inter-municipal planning body could be organised in the Mexican administrative, legal and political landscape. Although the Metropolitan Area of Guadalajara is located in a single state and the Valle de México spans the territory of three entities, IMEPLAN could provide valuable information for the organisation and management of a similar institute in the ZMVM.

### Box 5.4. Metropolitan planning institutes in the Île-de-France, Barcelona and Guadalajara

In France, the **Institut d'Aménagement et d'Urbanisme de Île-de-France** (IAU) was established as a public interest organisation (a foundation) in 1960, as the urban institute for the Paris Region. In 1982, the IAU became an associated body of the Regional Council. Although focused on the territory of the Île-de-France Region, the mandate of the IAU is to identify critical challenges faced by the region, from local to regional (that is from the Paris Basin to Europe). Its task is to formulate planning and development policies to take advantage of opportunities and face development challenges. Planning activities of the IAU include: preparation and implementation of master plans for regional and urban land use; regional sector development plans; research on population and economic development; consultancy and research services for various sub-national authorities; and gathering and disseminating information on regional development issues. The IAU is managed by a Board of Directors that includes four representatives of the national government, the members of the Regional Council of the Île-de-France, two members from the Economic and Social Regional Council and four founding members of the institute. The IAU has a multi-disciplinary team of specialists including architects, urban planners, engineers (agricultural, transport, sanitation and computer scientists), economists, demographers, geographers, experts in the areas of law, the environment and health, specialists in infographics and mapping, demographers, statisticians and librarians. The Regional Council covers 80% of the institute's annual budget and the remaining 20% comes from contracts and central government subsidies.

### Box 5.4. Metropolitan planning institutes in the Île-de-France, Barcelona and Guadalajara *(continued)*

In 1993, Barcelona's City Council, along with nine public shareholders including the Metropolitan Area of Barcelona, the Port of Barcelona, the Airport of Barcelona and the Consortium for Barcelona's Free Trade Zones, created **Barcelona Regional** as a public institution dedicated to strategic, urban and infrastructure planning. It was established on the accumulated experience that emerged from the urban transformation of the city of Barcelona during the Olympic Games in 1992. Over the years, the agency's main projects have centred on the metropolitan area and the large-scale projects that remade the metropolitan area. Its projects have included the environmental recovery of the Besòs River, the Universal Forum of Cultures in 2004 and its related urban development plans, the Action Plan for the development of infrastructure in the Poblenou district and the new generation district called @22, as well as the planning of the high-speed railway lines, accessing the Sagrera and Sants stations. Barcelona Regional has a multidisciplinary team of 60 people with architects, urban planners, engineers, geographers, economists and biologists.

In Mexico, **the Metropolitan Planning Institute of the Metropolitan Area of Guadalajara** (IMEPLAN) is an inter-municipal body that seeks to co-ordinate public service delivery across the eight municipalities that integrate the metropolitan area of Guadalajara under the stewardship of the state government of Jalisco. Its goal is to promote inclusive metropolitan development while preserving the environment. IMEPLAN is a collegiate organ, and its co-ordination board includes the eight municipal presidents and the state governor. It has several planning instruments, including the Metropolitan Development Plan, the Metropolitan Zoning Plan, a Metropolitan Risk Map, a Metropolitan Information System and the Metropolitan Zoning Plan.

*Note*: For more information on the Institut d'Aménagement et d'Urbanisme Île-de-France, see: www.iaurif.org (accessed 15 June 2015); for more information on Barcelona Regional, see: www.bcnregional.com/en (accessed 15 June 2015); for more information on IMEPLAN, see: http://imeplan.mx (accessed 15 June 2015).

Following the experience of Australian cities, the transition to better metropolitan governance could be carried out in stages rather than instituted in one reform package. At this point, the political reform of the Federal District could be an important part of this process. In a first phase, the Metropolitan Development Agency could be established, with jurisdiction over matters outlined in the third section of Table 5.4, reporting to a forum such as the CECM. In a second phase, the Metropolitan Development Agency could be given authority to plan and finance major roads, public transport, major open space, major water cycle infrastructure and urban regeneration functions. This would include two assumptions: 1) it must have separate bond-raising/fiscal powers; and 2) some metropolitan commissions would delegate their work to the agency.

### *The metropolitan commissions require a subsidiarity mandate*

Another feasible way to improve cross-sectoral work and governmental co-operation in the Valle de México is to capitalise on the different metropolitan commissions already in place. The revival of the CECM with the integration of the federal government and the state of Hidalgo is a positive step towards better metropolitan governance. However, as a first step, Mexican authorities may wish to ensure that all metropolitan commissions (CECM, COMETRAVI, COMETAH, CAMe, CADAM, COMEPROC) are operational, have a permanent technical secretariat led by professional staff and are guaranteed the financial means to pursue their work. Schemes similar to the one used to finance the

CAMe could be used for other commissions (see Chapter 4). A second aspect is to ensure

Table 5.4. **Subsidiarity and planning governance**

| Level | Examples of activities or decisions for this level |
|---|---|
| National level | – Improving national consistency of planning and building regulation<br>– Resolving cross-border issues such as water supply, ports and transport connections<br>– Environment, heritage issues of national significance |
| State/territory level | – Maintaining the state-wide land use and development regulation system<br>– Maintaining the administrative and judicial review process<br>– Overseeing planning institutions<br>– Development planning and development determinations for sites or projects of state-wide significance |
| Regional/ metropolitan level | – Prioritising and investing in strategic infrastructure of metropolitan significance<br>– Designing major activity centres and facilitating development in these centres<br>– Designing and managing major transport corridors<br>– Identifying and developing key economic strategies, including employment nodes<br>– Formulating land release schedules in growth areas<br>– Protecting environmental and cultural assets of regional significance<br>– Maintaining efficient land supply for housing |
| Local level | – Neighbourhood structure planning<br>– Regulating housing development and redevelopment within applicable state and regional guidelines<br>– Regulating development in all lower-order activity centres |

*Source*: Gleeson, B., J. Dodson and M. Spiller (2010), *Metropolitan Governance for the Australian City: The Case for Reform*, Urban Research Program, Issues Paper 12, available at: www.griffith.edu.au/__data/assets/pdf_file/0012/199299/urp-ip12-gleeson-et-al-2010.pdf.

that all decisions reached within the commissions are legally binding on all governments and agents. A revision and update of the covenants that led to the creation of the commissions is essential to ensure the political and legal commitment of all governments taking part in the commission. A third aspect is to ensure that the commissions have the authority to monitor, assess and establish some form of sanctions or penalties for poor performance or under-delivery on the different urban development projects. It is important that the commissions guarantee openness and transparency in their decision making and in the implementation of the investment projects. To ensure a long-term vision and continuity, the commissions would have to operate independently of the political calendar. Thus, the technical secretary for each commission should be appointed for a period longer than the electoral cycle, with the possibility of renewal. Since the electoral calendars of the Federal District and the states of Mexico and Hidalgo are not synchronised, a fixed-term appointment of the technical secretary would ensure continuity of co-ordination despite changes in government. Alternatively, the members of the commissions' boards could be elected following the proposal made above for the Metropolitan Development Agency. These commissions should also have a subsidiarity mandate from the state-level governments, while remaining independent.

In particular, the CECM should be given a more strategic role. It should ensure dialogue across the different commissions, and identify ways to combine successful project-based sectoral initiatives with long-term, cross-sectoral strategic planning, to assess progress and update the metropolitan agenda. The CECM should be responsible for assessing the work of the different sectoral commissions and the management of their resources, and ratify or reconsider any sanction imposed by sectoral commissions in case of disagreement. This Executive Commission should also be a forum for discussing metropolitan financing means such as the Metropolitan Fund. There are three specific areas where the CECM could function as an advocate: 1) promote making the legal framework uniform across entities and levels of government, to facilitate co-ordination for urban development; 2) promote a constitutional reform to recognise the "metropolitan zone", its inclusion in the corresponding laws, and make inter-governmental co-operation compulsory in the metropolitan zone; and 3) promote the inclusion in all legal frameworks of consulting citizens on urban-related affairs before and after decision making.

### *Inter-municipal arrangements have the potential to address administrative fragmentation*

Mexico may wish to re-evaluate and adjust the governance structure of the Valle de México to one that is more functionally driven. This could help ensure that the local services delivered and the methods for delivery match citizens' needs and are delivered according to municipal capacity. The functional model of metropolitan governance has been promoted in many OECD countries (i.e. Germany, the United Kingdom and the United States). It is based on governance at a functional economic area level, and built around cross-sectoral competitiveness and competences (i.e. not restricted to a specific sector or service) in areas with a metropolitan logic (e.g. transport, housing, investment promotion, water supply and tourism). It aims to achieve economies of scale generated by larger, unified service delivery areas, better cost equality and less social segregation across the entire metropolitan zone, as well as more strategic planning and integration of sectoral policies.

Structurally, this can take the form of large-scale amalgamations, establishing metropolitan authorities (i.e. the Stuttgart Regional Association in Germany; the Greater London Authority in the United Kingdom; and the Portland Metropolitan District in the United States), or promoting inter-municipal joint authorities. The first two options have the advantage of building scale and unifying service delivery, for example, but may also dampen competition and public choice. Creating an elected metropolitan government authority, as in London and Stuttgart, could be politically and technically more challenging for Mexico, given the sovereignty of states and the autonomy of the municipalities, and given that the constitutional arrangements in Mexico do not provide for a metropolitan government.

Inter-municipal institutional arrangements could be more appropriate for the Valle de México and effective at managing the impact of administrative fragmentation, particularly for service delivery, than creating a supra-municipal authority. This is due to the particularities of the politico-administrative system described at the beginning of this chapter. Inter-municipal arrangements are based on obligatory and/or voluntary co-operation among the municipalities comprising the functional urban area. Their success, however, requires effective horizontal and vertical networks among urban actors (Klink, 2008). This arrangement is more flexible than that of a supra-municipal authority model. Inter-municipal arrangements can take the form of metropolitan-wide (city-wide) or single-purpose bodies (Lefèvre, 2008). Metropolitan-wide or city-wide joint authorities are a more comprehensive form of inter-municipal arrangement. Setting up special-function councils or inter-municipal institutional arrangements to encourage collaboration in metropolitan areas could be a starting point. This model can develop organically over time, for example with the support of legislation promoting inter-municipal co-operation; alternatively, their development can be fostered by federal government incentives such as the Metropolitan Fund. In Canada, the Metropolitan Community of Montreal was created by an upper level of government, while in

Vancouver, the Greater Vancouver Regional District came about through voluntary co-operation. In addition, metropolitan-wide joint authorities tend to have their own administrative and financial resources, and enjoy sufficient funding for their operation and management. Grants from upper levels of government and/or fees from members' local governments would be some options for financing.

Inter-municipal joint authorities can either be single-purpose, that is, tasked with the delivery of only one service such as transport – or they can be multiple-purpose metropolitan bodies that perform a wide range of functions such as planning and co-ordination, and sometimes public service delivery. This would not necessarily mean adding a new tier of government. In some cases, not only can they deliver economies of scale in specific policy areas, but they can also equalise the sharing of service costs across the metropolitan region and allow for a more harmonious distribution of resources. The main disadvantages of a single-purpose agency are that it raises the problem of co-ordination among different sectoral agencies and increases the risk of the emergence of constituencies that will defend sectoral interests. However, they would cover the whole metropolitan area from the perspective of their domain. Barcelona's experience in metropolitan governance could provide a valuable example of how to deal with sectoral bodies. In 2011, the parliament of Catalonia set up the Ãrea Metropolitana de Barcelona (AMB), which brings together three sectoral inter-municipal authorities (a planning authority, a transport authority and an environmental authority). This ensures co-ordination and collaboration among the different authorities. Its Metropolitan Council is composed of the mayors of all 36 municipalities (including the city of Barcelona) covered under the strategic metropolitan plan. The AMB is in charge of planning, transport, water, waste treatment, social cohesion and economic development (OECD, 2015a). In the Valle de México's context, where co-operation across sectoral borders has been more complicated than across state borders, this would seem to be a major step forward.

Engaging in regional strategic planning could be a way to encourage co-ordination and collaboration in the Valle de México. For example, the elaboration of the first strategic plan at metropolitan level of the city of Turin, in Italy, facilitated the creation of a metropolitan authority. This case also shows that metropolitan governance should be viewed as a process, with the strategic plan as the instrument used in reaching a consensus among the most significant actors in the metropolitan area (Box 5.5).

Current discussions to update the General Law on Human Settlements (LGAH) could include reference to setting up metropolitan-wide joint authorities and allowing local jurisdictions to work together for certain common services or investments. This could be a way to put the Constitution's precepts into action. These arrangements would potentially incentivise better co-ordination for urban policy design among municipal-level governments and increase policy coherence across the metropolitan area. A strong cost-control incentive should be created for such an agency/body for objective case handling. Creating the incentives for co-operation – such as greater tax autonomy – is necessary to ensure that the scheme is viable. Accountability mechanisms are also essential. Joint authorities could report to local or municipal legislatures, or even to joint municipal boards. An inter-municipal joint authority in the Valle de México would require new institutional executive arrangements reporting to two legislative chambers: the Legislative Assembly of the Federal District and the State of Mexico Congress in Toluca. The key questions here are to what extent local/municipal authorities in the Valle de México would be prepared to give up authority in the name of a regional interest and what incentives should be put in place in exchange. This is important, because the joint authority could eventually be given competencies in transport, water management and waste management. To be effective, Ward and Robles (2012) argue that these arrangements would require some constitutional changes, to create a mandate that would ensure it is: 1) appropriately funded; 2) sustainable beyond electoral term limits; and 3) not subject to different ideologies operating in the individual units. The experience of OECD countries shows that the mandate of the metropolitan-wide joint authorities should be restricted to macro-level activities that are in the common interest of all municipalities, for example, risk management (OECD, 2013c).

### Box 5.5. Strategic planning to establish a metropolitan authority: The case of Turin

With the 2006 winter Olympics in view, the Turin Plan, the first strategic plan at the metropolitan level in Italy, was elaborated between 1998 and 2000 and approved that year. Following its approval, a public agency was established, Torino Internazionale, with the goals of co-ordinating and monitoring the activities approved in the plan; controlling the implementation of the projects included in the plan; and updating the plan through 2010. Torino Internazionale has 122 members: local governments (the province, the central city and 37 other suburban municipalities), development agencies, cultural associations, universities, the airport authority, trade unions, etc. It is led by the Mayor of Turin and administered by an assembly of partners, which appoints a nine-member board. The plan consists of the following strategic orientations, managed by six board members and six working groups: 1) integrating Turin within the world system (major infrastructure such as the high-speed train and airport); 2) building a metropolitan government; 3) research and education; 4) culture, commerce, tourism and transport; 5) urban quality of life (social integration, urban regeneration); and 6) employment and enterprises.

The strategic plan led to the signing of a pact between all local governments. In 2000, a metropolitan conference was established, comprised of the 22 municipalities of the first ring of the metropolitan area. This conference, chaired by the province of Turin, is considered the first step towards a metropolitan city. In 2002, a permanent working group was constituted, which was composed of the city of Turin, the province and Torino Internazionale; and was designed to organise and support the activities of the metropolitan conference. In 2014, the Italian parliament passed a law (Law n.56/2014), which identified a roadmap to establish the *città metropolitane*. The territories of the corresponding provinces are taken as the territories of the *città metropolitana*. On 14 April 2015, the Statute of the Metropolitan City of Turin (*Città Metropolitana di Torino*) was approved. The *Città Metropolitana* conducts general regional planning and co-ordinates its implementation. This plan can be adapted to different zones of the region.

*Sources:* Lefèvre, C. (2008), "Democratic governability of metropolitan areas: International experiences and lessons for Latin American cities" in: Rojas, E., J.R. Cuadrado-Roura and J.M. Fernández Guell (eds.), *Governing the Metropolis: Principles and Cases*, Inter-Americn Development Bank, David Rockefeller Center for Latin American Studies, Harvard University City, pp. 137-192; OECD (2015a), *Governing the City*, OECD Publishing, Paris, http://dx.doi.org/10.1787/9789264226500-en; Città Metropolitana di Torino (2015), Statuto della Città Metropolitana di Torino, available at: www.cittametropolitana.torino.it/speciali/2015/statuto_citta_metro/dwd/testo_definitivo.pdf.

As in many OECD countries, Mexico's federal government could play a key role in initiating inter-municipal co-operation agreements through the use of fiscal or legal instruments. For instance, in 2005, the government instituted a Gas Tax Fund (GTF) to share half the revenue from the federal excise on gasoline with 3 600 municipalities across the country, in order to fund sustainable municipal infrastructure, including for public transit and waste disposal. To access the funds, municipalities must apply jointly. The programme has resulted in the construction of regional water filtration plans, community co-generation systems and transport initiatives. In the United Kingdom, for instance, the government has offered to devolve new powers to cities over transport, infrastructure, business development, education and planning issues if cities put in place stronger governance arrangements, like a stronger community of existing local authorities.

Guidelines for the appointment of the head of an inter-municipal joint authority would be needed. These would predominantly include an open selection process, in which all municipalities play a role in selecting and appointing the head of the joint authority. The term of the appointment should be longer than the municipal three-year term, with the possibility of renewal based on performance. A clear job profile should define the skills and competences of such a position to ensure the recruitment of a highly professional, experienced manager, rather than a politician.

### *The New Mexico City International Airport as a lever to promote metropolitan co-ordination*

The New Mexico City International Airport (NAICM) is a tangible project that has the potential not only of boosting economic development, urban regeneration, social inclusion and positioning Mexico City as an international destination hub, but also as a catalyst for better inter-governmental co-operation in the Valle de México. The experience of OECD countries such as Estonia (co-ordinating EU affairs), Spain (comprehensive public administration reform), and cities such as Athens, Barcelona and Turin (the Olympic games) and Lille and Marseille (EU Capital of Culture in 2004 and 2013 respectively) shows that co-ordination is sometimes easier to achieve when it revolves around a specific and often time-limited initiative.[16] There often seem to be greater co-ordination opportunities at the technical rather than ministerial level. The challenge for authorities in the Valle de México is to develop the ability to motivate and encourage diverse actors to work together, or at a minimum to be moving in the same direction. There are local examples of co-ordination around specific initiatives in the Valle de México, such as the ProAire programme to improve the air quality in the metropolitan area. The implementation and relative encouraging results of the ProAire show that co-operation around a specific issue is feasible (see Chapter 4).

This new opportunity for metropolitan co-operation is a large-scale infrastructure project whose immediate impact will be felt in 11 municipalities of the State of Mexico and 3 *delegaciones* of the Federal District. The implementation of the integral plan of the project requires the collaboration of a large number of federal ministries and the governments of the State of Mexico and the Federal District, as well as municipal governments. Nonetheless, the NAICM project has so far been a federal government project without the active involvement of other actors such as municipalities, the private sector and civil organisations. This is partially explained by the fact that previous attempts to build the airport faced strong opposition. An insufficient exchange of information seems to be giving rise to misunderstandings, co-ordination gaps, negative perception of the project's management, and insufficient transparency and ownership. Even within the federal government, information does not seem to be flowing in a timely and systematic manner.

The key question the federal government must resolve is how to work with sub-national governments, the private sector and civil society organisations on building the airport and capitalising on this project for the economic and social benefit of the metropolitan zone. The federal and state governments in the Valle de México could adopt a network approach that focuses on formal and informal contacts across the public sector, building on current practices for problem solving (within the legal framework). The ability of actors within the national and sub-national governments in the Valle de México to work in a co-ordinated manner will be a key element in the successful construction and sustainability of the NAICM, the regeneration of the eastern region of the metropolitan zone and achieving a single vision for the Valle de México. To use the airport project to improve metropolitan governance, Mexican authorities could consider the following points:

- The federal government needs to be more inclusive, and willing to draw more broadly on knowledge, experience and perspectives of non-government actors and society as a whole. However, it is critical to decide who takes the final decision, after extensive consultation with supporters and opponents. Government should be open to receive unsolicited and solicited feedback from other levels of government and citizens through comment periods and actions, focus groups, letterboxes, surveys, public hearings and citizens' panels. To encourage active participation and consensus, conferences or citizens' juries could be organised; and experts could be involved through evaluation by stakeholders, tripartite commissions and joint working groups, and even dialogue processes. The new runway for Frankfurt Airport in Germany was built only after an extensive consultation process ensuring that the final decision took the views and concerns of the majority into account.
- Transparency and accountability are essential. The government should take the initiative to inform citizens on the different aspects of the project, through official documents, reports, guides, leaflets, information centres and co-operation with civil society organisations. Impact studies on different policy domains need to be made available to citizens (on the official websites at the very least), and special materials for a wider audience need to be prepared so that citizens can participate with adequate information. Details on how the different goals will be achieved are paramount, as well on how, why and to whom contracts for construction were awarded.
- Networks of relevant ministries (i.e. communications and transport, or urban development) actors, agencies, local authorities and external actors (i.e. municipal associations, academics, civil society organisations, social partners, etc.) could be formed to pool practical knowledge, identify and anticipate policy issues and practical problems, and come together to develop a consensus position. This can lead to more innovative solutions, with greater commitment behind them.
- The master plan of the NAICM should have a metropolitan, and even megalopolitan, vision developed with the input from public, private and civil society stakeholders. The NAICM should, in fact, be part of strategic planning for the region, given how it will affect the social, economic and natural environment. As a starting point, the NAICM should be part of the state and municipal development plans, and work to formulate a metropolitan/regional development plan with the NAICM as its central element. Some municipalities, however, do not have an urban development plan or have one that is clearly outdated (OECD, 2015b).
- A process of urban strategic planning aligned with the NAICM project can lead to greater consistency in policy action on the part of local and municipal governments. It can be the blueprint for action and encourage more effective

communication across all levels of government on how to meet objectives and raise effectiveness.

- The federal government should reinforce its role of leadership, but also assume the role of stewardship for this project. As a leader it should be the advocate for the project, articulating and communicating the vision behind the project in a way that it is easy to understand and motivate key external actors. As a steward, it should guide and co-ordinate, not control or direct, the actions of all those involved in the process. It can do so by making available and accessible all information, consulting the public and encouraging their engagement. It should be the arbiter of conflict between different bodies and nodes of activity.
- The magnitude of the project will require moving from co-ordination (i.e. shared information) to co-operation and collaboration (i.e. joint action). A senior executive programme for national and sub-national public and private senior managers – specifically for the NAICM – could be established to agree on a shared understanding and vision for the airport, the challenges ahead and the ways of managing them. Seminars, forums of discussions, learning cafés and workshops are some options for building networks. Finland's Finwin programme is an excellent example for Mexico in this respect (see Box 5.2).
- Building the airport and related urban infrastructure requires effective public investment across levels of government. Mexican authorities may refer to the OECD's *Recommendation of the Council on Effective Public Investment Across Levels of Government*, which is intended to help governments assess the strengths and weaknesses of their public investment capacity in a multi-level governance perspective and set priorities for improvement (OECD, 2014a).

Forming high-level councils/committees for the specific project could be a way to achieve coherence and speak with a single voice, improving efficiency. It could also be the starting point for developing a collaborative culture. A Metropolitan Co-ordination Council for the NAICM could be established to co-ordinate and monitor the implementation of the master plan of the airport. It could also oversee the activities of the regional development plans and/or the state and municipal development plans that have an impact on the airport or will have an impact due to the airport construction (Table 5.5). It is essential that the groups formed do not become exclusive, as they should remain open to voices of dissent.

### *Better inter-governmental co-ordination may lead to more effective metropolitan public investment*

Co-ordination for better investment in the Valle de México is a challenging issue, because of the cross-sectoral, cross-jurisdictional and inter-governmental features of the metropolitan area. It involves a large constellation of actors with different priorities. Moreover, the budget and financial regulatory framework do not seem to be compatible with the co-ordination needs for better investment. OECD countries have found that more effective public investment has a critical role to play to address inequalities, rebuild trust, restore growth and enhance well-being. The impact of public investment depends to a significant extent on *how* governments manage this shared competency across levels of government. Effective public investment requires substantial *co-ordination* across levels of government to bridge information, policy or fiscal gaps that may occur, as well as critical *governance capacities* at different levels to design and implement public investment projects.

Table 5.5. **Proposal for a Metropolitan Co-ordination Council for the NAICM**

| | |
|---|---|
| **The Executive Board of the Metropolitan Co-ordination Council for the new airport (NAICM)** | Co-chaired by the SCT and SEDATU. Other members would include SEDUVI and SEMOVI from the Federal District and the Ministries of Urban Development and Mobility from the State of Mexico. The municipality of Texcoco should also be a member of the board. It should provide the top-level strategy/vision on the airport construction and the required urban works. |
| **Co-ordination Secretariat** | Provided by SEDATU and the SCT in the first instance. They should be in charge of the organisation of the work of the Metropolitan Co-ordination Council. |

- **Working Group 1:** *Urban regeneration and housing*
- **Working Group 2:** *Water management*
- **Working Group 3:** *Mobility strategies*
- **Working Group 4:** *Economic promotion and green growth*
- **Working Group 5:** *Health and risk management*
- **Working Group 6:** *Strategic investment and prospective*

Membership of the Metropolitan Co-ordination Council for the NAICM could be open to public, private, academic organisations as well as NGOs and think-tanks. Every working group could be co-chaired by state-level authorities, depending on the area of specialisation. For example, the Working Group on Mobility could be co-chaired by SEMOVI and its counterpart from the State of Mexico. They could have monthly meetings to discuss the different investment projects required to make the NAICM operational, following the strategic orientations provided by the Executive Board. The challenges and the different alternatives for facing them should be discussed. Working Group 6 on Strategic Investment and Prospective could provide guidelines on the key investments needed not for the airport per se but on urban development in general for the short, medium and long terms. The aims of this Metropolitan Co-ordination Council for the NAICM are:

i) To ensure that all decisions on the new airport are acceptable to state- and municipal-level authorities, as well as private and civil stakeholders.

ii) To balance decision-making power with civil experts' and citizens' participation, ensuring that everyone is on board.

iii) To clarify responsibilities and sources of income. Everyone should know how they are contributing to the airport project and what benefits they are getting.

iv) To implement the regional development plans and set up a general framework for collective action.

In the current context of sluggish economic growth in Mexico (OECD, 2015f), public investment is under pressure to compensate for the reduction of income as a result of low oil prices. Mexican authorities have to do better with less, by spending smarter. Authorities in the Valle de México need to define a strategy to identify investment priorities, based on the particularities of each zone of the metropolitan area. The starting point should be a shared, politically supported project for the ZMVM. The 2014 OECD *Recommendation of the Council on Effective Public Investment Across Levels of Government*[17] contains a series of principles for an efficient and effective use of resources dedicated to public investment for territorial development (Box 5.6). The purpose of these recommendations is to help governments assess the strengths and weaknesses of their public investment capacity in a multi-level governance perspective, and set priorities for improvement. Effective public investment is important because it shapes choices about where people live and work, influences the nature and location of private investment, and affects quality of life. Moreover, most of the sub-national public investment goes to areas of critical importance for future economic growth, sustainable development and citizens' well-being, such as transport, energy and construction). This could be a useful instrument for authorities in the Valle de México to assess their public investment practices.

### Box 5.6. Recommendation of effective public investment across levels of government

OECD member countries should take steps to ensure that national and sub-national levels of government effectively utilise resources dedicated to public investment for territorial development, in accordance with the principles set out below:

**Pillar I: Co-ordinate public investment across levels of government and policies**

- Invest using an integrated strategy tailored to different places (e.g. Japan's National Spatial Strategy outlines the principles for integrated territorial and infrastructure development and is the guiding strategy for national and regional plans in these areas. Mexico's National Development Plan is the guiding strategic document for sub-national governments).
- Adopt effective co-ordination instruments across national and sub-national governments (e.g. the Austrian Conference on Spatial Planning [ÖROK] has served as a common platform of spatial planning co-ordination. It involves all federal ministries, the *Länder*, and the umbrella association of municipalities and social partners).
- Co-ordinate among sub-national governments to invest at the relevant scale (e.g. the 2007 Danish local government reform has contributed to reducing fragmentation of investment strategies through municipal mergers and the creation of regions).

**Pillar II: Strengthen capacities for public investment and promote policy learning across levels of government**

- Assess up front long-term impacts and risks of public investment (e.g. in Australia, the state of Victoria uses *ex ante* monitoring mechanisms such as the High Value/High Risk, or HVHR, process to assess investment projects with a value above a defined value or which are deemed to be high risk).
- Encourage stakeholder involvement throughout the investment cycle (e.g. the decision to build a new runway for Frankfurt's Airport in Germany was accompanied by a mediation process and an extensive consultation prior to the decision, with proponents and opponents).
- Mobilise private actors and financing institutions to diversify sources of funding and strengthen capacities (e.g. in the United Kingdom, the government launched the Local Enterprise Partnership between local authorities and business, to decide on local priorities for investment in roads, buildings and facilities).
- Reinforce the expertise of public officials and institutions throughout the investment cycle (e.g Estonia has carried out several studies examining local governance capacity since 2008; the studies measure: institutional capacity, financial capacity and capacity to provide public services at the local government level).
- Focus on results and promote learning (e.g. the United States has developed a tool named "Pay for Success", which shifts the focus onto outcomes, by aligning financial incentives with actual success).

**Pillar III: Ensure sound framework conditions for public investment at all levels of government**

- Develop a fiscal framework adapted to the investment objectives pursued (e.g. the Finnish government developed a new steering system for local government finances, to be implemented from 2015. Its aim is to ensure that, in the future, municipalities'' responsibilities match the available funding).

Box 5.6. **Recommendation of effective public investment across levels of government** *(continued)*

- Require sound, transparent financial management (e.g. Ireland plans to introduce a National Oversight and Audit Commission for Local Government to provide independent, high-quality examination of local government performance in meeting national, regional and local mandates and providing value for money in service delivery).
- Promote transparency and strategic use of public procurement at all levels of government (e.g. at the regional level, Galicia, in Spain, has developed a web platform for public procurement procedures for all public entities, including municipalities, to integrate all public entities and private companies in a one-stop shop for public procurement).
- Strive for quality and consistency in regulatory systems across levels of government (e.g. the Korean Ministry of Land, Infrastructure and Transport recently charged municipal authorities with having too many "hidden" local regulations that impede private investment in construction).

*Source:* OECD (2014a), *Recommendation of the Council on Effective Public Investment Across Levels of Government*, adopted on 12 March 2014, OECD, Paris, available at: www.oecd.org/regional/regional-policy/Principles-Public-Investment.pdf and www.oecd.org/effective-public-investment-toolkit.

## Strengthening institutional capacity

If state- and municipal-level governments in the Valle de México are to guarantee an efficient and effective delivery of public services to a growing population, they need a qualified public workforce and adequate means of obtaining sufficient financial resources. Citizens' participation needs to be valued as a source of feedback and innovation.

### *The public workforce should be an asset and not a cost*

Authorities in the Valle de México need to invest in the skills, leadership and management capacity of the public service. Professionalising the public service and planning the workforce needs strategically is a way to minimise disruption due to changes in government, and to protect capacity, enhance resilience, ensure continuity of service and avoid eroding citizens' trust in government.

#### *The management of the public workforce needs to be efficient and fair, and promote professionalism…*

State- and municipal-level authorities in the Valle de México need to invest in improving the management of the public workforce to enhance their capacity for urban development. Bahl et al. (2013: 9) argue that a "major reason for the lack of capacity at the local level is the inadequacy of the civil service system, which often accords local government officials a lower status, including lower salaries and fewer chances for advancement, and generally a system that does not encourage professionalism." To ensure that state- and municipal-level governments have sufficient institutional capacity to develop complex functions that require a long gestation period (i.e. urban development projects), they must have a solid legal foundation and organised procedures to manage personnel. To ensure an effective administration of personnel, state- and municipal-level governments in the Valle de México require: 1) a career civil service system that, along with eliminating favouritism in designating government employees, promotes its specialisation and professional development; and 2) a system of personnel management that promotes the career civil service system, while granting flexibility to elected authorities to adjust budget allocations and fulfil the designated tasks.

The 2015 *OECD Urban Policy Review of Mexico* and the 2011 *OECD Public Governance Review of Mexico* have already recommended some measures to modernise the municipal administration, considered the weakest link in the multi-level structure of government. The need for sufficient capacity and professionalism in local and municipal governments will grow in the light of urban development needs. It is in the interests of all levels of government to develop a merit-based human resource management system based on strategic workforce planning. Box 5.7 highlights the main recommendations in this regard that are applicable to the public workforce at different levels of government in the Valle de México.

### Box 5.7. **Professionalising the local public workforce in Mexico: Key recommendations**

The lack of professionalisation and the constant renewal of elected and appointed municipal authorities weaken the capacity of the public administration to promote appropriate urban development policies. Dealing with these challenges requires redesigning municipal administrations to make them suitable to a new context that requires a strong knowledge base and experience on the part of the workforce, as well as fairness and transparency in the management of public employees. To this end, it would be desirable to:

- Encourage merit and develop strategic workforce practices. This implies developing a merit-based recruitment process focused on competencies and through the development of standardised job profiles.
- Improve forward-looking management and planning. This involves engaging in strategic workforce planning to anticipate future developments and to maintain a well-structured workforce of appropriate size.
- Enact legislation for the professionalisation of the public workforce at local and municipal level. The federal Professional Career Service could be used as a model.
- Make training more strategic, focusing on ongoing skill development, the certification of competencies (i.e. those of urban planners), and the training of middle and senior managers.
- Create a body for professionalisation of the workforce that could also promote teaching and research on urban development.
- Institutionalise collaboration across levels of government for professionalisation.

*Sources*: OECD (2015c), *OECD Urban Policy Reviews: Mexico 2015: Transforming Urban Policy and Housing Finance*, OECD Publishing, Paris, http://dx.doi.org/10.1787/9789264227293-en; OECD (2011b), *Towards More Effective and Dynamic Public Management in Mexico*, OECD Public Governance Reviews, OECD Publishing, Paris, http://dx.doi.org/10.1787/9789264116238-en.

In addition, local and municipal authorities in the Valle de México may consider two additional points. First, the creation of a metropolitan system for qualified personnel for the public service in the metropolitan zone in the medium- to long term. The aim should be to attract, train and retain technical and professional staff to ensure the development of a strong and knowledgeable professional base of public servants to work in different municipalities or *delegaciones* within the metropolitan zone. This would require enforcing uniform hiring rules and compensation levels. Second, authorities may wish to align the management of the public workforce to the needs of urban development. The importance of having a competent, skilful and diverse public workforce should be emphasised in all strategic urban development documents. It involves linking strategic workforce planning to urban planning, budgeting and urban investment projects. This implies viewing the workforce as an asset to achieve organisational objectives, rather than a cost. This would provide clarity on the size and the profile of the public workforce that is needed to achieve urban development goals.

### *... while, at the same time, ensuring high ethical standards of public employees*

A critical issue for national and local authorities in the Valle de México is to ensure high levels of ethical behaviour of public officials. In Mexico, the public sector in general is perceived as being highly corrupt, affecting trust in government on the part of citizens, as Figure 5.2 shows. Corruption is a betrayal of trust and diminishes the legitimacy of the state and the moral stature of the bureaucracy in the eyes of the population (taxpayers). Dealing with corruption is critical, as corruption undermines government revenue, due to disincentives to investment and, therefore, limits the ability of the government to invest in productivity-enhancing areas. Where corruption is endemic, citizens will view paying taxes as a questionable proposition. The system works reasonably well when those who pay taxes feel that there is a good chance that their money will be used in a way that benefits them, e.g. through improvements in the city's infrastructure. For instance, if citizens perceive that the underground service has improved, they are less likely to oppose increases in tariffs. Moreover, corruption can distort spending decisions, as large capital projects provide tempting opportunities for corruption if adequate control and monitoring systems are not in place.

Figure 5.2. **Mexico's public sector is perceived as highly corrupt**

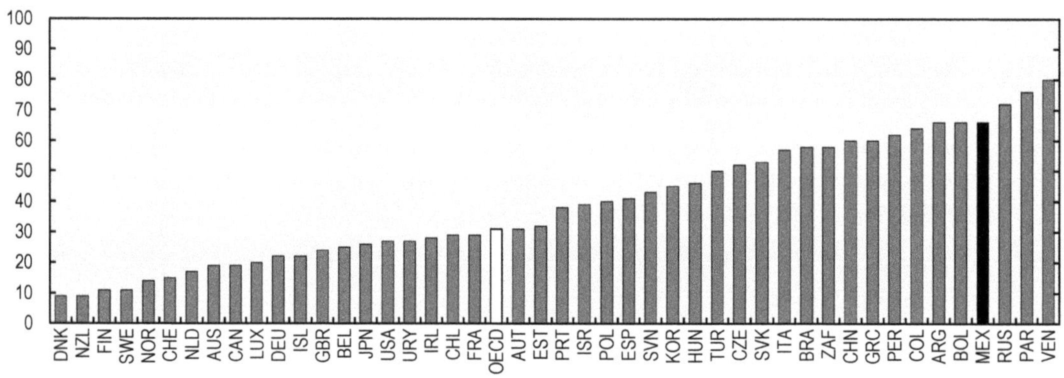


*Source*: OECD (2015f), *OECD Economic Surveys: Mexico*, OECD Publishing, Paris, http://dx.doi.org/10.1787/eco_surveys-mex-2015-en, based on Transparency International data.

The new National Anticorruption System, which not only requires asset disclosure but also private interests of public officials, could help to promote clean government.[18] It includes the creation of an anticorruption watchdog with a presence in every state of the country. Under this new system, the federal Constitution will acknowledge that both government and citizens are responsible for dealing with corruption. This is in line with the new antifraud or anticorruption offices that have been set up in other OECD countries, such as the Serious Fraud Office in the United Kingdom, the Independent Commission against Corruption in New South Wales (New Zealand), the Commissions on Integrity in the United States and the Antifraud Office in Catalonia (Spain). To regain trust in public service, it is important that administrative and legal sanctions accompany political sanctions in cases of proven corruption of public servants – particularly for those in political positions. Such sanctions would send the message that wrongdoing has both political and legal consequences. Normally, officials tend to be simply removed from office, without facing administrative and legal charges for wrongdoing. Mexico's actions to promote ethics and integrity in the public service could be further enhanced by aligning those efforts with the OECD's *Principles for Managing Ethics in the Public Service* (OECD, 1998) and the OECD *Guidelines for Managing Conflicts of Interest in the Public Service*.

### *Paying for better public services*

The poor record of service delivery by local and municipal-level governments in the Valle de México results from a combination of weak personnel management, inadequate management systems, an inability to capture economies of scale, expenditure mandates imposed by higher levels of government and an inadequate revenue base. In the case of the Valle de México, the institutional weaknesses of the state- and municipal-level governments (municipalities and *delegaciones*) – such as the lack of a civil service system – are an even bigger problem than the shortage of resources. Nevertheless, expanding the revenue base would certainly contribute to better services, such as improved infrastructure, both properly established and well maintained.

Implementing a strategy of increasing local revenues in the Valle de México will be difficult because of the heterogeneous fiscal regulatory framework and the political costs of increased taxation. Moreover, as discussed earlier in this chapter, sub-national governments in Mexico have limited taxing power, and often underuse the taxing power that they do have (OECD, 2015c). In the Valle de México, the efficient provision of public services and their financing has outgrown the jurisdictional boundaries of the city core. A new approach is required to cover these metropolitan-wide governance and finance challenges. One possible option is that the new mix of service provision and financing includes regional taxes, delivery of at least some services on a regional basis and a revenue model for the Valle de México that focuses on greater financial independence.[19] Region-wide taxes could be taxes on income or motor vehicles. That is why making the car ownership tax (*tenencia*) uniform across the metropolitan zone would be a positive step in this direction. Regional taxes could be collected by state governments and then distributed by formula among the legible municipalities in the area. Making more and better use of user and benefit charges is critical to increasing revenue. Some other options could be the capture of increasing land value resulting from public infrastructure investments (*contribuciones de mejora*) as Mexico City is beginning to do; and the removal of subsidy elements in the present system of user charges, so as to levy charges at or at least closer to cost-recovery levels (i.e. transport pricing, see Chapter 3). Recent progress in phasing out gasoline subsidies could be used to pass the extra resources to sub-national governments for urban projects such as urban transport. Authorities in the Valle de México may wish to use the "*transferencia de potencialidades de desarrollo urbano*" more strategically and frequently. São Paulo's Certificates of Additional Construction Potential (*Certificados de Potencial Adicional de Construção*, CEPAC)[20] in Brazil[21] and Colombia's *participación en plusvalía* exemplify the potential of this instrument. Property owners are obliged to pay a percentage of the increment in the value of the land due to the construction of infrastructure projects, changes in land use (from rural to urban use for example), and the authorisation to a major land use in buildings, either by raising the occupancy rate or the rate of construction, or both at once.[22]

Modernisation of the cadastre to charge for better and fairer property tax is indispensable, and more municipalities in the State of Mexico should take steps in this direction. A three-year revaluation cycle could be adopted so as to keep an up-to-date database. Eliminating exemptions and preferential treatments in property tax can lead to a significant increase in revenue productivity, but political resistance could be a deal-breaker in property tax reform (Bahl et al., 2013). Renting out public space to individuals and companies for activities such as trade or advertisement could be an important source of revenue, but contracts need to be public and granted only through a transparent public procurement process.

The amounts spent for public services in the Valle de México are much larger than own resources of the local governments, making them largely dependent on inter-governmental transfers. But since the current system does not encourage more local revenue collection and does not provide for a differential structure of transfers to metropolitan and non-metropolitan areas, or among metropolitan areas, the Valle de México receives less in per capita terms (i.e. through the Metropolitan Fund). Restructuring the inter-governmental transfer system in light of a metropolitan strategy could be a way forward. A first step in this direction could be weaning the metropolitan area from transfers but giving them enough authority to tax and impose user charges. A hard budget constraint with no back door for financing deficits could be part of this measure. Financing infrastructure investment could be done via debt financing, and borrowing could be supported by locally raised revenues (Bahl et al., 2013; OECD, 2013a). Moreover, the transfer system could be redesigned to be asymmetrical (OECD, 2015c), with the Valle de México handled under a different regime from other metropolitan areas and local governments in the country. The tricky issue for the Valle de México is how to treat the municipalities in the State of Mexico. The entire territory of Mexico City is part of the metropolitan zone, but only 59 out of 125 municipalities of the State of Mexico are part of the Valle de México. A formula would need to be designed to calculate the amount of the transfers, and the Metropolitan Fund would have to be used only for joint metropolitan projects, as discussed above.

Financing for large infrastructure projects such as underground, the water and sewage system, roads, etc. is often well beyond the financial reach of the local governments in the Valle de México. To increase the resource base for infrastructure finance, the focus could be on: 1) increasing own-source revenues, in which Mexico City is making progress, whereas the State of México is lagging behind – perhaps the improvement in property tax and the use of selective non-property taxes could be a way forward; 2) debt financing, which could be limited to capital projects with a long life; 3) transfers, which can be used to fund infrastructure projects; and 4) public-private partnerships. However, it will be necessary to ensure that local governments have the capacity for managing them.

### *Citizens as a source of legitimation, feedback and innovation*

The Valle de México needs efficient mechanisms to encourage the community's participation in the decisions that affect them, as well as the need to exercise an effective oversight of expenditure. "A democratic, transparent local government promotes community participation and has a better chance of satisfying the interests of the majority, while respecting the rights of the minorities, than a bureaucratic government, whose management is concentrated within its cupola" (Rojas, 2008: 15). Mexico needs federal regulations to ensure minimum guarantees for citizens' participation in public affairs. The federal framework should co-ordinate and harmonise local laws on the topic. That would ensure that citizens living in any part of the ZMVM have the same basic rights of public participation. State laws should include response times and appeal mechanisms, avoiding vague participatory frameworks (Peñalva and Medina, 2014). It is important that federal and state laws make public consultation on urban development issues a legal obligation, with administrative consequences to ensure effectiveness. The experience of OECD countries suggests that citizens' and communities' participation in the early stages of the policy-making process can build or reinforce a sense of belonging to the metropolitan area, legitimising public policies, helping to improve trust in metropolitan authorities (OECD, 2015a).

In the Valle de México, a main concern over citizens' participation is to develop a sense of belonging to the area, generating an identity. It is encouraging that there are efforts to include citizens' views in planning (*planeación participativa*) in Mexico City, through forums, discussion groups, workshops etc. on areas such as environmental protection. Although time-consuming, these activities should continue, as public participation gives a mandate to act. The key issue for Mexico is to incentivise public participation in public affairs that goes beyond political elections. There are different stages of citizens' engagement in metropolitan affairs: 1) citizen information – communicating information to citizens on decision making, policy development and implementation puts governments in a position to be scrutinised and builds citizen trust; it also helps to educate citizens about their rights and entitlements (websites, granting access to public records and data); 2) citizen consultation – by asking for citizens' views and opinions on government's initiatives, decision making can be improved, innovative ideas taken into account and new arrangements made workable (opinion surveys, focus groups, workshops/seminars, public hearings etc. can be some mechanisms for consultation); 3) citizen participation and empowerment – information is exchanged two ways, between the public and the government, through a dialogue into which the opinions of both parties feed, in a spirit of participation (citizen juries and citizen forums are examples of participatory mechanism) (OECD, 2014b).

Authorities in the Valle de México could capitalise on the fact that the most important universities in the country are located in the metropolitan zone. They constitute a source of feedback and innovative ideas and can reinforce the metropolitan-oriented collaborative dynamics, as the cities of Copenhagen, Barcelona, Montreal and Portland have done by benefiting from the expertise of the university sector (OECD, 2015a). For example, the University Programme on City Studies (*Programa Universitario de Estudios sobre la Ciudad*, PUEC) of the National Autonomous University of Mexico (UNAM), the Centre for Economic Research and Teaching (CIDE) and the Autonomous University of the State of Mexico (UAEM) have conducted a number of valuable studies on the Valle de México and taken part in a several discussions on how to face the urban development challenges of the metropolis. Research bodies and think-tanks such as the Centro Mario Molina, the Mexican Institute for Competitiveness (Instituto Mexicano para la Competitividad, IMCO), the Institute for Transportation and Development Policies (Instituto de Políticas para el Transporte y el Desarrollo, ITDP) and others have even collaborated with local authorities in developing strategic documents such as the climate change action programmes or municipal development plans. The CIDE's recommendations to improve the Metropolitan Fund and the Observatorio Ciudadano for the NAICM constitute two recent examples of how local universities and think-tanks can contribute with objective, tailored and informed proposals of action that should be seriously taken into consideration by policy makers in the metropolitan zone.[23] The Environmental Commission for the Megalopolis (CAMe) is even considering developing benchmarks to assess the performance of the six local governments in the region on environment-related issues. To assess progress on a comparative basis is a good idea, but all actors will need to agree on the methodology, so that results are not challenged and can be accepted by everyone.

## Conclusion

Transforming the Valle de México into a dynamic functional urban area requires effective institutional and organisational arrangements. Good governance must guide and enact the planning of safe urban trajectories. However, the present urban governance mechanisms are deeply fragmented, compromised and under-resourced and therefore cannot play this role. The implementation of urban development projects – including urban regeneration, housing, mobility and environmental protection – and the achievement of the desired results will depend to a large extent on how the metropolitan zone is organised and how the different agents in different sectors work together as a team or interact as part of a network. The current governance arrangements, which are the product of historical developments, are at odds with the idea of a functional metropolitan zone. Administrative fragmentation, sectoral planning and institutional capacity weaknesses are just some of the key challenges to overcome. To achieve this, the authorities in the Valle de México could capitalise on the political reform of the Federal District to lay the foundation for better inter-governmental co-ordination, and in the construction of the New Mexico City International Airport, which could bring together a wide variety of actors around a common project with ramifications in many areas of urban life. In addition, shifting to a networked governance model that allows for better information and knowledge flows, constant communication among peers, and a renewed and more inclusive working culture in the public sector, is a practical option to deal with administrative fragmentation. Regional planning based on a metropolitan vision and linked to long-term financial means should be the basis for metropolitan co-ordination. Giving authority to the metropolitan commissions and financial means to ensure their operations would help to improve metropolitan co-ordination and governance. To address the institutional flaws, investing in the professionalisation of the sub-national public workforce and expanding the revenue base of state and municipal governments are two essential tasks. These could provide a solid foundation for sub-national governments in the metropolitan zone to engage in urban development. Citizens should be consulted and government should be open to voices of dissent if urban development projects are to be bought in by the majority of stakeholders.

The Valle de México is well positioned to improve its governance architecture. It has the foundations and a critical mass to establish a much-needed metropolitan governance framework. Ensuring success can take time, will require some experimentation, and will rest on governments' capacity and willingness to work with each other. All parties involved in urban issues will need to sharpen their strategic focus, and identify ways to combine successful project-based sectoral initiatives with long-term, cross-sectoral strategic programming. Adopting such an approach can enhance urban development and improve residents' quality of life.

# Notes

1. The General Law on Human Settlements (LGAH) is the main regulation governing the management of metropolitan areas in Mexico since the mid-1970s, providing the legal basis for the establishment of institutions of inter-municipal and inter-regional co-operation.
2. For further information see Government of Mexico (2014).
3. In 2008, the state of Hidalgo joined the CECM.
4. For further information see: Government of the State of Mexico (1998) and Government of the Federal District (2008).
5. The Ministry of Communication is in charge of motorways and mass transit (BRT system Mexibús) while the Ministry of Mobility is responsible for regulating low-capacity concessioned public transport (Chapter 3).
6. For further information, see Government of Mexico (2014), Art. 115 Fr III and V.
7. In 2015, the Federal District was authorised to contract debt for up to MXN 5 billion.
8. Decentralised organisms are those that do not depend hierarchically on the central government and have legal and financial autonomy.
9. For further information, see Government of Mexico (2015a).
10. The state of Hidalgo receives MXN 3 425 per capita, whereas the State of Mexico and the Federal District receive MXN 327.9 per capita and MXN 457.6 per capita respectively.
11. The Federal District received in 2015 MXN 3 500 million from the *fondo de capitalidad* to be used for the Metrobús Line 6, public lights and urban infrastructure. This fund is included in the national budget and is intended to compensate the Federal District, as the capital of the country, by giving it access to a lump sum to be used in infrastructure, education, public security and other areas. For further information, see Government of Mexico (2015b).
12. For example, for 2015, the Metropolitan Fund for the Valle de México amounts to MXN 4 052.3 million, of which MXN 1 890 million corresponds to the Federal District, which will use the resources in transport, waste management and public lighting.
13. For further information, see: www.comune.roma.it/PCR/resources/cms/documents/delib_N_11_del_11_03_2013.pdf.
14. "Whole-of-government" is associated with a desire to ensure the horizontal and vertical co-ordination of government activity in order to improve policy coherence, use resources more effectively, promote and capitalise on synergies and innovation that arise from a multi-stakeholder perspective, and provide seamless service delivery to citizens and business. It requires government bodies, regardless of type or level, to work across portfolio boundaries to achieve shared goals and to provide integrated government responses to policy issues (based on OECD, 2011b).

15. For further information, see Viet Nam Urban Forum (2012).

16. See OECD (2015a, 2014a, 2011b) and Lefèvre (2008) for further details.

17. A Recommendation is an OECD instrument adopted by the Council. Recommendations are not legally binding, but practice accords them great moral force, as representing the political will of member countries.

18. The National Anticorruption System is currently under discussion in the local congresses. If approved by the majority, it will translate into a constitutional reform, and the secondary legislation for its implementation will then be enacted.

19. See Bahl et al. (2013) for a wider discussion.

20. Certificates of Additional Construction Potential.

21. For further information on the CEPACs see: www.prefeitura.sp.gov.br/cidade/secretarias/desenvolvimento_urbano/sp_urbanismo/cepac/index.php?p=19456.

22. For further information, see: www.shd.gov.co/shd/participacion-en-plusvalia.

23. The federal Ministry of Finance (SHCP) took part in the evaluation of the metropolitan and regional funds conducted by CIDE (see Iracheta Cenecorta and Iracheta Carroll, 2014). The Observatorio Ciudadano for the NAICM involves three civil organisations: the Mexican Institute for Competitiveness (IMCO), the Mexican Centre for Environmental Law (CEMDA) and CTS EMBARQ México. It has produced a report that takes into account experts' and citizens' concerns on the impact of the NAICM regarding environmental competitiveness and economic development, urban development and mobility, and social inclusion. It formulates recommendations that could improve and enrich the project of the airport. No public authority is part of this exercise, but the federal government could certainly analyse the proposals to incorporate them into their planning and project management plans.

# *Bibliography*

ANZSOG, Australia and New Zealand School of Government, www.anzsog.edu.au/about-us/about-anzsog (accessed 15 June 2015).

Bahl, R.W. et al. (2013), "Governing and financing metropolitan areas in the developing world", in: Bahl, R.W, J. Linn and D. Wetzel (eds.) (2013), *Financing Metropolitan Governments in Developing Countries*, Lincoln Institute of Land Policy, Cambridge, Massachusetts, pp. 1-30.

Città Metropolitana di Torino (2015), Statuto della Città Metropolitana di Torino, available at: www.cittametropolitana.torino.it/speciali/2015/statuto_citta_metro/dwd/testo_definitivo.pdf.

Gleeson, B., J. Dodson and M. Spiller (2010), "Metropolitan governance for the Australian city: The case for reform", Urban Research Program, Issues Paper 12, available at: www.griffith.edu.au/__data/assets/pdf_file/0012/199299/urp-ip12-gleeson-et-al-2010.pdf.

Government of Mexico (2015a), "Reglas de Operación del Fondo Metropolitano", *Diario Oficial de la Federación*, 31 March, available at: www.shcp.gob.mx/lashcp/MarcoJuridico/documentosDOF/2015/marzo/reglas_31032015.pdf.

Government of Mexico (2015b), "Lineamientos de Operación del Fondo de Capitalidad", *Diario Oficial de la Federación*, 30 January, www.dof.gob.mx/nota_detalle.php?codigo=5380014&fecha=30/01/2015 (accessed 15 June 2015).

Government of Mexico (2014), *Constitución Política de los Estados Unidos Mexicanos*, Cámara de Diputados, www.diputados.gob.mx/LeyesBiblio/htm/1.htm (accessed 15 June 2015).

Government of the Federal District (2008), "Primer convenio modificatorio al convenio por el que se crea la Comisión Ejecutiva de Coordinación Metropolitana que celebran el Distrito Federal, el Estado de México y el Estado de Hidalgo", *Gaceta Oficial del Distrito Federal*, No. 401, 18 August, available at: www.ordenjuridico.gob.mx/Estatal/DISTRITO%20FEDERAL/Convenios/DFCONV37.pdf.

Government of the State of Mexico (1998), "Comisión Ejecutiva de Coordinación Metropolitana", *Gaceta del Gobierno*, 23 March, available at: www.edomex.gob.mx/desarrollometropolitano/docs/cecm.pdf.

Huerta Melchor, O. (2008), "Managing change in OECD governments: An introductory framework", *OECD Working Papers on Public Governance*, No. 12, OECD Publishing, Paris, http://dx.doi.org/10.1787/227141782188.

IMCO/CEMDA/CTS EMBARQ (2015), *Observatorio Ciudadano del Nuevo Aeropuerto de la Ciudad de México*, Instituto Mexicano para la Competitividad, http://imco.org.mx/competitividad/observatorio-ciudadano-naicm-ejes-de-monitoreo (accessed 15 June 2015).

INEGI-CONAPO-SEDESOL (2010), *Delimitación de las Zonas Metropolitanas de México 2010*, Government of Mexico, www.conapo.gob.mx/es/CONAPO/Zonas_metropolitanas_2010 (accessed 15 June 2015).

Iracheta Cenecorta, A. (2003), "Gobernabilidad en la Zona Metropolitana del Valle de México", *Papeles de Población*, Vol. 9, No. 36, April-June, pp. 211-239, Universidad Autónoma del Estado de México, available at: www.redalyc.org/pdf/112/11203609.pdf.

Iracheta Cenecorta, A. and J.A. Iracheta Carroll (2014), *Evaluación de los Fondos Metropolitano y Regional del Gobierno Federal Mexicano*, CIDE, Centro CLEAR para América Latina, SHCP, BID, Colegio Mexiquense, Centro Eure, Mexico.

Klink, J. (2008), "Recent perspectives on metropolitan organization, functions and governance", in: Rojas, E., J.R. Cuadrado-Roura and J.M. Fernández Guell (eds.) (2008), *Governing the Metropolis: Principles and Cases*, IDB, David Rockefeller Center for Latin American Studies, Harvard University City, pp. 77-134.

Lefèvre, C. (2008), "Democratic governability of metropolitan areas: International experiences and lessons for Latin American cities" in: Rojas, E., J.R. Cuadrado-Roura and J.M. Fernández Guell (eds.) (2008), *Governing the Metropolis: Principles and Cases*, IDB, David Rockefeller Center for Latin American Studies, Harvard University City, pp. 137-192.

Meza Urías, J. (2004), "La co-ordinación intergubernamental para el desarrollo metropolitano en el Estado de México: El caso de la Zona Metropolitana del Valle de México", IX CLAD International Congress on Reform of the State and Public Administration, Madrid, 2-4 November, unpublished material.

OECD (2015a), *Governing the City*, OECD Publishing, Paris, http://dx.doi.org/10.1787/9789264226500-en.

OECD (2015b), *The Metropolitan Century: Understanding Urbanisation and its Consequences*, OECD Publishing, Paris, http://dx.doi.org/10.1787/9789264228733-en.

OECD (2015c), *OECD Urban Policy Reviews: Mexico 2015: Transforming Urban Policy and Housing Finance*, OECD Publishing, Paris, http://dx.doi.org/10.1787/9789264227293-en.

OECD (2015d), "Sub-national governments in OECD countries: Key data" (brochure), OECD, Paris, available at: http://www.oecd.org/regional/regional-policy/Subnational-governments-in-OECD-Countries-Key-Data-2015.pdf.

OECD (2015e), *OECD Urban Policy Reviews: China 2015*, OECD Publishing, Paris, http://dx.doi.org/10.1787/9789264230040-en.

OECD (2015f), *OECD Economic Surveys: Mexico*, OECD Publishing, Paris, http://dx.doi.org/10.1787/eco_surveys-mex-2015-en.

OECD (2014a), *Recommendation of the Council on Effective Public Investment Across Levels of Government,* adopted on 12 March, OECD, Paris, available at: www.oecd.org/regional/regional-policy/Principles-Public-Investment.pdf.

OECD (2014b), *How's Life in Your Region? Measuring Regional and Local Well-being for Policy Making,* OECD Publishing, Paris, http://dx.doi.org/10-1787/9789264217416-en.

OECD (2014c), *Spain: From Administrative Reform to Continuous Improvement*, OECD Public Governance Reviews, OECD Publishing, Paris, http://dx.doi.org/10.1787/9789264210592-en.

OECD (2013a), *OECD Economic Surveys: Mexico 2013*, OECD Publishing, Paris, http://dx.doi.org/10.1787/eco_surveys-mex-2013-en.

OECD (2013b), *OECD Territorial Reviews: Puebla-Tlaxcala, Mexico 2013*, OECD Publishing, Paris, http://dx.doi.org/10.1787/9789264203464-en.

OECD (2013c), *OECD Urban Policy Reviews, Chile 2013*, OECD Publishing, Paris, http://dx.doi.org/10.1787/9789264191808-en.

OECD (2013d), *OECD Territorial Reviews: Antofagasta 2013*, OECD Publishing, Paris, http://dx.doi.org/10.1787/9789264203914-en.

OECD (2013e), *Investing Together: Working Effectively across Levels of Government*, OECD Publishing, Paris, http://dx.doi.org/10.1787/9789264197022-en.

OECD (2012), *Value for Money in Government: Denmark 2011*, Value for Money in Government, OECD Publishing, Paris, http://dx.doi.org/10.1787/9789264130746-en.

OECD (2011a), *Estonia: Towards a Single Government Approach*, OECD Public Governance Reviews, OECD Publishing, Paris, http://dx.doi.org/10.1787/9789264104860-en.

OECD (2011b), *Towards More Effective and Dynamic Public Management in Mexico*, OECD Public Governance Reviews, OECD Publishing, Paris, http://dx.doi.org/10.1787/9789264116238-en.

OECD (2001), *Citizens as Partners: OECD Handbook on Information, Consultation and Public Participation in Policy-Making*, OECD Publishing, Paris, http://dx.doi.org/10.1787/9789264195578-en.

OECD (1998), *Recommendation of the Council on Improving Ethical Conduct in the Public Service Including Principles for Managing Ethics in the Public Service*, C(98)70/FINAL, 23 April, OECD, Paris, http://acts.oecd.org/Instruments/ShowInstrumentView.aspx?InstrumentID=129&InstrumentPID=125&Lang=en&Book (accessed 15 June 2015).

Orozco, M. and A. Palmerin (2011), "Reporte de la gestión del Fondo Metropolitano", Institute for Transport and Development Policies, available at: http://mexico.itdp.org/wp-content/uploads/Reporte-Fondo-Metropolitano.pdf.

Peñalva, A.P. and S. Medina (2014), "Leyes que bloquean a la ciudadanía", Nexos, 1 September, available at: www.nexos.com.mx/?p=22324.

Rojas, E. (2008), "The metropolitan regions of Latin America: Problems of governance and development", in: Rojas, E., J.R. Cuadrado-Roura and J.M. Fernández Guell (eds.), *Governing the Metropolis: Principles and Cases*, Inter-American Development Bank, David Rockefeller Center for Latin American Studies, Harvard University, Cambridge, United States, pp. 3-22.

Rosique Cañas, J.A. (2006), "Delegaciones del Distrito Federal: Una reforma política pendiente", *Revista Veredas*, No. 13, Segundo Semestre, UNAM Xochimilco, pp. 121-143.

Viet Nam Urban Forum (2012), "Viet Nam Urban Forum", Version 6, Ministry of Construction, Ha Noi, 19 May, www.geoviet.vn/FM/GetFile.aspx?ID=a2167cb2-8b36-4015-9af4-b68ca64d0db2 (accessed 15 June 2015).

Ward, P. and H. Robles (2012), "Metropolitan governance in Mexico: Mission impossible?", in: Spink, P., P. Ward and R. Wilson (eds.), *Metropolitan Governance in the Federalist Americas: Strategies for Equitable and Integrated Development*, University of Notre Dame, South Bend, Indiana, pp. 141-170.

# ORGANISATION FOR ECONOMIC CO-OPERATION AND DEVELOPMENT

The OECD is a unique forum where governments work together to address the economic, social and environmental challenges of globalisation. The OECD is also at the forefront of efforts to understand and to help governments respond to new developments and concerns, such as corporate governance, the information economy and the challenges of an ageing population. The Organisation provides a setting where governments can compare policy experiences, seek answers to common problems, identify good practice and work to co-ordinate domestic and international policies.

The OECD member countries are: Australia, Austria, Belgium, Canada, Chile, the Czech Republic, Denmark, Estonia, Finland, France, Germany, Greece, Hungary, Iceland, Ireland, Israel, Italy, Japan, Korea, Luxembourg, Mexico, the Netherlands, New Zealand, Norway, Poland, Portugal, the Slovak Republic, Slovenia, Spain, Sweden, Switzerland, Turkey, the United Kingdom and the United States. The European Union takes part in the work of the OECD.

OECD Publishing disseminates widely the results of the Organisation's statistics gathering and research on economic, social and environmental issues, as well as the conventions, guidelines and standards agreed by its members.

OECD PUBLISHING, 2, rue André-Pascal, 75775 PARIS CEDEX 16
(04 2015 08 1 P) ISBN 978-92-64-24516-7 – 2015-17

www.ingramcontent.com/pod-product-compliance
Ingram Content Group UK Ltd.
Pitfield, Milton Keynes, MK11 3LW, UK
UKHW051458290926
15471UKWH00008B/1272

9 789264 245167